New Directions in Education

Policy Implementation

New Directions in Education Policy Implementation

Confronting Complexity

Meredith I. Honig

State University of New York Press

Published by
State University of New York Press, Albany

For information, contact State University of New York Press, Albany, NY
www.sunypress.edu

Production by Michael Haggett
Marketing by Michael Campochiaro

Library of Congress Cataloging-in-Publication Data

New directions in education policy implementation : confronting complexity /
[edited by] Meredith I. Honig.
        p. cm.
    Includes bibliographic references and index.
    ISBN 0-7914-6819-4 (hardcover : alk. paper)—ISBN 0-914-6820-8 (pbk. : alk. ppaer)
1. School improvement programs—United States   2. Educational change—United States.
3. Educational Leadership—United States.   I. Honig, Meredith I., 1971–

LB2822.82.N48   2006
379.15´0973—dc22

ISBN–13: 978-0-7914-6819-7 (hardcover : alk. paper)
ISBN–13: 978-0-7914-6820-3 (pbk. : alk. paper)

2005024130

10 9 8 7 6 5 4 3 2 1

Some, I am sure, find the world of political pressures, ambiguity, and messiness untenable and believe that it is time for intellectuals to retreat to their ivory towers. . . . I do not believe that most of us would accept that pathway. However, I do believe that these changes [in policy research and practice] require us to reflect on the developments and become more self-conscious about the way we operate within a changing world. Historians have developed a subfield called historiography to reflect on the development of the history field. We need something of that sort—an analysis of our analyses. We should expand our scholarship to include an examination of our own work.

—Radin, 1997

Contents

Acknowledgments   ix

1. Complexity and Policy Implementation: Challenges and
    Opportunities for the Field   1
    Meredith I. Honig

2. Communities of Practice Theory and the Role of Teacher
    Professional Community in Policy Implementation   25
    Cynthia E. Coburn and Mary Kay Stein

3. Policy Implementation and Cognition: The Role of Human,
    Social, and Distributed Cognition in Framing Policy
    Implementation   47
    James P. Spillane, Brian J. Reiser, and Louis M. Gomez

4. Language Matters: How Characteristics of Language
    Complicate Policy Implementation   65
    Heather C. Hill

5. Revisiting Policy Implementation as a Political Phenomenon:
    The Case of Reconstitution Policies   83
    Betty Malen

6. Connections in the Policy Chain: The "Co-construction" of
    Implementation in Comprehensive School Reform   105
    Amanda Datnow

7. Building Policy from Practice: Implementation as Organizational
    Learning   125
    Meredith I. Honig

8. Toward a Critical Approach to Education Policy
    Implementation: Implications for the (Battle)Field   149
    Michael J. Dumas and Jean Anyon

9. An Economic Approach to Education Policy Implementation   169
    Susanna Loeb and Patrick J. McEwan

10. Social Capital and the Problem of Implementation   187
    Mark A. Smylie and Andrea E. Evans

11. Implementation Research in Education: Lessons Learned,
    Lingering Questions and New Opportunities   209
    Milbrey W. McLaughlin

Bibliography   229

Contributors   271

Author Index   277

Subject Index   285

Acknowledgments

I am fortunate to have had the assistance of many people while developing this volume. First, thank you to the authors, many of whom cheerfully worked through multiple drafts of their own work to help enhance the coherence of the overall project. Promises of anonymity prevent me from thanking them individually, but many close colleagues, acquaintances, and strangers spent considerable time providing formative reviews of these chapters; the thoroughness of those reviews and the care with which they were written surely strengthened this work. Allan Odden's 1991 book on education policy implementation provided the inspiration for this volume. Lisa Chesnel and others at SUNY Press have been a pleasure to work with on this volume from start to finish. Betty Malen offered helpful comments on various versions of my own chapters and consistently calls my attention to the persistent, pesky nuances of politics and public life.

Milbrey McLaughlin believed in and encouraged this project from the beginning. Our many conversations about policy implementation over a decade have been among my most important and valued professional experiences; for those and other things I am truly grateful.

Chapter 1

Complexity and Policy Implementation
Challenges and Opportunities for the Field

Meredith I. Honig

Education policy implementation as a field of research and practice for decades has amounted to a sort of national search for two types of policies: "implementable" policies—those that in practice resemble policy designs—and "successful" policies—those that produce demonstrable improvements in students' school performance. This focus on what gets implemented and what works makes sense especially in education. After all, education has become a high-stakes, big-budget policy arena. Education commands a lion's share of state and local budgets to levels that beg hard questions about the feasibility and value added by education policies. Given its promise to serve as a significant lever of change in an institution intended to serve all children and youth, education policy affects multiple dimensions of social welfare. And given these high stakes, education policy implementation warrants careful scrutiny.

However, recent trends in education policy signal the importance of reexamining what we know about what gets implemented and what works. In practice, education policy demands arguably have become more complex. School systems now are held accountable for demonstrable improvements in the academic achievement of all students in ways barely imagined just 20 years ago. Across the country, the increasing ethnic and racial diversity of public schools (Ladson-Billings, 1999; Villegas & Lucas, 2002), a shrinking base of resources for education in many states and districts, and new systems of negative sanctions for underperforming schools (Massell, 2001; O'Day, 2002) only add to the urgency and challenge of meeting those standards. Contemporary public school systems vie for resources in competitive and contentious political arenas against projects for roads and sewers, prisons, and health care as well as school alternatives such as vouchers, charters, private schools, and home schooling. Research and experience continue to deepen knowledge about how students' experiences in school are highly dependent on conditions in their neighborhoods, families, and peer groups in ways that up the ante on school

1

improvement efforts to look beyond school walls for key reform partners (Honig, Kahne, & McLaughlin, 2001). The federal government, states, school districts, mayor's offices, and others each promote various educational reform agendas that typically converge on schools simultaneously (Honig & Hatch, 2004; Knapp, Bamburg, Ferguson, & Hill, 1998).

In such contentious, interconnected, and multidimensional arenas, no one policy gets implemented or is successful everywhere all the time; on the bright side, some policies are implemented and successful some of the places some of the time. For example, some research on class size reduction links smaller class sizes with increases in student performance but other research reveals no improvement (Finn & Achilles, 1990; Gilman & Kiger, 2003; Hanushek, 1999; Illig, 1997; Smith, Molnar, & Zahorik, 2002; Zahorik, Halbach, Earle, & Molnar, 2004). Linking student support services to schools has been shown not to expand students' opportunities to learn but under certain conditions it has been associated with various positive youth development and learning outcomes (Honig et al., 2001; Mathematica Policy Research & Decision Information Resources, 2005). In some districts charter schools outperform neighborhood public schools but nationwide their performance has been mixed (Mishel, 2004, September 23; Viadero, 2004a, 2004b). Single-sex schooling seems both to strengthen and to impede educational outcomes (Datnow, Hubbard, & Conchas, 2001; Lee & Bryk, 1986). Accountability policies and other central directives have limited impacts on teachers' practice in some settings but significant effects in others (Elmore & Burney, 1997; Firestone, Schorr, & Monfils, 2004; Louis, 1994a).

These realities of schooling in diverse communities nationwide suggest that those interested in improving the quality of education policy implementation should focus not simply on what's implementable and what works but rather investigate under what conditions, if any, various education policies get implemented and work. In this view, "implementability" and "success" are still essential policy outcomes, but they are not inherent properties of particular policies. Rather implementability and success are the product of interactions between policies, people, and places—the demands specific policies place on implementers; the participants in implementation and their starting beliefs, knowledge, and other orientations toward policy demands; and the places or contexts that help shape what people can and will do. Implementation research should aim to reveal the policies, people, and places that shape how implementation unfolds and provide robust, grounded explanations for how interactions among them help to explain implementation outcomes. The essential implementation question then becomes not simply "what's implementable and works," but what is implementable and what works for whom, where, when, and why?

The complexity of these policy dynamics poses a dilemma for policy analysts, policy researchers, and others who routinely produce information about implementation. On the one hand, primary audiences for implementation information—elected officials, public managers, school principals, and others—by many reports demand clear, actionable, and reliable information that can guide their decisions especially in complex policy arenas; clear information in such arenas is often considered that which limits complexity and provides unambiguous action steps and chains of command (Cohen & Weiss, 1977; Majone, 1989; Weiss & Gruber, 1984). For example, policy recommendations in this spirit might call for the implementation of a single district-wide reading curriculum to help ensure that all schools are on the same page and offering consistent, coherent instruction. Such recommendations might urge the development of "what works" lists and clearinghouses and seek relatively unambiguous verdicts regarding program success (http://www.whatworks.ed.gov). A more complex view of education policy implementation may appear particularly unwelcome in the high-stakes accountability environments of many states and districts where short timelines for producing demonstrable improvements put a premium on swift and confident action.

But on the other hand, if such information and recommendations gloss over public school systems' complex day-to-day realities they run the risk of missing their mark and actually undermining progress. Without detailed information about the conditions under which certain interventions work, decision makers will not know if the failure of a particular reading curriculum, for example, stemmed from their choice of curriculum or poor conditions for implementation. Lists of recommended programs that "work" may obscure the resources and practices that enabled those programs to work, inadequately explain implementation results, and otherwise fail to help educational leaders understand which "successful program" might actually be successful with their own staff and students in their workplaces and communities. Recent federal emphases on scientifically based approaches to improvement arguably up the ante on researchers and practitioners alike to better understand the value and applicability of particular educational research in specific educational contexts.

This book starts from two broad premises: confronting the complexity of policy implementation is essential to building the kind of instructive knowledge base that educational decision-makers demand; and strong theoretical and empirical guides are needed to help researchers and practitioners navigate this inherently messy terrain. The time is ripe for a compilation of studies that build on this perspective. Decades of education policy implementation research and experience have been pointing to the complexity of implementation (Elmore, 1983; Sizer, 1985) and, specifically, to policy, people, and places as essential interrelated influences on how implementation unfolds (Odden & Marsh, 1988). Some scholars have developed models theoretically consistent with such descriptors (e.g., Goggin, Bowman, Lester, & O'Toole, Jr., 1990). However, arguably for the first time in education, implementation studies that confront complexity have reached a critical mass and when examined together begin to elaborate what productively confronting complexity might entail.

This new generation of education policy implementation research is distinguished by three specific features: (1) the policies under investigation on the whole are significantly more comprehensive and varied than in previous decades; (2) the research aims to uncover the various dimensions of and interactions among policies, people, and places that help explain variations in policy results; and (3) the basic epistemological approach of the research reflects the importance of moving beyond universal truths about implementation (e.g., "you can't mandate what matters") to revealing implementation as a complex and highly contingent enterprise in which variation is the rule, rather than the exception.

This volume brings together scholars whose original empirical work contributes to this new generation of implementation research. No one chapter promises to present an overall model of policy implementation. However, when viewed together in combination with other contemporary education policy implementation studies, these chapters begin to add up to a portrait of education policy implementation as the product of the interaction among particular policies, people, and places. These studies suggest that education policy researchers and practitioners interested in improving the quality of education policy implementation should help build knowledge about what works for whom, where, when, and why.

To help elaborate the distinguishing features of these chapters and contemporary education policy implementation research more broadly, I first locate recent studies in the context of past generations of implementation research identified by many other researchers (e.g., Goggin et al., 1990; Radin, 2000; Wildavsky, 1996). My analysis of these research waves reveals that contemporary implementation research in many ways builds directly on lessons learned from the past and seeks to deepen past findings. In doing so, contemporary research breaks from the past along particular dimensions that mark it as a distinct generation—one seeking more nuanced, contingent, rigorous, theory-based explications of how implementation unfolds. I highlight throughout the next sections how each chapter in this volume illuminates this approach and I conclude with implications for implementation research and practice.

A BRIEF HISTORY OF EDUCATION POLICY IMPLEMENTATION

Generalizing about generations or waves of research in a multidisciplinary field such as education policy implementation surely obscures variations in the work underway at any given time. However, bodies of research during different time periods may reflect prevailing approaches and underlying assumptions that help mark distinct evolutions in knowledge. In scholarly reviews of education policy implementation research—and implementation research in other social policy arenas—there is remarkable agreement that the field has passed through at least three stages (Odden, 1991a; see also Goggin et al., 1990; Lennon & Corbett, 2003; Radin, 2000; Wildavsky, 1996). I find that scholars generally distinguish each stage by (1) particular features of policies enacted and examined and (2) predominant approaches to implementation research. A review of these stages with attention to selected outlying studies helps highlight that contemporary education policy implementation research both builds on and departs from all three past eras in ways that mark a distinct new phase of knowledge-building about implementation.

Wave 1: A Focus on What Gets Implemented

According to Odden and others, implementation research as a formal field of inquiry emerged in the 1960s. Early implementation studies mainly focused on federal Great Society Period policies such as the Elementary and Secondary Education Act (ESEA), then newly passed in 1965 (Murphy, 1971). These policies aimed to achieve broad societal goals such as eradicating poverty but implementers were evaluated along far more modest measures: namely, the extent to which schools delivered supplemental services to low-income students (Elmore & McLaughlin, 1988). Policy designs were largely distributive, categorical, and regulatory in nature. That is, they aimed to help spread particular resources (typically funding) to groups or categories of students who met particular eligibility criteria and to ensure the appropriate use of resources as specified by policy makers. These policy designs were generally top-down in orientation—based on assumptions that policy makers *should* develop policies for implementers to carry out and monitor implementers' compliance.

Supported in large part by federal contracts, many Great Society Period researchers conducted large-scale evaluations of these policies and were almost unanimous in their findings of implementation failure—schools and districts tended not to put programs in place in ways that faithfully resembled policy designs or, in economic terms, that could be predicted by policy designs. Researchers and others generally traced root causes of these failures to conflicts between policy makers' and implementers' interests and to implementers' overall lack of capacity and will to carry out those instructions (Murphy, 1971; see also, Derthick, 1972; Pressman & Wildavsky, 1984). Such assumptions stemmed in part from conventions of particular academic disciplines such as economics and political science—dominant in implementation research at that time—that viewed the individual implementer as the most meaningful unit of analysis and posited that these individuals were driven by individual self-interest to behave in ways not always congruous with policy designers' goals. Coalition building among implementers, stronger incentives, and clearer instructions for implementation were heralded as important strategies for closing policy design-implementation gaps (Bardach, 1977; Sabatier & Mazmanian, 1979).

Wave 2: Attention to What Gets Implemented over Time

In the 1970s, predominant policy designs reflected some continuity and some change. The federal Great Society Period programs persisted as a focal point for implementation research thanks in part to ongoing federal evaluation contracts. However, long-standing policies such as ESEA through multiple reauthorizations had come to include more specific regulations and other guidance. By the 1970s ESEA and its signature program, Title I, had become old-hat for many schools and districts that had been implementing its programs for almost a decade. In addition, the types of federal policies under study expanded to include other distributive, categorical, and regulatory policies such as those for special education students.

Research on these federal policies also followed a pattern of continuity and change. Research questions still probed fidelity of implementation. For example, Kirst and Jung demonstrated that over extended periods of time, federal programs in practice did resemble initial policy designs and they concluded that longitudinal approaches to policy making and policy research would improve implementation (Kirst & Jung, 1980; see also Farrar & Milsap, 1986; Knapp, Stearns, Turnbull, David, & Peterson, 1991). However, a handful of researchers began to concern themselves with variations in implementation and to forecast the importance of policies, people, and places as mediators of implementation.

For example, Peterson, Rabe, and Wong highlighted that policy designs differed not only in the details of their provisions but also in terms of their underlying mechanisms for allocating resources. They argued that the implementation of redistributive programs (those that required government to provide more services to certain generally underprivileged groups) led to more conflicts at various points in the policy process than developmental programs (those that made infrastructure investments and promised benefits for wider groups) (Peterson, Rabe, & Wong, 1986; Peterson, Rabe, & Wong, 1991. See also Lowi, 1969). Other studies began to cast implementers in a different light—not as individuals who lacked the motivation to change but as engaged actors trying to cope with the sheer number of new policy requirements that converged on the "street level" (Weatherley & Lipsky, 1977) and to reconcile workplace demands with their personal and professional worldviews (Radin, 1977). The importance of attending to places or local context edged to center stage thanks in large part to the RAND Change Agent study. This study found, among other things, that implementation is shaped by macro- (policy-level) and micro- (implementation-level) influences; implementation unfolds as a process of "mutual adaptation" as implementers attempt to reconcile conditions in their microlevel context with macrolevel demands (Berman & McLaughlin, 1976, 1978).

These and other landmark studies began to herald *that* variations among policy, people, and places mattered to implementation. However, studies during this period seldom elaborated *how* they mattered. For example, few disagreed that local context mattered to implementation but instructions to attend to context said little about the dimensions of context that mattered, under what conditions they mattered, whether context could be attended to, and if it could, how policy makers should do so (Kirst & Jung, 1980). Furthermore, the general orientation to knowledge-building about implementation during this decade reflected persistent concerns with closing the gap between policy makers' intentions and implementers' actions and reinforcing top-down command-and-control relationships between policy makers and implementers. New, "alternative" policy models and tools such as backward mapping and decision checklists for policy makers aimed to help policy makers anticipate implementers' deviations from policy makers' plans and to take steps to avoid such implementation "pitfalls" at the point of policy design (Elmore, 1979-80; Elmore, 1983; Sabatier & Mazmanian, 1979, 1980).

Wave 3: Growing Concerns with What Works

In the 1980s, policy demands shifted again thanks in part to the publication of *A Nation at Risk* in 1983, the growing maturity of the federal Great Society Period programs, and the emergence of states as designers of broad-based policy initiatives. Policy designs during this period not only aimed to ensure full implementation but to achieve demonstrable improvements in students' school performance through new attention to curriculum and instruction and teacher professionalism (McLaughlin, 1990b). As Fuhrman and others have noted, policy making and policy research in previous eras generally:

> . . . centered on individual programs many of which were for special needs students and were more peripheral than central to core elements of schooling. They were discrete and amenable to study. By contrast, the current [Wave 3] reforms deal with central issues of who shall teach and what shall be taught and in what manner. (Fuhrman, Clune, & Elmore, 1988, p. 239)

Some of these policies stemmed from state educational agencies which emerged in many regions across the country as significant education reform leaders. State policy development focused in part on the categorical federal programs of the prior decades but also on curriculum (Anderson et al., 1987). For example, during this decade California launched a major effort to develop curriculum frameworks and grade-level initiatives to guide school decisions and teacher professional development (Knapp et al., 1991; Marsh & Crocker, 1991; Odden & Marsh, 1988). States and districts passed and promoted prominent initiatives that called for school restructuring and school site-based management (David, 1989; Malen, Ogawa, & Kranz, 1990) and other strategies to reshape basic, usually formal school structures based in part on the theory that such restructuring would contribute to better decisions about various school operations. A related strand of policy making emerged from a host of other and relatively new "policy makers" including "whole school reform designers" such as the Coalition for Essential Schools, Accelerated Schools, and Comer Schools who aimed in part to develop schoolwide improvement strategies they could replicate across multiple schools.

Lessons from education policy implementation research during this period extended some of the past. For example, many studies of state policy implementation echoed previous waves' federal policy studies in their findings that mismatches between policy makers' and implementers' incentives impeded implementation (e.g., Anderson et al., 1987). However, more nuanced understandings of the significance of policies, people, and places also began to take shape. For example, McDonnell and Elmore expanded on the notion that differences in policy design matter to implementation by distinguishing policies by their "instruments" or tools (McDonnell & Elmore, 1987). They highlighted that policy instruments—mandates, incentives, capacity building, and systems change in particular—reflected different underlying assumptions about how to motivate implementers to change. They argued that an analysis of policy designs at this level would help reveal why policies of certain types were more or less effective. (See also Schneider & Ingram, 1990.)

A wider range of people emerged in implementation studies as consequential to implementation. For example, various researchers began to illuminate the importance of state educational agency leaders and staff as designers and implementers of policy (Cohen, 1982; Fuhrman, 1988; Fuhrman et al., 1988). While schoolteachers and principals long had been topics of study in the fields of teacher education and educational leadership, research explicitly located within the field of policy implementation began to explore how these school-based professionals shaped implementation processes and outcomes (Elmore & McLaughlin, 1988; McLaughlin, 1991a, 1991b; Rosenholtz, 1985). For example, Clune and others revealed policy implementation as a negotiated process involving at least the federal government, states, and local districts through which the terms of policy compliance were constructed (Clune III, 1983). Consistent with conventions of terminology in federal legislation, studies during this period tended to refer to implementers by broad categories such as "teachers" and "state educational agencies" and not to explore how differences among individuals within these broad categories shaped implementation. Nonetheless, this research helped solidify a focus on implementers' agency as an important avenue for implementation research.

Studies in the 1980s also began to elaborate the places that mattered to implementation in several respects. For one, places included geographic locations and jurisdictions such as states that had received little attention in prior waves of reform and research. Studies revealed that these locations and jurisdictions varied in terms of their politics, culture, and histories in ways that helped to explain their differing responses to policy directives (Fuhrman et al., 1988, p. 64). Places also included new units of analysis such as "teacher networks" and "communities" and studies in this vein revealed these nonlegislated associations among implementers as powerful influences on implementers' work (Anderson et al., 1987; Fuhrman et al., 1988; Lieberman & McLaughlin, 1992; Little, 1984; Marsh & Crocker, 1991).

Some implementation researchers went so far as to make places rather than policies their main concern. That is, past decades' implementation studies generally asked whether or not a given policy was implemented. By the 1980s, a growing cadre of implementation researchers focused on high performing schools and asked: "What are the policy and other conditions in those places that explain that performance?" This approach of tracking backwards from practice to policy was a particular hallmark of the effective schools movement (Purkey & Smith, 1983; Sizer, 1986). Reinforcing this approach, McLaughlin argued that implementation researchers should move away from mainly trying to understand which policies get implemented to elaborating the various conditions that matter to enabling effective practice (McLaughlin, 1991b).

In sum, the history of education policy implementation research may be divided into three waves that correspond roughly with the decades between 1960 and 1990. These waves may be distinguished by changes in policy demands that grew progressively more varied and complex. Policy implementation research followed suit by beginning to highlight that variations in policies, people, and places matter to how implementation unfolds.

THE CURRENT STATE OF THE FIELD:
CONFRONTING COMPLEXITY

(W)e have learned that there are few "slam bang" policy effects. This is because policy effects necessarily are indirect, operating through and within the existing setting. Thus policy is transformed and adapted to conditions of the implementing unit. Consequently, local manifestations of state or federal policies will differ in fundamental respects and "effective implementation" may have different meanings in different settings. (McLaughlin, 1991, p. 190)

Education policy implementation research over the past 15 years has continued to build on lessons and insights from previous waves. However, as with previous waves, two developments mark contemporary education policy implementation research as a new generation of implementation inquiry: focal policy designs that differ significantly from those of previous eras and growing attention to how policy, people, and places interact to shape how implementation unfolds. In addition, contemporary research aims to build knowledge about implementation processes in ways that mark a distinct epistemological departure from past waves' research. I discuss each of these three trends in the following subsections.

New Policy Designs

Contemporary education policies differ from those of all three previous eras in terms of their basic design. Policies with similar designs may be found in previous decades and policies with past decades' characteristics can be found throughout contemporary educational systems. However, policies with certain features have reached a critical mass in recent years and have come to constitute a distinct trend. Table 1.1 elaborates on these major policy design distinctions.

Goals
To elaborate, the goals sought by policies of various stripes have exploded to address systemic, deep, and large-scale educational improvement. To be sure, certain past federal policies aimed to tackle such ambitious problems as societal disadvantage. However, by and large, the formal goals of even those policies focused on schools' delivery of particular discrete programs, procedural changes in schools, and students meeting basic minimum standards. Title I of the Elementary and Secondary Education Act (ESEA) reflects this distinction. In its early years, Title I of ESEA aimed to reach the long-term goal of reducing poverty and disadvantage by achieving the short- and mid-term goals of encouraging schools to provide supplemental services to help low-income, low-achieving students meet basic minimum performance standards. By 2001, Title I of ESEA had become a leg in the so-called systemic or standards-based reform movement. In conjunction with other components of ESEA, now called the No Child Left Behind Act, Title I aims to help all students achieve to high-performance standards. In the short term, it focuses on helping to develop systems of schools with

TABLE 1.1
Changes in Policy Designs "Then" and "Now"

	Then (1965–1990)	*Now (1990–early 2000s)*
Change Goals	**TO HELP CERTAIN STUDENTS REACH BASIC MINIMUM STANDARDS through discrete programs and procedural changes** Focus mainly on adding programs on to the regular school day for specific categories of students.	**TO ENSURE ALL STUDENTS ACHIEVE HIGH STANDARDS through systemic, deep, large-scale change initiatives** Aim to change professional practice throughout schools, districts, and states and students' various communities.
Targets	**SCHOOL ACTORS** Mainly school staff.	**ACTORS SYSTEMWIDE & BEYOND** People and organizations at school, district, state, and federal levels. Actors across institutions that matter for student learning, such as families, neighborhood services organizations, and youth agencies.
Tools	**LIMITED** Mainly federal mandates and incentives and other instruments that assert top-down command-and-control relation-ships in hierarchical education systems.	**SIGNIFICANTLY EXPANDED** New tools reinforce traditional control models (e.g., threat, sanctions, high stakes) but also depart from them (e.g., capacity building, systems change, learning, and community). **MULTIPLE** Tools with conflicting logics or theo-ries about how to effect change now more likely operate within single omnibus policies or otherwise con-verge on schools.

aligned content and performance standards, student performance assessments, data-driven decision making, penalties for failure to meet adequate yearly progress, major investments in supplemental services (many of which are pro-vided outside public school systems), and school choice provisions.

Likewise, contemporary education policies aimed at fostering teacher pro-fessional learning communities and improved instruction in math, science, and reading move beyond past decades' effort to distribute programs and seek fun-damental or core changes in the beliefs and practices of schoolteachers and district central office and state administrators (Coburn, 2003; Cohen & Ball, 1990; Elmore, 1996). Education policy goals sometimes extend to a scale beyond formal school systems to address the quality of learning opportunities in students' families and communities (Honig & Jehl, 2000).

Targets

The targets—people and organizations named in policy designs as those slated for change—once resided almost exclusively in schools. Contemporary policy designs now more routinely include targets who sit throughout and beyond formal educational systems. For example, as noted above, systemic reform initiatives focus on the decisions of leaders in schools, school district central offices, and state educational agencies consequential to the alignment of curricular content, instruction, and assessments. Likewise, state agencies and district central offices have launched accountability policies that place various demands on schools but that also call for the marshalling of their own staff to participate in implementation (Massell & Goertz, 2002). In other words, those targeted to implement educational policies may very well be the policy makers themselves.

Many policy designs also no longer exclusively focus on schools but rather now target various organizational actors across institutions that seem to matter for improved school performance including those in families, neighborhoods, businesses, community organizations, the courts, and service systems (Crowson & Boyd, 1993; Mawhinney & Smrekar, 1996). For example, federal policies related to science programs, bilingual education programs, after-school partnerships, and parental involvement ask schools to collaborate with families and various community-based organizations to develop and implement reform efforts (Honig & Jehl, 2000). Statewide school restructuring in Kentucky and districtwide reform in Philadelphia include community service organizations as key education policy implementers. In Chicago, low-performing schools on probation must utilize a school-level support system that includes "an external partner" such as a university or professional development organization (Burch, 2002; Finnigan & O'Day, 2003). For almost a decade, the Comprehensive School Reform Demonstration Program has required that schools work with school reform support providers in the implementation of comprehensive school reform designs (Berends, Bodilly, & Kirby, 2002; Bodilly, 1998).

Tools

Perhaps not surprisingly given these changes in goals and targets, the policy tools or underlying levers of change employed by policy makers have expanded significantly (McDonnell & Elmore, 1991). Prior to the 1990s federal, state, and other policy makers primarily relied on mandates and incentives —tools consistent with top-down command-and-control models of decision making. The 1990s and beyond have witnessed a broader set of policy tools in practice. For example, systems change tools (instruments that aim to effect change primarily by shifting authority among various parties) have appeared more prominently in recent years as part of school choice and site-based decision-making policies (e.g, Bryk, Kerbow, Rollow, & Sebring, 1993), school-linked services efforts (Smithmier, 1996), and new small autonomous schools initiatives. Teacher professional development initiatives throughout educational systems often rely on capacity building tools (instruments that aim to build resources and capabilities for future use) to increase teacher supply and quality.

Still other contemporary policies seem to represent policy instruments not specifically identified in previous catalogs of education policy tools. Various school improvement planning and waiver processes support schools' collection and use of student performance and other data to develop strategies for educational improvement (United States Department of Education, 1998b; United States General Accounting Office, 1998). Accordingly, these policies employ what Schneider and Ingram referred to as "learning tools"—tools that reflect that policy makers do not necessarily know which strategy will improve outcomes and their willingness to fund implementers to invent such improvement strategies (Schneider & Ingram, 1990). The bully pulpit or hortatory policy tools—tools that rely on the sheer power of argument and persuasion—have grown in prominence especially in the context of the 1990s standards-based reform efforts that used such slogans as "all students can learn" and "it takes a village to raise a child" as primary levers of change (Smith, Levin, & Cianci, 1997). Arguably, standard-setting and credentialing constitute a distinct policy tool, particularly prominent in the 1990s and beyond, that relies on performance targets themselves as the main lever for change (Mitchell & Encarnation, 1984). Some high-stakes testing, reconstitution, and accountability policies stem from the premise that schools will reform and improve under threat of penalty and takeover to lengths that seem quite distinct from negative incentives (Mintrop, 2003; O'Day, 2002). Still other policies use the formation of "communities" or partnerships to leverage change in various settings (Rochefort, Rosenberg, & White, 1998).

Adding to the complexity of contemporary policy designs, policies with different tools or theories of change converge on schools, districts, and states (Chrispeels, 1997; Hatch, 2002; Honig & Hatch, 2004; Knapp et al., 1998; Newmann, Smith, Allensworth, & Bryk, 2001). Schools and other implementing organizations always have managed multiple policies at the same time. However, the diversity of policy tools simultaneously at play in contemporary public educational systems means that implementers now juggle an arguably unprecedented variety of strategies, logics, and underlying assumptions about how to improve school performance in ways that significantly complicate implementation (Hatch, 2002). For example, some schools participate in new small autonomous schools or site-based management initiatives that promise considerable new autonomy for schools over curriculum, instruction, and other operations and accordingly rely on systems change or learning tools as the main levers of change. These same schools may also face mandates to participate in districtwide reading programs or professional development opportunities. Accordingly, such schools face demands both to set their own curriculum *and* follow others' decisions about curriculum. The convergence of such demands that rest on fundamentally different theories of change can create significant confusion regarding who ultimately decides and, if not managed strategically, can frustrate educational improvement goals (Honig & Hatch, 2004).

New Approaches to Implementation Research

Whereas past implementation research generally revealed *that* policy, people, and places affected implementation, contemporary implementation research specifically aims to uncover their various dimensions and *how and why interactions among these dimensions* shape implementation in particular ways. I outline these dimensions in Figure 1.1.

Policy
Contemporary studies generally suggest that policy designs have three key dimensions—goals, targets, and tools—and aim to uncover how differences at this analytic level influence implementation. For example, researchers now commonly highlight that policies with *goals* related to the core of schooling— teachers relationships with students, their subject matter, and their work-places—pose fundamentally different implementation challenges than policies that seek more peripheral changes such as new course schedules or classroom

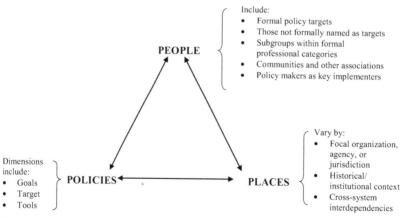

FIGURE 1.1.   Dimensions of contemporary education policy implementation in practice and research.

seating arrangements (Cuban & Tyack, 1995; Elmore, 1996; Lee & Smith, 1995; McLaughlin & Talbert, 2001; Siskin, 1994). Goals also differ by scope: Policies that aim to impact schools districtwide require a different degree of engagement by district central offices than policies that focus on a limited number of schools. Policies that focus on changes in the short term have different consequences in implementation than those that allow for a longer implementation horizon. For example, Hess highlights that accountability policies in general aim to deliver diffuse benefits over the long term; but because costs in the short term are so high, implementation of such policies typically meets strong immediate resistance, particularly among the communities the policies aim to benefit over the long term (Hess, 2002). Failure to attend to the different challenges and opportunities such policies present in short and long terms may significantly curb implementation.

Certain goals also are more or less attainable depending on implementers' starting capacity or current performance relative to the goal. For example, schools that are labeled as low-performing but that are on the cusp of meeting required performance standards face different challenges in reaching those standards than schools performing at lower levels (Mintrop, 2003). Similarly, adopting particular standards for the teaching of mathematics for some teachers may constitute a core change in their practice but for others such adoption may involve a more peripheral change (Hill, this volume).

Policy designers' choices of policy *targets* appear in implementation research as influences on implementation in their own right. For example, Malen in this volume highlights that those who stand to win or lose from particular policies significantly shape the mobilization of groups either in support of or against implementation. (See also Hess, 2002; Stone, 1998.) How various groups are named or labeled in policy designs sends signals about the targets' value in ways that significantly influence policy outcomes (Mintrop, 2003; Schneider & Ingram, 1993; Stein, 2004). For example, Pillow argues that the social construction of teen mothers as a target group within education policies has systematically denied them access to educational opportunity despite the provision of other resources (Pillow, 2004. See also Schram, 1995). Stein has revealed implementers' themselves as significant creators and reinforcers of group labels and has demonstrated how such labels may function to frustrate precisely the equity and other policy goals that implementers aim to advance (Stein, 2004; see also Datnow et al., 2001).

Tools also exert their own influences on implementation and have differential benefits depending on other implementation conditions. For example, in this volume, Coburn and Stein demonstrate how in some settings the implementation of teacher professional communities may be reinforced by central mandates whereas in other districts such mandates are unnecessary or prohibitive. (See also McLaughlin & Talbert, 2001.) The same accountability policies are met with different degrees of resistance within states depending on teacher motivation, capacity, incentives, and other factors (Mintrop, 2003). Honig has highlighted that bottom-up reform initiatives as designed generally rely on systems change and learning tools and at a minimum can spark a rethinking of relationships between school district central offices and schools; however, their strength as levers of change seems to depend on supportive contextual conditions, the starting capacity of district central offices and schools, and the assistance of intermediary organizations (Honig, 2001).

People

The people who ultimately implement policy significantly mediate implementation in a wide variety of ways that have begun to take center stage in contemporary implementation studies. First, to be sure, researchers continue to examine how those targets formally named in policy designs respond to policy demands. But given the expansion of the types of formal policy targets noted above, a focus on targets now means that contemporary studies are more likely than those of past decades to consider a host of individuals both inside and outside the formal education system including parents, youth workers, health and human service providers, and comprehensive school reform designers to name a few (e.g., Honig et al., 2001). A battery of new policy initiatives and related research highlight school district central office administrators as key mediators of policy outcomes (e.g., Burch & Spillane, 2004; Hightower, Knapp, Marsh, & McLaughlin, 2002; Honig, 2003; Spillane, 1996).

Second, researchers also focus on individuals who are not formally named as targets in policy designs but who nonetheless participate in and otherwise influence implementation. For example, Shipps has shown how business leaders had a profound effect on the implementation of various Chicago reform efforts over the course of nearly two decades even though they were not named specifically in policy designs as targets (Shipps, 1997). City mayors play increasingly prominent roles in education policy implementation not only as policy makers but as primary influences on the implementation of policies passed by state and local school boards (Cuban & Usdan, 2003; Katz, Fine, & Simon, 1997; Kirst & Bulkley, 2000).

Third, past decades' research tended to focus on groups of implementers based on their formal professional affiliations (e.g., "teachers," "central office administrators") and to assume that such groups on the whole held certain interests, beliefs, values, ideas, knowledge, and other orientations that shaped their participation in implementation. Contemporary studies are more likely to probe differences among sub-groups within these broad categories. Louis has demonstrated that implementers' functional roles—such as stimulator, storyteller, networker, and coper—reveal important implementation dynamics not always obvious from formal employment categories such as "teacher"

(Louis, 1994a). Likewise, school district central offices are less likely to appear, in Spillane's words, as "monolithic" but rather to be viewed as consisting of frontline and midlevel administrators among others who each face different demands, opportunities, and constraints in implementation (Spillane, 1998b; see also Burch & Spillane, 2004; Hannaway, 1989; Honig, 2003).

Research in this vein sometimes highlights the processes whereby various individual and group orientations shape implementation. For example, Spillane, Gomez, and Reiser in this volume build on their previous publications to reveal that implementers' identities and experiences extend well beyond their formal professional positions; these authors elaborate the individual, group, and distributed sense-making processes through which implementers draw on various identities and experiences to shape their choices during implementation. In this view, opportunities for people—policy makers and implementers alike—to learn about policy problems, policy designs, and implementation progress essentially shape how implementation unfolds (Cohen & Hill, 2000; Louis, 1994a; O'Day, 2002; see also Honig, this volume).

Fourth, researchers have come to reveal that people's participation in various communities and relationships is essential to implementation. For example, researchers have shown that teachers within schools and districts are situated in professional communities that help shape their beliefs and worldviews and ultimately their interpretations of policy messages (Cobb, McClain, Lamberg, & Dean, 2003; Coburn, 2001a; McLaughlin & Talbert, 2001; see also Coburn & Stein, this volume). Hill in this volume argues that teachers and others belong to different discourse communities that significantly shape their responses to ambitious standards-based reform demands. Pollocks' school-based ethnography examines in part how such communities in schools influence how teachers talk about and act on potentially racially charged issues in their educational improvement efforts; she recounts multiple instances in which teachers aimed to use race-neutral language in an effort not to generate negative racial stereotypes of students but in the process actually reinforced the very categories they sought to avoid (Pollock, 2001). Smylie and Evans (this volume) discuss how other forms of social interactions and trusting relationships both fuel and frustrate reform (see also, Knapp, 1997).

Importantly, contemporary education policy implementation research also continues to move beyond traditional distinctions between policy makers and implementers and teaches that both are consequential sets of people who shape how a policy is designed and implemented. For example, in this volume, Malen reveals how policy design and implementation are overlapping processes that unfold in a series of games through which those in formal designated policy-making roles and those in implementation roles shape both processes—even in cases such as school reconstitution in which traditional top-down control dynamics are a fundamental aspect of policy design. Also in this volume, Datnow elaborates on her prior work to reveal education policy systems as nested systems in which local, state, and federal actors play key roles in co-constructing policy design and implementation. Honig in this volume and elsewhere flips these traditional policy-making and implementing roles on their heads to reveal implementers as significant drivers of policy and policy makers as key implementers.

Places

Contemporary researchers build on Wave 3 studies in elaborating dimensions of places as fundamental to implementation outcomes in several respects. First, as in the past, these researchers find that governmental organizations such as state educational agencies are important settings where implementation unfolds (Hamann & Lane, 2004; Lusi, 1997). As noted above, a growing cadre of researchers explores school district central offices as central implementation sites. However contemporary studies are more likely than those of the past to probe differences in how formal organizational systems operate in the implementation process. For example O'Day revealed how district central offices function as complex systems in ways that lead to particular implementation processes (O'Day, 2002). Similarly, an emerging literature on *urban* districts teaches that these districts have particular political and institutional resources for implementation that mark them as a distinct subset of districts (Kirst & Bulkley, 2000; Orr, 1998; Stone, 1998).

Second, many contemporary researchers name their districts and states in their studies in an effort to build a body of knowledge about how implementation unfolds in these locations and to call attention to how deep-seated historical institutional patterns shape implementation outcomes. For example, the implementation literature now includes a substantial substrand concerning Chicago school reform (e.g., Bryk & Sebring, 1991; Bryk et al., 1993; Katz et al., 1997; O'Day 2002). In this volume, Dumas and Anyon reveal implementation as significantly shaped by race- and class-based tensions that may seem familiar nationwide but that are deeply rooted in the local educational, economic, and political institutions of New Jersey's cities (see also Anyon, 1997).

Some contemporary research—what I call "place-based studies"—builds on the effective schools tradition in that it focuses on particular geographic locations as a main concern and asks which policies and other conditions account for education outcomes in those settings. For example, Anyon's research for *Ghetto Schooling* began as an investigation into the school experiences of students in Newark, New Jersey's elementary schools and ultimately revealed important lessons about Marcy School's main policy implementation challenge at that time—school restructuring (Anyon, 1997). Orr's examination of Baltimore addressed the trajectory of multiple policies in which the city was engaged over more than a decade to highlight not only how particular policy initiatives fared but also more broadly how Baltimore as a community and urban system managed change (Orr, 1998, 1999).

Some of this "place-based" research has shown that schools are inextricably linked to other places—namely the urban institutions they operate within and alongside—despite Progressive Era reforms and other efforts to separate "school" from "city" (Bartelt, 1995; Yancey & Saporito, 1995). Such interdependencies mean policy makers, researchers, and others should cast a broad net when considering which places matter to implementation. On the flipside, they should aim to uncover the educational impact of policies in other sectors such as community development, health care, and social services (Anyon, 2005).

Overall, these three dimensions of implementation—policy, people, and places—come together to form a conception of implementation as a highly contingent and situated process. In this view, the benefits or limitations of one dimension cannot be adequately understood separate from the other. For example, as noted above and in the chapters by Hill and Spillane and associates, how teachers and central office administrators make sense of standards-based curricular reform depends on the policy tool employed within the given policy design, their own prior knowledge and experiences, and the broader institutional setting in which they operate. Maryland superintendents such as the one featured by Malen (this volume) seem to face different obstacles to implementing high-stakes accountability policies than the Chief Executive Officer in Chicago (Finnigan & O'Day, 2003) or state-level leaders (Massell, 2001). In these studies, variation in implementation outcomes is not the exception but the rule and researchers aim to understand how different dimensions of policies, people, and places combine to shape implementation processes and outcomes.

In the process, this generation of research is beginning to move from a static to a dynamic and contingent view of implementation capacity. That is, researchers are less likely than in the past to view capacity as a set of resources with a fixed value and more likely to conceptualize capacity as including a variety of supports whose value depends on what particular people in certain places are trying to and are currently able to accomplish. For example, past generations of researchers tended to suggest that resources such as strong leadership or increased funding were universally important to implementation and aimed to identify the specific dimensions of leadership and the total amount of funding necessary for implementation across sites. Contemporary researchers more often highlight that the importance of such resources varies depending on many factors, including what people already know and can do, the historical patterns of opportunity in particular jurisdictions, and the stakes associated with implementation outcomes. As Smylie and Evans demonstrate in the context of the Chicago Annenberg Challenge (this volume), social capital—defined in part as trusting relationships among key actors—is often highlighted as essential to implementation; however, in their case, social capital did not support implementation across the board and in some instances was actually marshaled against policy goals. Loeb and McEwan (this volume) cite numerous examples of the relative value of various resources in the context of implementing school choice and accountability policies.

In part by broadening their view of capacity, contemporary researchers have revealed a range of previously hidden or unnoticed resources necessary for implementation including various forms of cultural, political, social, technical, and institutional capital (Honig, this volume; Orr, 1998; Schram, 1995; Spillane & Thompson, 1997). The ability to learn new ideas appears as a distinct resource essential to implementation in complex policy environments; some researchers argue that this ability is so important that policies should be evaluated by the extent to which they build policy actors' capacity to learn (Cohen & Hill, 2000; Elmore, 1983; McLaughlin, this volume) and otherwise to evaluate, negotiate, and craft the fit between policies, people, and places over time (Honig & Hatch, 2004).

Distinct Approach to Knowledge-Building

The discussion above reveals that contemporary education policy implementation research also may be distinguished epistemologically—by its orientation to the nature of knowledge and knowledge-building about implementation. First, as already noted, contemporary researchers are less likely than those in past decades to seek universal truths about implementation. Rather, they aim to uncover how particular policies, people, and places interact to produce results and they seek to accumulate knowledge about these contingencies. These researchers seem to take to heart McLaughlin's admonition that "generalizations decay"—few if any findings hold true across all contexts or across all time. For example, in the early years of education policy implementation research some researchers argued that policy makers could not mandate what matters to educational improvement—that mandates were insufficient instruments for changing teachers underlying beliefs about and engagement in their work; however, over time researchers have shown that sometimes policy makers could mandate what mattered—that given certain conditions mandates did in fact leverage core changes in schools (McLaughlin, 1991b). This orientation to uncovering contingencies—what I refer to here as confronting complexity—stems not from a lack of rigor or scientific-basis for educational research but rather from the basic operational realities of complex systems in education and many other arenas. In light of these realities, education policy implementation researchers aim to uncover the various factors that combine to produce implementation results and to accumulate enough cases over time to reveal potentially predictable patterns (Majone, 1989).

Second, contemporary research increasingly reflects the orientation that variation in implementation is not a problem to be avoided but part and parcel of the basic operation of complex systems; variation should be better understood and harnessed to enhance the "capacity of program participants to produce desired results" (Elmore, 1983, p. 350; see also Honig, 2003; O'Day 2002). This view stems in part from contemporary research on student and teacher learning that suggests one size does not fit all when it comes to educational improvement, especially in diverse urban school systems; supports provided to students should vary depending on what students, teachers, and other implementers already know and can do (Darling-Hammond, 1998; Villegas & Lucas, 2002). This orientation also reflects relatively recent education policy implementation findings about sense making, interpretation, and learning as unavoidable dimensions of implementation processes. Studies in this vein uncover how individual, group, and cognitive processes contribute to implementers' variable policy responses and, for certain implementers in some settings, the achievement of policy goals (Spillane et al., 2002).

Third, contemporary research is more deeply theoretical than in past decades in keeping with conventions that define rigorous quantitative and qualitative research. As the subsequent chapters demonstrate, theory provides criteria for site selection, guides data collection and analysis, and, importantly, helps explain why certain interactions among policy, people, and places contribute to particular implementation outcomes. Such research aims not to develop a universal theory about implementation as an overall enterprise but to use theory to illuminate how particular dimensions of policies, people, and places come together to shape how implementation unfolds.

The theories on which education policy implementation researchers now draw come in part from disciplines familiar in implementation arenas such as political science and economics but researchers have begun to apply those theories in new ways. For example, economic analyses of policy implementation have tended to assume a singular implementation actor with certain almost automatic responses to policy demands. But as Loeb and McEwan reveal in their chapter, many contemporary applications of economic theory to implementation include significantly deeper explorations of how implementers' agency and context matter to implementation. At the same time, the field of education policy implementation research has expanded to embrace theoretical constructs from disciplines not traditionally applied to implementation such as those from anthropology, cognitive science, psychology, and learning theory. Critical and sociocultural theories have contributed to particularly vibrant lines of analysis (Anyon, 1997; Lipman, 2004; Stein, 2004; Sutton & Levinson, 2001).

Perhaps in a related development, qualitative research designs and methods have become important sources of knowledge for implementation researchers. In particular, strategic qualitative cases—cases that provide special opportunities to build knowledge about little understood and often complex phenomena—have long informed implementation in other fields and seem to be becoming more standard fare within education. Such methods and research designs, especially when well grounded in theory, have allowed contemporary researchers to elaborate the dimensions of and interactions among policy, people, and places that comprise implementation in contemporary educational systems. In fact, the more complex portrait of implementation processes advanced here may have become possible only recently thanks in part to the use of theoretically grounded qualitative methods for capturing such complexity.

PROGRESS OR POOR GUIDES FOR PRACTICE?

Critics of contemporary education policy implementation research and education research more broadly occasionally argue that educational researchers paint such complex portraits of the world that they obscure what is implementable and what works and serve up poor guides for practice. To the contrary, the chapters in this book suggest a deep interest on the part of researchers, their funders, and others in building a base of knowledge that can guide practice in informed, responsible, and productive ways. These chapters reflect the orientation that those who aim to produce "usable" knowledge should seek to highlight and sort through the complexity that is fundamental to implementation in contemporary education policy arenas—that implementation studies should keep pace with and reflect, not minimize, or ignore the complexity of contemporary policy demands and implementation processes. Accordingly, critics might consider that confronting complexity has been a positive development. As organizational theorists have long shown, complexity in its various forms—including variation—can serve as a stimulus for innovation and improvement especially given the diverse and sometimes unpredictable circumstances under which educational leaders routinely operate.

This volume represents a small but important sampling of how, over the course of the past four decades, education policy implementation researchers increasingly have confronted the complexity of implementation. In her important concluding chapter to this volume, McLaughlin elaborates how researchers can continue to build on this tradition. She emphasizes in particular that in confronting complexity future education policy implementation research should aim to deepen knowledge about how entire systems—those within and beyond the formal educational system—matter to educational outcomes and about the learning processes that are and should be fundamental to how implementation unfolds. In short, future researchers should delve deeper into the complexity.

The view of implementation advanced here increases the urgency for educational leaders to become more savvy consumers of research. It suggests that at this stage of knowledge development about education policy implementation leaders should look to research not for prescriptions or to light a direct path to improvement in their own local communities. Rather, they should mine the research for ideas, evidence, and other guides to inform their deliberations and decisions about how lessons from implementation research may apply to their own policies, people, and places. For example, leaders could ask whether the transformation of large high schools into multiple smaller schools contributes to educational improvement. But a search for answers would yield many studies that reveal positive results and also some important confounding cases. Rather, a more productive question might be: under what conditions within my own district, school, or organization might small schools yield positive results for my particular students? When viewed in this way contemporary education policy implementation research seems to reflect an underlying belief that educational leaders and other practitioners are willing and able (or can become willing and able) to confront complexity and to draw on a variety of increasingly nuanced research findings and other evidence to help inform their own work. This then is an optimistic book.[1]

NOTE

[1]This line refers in part to Bardach's (1980) seminal work, *The implementation game*. The introductory chapter of Bardach's book summarizes and generally laments the various ways implementation deviates from policy design and concludes: "This is not an optimistic book" (p. 6).

Chapter 2

Communities of Practice Theory and the Role of Teacher Professional Community in Policy Implementation

Cynthia E. Coburn and Mary Kay Stein

Since the 1990s, implementation researchers have increasingly come to see the problem of educational policy implementation as one of teacher learning. Scholars point to the ways that new federal, state, and local policies often require implementers to learn new ways of carrying out their work (Cohen & Barnes, 1993). They further argue that learning demands on teachers have been especially intense because state and district policy makers typically focus their attention on classroom instruction and put forth visions of instruction that depart substantially from many teachers' existing practice (Cohen & Hill, 2001; Spillane, Reiser, & Reimer, 2002). To date, most research that views implementation as involving learning has focused on teachers as individual learners. Drawing on cognitive learning theory, scholars argue that teachers understand new, often very challenging forms of instruction through the lens of their preexisting knowledge, beliefs, and experiences (Grant, 1996; Jennings, 1996; Spillane, 2000; Spillane & Callahan, 2000; Spillane & Jennings, 1997). Thus, they are likely to gravitate toward approaches that are congruent with their prior practices (Spillane, 2000), focus on surface manifestations (such as discrete activities, materials, or classroom organization) rather than deeper pedagogical principles (Coburn, 2004; Spillane, 2000; Spillane & Callahan, 2000; Spillane & Zeuli, 1999), and graft new approaches onto existing practices without altering classroom norms or routines (Coburn, 2004; Cuban, 1993).

Alongside this largely individualistic analysis is a small but growing body of research that has begun to focus on the social aspects of teacher learning. These studies point to teachers' professional communities as a crucial site for implementation (Little, 1982; Little, 2003; McLaughlin & Talbert, 2001; Smylie & Hart, 1999) and provide evidence that teachers' organizational context and patterns of interaction shape how they learn (Coburn, 2001a; Hill, 2001; McLaughlin & Talbert, 2001; Spillane, 1999).

However, this research has paid scant attention to the process by which learning in community occurs.

It is within the field of learning theory that the processes and dynamics of socially situated learning have been investigated. In contrast to conventional views of learning as an individual psychological process, sociocultural theorists argue that learning occurs as individuals participate in the social and cultural activities of their communities (Rogoff, 1994). Researchers interested in teacher professional communities have begun to draw on one stream of sociocultural learning theory—the communities of practice perspective (Lave & Wenger, 1991; Wenger, 1998)—to illuminate the social processes that shape teacher learning (Cobb, McClain, Lamberg, & Dean, 2003; Franke & Kazemi, 2001; Little, 2003; Stein & Brown, 1997; Stein, Silver, & Smith, 1998). But most of this research has yet to make the links between learning processes in communities and teachers' classroom practice. Furthermore, few have explored the implications of this approach for the ways teachers implement instructional policy. (Gallucci, 2003, is an exception.)

Here, we use the conceptual tools of communities of practice theory to investigate and elaborate the underlying mechanisms by which participation in teacher communities shapes how teachers come to understand and act on instructional policy. We view policy implementation as a process of learning that involves the gradual transformation of practice via the ongoing negotiation of meaning among teachers. We elaborate how teachers develop responses to policy by interacting with colleagues in informal communities forged through mutual engagement, joint enterprise, and shared repertoires of practice. How teachers shift their practice—that is, how they learn in response to their engagement with policy—depends on their shared history of practice. These processes, in turn, depend crucially on the connections between communities of practice in schools and the communities of practice from which policy emerges.

We illustrate these ideas with examples from two separate studies of the implementation of literacy policy. We draw on a study of statewide reading policy in California to show how the dynamics of teacher professional community *within* schools shapes what and how teachers learn in response to changing policy. We then highlight research on New York City Community School District 2's efforts to improve elementary literacy instruction to explore the ways that communities of practice *among and between* schools and districts shape implementation on a districtwide scale. Both these policies put forth visions of instruction that required significant new learning on the part of teachers and administrators at multiple levels of the system. By taking these two examples together, we advance a conception of policy implementation as a social process of learning within and between communities of practice.

TEACHERS' PROFESSIONAL COMMUNITY AND POLICY IMPLEMENTATION: WHAT DO WE KNOW?

A growing body of policy research supports the notion that teachers' professional relationships play an important role in teacher learning (Little, 2003; Smylie & Hart, 1999). This work suggests that teachers' social relations influence both the degree to which and manner in which they act on policy messages. Numerous studies have found that the strength of teachers' professional relationships influences the degree to which they change their practice. These studies argue that teachers in schools with shared goals, collaboration, a focus on student learning, shared responsibility, and social trust are more likely to make changes in their instructional practice (Elmore, Peterson, & McCarthey, 1996; Louis, Marks, & Kruse, 1996; Louis & Marks, 1998; Newmann et al., 1996; Newmann, King, & Youngs, 2000) and show increases in student learning (Lee & Smith, 1996; Louis & Marks, 1998; Rosenholtz, 1991; Yasumoto, Uekawa, & Bidwell, 2001) than teachers in schools with weak communities.

Other studies suggest that how teachers enact policy is shaped by pedagogical assumptions and preexisting practices of their colleagues (Coburn, 2001a; Hill, 2001; Gallucci, 2003; McLaughlin & Talbert, 2001; Talbert & McLaughlin, 1994). This scholarship explores variability within schools, providing evidence that teachers in microcommunities with different conceptions of appropriate instruction enact the same policy in substantively different ways (Coburn, 2001a). It also suggests that teachers in strong communities whose approaches are noncongruent with particular policies may be more likely than teachers in weaker communities to enact them in ways that depart from policy makers' intentions (Gallucci, 2003).

However, existing research provides little insight into the processes and dynamics by which teachers' interactions with colleagues create opportunities for learning that facilitate or constrain policy implementation. As a result, as Little (2002; 2003) points out, the role of teacher professional community in teacher learning and ultimately classroom change continues to remain something of a black box. Furthermore, most research focuses attention on communities of practice within schools, paying little attention to the way professional community within schools is influenced by teachers' connections with colleagues and others beyond their own schools. Yet we know from studies of professional development that some teachers are involved in professional communities outside of schools (e.g., professional development networks or with district activities) that play a key role in implementation (Coburn, 2005; Spillane, 1999) and learning (Cobb et al., 2003; Lieberman & Grolnick, 1996; Lieberman & Wood, 2001). Here, we turn to the communities of practice perspective (Brown & Duguid, 1991; Lave & Wenger, 1991; Wenger, 1998) to help us understand the process by which learning unfolds in teachers' interactions with their colleagues inside and outside of schools during policy implementation.

COMMUNITIES OF PRACTICE AS A THEORETICAL LENS

In the communities of practice perspective, learning occurs not inside the mind of individuals, but rather in the fields of social interaction between people (Hanks, 1991). Implementation, therefore, may be explained by examining these interactions. The term "community of practice" refers to a group of individuals who, through the pursuit of a joint enterprise, have developed shared practices, historical and social resources, and common perspectives. Rather than assuming that communities reside in formal organizational structures (such as grade levels, subject matter departments, or even entire schools), it locates community any place individuals opt into relationships with one another. Often, but not always, communities of practice develop as networks of informal relationships that are not congruent with formal organizational structures (Brown & Duguid, 1991; Coburn, 2001a; Wenger, 1998; Vaughan, 1996).[1] Individuals can—and usually do—participate in more than one community at a time. Communities of practice are neither intrinsically beneficial nor intrinsically harmful. Rather, they constitute the *places* in which organizational and individual learning unfolds.

Wenger (1998) contends that three dimensions characterize communities of practice: mutual engagement, a joint enterprise, and a shared repertoire (p. 73). *Mutual engagement* connotes deep involvement in activities that are significant components of daily work and important for how individuals experience the world. For example, Cobb et al. (2003) document how mathematics teachers in a district leadership team developed mutual engagement as they moved from working in isolation under a strong norm of privacy toward planning lessons together, observing each other's instruction, and watching and jointly analyzing videotapes of their classrooms.[2] Second, *joint enterprise* is the community's definition of and response to its shared situation. This enterprise is negotiated among community members and binds the community together. Stein and Brown (1997) provide an example of a group of middle school math teachers whose initial response to a reform mathematics project was to hold tight to their joint enterprise of increasing students' test scores on standardized tests. As various organizational and political factors changed, they gradually negotiated a new joint enterprise, one that was oriented toward providing high-quality, meaningful mathematics instruction. The final dimension is a *shared repertoire of practice*—the routines, rituals, ways of doing things, definitions of the situation, or particular concepts or ways of thinking that participants in a community develop in their interactions with one another

(Vaughan, 1996; Wenger, 1998). In her investigation of high school teachers' interaction in two subject matter departments, Little (2003) describes how teachers in one department invoke, challenge, and redefine ways of categorizing students (i.e., "fast" and "slow" students) as they made sense of a problem of practice. This example illustrates how systems of categorization, as part of a shared repertoire, "organize ways of talking and thinking about students, subjects, and teaching" (p. 928).

Conceptualizing Learning in Communities of Practice

In the communities of practice perspective, learning is conceptualized as the ways in which communities gradually transform their practices through ongoing negotiation of meaning as they engage with one another and respond to changing conditions in their environment. In so doing, community members evolve new ways to interact and new forms of mutual engagement, fine-tune their enterprise, and further develop their repertoire. These changes can thus be seen as a community's shared history of learning (Wenger, 1998).[3]

The negotiation of meaning is the central mechanism for driving changes in practice, or learning. Wenger (1998) suggests that negotiation of meaning occurs through the dynamic interrelationship of participation and reification where participation is active involvement in the social world and reification is "the process of giving form to experience by producing objects that congeal the experience into thingness" (p. 58). For example, in the case of instruction, reifications can include tools such as lesson plans, curricula, or assessment instruments; processes such as procedures for student placement; routines such as patterned ways of interacting with students; and conceptual categories such as ways of representing student achievement (e.g., "at risk" or "proficient").

Reifications emerge from social processes and provide a concrete representation of the processes that produced them by capturing and embodying experience in fixed form. However, they require participation from a community in order for the community to appropriate them into its ongoing practice. For example, the meaning and implications of a new textbook series or new assessment tool (both reifications) are not self-evident. Rather, teachers must engage with the tool and each other to construct an understanding of the approach and its implications for practice (Coburn, 2001a; Coburn, 2001b). It is this understanding that emerges from participation with the textbook that becomes part of practice, not the intentions of the curriculum developers that are instantiated in the reification. Thus, once created, reifications take on a life of their own, often losing connections with the process that created them.

By the same token, participation also requires reification to be meaningful. Unless participants create some record of their work with one another or some

shared understandings, it is difficult to build on previous interaction and participation can become meaningless or circular. Thus, it is the interplay of reification
and participation that creates new possibilities for the negotiation of meaning
and new opportunities for communities to adjust their participation, renegotiate
their enterprise, and continue to develop their shared repertoire over time.

Finally, communities of practice within schools are not islands. Rather they
exist in a social landscape comprising multiple and overlapping communities
that stretch within and beyond schools. Members of communities "bump up
against" reifications and people from other communities of practice, which
Wenger refers to as boundary objects, brokers, and boundary practices. Boundary objects are reifications—artifacts, terms, concepts, or documents—that reach
across the boundaries of one community into another. Brokers are individuals
who use their memberships in multiple communities to carry reifications
between them. Boundary practices are regular, ongoing forums for mutual
engagement for individuals from different communities, the purpose of which is
to sustain a connection across boundaries. All three are mechanisms to organize
the interconnections between communities. As boundary objects and brokers
move into new communities, they may introduce what Wenger refers to as "discontinuities" or interruptions into a community's ongoing practices. Such discontinuities hold the potential to open up new meanings and thus spur learning.

Policy Implementation as Learning in and Across Communities of Practice

Policy can be seen as an attempt by members of one community of practice
(policy makers) to influence or coordinate the practice of others (communities
of practice within schools) via boundary objects, brokers, or boundary practices. To reach schools, policy must often travel across the boundaries of many
communities. In the case of state policy, for example, policy may travel across
district policy communities, professional development providers, professional
associations, and school leaders, to name a few. Furthermore, to appropriate
policy into practice, communities of practice within schools must participate
with boundary objects or brokers and negotiate their meaning in ways that
have the potential, but not the guarantee, to alter their patterns of mutual
engagement, their enterprise, or their shared repertoire.

This process of negotiation depends crucially on the nature and configuration of communities of practice within schools. When policy enters schools,
it enters into multiple, overlapping communities that have developed their
own norms of mutual engagement, joint enterprise, and repertoires of practice.
In many cases, policy seeks to interrupt or reconfigure this practice, creating

what Wenger (1998) refers to as alignment, or "bridg[ing] time and space to form broader enterprises so that participants become connected through the coordination of their energies, actions, and practices" (p. 179). For example, subject matter standards in states across the country seek to shift school communities' goals for instruction (joint enterprise) and repertoire of instructional practices so that they are more aligned with the vision of state policy makers and coherent across the state.

However, communities are inherently invested in the continuity of their practice (Wenger, 1998). Thus, while communities may "reorganize their history" (p. 98) around external reifications, they are likely to do so in ways that preserve the continuity of their practice. This suggests that what communities learn from their participation with policy—how they shift their practice—depends crucially on the history of practice that they bring to this process. Hence, microcommunities within schools with different preexisting practices implement policy in significantly different ways (Coburn, 2001a; Gallucci, 2003; McLaughlin & Talbert, 2001).

The process of policy implementation also implicates the nature of the connections between these communities of practice within schools and communities of policy makers outside of schools. Frequently, communities of practice within schools are connected to the policy community in ways that rely heavily on reification—for example, some teachers encounter policy solely through boundary objects such as standards documents, subject matter frameworks, or curricular material. Wenger (1998) suggests that reifications alone, while efficient for reaching large numbers of people, have limited effectiveness in coordinating meanings because there is not enough overlapping experience between the communities that create the reification and the community that encounters it to enable a "coordinated, relevant, or generative meaning" (p. 65). At times, though, teacher communities encounter boundary objects in conjunction with opportunities to participate with the communities that created them via brokers or boundary practices. These more participatory connections potentially provide opportunities for joint negotiation of meaning and coordination of perspectives across communities, leading to greater alignment between policy and practice.

Connections between the policy community and communities of practice in school are also shaped by what Wenger calls "negotiability," or ability, legitimacy, and authority to take responsibility for and shape meaning.[4] In the case of education policy, negotiability refers to the authority to define valued ends for instruction, create programs or approaches, adapt programs to local circumstances, or construct accounts of new events or information. There is often a tension between the call for alignment on the part of policy makers and local negotiation of the meaning of approaches in schools. Policy makers' press for coordination and alignment of policy and practice requires some control on their part over the negotiability of meaning. Encouraging local communities to move toward particular visions of appropriate practice means privileging policy makers' definitions of this practice. Yet in order for local communities to integrate new approaches into their local practice, they too need the authority to negotiate meaning. Absent this authority, communities are likely to respond to pressures to align practice with compliance or proceduralization, which, Wenger argues, does not equip local communities to respond to change, unforeseen circumstances, or local variability (Wenger, 1998). On the other hand, negotiability for local communities in the absence of mechanisms for alignment works against the goal of coordination within and across communities.

In any given interaction between the policy community and communities of practice in schools, the authority to negotiate the meaning of policy might be configured differently. This suggests that in order to examine the role of teacher professional communities in policy implementation, it is important to look not only within schools at the patterns and dynamics of communities of practice, but also beyond schools at the ways within-school communities are connected in overlapping and interlocking ways to the broader policy community.

USING COMMUNITIES OF PRACTICE THEORY TO UNDERSTAND POLICY IMPLEMENTATION

To illustrate how communities of practice theory can illuminate policy implementation, we provide examples from two empirical studies. In the first example, we draw on research on how teachers in one urban California elementary school responded to dramatic changes in state reading policy. It reveals how the nature and configuration of communities of practice within the school as well as the connections between these communities and the policy environment influenced how teachers responded to policy. In the second illustration, we draw on research on New York City Community School District 2's systemwide effort to implement the Balanced Literacy Initiative. We explore how the district central office used brokers, boundary objects, and boundary practices to align perspectives across multiple communities. Taken together, these two examples illustrate how teachers' learning in response to instructional policy is shaped by multiple, overlapping communities of practice within schools and between schools and districts.

Implementing Reading Policy in California

In 1995, the state of California launched a reading initiative that put forth a vision of instruction rooted in epistemological assumptions about the nature of teaching and learning fundamentally different from previous state policy. Backed by tremendous material resources, the initiative was exceptionally comprehensive and wide reaching. By the late 1990s, teachers in elementary schools throughout the state had encountered this new policy in multiple forms, including a new textbook series, state policy documents such as standards and a new framework for reading instruction, extensive professional development, and a new high stakes standardized test. To understand how teachers' relationships influenced how they implemented new reading policy, the first author embarked on a year-long, ethnographic study of early grades teachers in two urban elementary schools.[5] Here, we use data from one school—Stadele Elementary[6]—to provide an up-close look at the processes by which teachers negotiated the meaning of new reading policy through the interplay of reification and participation in the contexts of their multiple and overlapping communities of practice.

How the early grades teachers in Stadele Elementary responded to their encounters with shifts in reading policy depended crucially on the nature of their relationships with their colleagues. As suggested by Wenger, communities of practice in Stadele did not necessarily correspond with the formal organizational structures in the school, which relied heavily on grade-level groups. Instead, teachers forged their own communities of practice with like-minded colleagues outside the bounds of their grade level group where they discussed their work, made meaning of new events and information (like policy directives), and jointly constructed their practice. Figure 2.1 provides a representation of teachers' membership in overlapping communities of practice in Stadele Elementary. For example, three first-grade teachers and one kindergarten teacher (teachers F, G, H, and M in Figure 2.1) constituted one community of practice. This group was constituted through their mutual engagement around reading instruction. They met weekly on their own for planning, ate lunch together nearly every day, and were constantly popping in and out of each other's classrooms to discuss issues about reading. Through a process of reciprocal influence, they developed a common set of goals and beliefs rooted in behaviorist assumptions that emphasized learning to read as mastering a sequence of skills. This joint enterprise guided their work, as they shared ideas about pacing skill development and worksheets so that children could practice skills to attain mastery. They also developed a mutual repertoire of practices, including a set of classroom practices (learning centers, lesson structures in reading groups, procedures for grouping students) and norms of interaction that guided their work with one another. Their shared sense of their practice was so strong that teachers consistently used "we" rather than "I" when referring to their individual beliefs and classroom practice. For example, during one interview with Teacher F, Teacher G came in the room and joined the conversation while Teacher F was explaining how she used the textbook in reading groups:

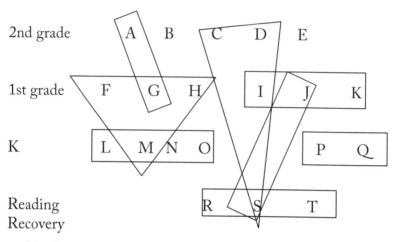

FIGURE 2.1.   Communities of practice among early grades teachers in Stadele Elementary.

F: We go through the skill work, using the charts. So this is really important. We each go through a story a week. [Teacher G enters the room and sits down. Teacher F repeats the interview question to Teacher G.]
G: We do a lot of work with blends, the vowels and . . .
F: . . . the consonants. You do the skill work, you read the story one day, and you do comprehension and you do worksheets each day . . .
G: . . . and then we do writing in learning centers to follow up.

These communities of practice—and not grade-level teams or the school as a whole—constituted key sites for negotiation of the meaning of policy reifications such as textbooks and curriculum frameworks. For example, during the year of the study, teachers received new textbooks from the recent state adoption. These textbooks can be considered a reification of the approach to reading instruction promoted by state policy. For teachers at Stadele Elementary, the textbook represented an interruption or, in Wenger's terms, a discontinuity in their ongoing practice of teaching reading.

Because different communities had different histories of practice, their engagement with the textbook varied and therefore had different implications for how they shifted their practice. Teachers F, G, H, and M had a history of using textbooks to drive their reading instruction and had developed a structure for reading groups that emphasized introducing a skill, practicing it by reading the story, and reinforcing it by doing worksheets.[7] In early planning meetings, they reviewed individual units in the textbook, reading through the stories, identifying the key skills they wanted to introduce at the beginning of the story, and finding the worksheets they could use for practice. However, the new textbook series made it difficult for teachers to do their lessons their usual way because its organization was rooted in a different theory of learning. Rather than introducing skills for each story and providing worksheets at the end, the text suggested that teachers introduce stories by building prior knowledge, work on skills in the context of the story using particular questioning strategies, and follow up with writing activities. After reviewing and jointly planning lessons for three units, teachers decided that the new reading series did not fit either with their conceptions of appropriate reading instruction or with the way they organized instruction in reading groups. One teacher declared that "you can't teach kids to learn to read" with the new textbook and the group decided to continue using their previous textbook. Thus, this group of teachers preserved the continuity of their practice and the focus of their joint enterprise by maintaining the essential core of their program in the face of a reification of a very different vision of reading instruction.

Teachers in other microcommunities of practice in the school negotiated the meaning of the same textbook series in different ways. For example, teachers C, D, and I had a shared history of teaching reading using thematic units intended to foster student construction of meaning across subject areas. Rather than using a textbook and following it in order, they created thematic units and pulled stories from the textbook and other sources that fit with the theme. They did not follow the textbook's structure for lessons, preferring to use an approach they learned in professional development a few years earlier in which children read stories individually while the teacher circulated and listened in. At the end of the story, the teacher focused on one or two teaching points, usually on things the teacher noticed the children were having difficulty with, followed by open-ended and reflective questions about the story to foster reading comprehension.

Initially, C, D, and I focused on fitting the new textbooks into their ongoing instructional routines, as they traded information about which stories in the textbook they could use with their thematic approach. However, as the year progressed, they began to pay greater attention to the instructional scripts in the teachers' manual as they struggled to find ways to increase students' ability to comprehend. One teacher eventually suggested that they turn to the text for ideas about questions that elicit comprehension:

TEACHER D: Let's look at the unit on animals from [the textbook] because there are a lot of questions that go along with the text listed in the teachers' manual and some of the questions are pretty good. Maybe we could pull from that.
TEACHER C: Are you talking open-ended at the end or along the way? [referring to whether they should ask questions at the end as they are

accustomed or along the way as suggested by the teacher scripts in the text]

TEACHER D: They [the text] say we should do it along the way. We need to ask what do you think and why.

TEACHER I: We could try it. Do they work?

TEACHER C: It's supposed to stop and make them think along the way.

Following this conversation, one teacher began to experiment using the questions from the script in the teacher's manual. After describing her experimentation to her colleagues, they also tried it in their classrooms, providing further suggestions about which aspects of the scripts to follow and which to ignore. Classroom observations later in the school year revealed that all three teachers were using some of the strategies for questioning from the textbook scripts. Rather than having children read through the stories on their own and asking reflective questions at the end, all three stopped students along the way to ask children questions focused on summarization and prediction provided by the teacher scripts in the textbooks. Thus, through their engagement with each other and the text, they shifted their practice to include selected stories from the new textbook, and shifted their overall strategy for comprehension to include some of the questioning strategies offered by the text.

In both instances, the textbook served as a point of focus for negotiating meaning. But their differing shared history of practice framed communities' engagement with this reification. Teachers incorporated the texts into their practice, constructing its meaning in ways that maintained continuity with existing practice. They incrementally shifted their shared repertoire and, in the case of teachers C, D, and I, their vision of effective comprehension instruction. However, ultimately neither community's practice was in alignment with the meaning reified in the text, or the approach promoted by policy makers.

It is important to note that teachers in Stadele Elementary School encountered the textbook as a boundary object with virtually no opportunities to participate with others who were more closely connected with the policy community that created and sanctioned it. Teachers had only limited professional development related to the textbook late in the year. Thus, the policy community distributed meaning via a heavy emphasis on reification in the form of a boundary object and a light emphasis on participation accompanying the object. As such, it lacked a social infrastructure to encourage coordination and alignment between policy and practice.

However, teachers encountered other aspects of state policy with different balances of reification and participation. When these encounters involved what Wenger calls "participative connections" between the policy community and communities of practices in schools, teachers were more likely to negotiate the meaning of policy in ways that resulted in shifts in practice better aligned with policy. For example, shortly after the state adopted new text-books, it also put forth a new framework for reading instruction that empha-sized using reading assessments to guide instruction in an ongoing manner, among other things. In Stadele's district, professional development leaders relied on teachers and teacher leaders trained in Reading Recovery to provide professional development on this aspect of the framework.[8] Two of Stadele's three Reading Recovery teachers (R and S in Figure 2.1) provided the school with training on an assessment instrument called the running record.[9] The professional development encouraged teachers to use running records to pro-vide a window into children's thinking to guide their instruction (formative assessment), rather than to solely assess at the end of a unit to ascertain if stu-dents "got it" (summative). The structured and analytic approach to assessment embodied in running records represented a substantial departure from existing assessment practice of nearly all of the early grades teachers in the school, who tended to use a more informal and intuitive approach to assessment, empha-sizing the summative rather than the formative.

In contrast with their encounter with the new textbook, teachers encoun-tered assessment policy through a balance of reification in the form of the run-ning record tool and participation in the form of conversations with key brokers—the Reading Recovery teachers—who spanned the community of district policy makers, the broader Reading Recovery community, and com-munities of practice in the school. Furthermore, different communities in the school had different levels of participation with the Reading Recovery teach-ers, depending on the nature of the connections between their community of practice and the Reading Recovery teachers' community of practice. Teachers F, G, and H participated with Reading Recovery teachers during the on-site professional development, but, for the most part, these teachers made sense of the professional development and the tool in the context of their own bounded community. They began to appropriate the running record into their practice but tended to use them in a summative manner rather than to provide forma-tive feedback or to guide instructional decisions.

Teachers C, D, and I had more intense participation with these brokers of assessment policy because one of the Reading Recovery teachers, Teacher S, often participated in conversations as part of their community of practice (see Figure 2.1). Thus, they not only participated with key brokers during profes-sional development, but also in the ongoing contexts of their work. Teacher S played a crucial role as they constructed the meaning of running records by pro-viding feedback when teachers experimented with the assessments in their classroom and serving as a resource for analyzing the results of the assessment and considering implications for practice. In so doing, Teacher S acted as a bro-ker, providing a bridge between the perspectives and learning of the broader community of Reading Recovery teachers for whom running records is a central element of their practice and the perspectives and learning of teachers C, D, and I. The teachers gradually incorporated running records into their practice, renegotiating the purposes and role of assessment in their broader program from a summative use to a formative one as they began to use assessment to guide instructional decision making. Thus, the interaction between the teachers, the broker, and the reification brought the practice for teachers in this community in greater alignment with visions of practice in district and state policy.

Balanced Literacy in New York City's Community School District 2

Research on New York City's Community School District 2's[10] systemwide implementation of the Balanced Literacy Program illustrates how entire districts function as multiple, overlapping communities of practice. We show how district policy makers used brokers, boundary objects, and boundary practices to coordinate and align the actions, energies and practices of disparate communities, while at the same time allowing for local appropriation and meaning making. As such, this case illustrates how negotiability can be distributed across a system as part of the social infrastructure that coordinates learning across multiple communities.

District 2 began its systematic effort to improve elementary literacy instruction in 1989 with the selection and adaptation of the Balanced Literacy Program (Fountas & Pinnell, 1996; New Zealand Ministry of Education, 1996).[11] When the second author began a multiyear study of the district[12] in 1996, the Balanced Literacy initiative had been in effect for nearly eight years. The practices, tools, and ideas that supported it were mature and a shared language permeated the district, from district leadership to the classroom teacher (Elmore & Burney, 1999). The array of support and resultant shared language led to instructional practices across the district that were remarkably aligned with key features of the program (D'Amico, Stein, & Harwell, 2001; Harwell, D'Amico, Stein, & Gatti, 1999; Stein, Harwell, & D'Amico, 1999; Stein & D'Amico, 2002). Although local variations in literacy practices existed, they existed within and were given meaning by the district's overall model.[13]

Most districts comprise many distinct communities of practice including but not limited to a district leadership community, a school principal community, a community of staff developers, and a whole host of teaching communities (Cobb et al., 2003; Spillane, 1998a; Wechsler, 2001). Often, communities' shared histories of learning create boundaries between members and nonmembers (Wenger, 1998). These boundaries are especially pronounced between different levels of the system because the nature of their enterprises and shared repertoires are so distinct (e.g., district leadership communities are concerned with organizing for systemic change while teacher communities are concerned with teaching children to read). In contrast, in District 2, district leaders used brokers, boundary objects, and boundary practices to create connections among these often disparate communities. These connections functioned to align learning opportunities and perspectives between policy communities and school-level communities.

First, District 2 used brokers to work across multiple communities to provide human, participatory links between communities, thus catalyzing socially organized learning. For example, staff developers tended to work in two to three schools and by virtue of their multimembership in various teacher communities, these individuals were in the position to carry elements of practice from one community into another. Often, staff developers connected less-experienced teachers with more accomplished practitioners of the Balanced Literacy Program. They were very skilled at assessing individual teachers' needs and identifying resources inherent in the practices of other teacher communities that could be used as learning resources (Stein & D'Amico, 2002). Beyond simply sharing pedagogical practices verbally, they usually arranged a visit to the other community so that teachers could observe the instructional practice and have the opportunity to talk to the observed teacher. Staff developers would accompany teachers on these visits, helping them to focus on those aspects of the practice that would be most helpful and conduct follow-up sessions with the teachers, helping them to make connections back to their own practices. In other words, this cross-community visitation accompanied by opportunities for reflection with a broker created multiple and overlapping opportunities for teachers to participate with reifications such as the Balanced Literacy framework. These participatory connections thus encouraged the development of both local and coordinated negotiations of meaning. In the words of one teacher who participated in this process:

> [Being in another teacher's classroom] really helped me sort of pull things together. I think midway through the year, I had really sort of lost sight of the importance of process and teaching kids how to do things . . . And so being in Teacher X's class sort of helped me rethink that and I also got a better sense of how to make the learning more sort of comprehensive; everything sort of like stretching. What's the best way to describe it? Sort of like making everything cohesive and relate it to each other.

District 2's leadership also used boundary objects to reach across and coordinate the practices of multiple communities of practice. The Balanced Literacy Framework—a one-page depiction of the instructional components of the Balanced Literacy Program along with a suggested order and amount of time to devote to each component[14]—was used extensively and purposefully in the practices of many disparate communities in the district. District leaders used the framework to communicate their expectations to principals and to guide what they looked for when visiting classrooms (Fink & Resnick, 2001). It helped principals guide their own observations of classrooms, to evaluate and arrange tailored support for new teachers, and to judge the "fit" of potential new programs (D'Amico & Stein, 1999). Staff developers used the framework to help teachers keep in view the entire range of assistance that must be provided to students every day. Finally, teachers used the framework to plan their day's activities and to orient themselves and their students to where they were at any given point in the literacy block. Thus, this boundary object was well positioned to play a role in coordinating the work of multiple communities across the district.

Despite its ubiquity, the framework was not taken up and used in exactly the same way across communities. Its meaning was not fixed; rather, it became a point of focus around which meaning was negotiated. In some cases, district leaders held tight to their "privileged" notion of how the framework should be applied. For example, they believed that the mostly inexperienced teachers in their lowest-performing schools (Focus Schools) should apply the framework quite faithfully. According to the director of professional development, "we really expect that the framework is adhered to [in Focus Schools] . . . It really gives [teachers] a solid base and foundation in which to know that they are doing a good job until they gain enough experience and enough strategies and enough of a repertoire where they can then flex." Once district leaders were convinced that teachers had a strong understanding of the Framework's underlying tenets and after students had shown that they were on the way to becoming proficient readers, they were allowed to use it more flexibly.

Thus, the Balanced Literacy Framework was not prescribing practice or limiting responsibility for creating a practice that would be responsive to communities' needs, context, and history of practice. The literacy practices across multiple communities in District 2 were coordinated and aligned through the use of the Balanced Literacy Framework. However, the flexible use of the framework—that is, local communities' ability to negotiate its meaning—meant that negotiability was distributed across the system, as opposed to being held completely by the policy community. Furthermore, the distribution of negotiability did not occur in a random manner, but rather in a way that allowed more negotiability as a function of more experience and better student learning results.

Finally, District 2 also used boundary practices—recurrent practices at the intersection of communities—to foster alignment between district policy communities and communities of practice in schools. Boundary practices took a variety of forms in District 2 such as three-week instructional residencies of inexperienced teachers with teacher communities whose practices were more aligned with Balanced Literacy, regularly scheduled visits between different communities, and meetings attended by representatives from several communities. Here, we discuss one boundary practice—the walk-through—and show how it provided a place for members of different communities to learn about each other's practices.

At least twice per year, a representative from the district leadership community (usually the deputy superintendent) and the director of professional development visited each school in the district. Known as a walk-through, this practice represented the intersection of four communities of practice: district leadership, staff developers, principals, and teachers. The half-day visit began with a conversation with the principal during which each teacher's practice, including any changes since the last visit, was discussed. Then the threesome would visit each classroom, noting the kind and quality of literacy instruction and student learning. Afterward, they returned to the principal's office, debriefed the observations, and made plans for actions to be taken before the next visit. Although the walk-through was almost always initiated by district leadership and thus can be interpreted as a one-way "monitoring" visit, our observations and conversations with teachers, principals, and district leaders convinced us otherwise.

The official purpose of walk-throughs is to help principals learn how to assist their teachers' learning of the instructional practices associated with the Balanced Literacy Program (Fink & Resnick, 2001). However, this goal is carried out to meet the specific needs of teachers and children in the particular schools being visited. Efforts are made to understand the context of the particular school (i.e., the developmental level of teachers, the organization of various microcommunities of practice within the school, and the background and needs of the students) and to negotiate the meaning of Balanced Literacy within that context. In this way, district leadership acknowledged that the enactment of district policy must move beyond literal compliance. That is, local communities must, in the end, take responsibility for owning and negotiating the meaning of Balanced Literacy within their school.

When viewed as an example of an established boundary practice, the walk-through illustrates how regularly occurring forums that span communities (especially the policy and teacher communities) can surface both problems of and possibilities for policy implementation. For example, because walk-throughs occurred at least twice per year, the "drift" toward nonalignment that often happens over time in policy implementation was typically "caught" and discussed before major disjunctures occurred. Similarly, during walk-throughs the director of staff development often identified common implementation problems "on the ground," which in turn fed into the design of ongoing districtwide professional development that principals were urged to send particular kinds of teachers to (e.g., first-year teachers, teachers who are struggling with Guided Reading). During walk-throughs, promising practices from teacher communities also had a chance to "bubble up" to district leaders and influence their learning thereby demonstrating that learning can occur not only from district leadership to local communities but also from local communities to district leadership. Sometimes this learning led to a modification to the Balanced Literacy Framework itself (as happened with the addition of the Word Study component) and sometimes it took the form of the creation of new brokering arrangements between schools.

Thus, the walk-through and other boundary practices served as mechanisms for learning in practice and for seeding practices across communities. Because district leaders recommended how various communities should interact with one another (both within and between schools), they retained some control over the opportunities for learning, including into which communities new practices were seeded and how. In that way, coordination and alignment remained largely under district leaders' purview. However, the walk-through and other boundary practices were accompanied by time and space for the local negotiations of meaning as well.

IMPLICATIONS FOR POLICY AND RESEARCH

Our conceptualization of policy implementation as learning within and between communities of practice has a number of implications for policy makers and policy researchers. It suggests that policy makers must not only put forth the shifts in practice they seek to engender and expect them to be implemented; they must also design what Wenger (1998) calls a "social infrastructure to foster learning" (p. 225) that enables teachers and others to move toward these practices. As the case of reading instruction in California illustrates, while policy makers can design procedures, tools, processes, and accountability systems, they ultimately cannot control how local communities shift their practices in response to these reifications. Practice is always local, situated, emergent, and linked with prior practice. However, policy makers can indirectly influence shifts in practice by shaping the conditions under which learning unfolds.

To accomplish this task, policy makers can support the development of communities of practice focused on teaching and learning. This task is not at all straightforward. Because the communities that matter for the social negotiation of meaning are emergent and informal, policy makers cannot legislate the creation or architecture of communities (Gallucci, 2003; Wenger, 1998). However, if they recognize the existence and importance of networks of informal local communities, policy makers can create organizational structures that support and even build on these networks rather than work at cross purposes to them. For example, district leaders in Stadele Elementary's district were successful in reaching teachers to the degree that they called on teacher leaders who were connected in informal ways to multiple communities of practice in schools. Policy makers can also foster the development and growth of communities of practice by providing time and space to interact, joint activities, and occasions to exercise judgment. Further, as in the case of District 2, they can think strategically about mechanisms to connect communities and manage boundaries in ways that create opportunities for introduction of new practices.

Second, policy makers can shape the conditions for learning in communities by balancing reification, participation, and negotiability in policy design. Wenger (1998) suggests that in creating boundary objects, designers must always design for participation rather than use because local negotiation of the meaning of boundary objects in participation leads to shifts in practice, not the boundary object in and of itself. This means that policy makers must attend not just to the creation of policy documents such as standards or frameworks or tools such as textbooks or accountability and incentive systems, but also to the structures of participation—boundary practices or brokers—that accompany and interact with these reifications.

As policy makers seek to design mechanisms to create alignment between and across levels of the system, issues of who has the authority to define, interpret, and shape the meaning of policy come to the fore. Different distributions of negotiability in a policy design create very different conditions for learning in communities of practice. As illustrated by the District 2 case, policy designs must strike a balance between a reliance on reifications necessary to coordinate meaning across the multiple and overlapping communities of practice, and the structures of participation necessary to create the engagement required for local communities to participate in the negotiation of meaning.

The community of practice perspective on implementation also has important implications for research design. First, it focuses attention on a new unit of analysis for studying the process and outcome of policy implementation. Typically, studies of policy implementation treat either the school or individual teacher as the key analytic unit. However, this theoretical approach suggests that communities of practice are the social location where meanings are negotiated, actions are undertaken and interpreted, and implementation unfolds. Because communities of practice exist in dynamic tension and interaction with organizations and individuals, the process and dynamics that unfold within and between communities implicate both organizational change and individual learning. As such, they offer a strategic site to understand the social and organizational mechanisms underlying implementation.

Further, this perspective suggests that the location of communities of practice is not something that can be prespecified in a research design. Because they are emergent rather than designed, the identification of communities of practice is itself an object of empirical study. Thus, the first step in any study of the role of communities of practice in policy implementation is to identify the relevant communities and the connections between them (see, for example, Cobb et al., 2003 and Coburn, 2001a). This approach departs and indeed challenges most existing research on teacher professional community and implementation, which tends to investigate social interaction in prespecified formal organizational units such as schools, grade levels, or subject matter departments.

Third, by viewing the connections between policymakers and teachers as a series of multiple, overlapping communities, communities of practice theory pushes studies of teacher professional community up and out of schools. Most studies in this area have remained firmly situated within schools (Cobb et al., 2003 and Wechsler, 2001 are exceptions). Yet, as this chapter illustrates, learning within communities of practice in schools is linked with and shaped by connections with other communities that stretch beyond the school walls. Boundary objects, brokers, and boundary practices create connections, disconnections, and fundamentally different conditions for the negotiation of meaning necessary for policy to move in and through the system and for teachers to appropriate policy into their ongoing practice. Understanding these dynamics is crucial to illuminating the key role that communities of practice play in policy implementation.

NOTES

We wish to thank Meredith Honig, Nathan MacBrien, and two anonymous reviewers for helpful comments on earlier versions of this chapter. Thanks also to Mika Yamashita and Gabriela Silvestre for research assistance.

[1]Research on teacher professional communities suggests communities of practice are more likely to coincide with formal organizational structures in high schools (e.g., subject matter departments) (Bidwell & Yasumoto, 1999; McLaughlin & Talbert, 2001; Siskin, 1994; Yasumoto et al., 2001) than in elementary schools (e.g., grade levels) (Coburn, 2001a).

[2]It is important to note that mutual engagement does not imply homogeneity of practice. Individuals engaged in ongoing interaction may play different roles, or play similar roles in different ways. What is important for mutual engagement is that individuals engage with one another to negotiate understandings of the work.

[3]*Individuals'* learning can be conceptualized as trajectories within the community as they progress from the legitimate peripheral participation of newcomers to the fuller forms of participation of old-timers (Lave & Wenger, 1991; Stein et al., 1998). As they progress they acquire the skills, the identity, and the ways of acting and interacting valued by the community.

[4]Wenger's account moves away from traditional conceptions of power as involving conflict, domination, and competing interests. Rather, it focuses on what Wenger refers to as "economies of meaning," or the authority to take part in the construction of meaning within and across communities. This aspect of power becomes important as different meanings are produced in different places in the system, governing the ways policy implementation unfolds.

[5]The data for this section comes from a larger study of the relationship between changes in reading policy and early-grades teachers' classroom instruction in two urban elementary schools (Coburn, 2001b). During the 1998–1999 school year, the first author spent 130 hours observing teacher interaction during formal meetings and professional development, supplementing this with countless hours observing teacher interaction in informal settings such as lunchtime, before and after school, and in the hallways. Observation of teacher interaction was supplemented with fifty-seven interviews with eighteen classroom teachers and resources teachers and three interviews with the principal. Finally, to understand teachers' classroom practice, the first author conducted 106 hours of classroom observation with five first- and second-grade teachers and three Reading Recovery teachers. For further description of research methods, see Coburn 2001a; Coburn 2001b.

[6]Stadele Elementary is a pseudonym for a large, urban elementary school in a district in Northern California. At the time of the study, Stadele had 692 students, 32 certified teachers, and a single administrator. Ninety-seven percent of children were of color, 48 percent were classified as English Language Learners, and 67 percent qualified for free or reduced-price lunch.

[7]Teacher M did not participate in this aspect of their shared repertoire because she taught kindergarten and most of her children were yet to be independent readers.

[8]Reading Recovery is an intervention program for first graders focused on intensive, one-on-one reading instruction to students who are the lowest achieving readers in their class. It is a pull-out tutoring program in which trained teachers work with students for a half-hour every day, for from twelve to twenty weeks (Askew, Fountas, Lyons, Pinnell, & Schmitt, 1998; Neal, Kelly, Klein, & Schubert, 1997). Typically, Reading Recovery teachers in schools are linked with a Reading Recovery program at the district, which coordinates ongoing professional development called "continuing contact" for all Reading Recovery teachers. As such, Reading Recovery teachers in schools are always part of a broader community that stretches beyond the school to the district, region, and, at times, the national Reading Recovery network.

[9]Running records are a form of assessment that provides insight into both a child's reading process (What strategies are they using to decode?) and a child's reading level (What books can a child read on an "instructional" level?) (Fountas & Pinnell, 1996).

[10]District 2 was one of the thirty-two community school districts that, until 2003, comprised the elementary and middle school portion of the New York City public school system. The district was ethnically diverse with the number of students eligible for free or reduced-price lunch ranging from 10 percent to 99 percent.

[11]Balanced Literacy is a theory-driven, literature-based program that assists the learning-to-read process based on the assessment of children's reading levels and the provision of texts and instructional supports geared to those levels.

[12]The data for this section come from the High Performance Learning Communities Project (Resnick, Elmore, & Alvarado, 1996). From 1996 to 2000, researchers gathered both qualitative and quantitative data at all levels of the system. Qualitative methods included interviews with district leaders, school leaders, and classroom teachers as well as observations of principal and staff developer meetings, districtwide professional development sessions, school-level meetings and professional development, and classroom instruction. Quantitative methods included surveys of teachers and principals as well as the collection and analysis of student achievement data. For an overview of research methods, publications, and project reports, please see the High Performance Learning Communities Project Final Report (2001).

[13]For example, one school utilized partner reading instead of Guided Reading to accomplish similar goals. Another school integrated an interactive writing component into the district's overall writing model.

[14]As with all reifications, an incredible amount of information "sits beneath" this framework. Produced through months of interactions between District 2 leaders and the New Zealand-based experts that helped to adapt Balanced Literacy for the District 2 context, the framework takes into account a Vygotskian-based theory of how children learn to read, the kinds and amount of support children need on a daily basis to make progress toward independent reading, and how this support can be incorporated into a ninety-minute literacy block.

Chapter 3

Policy Implementation and Cognition

The Role of Human, Social, and Distributed Cognition in Framing Policy Implementation

James P. Spillane, Brian J. Reiser, and Louis M. Gomez

Scholars of implementation have developed many explanations for how policy does and does not get implemented. These explanations focus on everything from the design of policy to the resistance of those responsible for implementing policy in local jurisdictions such as schools and school districts. These accounts rest on assumptions that implementers understand a policy's intended messages and that implementation failure is a function of an unclear policy message or the mismatch between policy and the agendas and interests of local implementers.

Some recent work in implementation research has challenged these pervasive assumptions by showing that even when teachers and administrators heed higher-level policies and work hard to implement them implementation failures still persist (Cohen & Hill, 2000; Firestone, Fitz, & Broadfoot, 1999). This work suggest that viewing implementation failure exclusively as a result of poor policy clarity or deliberate attempts to ignore or sabotage policy neglects the complexity of the human sense-making processes consequential to implementation.

This chapter reviews and extends this growing body of implementation literature that applies cognitive frames to the study of policy implementation. Such frames also fall under such rubrics as "interpretation," "cognition," "learning," "sense-making," and "reading," (Ball, 1994; Cohen & Hill, 1999; Lin, 1998, 2000; Spillane, 2004; Weiss, 1989, 1990, 1993; Yannow, 1998). From a cognitive perspective, implementation hinges on whether and in what ways local implementing agents' understanding of policy demands impacts the extent to which they reinforce or alter their practice (Spillane, 2004; Spillane, Reiser, & Reimer, 2002).

Attention to how implementing agents interpret policy is especially relevant considering attempts over the past decade by public policy-makers to press for ever more complex changes in local behavior—changes that necessitate fundamental transformations of local practice. Among these attempts, the standards movement in education called for more intellectually demanding content for all American children and otherwise focused on enhancing all students' principled knowledge—that is, their knowledge concerning key ideas and concepts. Such calls for principled knowledge in the standards movement challenged popular conceptions of teaching, learning, and subject matter as well as deeply held beliefs about which students can do intellectually demanding work in school. Such policy designs present relatively complex ideas to teachers and other implementers and thereby throw into relief the importance of their interpretations to implementation. Furthermore, their implementation ultimately requires fundamental shifts in many implementers' views of their practice.

We structure this chapter around two questions. First, we consider what we have learned about policy implementation from applying cognitive frames to investigations of standards-based reform implementation. In doing that, we consider both the application of individual and social cognition frames to studies of policy implementation. Second, we explore where we might go next in using a cognitive perspective to understand policy implementation with a focus on the importance of a distributed cognition perspective. We argue that cognition is an essential lens for understanding education policy implementation, especially the implementation of policies that demand significant shifts in teachers' practice, but that investigations of the role of cognition in policy implementation to date, including some of our own investigations, have failed to grapple with cognition as a distributed practice. The prevailing framework for studying cognition in the implementation process centers on the cognitive scripts and understandings of the individual sense-maker or on the influence of social circumstances on individual cognition. We consider what a distributed cognition framework might add to studies of policy implementation.

RETROSPECTIVE: WHAT HAVE WE LEARNED
FROM A COGNITIVE PERSPECTIVE ON IMPLEMENTATION?[1]

Cognitive frames have been used in studies of policy implementation in education to investigate how various dimensions of human sense-making influence implementation. Some of this work concentrates on implementing agents' prior knowledge (Cohen & Weiss, 1993) and the analogies that implementing agents draw between new ideas and their existing understandings

(Spillane, 2000). Other work concentrates on how aspects of social situations—including organizational and community history (Lin, 2000; Yanow, 1996), organizational segmentation and professional expertise (Spillane, 1998b), professional discourse (Hill, 2000), and formal and informal networks (Coburn, 2001a)—influence implementing agents' sense making. We take up both separately below.

Implementing Agent's Cognition

Considering the role of human cognition in policy implementation underscores the importance of unintentional failures of implementation. What is paramount is not simply *that* implementing agents choose to respond to policy but also *what* they understand themselves to be responding to. The "what" of policy begins with the policy texts such as directions, goals, and regulations. Individuals must use their prior knowledge and experience to notice, make sense of, interpret, and react to incoming stimuli—all the while, actively constructing meaning from their interactions with the environment of which policy is part. As Cohen and Weiss argue, "When research is used in policy making, it is mediated through users' earlier knowledge," with the policy message "supplementing" rather than "supplanting" teachers' and other implementing agents' prior knowledge and practice (Cohen & Weiss, 1993, p. 227).

The fundamental nature of cognition is that new information is always interpreted in light of what is already understood (Brewer & Nakamura, 1984; Greeno, Collins, & Resnick, 1996). An individual's prior knowledge and experience, including tacitly held expectations and beliefs about how the world works, serve as a lens influencing what the individual notices in the environment and how the stimuli that are noticed are processed, encoded, organized, and subsequently interpreted.

Schemas are specific knowledge structures that link together related concepts used to make sense of the world and to make predictions. They represent understandings of complexes of ideas for everyday objects and events, such as "kitchen," "classroom," "going shopping," or "reviewing homework" (Mandler, 1984; Rumelhart, 1980; Schank & Abelson, 1977). Schemas encode causal explanations or theories about how the world operates (Keil, 1989; Markus & Zajonc, 1985; Murphy & Medin, 1985; Schank, 1986). Schemas also encode knowledge about the social world by representing associations of expectations about people and social situations (Cantor & Mischel, 1979; Cantor, Mischel, & Schwartz, 1982; Trope, 1986) such as how one interacts with others at a party or business meeting and how one expects librarians, musicians, and auto mechanics to appear and behave.

Schemas can guide the processing of information, help to focus information processing, and otherwise enable individuals to use past understandings to see patterns in rich or ambiguous information. Accessing a schema from memory affects comprehension by activating collections of expectations that are used to fill the gaps in what is explicitly said or observed, driving the "top-down" nature of comprehension, so that much of what is understood is in fact inferred from input that is only partially explicit (Brewer & Nakamura, 1984; Schank & Abelson, 1977). For example, understanding and memory involve accessing and using schemas to construct a network of coherent goals, events, and states, filling gaps between those goals, events, and states explicitly mentioned and the many plausible inferences "invited" by the schema (Bower, Black, & Turner, 1979; Bower & Morrow, 1990; Brewer & Nakamura, 1984). In policy terms, people naturally categorize what they see in terms of existing knowledge structures by encoding conceptions of types of people or behaviors (Kunda & Thagard, 1996; Trope, 1986). Once accessed, a schema can focus an interpretation, helping to resolve ambiguous information and thereby affecting the interpretation of information presented in that context (Higgins, 1996).

For example, people may interpret an ambiguous statement or facial expression on the basis of how they would expect a person to react in such a situation. People also tend to pay more attention to information that confirms rather than challenges or refutes their expectations (Klayman & Ha, 1987; Olson, Roese, & Zanna, 1996). Schemas allow memory to be reconstructed, using general knowledge to search for and infer likely contextual information from the partial information explicitly recalled (Kolodner, 1983).

Research on schemas also has stressed the mental representation of dynamic processes, called mental models (Gentner & Stevens, 1983). An important finding in this research is that people construct intuitive models from their experience, apart from formal instruction (Greeno, 1989; Vosniadou & Brewer, 1992), and use those models to envision a situation, essentially "running" the model to make predictions about its causes and outcomes. People build intuitive models of the physical world (Carey, 1985; Smith, diSessa, & Roschelle, 1993) and the world of social interactions (Cantor & Mischel, 1979; Cantor et al., 1982; Markus, 1977; Nisbett & Ross, 1980). For example, intuitive models allow people to predict what will happen when someone pushes a chair or bounces a ball, or how a potential employer will react to various kinds of behavior in a job interview. Similarly, people construct their own intuitive models that encode their biases, expectations, and explanations about how people think and how they learn (Dweck, 1999; Hammer & Elby, 2002). Intuitive models of learning and classroom interactions should strongly influence how agents interpret reforms. For example, when asked to interpret a proposed instructional practice, such as encouraging elementary students to explain their mathematical reasoning, one applies tacit knowledge about children and the discipline to mentally envision the situation and draw inferences about how effective that practice would be.

These concepts move implementation researchers beyond simply recognizing that lack of knowledge interferes with the ability to understand. It highlights that different agents will construct different understandings even when they have complete knowledge of reform demands and view new demands in terms of what they already know and believe. What implementers see is influenced by what they expect to see.

A second implication of this framework concerns the difficulty of accomplishing major restructuring of schemas as part of learning. In early accounts of learning and development, Piaget (1972) stressed the importance of what he termed "accommodation," or the restructuring of existing knowledge. But the complementary process of "assimilation," or encoding stimuli into existing knowledge frames, is often the central part of perception and action. Assimilation is a conserving process, as it strives to "make the unfamiliar familiar, to reduce the new to the old" (Flavell, 1963, p. 50). Later cognitive accounts of conceptual change stressed the difficulty of major restructuring and the need for continued engagement with problematic ideas as a catalyst for this restructuring (Carey, 1985). Thus the sense-making framework implies that learning new ideas such as certain standards-based instructional approaches is not simply an act of encoding these new ideas; it may require restructuring a complex of existing schemas, and the new ideas are subject to the danger of being seen as minor variations of what is already understood rather than as different in critically important ways.

A third implication of the sense-making framework for policy implementation concerns the mechanisms for accessing and applying knowledge structures. The concrete features of a situation are highly salient to human sense-making processes. Superficial aspects of a situation, although not the most significant for deep conceptual analysis, nevertheless are effective memory triggers for superficially similar situations. People often rely on superficial similarities when accessing related information from memory, even when knowledge structures connected through deeper principles might be relevant (Gentner, Rattermann, & Forbus, 1994; Ross, 1987). Experts can see deeper meaningful patterns in problem situations that may not be apparent to novices (Chase & Simon, 1974; Chi, Feltovich, & Glaser, 1981; Larkin, McDermott, Simon, & Simon, 1980; VanLehn, 1989).

Experts focus their attention on features of stimuli that are more significant conceptually. That is, they can see situations in terms of the "big ideas" and core principles of a specific domain. Consequently, experts are less likely to be distracted by similarities that are only superficial—they are less likely to "lose the forest for the trees" in solving problems—and can access situations connected by deeper principles (Novick, 1988). The difficulty this poses for reform is that agents with less expertise in the substance of the reforms may rely more than they should on superficial similarity and assume that two situations are similar in important principled ways because they are similar in salient superficial aspects. For example, mathematics teachers may not distinguish between two teaching scenarios that both use concrete manipulatives— one where the manipulatives form the basis for mathematics exploration and discourse in ways consistent with standards-based math reforms and one where the same manipulatives are used in a more procedural way (Cohen, 1990).

In the next three subsections, we examine how a cognitive sense-making framework helps explain the implementation of policies that urge fundamental changes in classroom instruction. First, we consider how top-down comprehension can lead to differences in interpretation of the same instructional policy messages. Second, we consider the obstacles to true restructuring of implementing agents' schemas and the dangers of seeing what should be partially new ideas as mere examples of what is already known. Third, we consider how implementing agents may be distracted by superficial similarities, becoming overconfident about their success in achieving the true principles of the reform.

Different interpretations of the same message

The Educational Policy and Practice Study's (EPPS) research on mathematics and language arts standards in California, Michigan, and South Carolina underscores how teachers' and administrators' prior knowledge and practice influence their ideas about changing instructional practice (Cohen & Barnes, 1993; Jennings, 1992; Spillane, 1996, 1998a). Even teachers who used the same language (e.g., "reading strategies") did not have the same ideas about revising reading instruction.[2] Some differences were due to the teachers' varying opportunities to learn about the policy, including the policy texts available, professional development workshops, and guidance and support from the district or school. Yet even teachers who encountered the policy from the same policy texts or professional development experiences constructed different understandings of the policy's message about revising reading instruction. Teachers' beliefs about subject matter, teaching, students, and learning were influential in what they interpreted from state and national standards about their practice. Differences in interpretation were more predictive of the level of implementation than of teachers' outright rejection of the reform.

Recent studies demonstrate similar trends in which misunderstandings about implementation cannot be attributed to lack of effort, incomplete buy-in or explicit rejection of the reform's ideas. Hill (2001) found that teachers working on a district committee to adopt materials to support the state's mathematics policy understood the reform ideas in ways very different from what the state intended. These teachers, perceiving little distance between their own position and the state's, assumed that a traditional curriculum was sufficient to implement great chunks of a state policy that was designed to press fundamental change in mathematics education. What is striking is that the teachers devoted substantial time to discussing and attempting to figure out the state's mathematics policy. Thus their misunderstandings of the reform proposals cannot be explained in terms of limited or perfunctory attention to the policy. Another study of the implementation of standards-based mathematics reforms in four Colorado school districts identified as leaders in standards-based reform also reveals the influence of individual interpretations on implementation (Haug, 1999). Although the four districts had had standards in place for several years, there was "great variability" in local educators' understandings, ranging from interpreting the state reform as a curricular checklist to understanding it as involving fundamental change in classroom practice (Haug, 1999, p. 256). The differences in interpretation were predictive of levels of implementation in these districts.

New ideas misunderstood as familiar interfere with change
Ideas may be seen as more familiar than they actually are. Thus, when implementing agents perceive an instructional idea in policy, the idea may be over-interpreted as essentially the same as the belief or practice that the teachers already hold. In this case, the influence of expectations from existing knowledge structures helps to focus understanding in ways that lead to rejection of information incongruous with those expectations (Chinn & Brewer, 1993; Keisler & Sproull, 1982). Fundamental conceptual change requiring restructuring of existing knowledge is extremely difficult (Strike & Posner, 1985). Understanding involves accessing relevant structures in memory and applying them to make sense of what is presented and the top-down nature of this process often causes inconsistencies or unexpected features to be overlooked.

In some situations, however, features that violate expectations can become the focus of attention; they may be noticed and remembered as inconsistent information when one is motivated to be attentive to all details (Stangor & McMillan, 1992), perhaps because the incongruities trigger explanatory reasoning to account for the violation of expectations (Schank, 1986). This kind of effort to explain discrepant cases is precisely what is needed for deep conceptual reorganization to occur (Carey, 1985; Strike & Posner, 1985). It takes more than a single discrepant event, however. A sustained engagement with a sequence of problematic ideas and an explicit goal of making sense of them and reconsidering what is already "known" are required (Smith, Snir, & Grosslight, 1992; Strike & Posner, 1985, 1992).

Recent implementation research suggests that seeing new ideas as familiar is indeed an obstacle to implementation. A recent study of school districts' responses to state and national mathematics and science policies suggests that district leaders were more likely to attend to familiar policy ideas than to the more novel ideas (Spillane, 2000; Spillane & Callahan, 2000). Reform ideas such as "hands-on mathematics" and "problem solving," popularized in previous reform waves and already part of practitioners' conversations about instruction, featured much more prominently in district officials' understandings of the policy message than did novel reform ideas such as "mathematics as communication" and "mathematics as reasoning." A similar pattern appears in studies of classroom implementation. For example, case studies of teachers' responses to the California Mathematics Frameworks show that teachers missed the unfamiliar and more fundamental transformation in mathematics content and pedagogy sought by the frameworks (Cohen, 1990). They noticed and attended to familiar ideas, such as group work and the use of manipulatives; however, lacking a mental framework to connect and explain the unfamiliar ideas, they devoted less attention to them and often overlooked them altogether.

Both the EPPS study and the Hill (2001) study described earlier underscore the conserving nature of teachers' sense-making with respect to state standards. For example, the EPPS researchers found that California teachers' understandings of that state's mathematics frameworks contained a blend of old and new ideas about instruction (Cohen, 1990). A study of the implementation of state and national assessment policy intended to challenge conventional ideas about mathematics and mathematics pedagogy involving schools in Maryland, Maine, England, and Wales also found that teachers tended to assimilate reformers' proposals into their existing frameworks (Firestone et al., 1999). For example, teachers interpreted complex assessment items requiring students to construct responses as chiefly requiring the memorization of simple formulas and algorithms. Thus the teachers constructed understandings of the reform ideas that fit within their existing models for mathematics and mathematics instruction rather than substantially rethinking them, leading to important differences between the intended policy and these teachers' understanding.

Studies of science teachers have revealed similar findings; teachers incorporate reform ideas into their existing beliefs and understandings of epistemology and learning, posing challenges for reform when teachers' tacit models conflicted with the intent of the policy (Beck, Czerniak, & Lumpe, 2000; Czerniak & Lumpe, 1996). Teachers see new policies in terms of their current understandings; they interpret science reforms such as standards-based teaching and inquiry in terms of access to more textbooks or emphasis on hands-on activities (Vesilind & Jones, 1998). Technology intended to bring inquiry pedagogy into science classrooms is often seen as simply an extension of library research and incorporated into existing practice rather than enabling students to play new roles of question posing, investigation, and argumentation (Songer, Lee, & Karn, 2002).

Understanding may focus on superficial features, missing deeper relationships
People can be misled by superficial similarities in situations. Only with substantial expertise do they look beneath the surface to recognize deeper principles. Understanding may focus on the superficial features in comparison and analogical reasoning. Consequently, agents may see important similarities between classroom activities and policy goals, but those similarities may be only superficial. One may perceive implementation to be as intended by policy makers because the core surface features such as "problem solving" or "using manipulatives" or "hands-on activities" are represented, even if deeper and more abstract principles such as changes in mathematical discourse or changes in students' epistemological stance toward science are not reflected. This is important when it comes to the implementation of policies that press for complex changes in extant behavior, because in such instances, most implementing agents are novices. Few are experts when policy charts new terrain.

A recent study examining prevalent patterns in implementing agents' understandings of mathematics and science standards shows that, when implementing agents encounter new ideas about their work through policy, they are more likely to draw surface-level connections to their prior experiences. Studying the local school districts' responses to state and national mathematics policy, this work highlighted how agents' understandings of the reform message tended to focus on surface features rather than the underlying structural ideas (Spillane, 2000; Spillane & Callahan, 2000; Spillane, 2004). In this study, four-fifths of district leaders expressed a "form-focused" understanding, in which the agents' interpretations of key reform ideas, such as problem solving in mathematics, focused on the surface-level forms rather than the underlying functions of the policy ideas. For example, their understandings of problem solving focused on the form of the mathematical problems; implementing the mathematics reforms involved making the story problems given to students more realistic and connected to real life situations, but did not involve any changes in the epistemological function of mathematics education. While problem solving did represent change for these district leaders, it did not involve fundamental change in what counted as mathematics. Drawing surface analogs and failing to access the deeper structural relations between the reform proposals and their experiences, district leaders interpreted the reform in ways that missed its core intent, contributing to superficial implementation of state and national mathematics policies.

A SOCIAL COGNITION PERSPECTIVE ON IMPLEMENTATION

While the previous set of concepts about individual sense-making is powerful for explaining certain dimensions of implementation, other research reveals that sense-making is not a solo affair; an individual's situation or social context fundamentally shapes how human cognition affects policy implementation. Adding the dimension of social context to discussions of human sense-making presses us to consider how knowledge—embedded in social contexts as the practices and common beliefs of a community—affects sense-making and action in implementation and how implementing agents encounter policy in a complex web of organizational structures, professional affiliations, social networks, and traditions.

An aspect of situation that has featured prominently in scholarship is the institutional sector—such as hospitals, schools, social service agencies—in which implementing agents work. Social agents' thinking and action is situated in institutional sectors that provide norms, rules, and definitions of the environment that both constrain and enable action (DiMaggio & Power, 1991; Scott & Meyer, 1991). Showing that individual cognition and agency are constrained by the institutional sectors in which they are situated, this work illuminates how different sectors structure work practices, innovation, and the implementation process. For example, almost three decades of scholarship on schools from an institutional perspective suggests, among other things, that schools "decouple" formal structure (i.e., administration and management) from core activities (i.e., teaching and learning) (Meyer & Rowan, 1977, 1978; Weick, 1976).

Some recent implementation studies have underscored the influential role of social interactions as part of social context in the implementation process. Studies of the mediating role of teachers' professional communities in teachers' construction of messages about their practice from policy and other sources emphasize the importance of socially mediated sense-making in the implementation process (Coburn, 2001a; Stein & Brown, 1997). As members of a community interact over time on problems of shared concern, they negotiate meanings about the nature of their work and in some instances they forge shared understandings. These shared understandings become a filter for ideas about revising extant practice that are pressed by policy and other sources. Coburn (2001a), for example, described how teachers' sense-making even within the same school could be situated in different formal and informal groups; these situations mattered because teacher groups often made different sense of the same policy messages. This underscores that human interaction patterns in schools and other delivery agencies are in part a function of organizational structure. Organizational arrangements can hamper or enable interactions among implementing agents about policy and practice. In schools, the prevailing "egg-carton" structure, in which teachers work chiefly as isolates with little interaction with colleagues, undermines opportunities for teachers to test or be exposed to alternative understandings of policy proposals (Lortie, 1975).

Dominant patterns aside, schools nevertheless vary in their ways of structuring the work of teaching, and especially in the extent to which their structural arrangements support interactions among staff about their work. Those arrangements are especially influential when it comes to innovation in schools (Bryk, Lee, & Holland, 1993; Driscoll, 1990; Little, 1982, 1990; Louis & Kruse, 1995). Consider, for example, Bouillion's (2000) effort to understand how nine school districts approached the task of implementing a project-based science reform. The districts varied along several dimensions, geographical setting, and students' socioeconomic status. Ostensibly, there was one common innovation for all the schools: a project-based education reform that required students to do work that was both relevant to school curricula and was coupled to a local community problem. Bouillion's analysis of implementation practices in these diverse schools revealed tremendous variation. Some school districts were able to accomplish highly articulated programs that connected students on a regular basis to outside partners, whereas other school districts were barely able to create an infrastructure where students had only the briefest contact with partners beyond the school building. In other cases, it was clear that the partnership arrangements developed between school and community had the appearance of peerage (i.e., equals negotiating with equals). By contrast, in other cases, it appeared as though students and teachers from schools considered their role to be one of client service to the outside community organization. Bouillion's analysis suggested that community setting had a lot to do with the selected implementation strategy. As a case in point, she suggests that implementers in the middle-class districts tended to treat outside partners as peers where this was less true in the districts of lower socioeconomic status.

Recent implementation research reveals that organizational arrangements are also a dimension of context consequential to the sense-making process. For example, a study of a district office's role in the implementation of state policy illuminates how organizational arrangements can contribute to the construction of multiple and sometimes contradictory understandings in the same office about the same policy on revising instruction (Spillane, 1998b). Specifically, responsibility for reading instruction in the district office is often divided among subunits such as an assessment office, a staff development office, a Title I office, and a curriculum office. District administrators' *situations* influenced their understandings of the reading policy; that is, organizational arrangements and the accompanying vertical and horizontal segmentation of responsibility enabled different parts of these school districts to construct the policy message differently and to respond separately and often in different ways. Different subunits took their cues from different parts of the school system, cues that influenced their particular missions. Efforts to enact the reading reforms varied among subunits because they construed and prioritized state policy through their distinct missions and responded to the policy in ways that reflected these different understandings (Spillane, 1998b). Different subunits sent teachers different, and at times conflicting, messages about reforming reading instruction.

In general, implementing agents' work is nested in multiple organizational contexts simultaneously (McLaughlin & Talbert, 1993b). This is especially true in education: schoolteachers and administrators work in schools that are nested in school districts, which in turn are nested in states, and so on. Overlapping contexts interact with each other and situate implementing agents' attempts to make sense of standards and other education policies. Similar to the characterization given by Bronfenbrenner (1979) for the developing organism, sense-making agents are local organizational ecological niches whose success or failure is shaped by multiple interacting contexts. For the most part, prior analysis of individual agents has not sought to characterize and specify the patterns of these interacting forces.

In thinking about the social nature of implementing agents' sense-making it is important to take into account not only the formal education system but also the extra system of textbook publishers, professional development providers, educational consultants, and the like. "Implementation networks" in the fields of law enforcement and education can influence implementing agents' sense-making during the implementation process (Hill, 2000). Actors within the extra system are especially influential in shaping school-level interpretations of district accountability policies (Burch, 2000).

Professional specializations are one potentially influential extra-system context for implementing agents' sense-making. The professional or occupational identities of workers influence their work with individuals in professional communities through reinforcing shared norms, knowledge, perspectives, commitments, and often a language or vocabulary, all of which influence their work in the organization (Clark, 1983; Van Maanen & Barley, 1984). Professional specializations frequently form the basis for connections with groups outside the organization as individuals network with other members of their professional communities (Clark, 1983; Scott & Cohen, 1995).

These professional affiliations *situate* implementing agents' efforts to interpret policy and may contribute to the construction of the different understandings of policy messages at the district level (Spillane, 1998b) and at the school level (Ball & Lacy, 1984; Little, 1993; McLaughlin & Talbert, 1993b; Siskin, 1991, 1994). For example, the study referred to earlier (Spillane, 1998b) illuminates how district central office staff in a segmented organization had very diverse professional associations and identities; they included reading specialists, assessment specialists, and staff development specialists. Staff members in the assessment unit, for example, were psychometricians and program evaluation specialists, and their specializations were the lenses through which they understood the state reading policy. These different lenses contributed to multiple understandings of the same state policy within one district office. Even within the same district office, district policy makers' efforts at sensemaking from and about state policy were situated differently, leading them to pursue divergent changes as they attempted to implement the policy.

A situation involves more than the here and now. As is the case with individually held beliefs, most of what people know about the cultures that they inhabit is tacit—learned primarily through experience and the unconscious integration of contextual cues from being immersed as a member of the community. It is this tacit knowledge—actively acquired through participation in a culture—that forms the basis of an individual's beliefs and expectations about how to act in a certain situation. Arguing for a person-centered approach to policy analysis, Lewis and Maruna (1998) suggest that individual life histories and biographies may be useful analytical tools for investigating the implementation of public policy. For example, a study of elementary school teachers' responses to a new mathematics curriculum that was consistent with the National Council of Teachers of Mathematics' Standards identified different types of mathematics life histories among teachers and showed how teachers' understanding of the curriculum depended on their story type. Teachers' understandings of the curriculum were situated in their mathematics life stories (Drake et al., 2001).

Organizations also have histories that can be especially influential in implementing agents' efforts to understand what a policy is asking of them. A recent study of the implementation of rehabilitation programs in prisons, for example, shows how each prison's unique history influenced the ways in which its programs were understood by staff and inmates (Lin, 1998, 2000). Arguing that implementation failure was a function of "a fundamental misunderstanding between policy makers and the implementing agents" (p. 35), Lin illuminates how the unique histories of the prisons she studied shaped implementers' understanding of the rehabilitation program and contributed to differential implementation across prisons.

PROSPECTIVE: A DISTRIBUTED COGNITION PERSPECTIVE ON IMPLEMENTATION

Although some recent implementation studies lean toward situated cognitive constructs, these perspectives are still rather novel in policy implementation research, and the conceptual tools that they offer are not exploited to the degree they could be. Furthermore, when implementation scholars do attend to the social aspects of cognition, most cast aspects of the social situation as one independent variable that affects how individuals make sense of information. Our review suggests that relatively few studies have exploited the full potential of a distributed perspective on cognition—a perspective that treats the situation more centrally—and that adapting conceptual tools from work in distributed cognition to frame implementation research is likely to contribute to investigations that yield important new insights into the implementation process. Below, we consider some of the core elements of a distributed perspective on cognition in implementation differentiating it from the more widely used social cognition perspective. We then use some examples from our own work to identify insights that the distributed frame offers for policy implementation research.

Scholars working in the distributed cognition tradition treat the situation as a defining element of human cognitive activity. Based on the work of Vygotsky, cognitive practice—rather than the individual—becomes the basic unit of analysis. That is, this work shifts the unit of analysis from an exclusive focus on the individual's knowledge structure to the activity or practice system. Building on Vygotsky, Leont'ev (1981) defined an activity as "a system with its own structure, its own internal transformations, and its own development . . ." (p. 46). In this view, sense-making practice is *distributed* in the interactive web of actors, artifacts, and situation, and this system becomes the appropriate level of analysis (Greeno, 1998b). The defining characteristic of this perspective is "its theoretical focus on interactive systems that are larger than the behavior and cognitive processes of an individual agent" (Greeno, 1998b, pp. 5–6). A "situation" in this sense includes both other people and the sociocultural context.

Recent investigations in distributed cognition have focused on ways in which cognition is distributed across or "stretched over" material and cultural artifacts (Rogoff, 1990). Artifacts include language, notational systems, tools of various sorts, and buildings (Gagliardi, 1990). Hutchins (1995a), for example, documents how the work of landing a plane can be best understood within a framework that includes the manufactured tools and social context of the cockpit that situate a pilot's activity. These features of the environment are not, argues Hutchins, merely "aides" to the pilot's cognition, rather they are essential features of a composite that has the cockpit as the basic unit of analysis. The situation then becomes an integral *constituting* component of, not just backdrop or container for, cognitive practice. Cognition is distributed through the physical environments' material and cultural artifacts and through other people in collaborative efforts to complete cognitive tasks (Latour, 1987; Pea, 1996). Individual, interpersonal, and cultural elements constitute each other.

Hence, Rogoff argues for simultaneous attention to three planes of analysis—individual, interpersonal, and community/institutional—and stresses that there are no boundaries between these entities (Rogoff, 1995).

Using Distributed Cognition to Frame Implementation Research

Guided by these ideas, some of our recent studies of instructional reform implementation focus on sense-making activity *as it unfolds* in the daily work of classrooms and schools, using a combination of field notes, interviews and videotapes to collect data (Kemp, Tzou, Reiser, & Spillane, 2002; Reiser et al., 2000; Reiser, Tabak, Sandoval, Smith, Steinmuller, & Leone, 2001; Tzou, Reiser, Spillane, & Kemp, 2002; Spillane, Diamond, Sherer, & Coldren, 2004). Rather than focusing exclusively on implementing agents' knowledge structures, beliefs, and networks, this work explores sense-making from a distributive perspective—as a system or systems of practice. This way of framing reform implementation focuses our research in at least three ways: (1) Because sense-making is stretched over teachers and school leaders, we examine how reform ideas are worked out in formal and informal school level practices such as grade-level meetings, faculty meetings, professional development workshops, and informal gatherings; (2) we treat classroom instruction as it is coproduced in the interactions among teachers and students—not simply as a dependent or outcome variable in the implementation process but rather as a site for sense-making practice about instructional reform; and (3) we examine how sense-making practice is stretched over the situation as represented by materials, routines, and structures of various sorts. We believe that focusing our research in these ways will generate new insights into how reform ideas get implemented in practice. We take up each of these ideas briefly below.

First, our ongoing research in schools in the Chicago area suggests that the social practices found in grade-level meetings, faculty meetings, and professional development workshops as well as informal interactions in the lunch room or between classes are sites for making sense of reform ideas. Reform ideas, as represented in standards documents, are not simply read and made sense of by teachers and other professionals in a single sitting. Rather, standards documents and related materials (e.g., student test data, curricula) are apprehended and used in various social practices in schools. Rather than carrying meaning directly to individual implementing agents, to varying degrees these documents and materials become the basis for discussion in particular social practices in schools. In this way, sense-making practice is stretched over teachers, specialists, and school administrators and is not purely a solo enterprise.

Our work in the Distributed Leadership Study in K–8 schools in Chicago shows that these social practices differ depending on the subject area. For example, the social practices of making sense of reform ideas are different in mathematics compared with language arts. Our ongoing analysis of these practices suggests that teachers are much more active participants in these social practices when they have to do with language arts compared with mathematics.

Treating sense-making as a coproduction of students and teachers, we have found that teachers' understandings of reform ideas evolve as they try out new instructional ideas and approaches in their teaching. Our work in middle-school science, for example, suggests that inquiry science *takes form* over time as teachers and students try out reform curricula in their daily work and in the process work out new understandings of what doing inquiry science entails. Understandings about instruction, subject matter, and the like are worked out in instructional practice. The practice of making sense of the reform ideas is stretched over students and the sense they make of the learning situation. For students the assessments or product requirements are paramount. Less tangible changes such as the nature of discussion in an activity are less apparent and less of a concern for students, than for example, change in the type of written work required in an activity. So students strongly shape the nature of the activity itself. Hence, what students say and do as new curricula are put into practice in their classrooms may serve to reinforce a teacher's focus on the activity itself rather than the classroom discourses.

Third, from a distributive perspective, materials, routines, and other structures also define sense-making practices. The concrete part of lesson plans such as specific activities are indeed easier to convey in text-based materials such as curriculum guides than in-class discussions. For example, if the goal of a lesson is for students to make a certain kind of graph, drawing from data tables, the procedures for this activity can be clearly specified in text. More difficult to convey is a lead-in discussion that is meant to create a sense of need—where students are involved in identifying questions they need to address using the data set that is available to further the investigation. Such discussions are much more difficult to represent for teachers than concrete procedures that include passing out handouts, explaining the goal of the activity, sharing graphs, and so on. Thus, while such materials may enable teachers to problematize aspects of subject matter or new activity content, they are less likely to create a sense of focus or concern about the nature of discussions.

While aspects of the situation such as materials, routines, and structures define sense-making practice, it is also the case that these aspects of the situation are defined in these same sense-making practices. So, a tool like student assessment data frames sense-making practice in a particular way in the schools in the Distributed Leadership Study – they focus it on content coverage. At the same time, this tool gets used in different ways depending on the social practices in the particular school. While some schools use achievement data merely to point out skills that teachers need to work on in the coming year, others reanalyze these data longitudinally and engage teachers in an effort to figure out what the problem is and how they might address this as a school. In this way, the situation both defines the practice of sense-making, and is defined by this practice.

CONCLUSION

As we have argued, implementation involves cognition. But cognition is inherently a social practice that can be conceptualized as stretched over people and key aspects of their situation. In this way, what is understood from and about policy is defined in the interactions among implementing agents and their situation. Reforms are complex ideas. Policy attempts to prescribe particular ways of responding to instructional situations. Any artifacts used to communicate these reforms encode representations of a set of ideas about the reform. For example, the reform idea may be represented as a curriculum to enact, a teaching approach as represented in professional development materials, or guidelines such as standards documents. However, these representations of the ideas in the reform are examples of implementations of the core ideas. Actual implementation requires thoughtful use of these artifacts in ways that involve understanding their underlying intent.

The cognitive perspective on implementation reviewed in this chapter is *not* proposed as an alternative to conventional models but rather is meant to supplement rather than supplant existing models of the implementation process. It is meant to characterize the way that sense-making practices can lead to the types of challenges observed in reform efforts.

NOTES

This chapter was made possible by support from Northwestern University's Institute for Policy Research and School of Education and Social Policy, the National Science Foundation (Grants No. OSR-9250061 and REC-9873583), the Spencer Foundation, the Consortium for Policy Research in Education (Grant No. OERI-R308A60003, U.S. Department of Education), and the James S. McDonnell Foundation. We are grateful to Hilda Borko, Patricia Burch, Cynthia Coburn, Corey Drake, Susan Fuhrman, Heather Hill, Dan Lewis, and Lisa Walker for their thoughtful suggestions on earlier drafts of this chapter. Additional information about some of the work discussed here can be found at http://www.distributedleadership.org. All opinions, findings, and conclusions expressed in this article are those of the authors and do not necessarily reflect the views of any of the funding agencies.

[1]This section has been adapted from: Spillane, J. P., Reiser, B. J., and Reimer, T. (2002). Policy implementation and cognition: Reframing and refocusing implementation research. *Review of Educational Research*, *72*(3), 387–431. Copyright (2002) by the American Educational Research Association. Reproduced with permission of the publisher.

[2]For an elaboration on the importance of policy language to policy implementation, see Hill's chapter in this volume.

Chapter 4

Language Matters

How Characteristics of Language Complicate Policy Implementation

Heather C. Hill

Scholars and policy makers agree that the results of standard-based reforms in mathematics education have been uneven at best. Published reports point mainly to differences between policy as designed and policy as implemented in classrooms. Specific findings suggest that teachers adopt new practices, such as cooperative grouping, but otherwise leave the heart of their practice unchanged (Cohen, 1990; Peterson, 1990) and transform novel curriculum materials to support more traditional forms of instruction (Collopy, 2003; Wilson, 1990). Standards tend not to be implemented deeply in classrooms and studies reveal a mismatch between teachers' reports of their engagement with standards-based mathematics practices and evidence from their classrooms (Kazemi & Stipek, 2001; Mayer, 1999; Spillane & Zeuli, 1999). Explanations for differences between policy as written and implemented typically locate problems in individual cognition (Spillane & Zeuli, 1999), in the contexts in which individuals work (McLaughlin & Talbert, 1993), in the professional communities and networks in which implementers participate (e.g., Coburn 2001a), in weak policy designs (Cohen & Ball, 1999), and in the weak capacity of the educational system to support change (Cohen & Spillane 1993). These explanations all make sense.

This chapter brings an additional lens to bear on the implementation of standards-based reform—language, or more specifically, the ways policy makers' and implementers' language for communicating about reform and *doing* reform affects the policy implementation process. To elaborate language-related dimensions of implementation, I take an exploratory approach using two insights from linguistics. First, the meaning and use of words is shaped heavily by context, especially the particular "discourse community" to which its users belong. This insight suggests that implementation scholars ought to consider carefully how individuals at specific levels of policy systems make meaning(s) out of policy and how meanings travel across boundaries and contexts. Second, discourse communities can vary in what I call their "grammar" – for instance, the extent of technical language, the use of slang or newly coined terms, or how precisely they define and use terms related to policy—in ways that are also consequential to implementation, especially when it comes to the precision with which different communities use policy language.

These theoretical and empirical observations are not entirely new; implementation scholars have long pointed to implementation challenges stemming from communication between actors at different levels of the federalist system (e.g., Goggin et al., 1990), from ambiguity and lack of specification in policy (e.g., Brodkin, 1990; Cohen & Ball, 1990), and from the use of language to communicate policy intent (see, in particular, Yanow, 1996). The aim of this chapter is to consolidate these observations and to lay groundwork for a theory of language and implementation.

Standards-based mathematics reform—specifically the adoption and adaptation of National Council of Teachers of Mathematics (NCTM) standards by various states and districts—further increases the urgency of understanding these issues. Both the 1989 and 2000 versions of those standards, as well as related state standards, place significant demands on teachers to transform their practice from one characterized by teacher presentation and student recitation to one distinguished by student exploration, reasoning, proof, and communication. Most standards-based reforms in mathematics rely principally on language as the medium for communication with implementers. Understanding the effects of these standards on teachers' mathematics instruction can be helpful in understanding standards-based or similar reforms in other educational and policy areas.

This chapter draws broadly on implementation theory, linguistic theory, and research into the nature of schools and teaching communities. Because this is exploratory research, I cast the empirical portion of this chapter as two investigations into whether and how language affects implementation. Investigation one focuses on different meanings policy makers and implementers attach to key policy terms. Investigation two focuses on an instance in which implementers were asked by policy to speak in a "grammar" not native to their profession. Insights from these investigations help identify reasons why standards-based reform may diverge from its intended pathways.

LITERATURE REVIEW

To support the first investigation into the meanings policy makers and implementers attach to policy terms, I begin with a model of policy implementation as communication (Goggin et al., 1990). In this perspective, implementers (in Goggin's case, state officials) are the subject of a barrage of messages from federal and state policy makers, local officials, and interest groups. This barrage creates the potential for the distortion of messages about policy (p. 33). In Goggin's positivist model, distortions are framed as resulting from differences between policy makers' and implementers' "interest and motives" (p. 20). More recent interpretive work, however, emphasizes that implementers do not distort policy messages but construct their meaning (Coburn, 2001a; Cohen, 1990; Cohen & Hill, 2001; Hill, 2001; Lin, 2000; Spillane, Reiser & Reimer, 2002; Yanow, 1996). This perspective traces variations in implementation to the cognitive processes individuals engage in as they attend to, understand, integrate, and act on policy messages.[1]

Much of the recent literature on implementation as cognition focuses on these processes and the contexts that shape them. However, the ways individuals and organizations construct meaning from policy also depends in part on how policies deliver their messages. Accordingly, research should attend not only to how individuals interpret policy but also to how policy is shaped and reshaped as it is transmitted via symbols, objects, and metaphors (Yanow, 1996), professional development and curriculum materials (Hill, 2000; 2001), professional networks (Coburn, 2001a), and other media. One key medium for the construction and expression of policy is language, or the medium used to scaffold human activity and affiliation (Gee, 1999). Studying how well policy language communicates policy intent is critical to understanding how implementation unfolds, especially because many social policies rely heavily on language—e.g., legislation, executive orders, rules, educational standards statements, and because such documents may be "translated" for practitioners via oral or written language (Yanow, 1996).

Basic principles from linguistics help illuminate how language shapes implementation. Linguists observe that particular terms have no inherent meaning. Instead, they signify ideas or actions ascribed to them by communities whether those communities are speakers of a language, workers in a technical field, or children on a playground. Often, one term holds different meanings for different communities. For example, the word "variance" means one thing to lawyers (discrepancies in statements during a proceeding), another to statisticians (the square of the standard deviation), and still another to the general population (the difference between what occurs and what is expected or a reprieve from local zoning regulations). How one interprets this word depends on the context in which one finds it and on the communities of meaning to which the reader or user has access (Bakhtin, 1981; Schwab, 1987). In certain circumstances this flexibility in the meaning of terms is of great benefit—for instance, in limiting the necessity for cultures to invent new terms for every community and context and otherwise enabling them to economize on the memorization of words, spellings, and so forth. But flexibility in the meaning of terms also complicates communication, particularly across boundaries of communities that differ significantly around what specific terms mean. In this view, implementation failure may stem from how language in these different discourse communities contributes to the assignation of different meanings to the same policy texts.

This work on the relationship between policy language and implementation also borrows from social theorists and linguists the premise that discourses help shape how implementation unfolds. By discourses, I mean conversations that occur within communities and in which the use of particular terms, grammar, and styles of speech (among other things) demarcate individuals as belonging to a given community. As Gee (1999) states, "Such socially accepted associations among ways of using language . . . (associations that can be used to identify oneself as a member of a socially meaningful group or 'social network') I will refer to as 'Discourses,' with a big D" (p. 17). Initiating oneself into a discourse community can serve class, social, or political interests (see Bourdieu, 1990), or it may simply serve to facilitate communication within a group of individuals with common interests in technical or esoteric topics. For instance, Freeman (1993; 1996) and Lampert (1999) use language to understand teachers' journeys from novice to professional, insider to outsider, apprentice to expert, or from local to more remote communities of meaning.

Linguists also highlight how cultural rules of language vary across communities—what I refer to here as the "grammar" of language use within different communities. In these analyses, sociolinguists study how language is "used 'on site' to enact activities and identities" (Gee, 1999, p.7).[2] Communities may differ in the amount of jargon or number of acronyms deployed, how new terms are coined and adopted by users, how different syntactic constructions are used to convey subtle meanings, or in other ways.

A key difference in "grammar" in implementation contexts concerns the degree of precision with which communities imbue terms with meaning and how communities regulate those terms' use within community boundaries. Some communities require precise use of terms by members and expend considerable energy inducting potential community members into the exact use of such terms through lengthy formal education (i.e., medicine and law), through licensing requirements or through apprenticeships with practitioners (e.g., drafting or carpentry). Other communities are more tolerant of members' nonstandard use of terms (e.g., education, policing) and still others actively support the cooptation of terms toward new meanings, particularly when the use of certain terms serves as a mark of membership in such a community (e.g., teenagers). Such community practices can affect policy implementation when policies require implementers to use terms with a particular degree of precision, implementers vary in their willingness or ability to do so. This idea is explored in the second investigation.

Several scholars have explored how language, and more specifically, discourse, affects educational enterprises. Jackson (1968), in a seminal work on the culture of teaching, argues that teaching has no "technical" language—no set of terms whose precise meanings are widely shared in the community. As a result, he conjectures, educators may have particular difficulty communicating effectively. More recent evidence is equivocal on this subject. In a study that asked both teachers and nonteachers to use an instructional log to record the same mathematics lesson, Hill (2005) finds that teachers do have a technical mathematical language. When nonteacher observers attempted to describe the lessons using the log's mathematical terms, they often missed the mark. "Ordering fractions," for instance, typically refers in curriculum and teachers' language to activities that ask students to place three or more fractions in ascending order—for example, "put 1/2, 1/8, and 3/4 in order." One observer, however, used this term to refer to counting with fractions (e.g., 1/2, 1, 1 1/2, 2). Though the result is, literally, ordered fractions, it is not what is meant by teachers who use the term "ordering fractions." By inserting nonteaching observers into classrooms, numerous examples of this "school mathematical language" emerged including "equivalent fractions," "inequalities," and "number patterns."

However, school mathematical language is different from the language used by professional mathematicians, and if teachers are asked to use the language of professional mathematicians but are not given access to that language, complications of implementation will likely ensue. As Hill (2005) notes, teachers regularly use terms mathematicians would not strictly approve, such as decimal numbers or mixed numbers (mathematicians reserve the term "number" for classes of numbers, like whole numbers, integers, and rationals). Some school mathematical terms have no mathematical analogue; "ordering fractions," as in the example above, has no precise mathematical meaning. And even when discussing elementary school content, mathematicians take great care in crafting phrases that are mathematically beyond reproach. As David Pimm (1987) argues, "One of the distinctive features of discourse about mathematics is the widespread use of technical vocabulary. Mathematicians have developed an accepted public language with which to communicate to others which has evolved primarily to meet the needs of expert users . . ." (p. 59). Similar observations about the nature of mathematical language with respect to teaching have been made by Austin and Howson (1979) and Smith (2002). Survey research scholars (e.g., Burstein et al., 1995; Mayer, 1999; Stigler et al., 1999) often note the obstacles a lack of technical language brings to their enterprise.

METHOD

To understand how language shapes policy implementation, I take an interpretive approach to research and theory building (Geertz, 1973; Glaser & Strauss, 1967). This approach is particularly appropriate to this inquiry because it calls on the investigator to reject the positivist view that there is one "true" and universally held version of reality. Rather, this approach recognizes that individuals will interpret the world in multiple ways based on their culture, experience, and other factors. Scholars using interpretive methods often conduct investigations about how actors understand particular situations, cultural practices, and so on. Using this approach, I seek to investigate the meanings different actors assign to particular terms. By terms, I mean words or phrases meant to indicate an object, a practice, or in this case, an element of policy. A key focus for inquiry is the terms used to describe policy and the associated results in classrooms.

The discourse communities included in this study constitute a kind of vertical sample of those involved in implementing a new mathematics education policy in one state that I refer to by the pseudonym Eastern. In 1998, when the data for this project were collected, Eastern had been engaged in mathematics reform for nearly two decades.

To learn how mathematics policies were interpreted at different levels of the policy system, interviews were conducted with state officials, district officials, and other policy leaders engaged in formulating this reform. Next, professional development and curriculum materials, both of which served as conduits or mediators between policy makers and teachers, were also examined. Finally, observational, interview, and survey data were collected from a sample (N = 46) of K–6 teachers in four districts. In the first investigation below, teachers involved in standards-based reform implementation reported on their use of particular reform-related mathematics instructional practices including "real-life problems" and "explanations." They then supplied examples of these practices and an observer watched for such practices in their classroom instruction. I compare teachers' use of these terms with the examples they supplied, their classroom practice, and ultimately policymakers' intentions for such terms, to reveal similarities and differences of meaning that may explain how standards-based reform is implemented. I use similar procedures to develop the second investigation that examines an element of policy requesting more authentic mathematical language in classrooms.

FINDINGS

Elements of the state reform will be described in detail below as part of the analysis of the different discourse communities. However, the broad outlines of Eastern's reform can help situate this work. One part of the state improvement effort offered educators a new definition of student proficiency in mathematics. Reformers characterized the current state of most students' mathematical knowledge as rule-bound and inflexible—the result of students' blind memorization of mathematical rules and facts. They contrasted this stark picture with "mathematically powerful" students. Per a state policy guide, mathematical power:

> ... denotes an individual's capabilities necessary to explore, conjecture, and reason logically as well as the ability to use a variety of mathematical methods effectively to solve non-routine problems. This notion is based on the fact that mathematics is more than a collection of concepts and skills to be mastered. It includes methods of investigating and reasoning, means of communication, and notions of context (NCTM, 1989 as cited in a 1997 state[3] document).

To achieve these more ambitious standards, policy documents suggested that teachers use innovative classroom techniques. Conventional mathematics classrooms, said a 1997 state document, place "an emphasis on memorization of isolated facts and procedures, and proficiency with paper and pencil skills." Yet, citing a National Research Council publication, it continued:

> Students simply do not retain for long what they learn by imitation from lectures, worksheets, or routine homework. Presentation and repetition help students do well on standardized tests and lower-order skills, but they are generally ineffective as teaching strategies for long-term learning, for higher-order thinking, and for versatile problem-solving (from NRC, 1989).

Instead teachers should create classroom environments that allow students to problem-solve, discuss mathematical ideas, and work together in small groups. Overall, state reformers reported substantial alignment between their products and the ideas contained in the standards of the National Council of Teachers of Mathematics (NCTM), a national professional association of mathematics teachers. The intention was, as one state official expressed, to prove that a state could use its wherewithal to implement the "vision of the NCTM standards."

Investigation 1: Interpreting Policy Terms

This vision of mathematics reform included more emphasis on real-life problem solving and "explanation" of mathematical ideas and procedures. Both emphases are explored here as an example of the ease with which terms can be redefined by cultures and communities for specialized use and how such redefinitions complicate implementation. First, I briefly explain what policy makers meant by these terms; then I explore how the meanings of these terms traveled across discourse communities and shaped implementation.

State policy documents repeatedly mention one "overarching core goal":

> By the end of grade 12, students will apply proficiently a range of numeric, algebraic, geometric and statistical concepts and skills to formulate, analyze, and solve real-world problems; to facilitate inquiry and the exploration of real-world phenomena; and to support continued development and appreciation of mathematics as a discipline.

Many teachers can legitimately claim a focus on real-world problems in the sense that most offer some contextualized problems for students to, for lack of a better word, solve. Take for example a type of third-grade problem often offered in textbooks: If Johnny had twenty-three rows of four apples, how many apples did he have altogether? This is a real-world situation that requires mathematical ideas and symbols to formulate and solve, yet it generally calls for a student simply to select an appropriate solution method, often from a set of memorized procedures.

By contrast, state policy documents use "real-world problems" in another sense. First, these documents suggest students should be encouraged to apply mathematical ideas and solutions to more nonroutine and student-relevant tasks, such as measuring the wall of a classroom to determine the amount of paint needed in a planned renovation, or conducting a survey of student lunch preferences. Second, such real-world problems are designed so methods for solving them are not necessarily clear; solutions may require multiple steps and address numerous mathematical topics (e.g., measurement and geometry) and surface new mathematical ideas or materials in the process.

One state policy document mentions real-life problem-solving no less than ten times in a variety of different ways, using language often associated with what I will call "complex" problem solving, including problems that "relate to (students') world" and "meaningful" and "nonroutine" problems. Documents and interviews with state leaders also suggest a focus on preparing students for careers in business and industries where complex problem-solving is in high demand; for instance, one document states that students "may be clustered at times in small teams to work together, as is done in business and industry, to solve problems. . . ."

Professional development offered by the state focused on providing teachers with examples of such complex problems. Examples included estimating and finding averages using the number of buttons worn by members of a class and making Venn diagrams representing individuals' places of birth. State documents also offered examples at every grade level. While state leaders likely did not mean to exclude more conventional (noncomplex) real-world problem solving entirely, policy documents do suggest a strong push toward using contextualized, challenging problems as a core element of the mathematics curriculum.

To probe the implementation of complex problem solving, I asked teachers to estimate the number of times each week students worked on "real-life[4]" mathematics problems and to describe the types of activities students did as part of this work. Evidence from teacher surveys suggests that many believed they emphasized real-life problems—65 percent of teachers reported focusing on real-life problem-solving daily, and another 17 percent reported doing it once or twice a week. However, in interviews, different conceptions about the nature of such problems emerged. When asked to name a real-life problem, many teachers referred to straightforward problems in their mathematics curricula such as the Johnny problem above or work with the calendar (e.g., how many days are there between now and next Tuesday?) and telling time. As one teacher said, real-life problems are textbook or problem-of-the-day exercises students "*might* come across in real life. That's what I consider real-life math problems" (emphasis added). A smaller group of teachers, by contrast, mentioned longer-duration activities that better fit policy makers' definition of more complex problems such as constructing a "checkbook" or budgeting for a class party. An even smaller group mentioned taking advantage of mathematical situations that arose in their classrooms such as tallying lunch money or making graphical representations of test scores.

Observations of lessons confirmed this impression. Nearly all teachers did enact "real-life" problems in their classroom. However, most such problems came as brief moments during mathematics "warm-up," as "problems of the day," as introduction to the major topic of the day or on a worksheet following daily instruction—not as the core of instruction as envisioned by policy makers. In many of these cases, students needed only to determine the appropriate mathematical idea or computation method for the contextualized problems and then compute. In one classroom, for instance, students solved "real-world" problems that stated, "There are 4 seals in the water. Three more dive in. How many seals are in the water?" By contrast, in only one-sixth of cases were teachers observed designing student tasks around complex problem-solving situations such as planning a Thanksgiving dinner or graphing different modes of student transportation to school—extended problems related to situations from the students' actual experience that require students to reason out the necessary methods, to engage in multiple steps, and to draw on numerous mathematical topics.

The same phenomenon occurred around another term that appeared frequently in Eastern's mathematics framework: "explain." State frameworks and supporting documents frequently requested that teachers have students "explain" things such as computational procedures, estimation strategies, and problem solving. By having students explain procedures, strategies, or problems, policy makers hoped students would move beyond rote execution and toward deeper understanding of the material they studied as called for in the NCTM standards. In interviews, 71 percent of sampled Eastern teachers said they had students provide explanations for ideas or answers almost every day. In these interviews, some teachers commented, "We do that daily. I'm always asking why."

However, observations suggested wide variation in whether and how this element of the policy was enacted. For instance, half the teachers who reported having students explain the reasoning behind an idea or answer almost every day did not do so during the lesson observed. For the remaining half, the student explanations left this observer unsure that students were in the process of constructing more understanding around mathematical ideas and procedures. For example, in presenting a lesson on multiplying multiples of ten, a teacher asked her sixth-grade students why $70 \times 20 = 1400$. A student replied "because you multiply seven times two and add two zeroes" and the teacher accepted this explanation and moved on. Though this teacher said she "always" had students explain the reason behind an idea or answer, the student's explanation in this case is a recitation of the procedure he used to find the correct answer—not an explanation for why you can first ignore the zeroes then reattach them after completing the calculation. Such a student explanation might have pointed out that 70×20 is the same as $(7 \times 2) \times (10 \times 10)$, or 14×100. This explanation might also have alluded to commutivity and associativity—the mathematical axioms that can justify this rearrangement of terms.

The importance of distinguishing explanation types is recognized by some scholarly and policy communities. For example, Kazemi and Stipek (2001) examined teaching practices that promote students' conceptual thinking and argue that:

> [a] fundamental focus of inquiry-based mathematics is that students explain their thinking. Many classrooms are governed by that norm. But, students can describe the steps they took to solve a problem without explaining why the solution works mathematically. To push students' conceptual thinking, teachers should ask students to justify their strategies mathematically (p. 64).

Policymakers in Eastern echoed this differentiation. One policy leader, for instance, said: "Right now the big, another big push is on valuable questioning techniques. How you question a child is very important. That you don't just go for a procedural type explanation from the child, that you really try to get to a content explanation. And we work on it. Because it's difficult." Teachers in this study, however, rarely made the same critical distinctions.

In sum, policies like Eastern's mathematics reform rely on written words to help practitioners connect policy goals to their everyday work. Yet many of the terms used in Eastern's policy do not hold the same meaning in policy makers' communities as in implementers' communities. Investigation 1 reveals that language as a medium for policy communication is of limited effectiveness when policy making and implementing communities do not share definitions of key terms.

Other data collected in Eastern suggests the lack of shared meaning between policy makers and implementers likely results from at least two phenomena. First, the teaching and policy communities in this case vary in their knowledge of mathematics and methods for teaching mathematics. Most policy makers but only a few teachers in this study had numerous opportunities to work with nationally known mathematics educators and mathematicians. During this time they might have learned new definitions for problem-solving and explanation and some mathematics to help support their own use of these new methods in the classroom. Teachers who had such learning opportunities alongside policy makers tended to use terms in ways consistent with policy makers. Yet most teachers did not have access to this community and interpreted and acted on terms with less consistency. Thus knowledge differences likely contributed to the differences in interpretation of policy terms.

Second, policy is less likely to carry its meaning across communities when policy is communicated solely through words and when policy makers fail to pay attention to meaning elements (Cohen and Ball 1999). Although professional development and supplemental materials provided to teachers supported problem-solving and student explanation through examples, relatively few teachers had access to such supports. And nowhere in the policy materials and professional development included in this project was explicit attention paid to definition and meaning. By negative example then, this case suggests an important footnote to this chapter's observations about language: more concrete examples, more support for using policy elements in classrooms, and quite simply, more "work" on the meaning of particular terms may help overcome the problems with policy language.

Investigation 2: How Community "Grammar" Affects Implementation Quality

Discourse communities vary in the "grammar" with which they enact activities and identities. Some educational and other social policies suggest or require that implementers use grammars from outside their own community, and implementers vary in whether and how they fulfill those stipulations of policy. The discourse community constituted of teachers, for instance, uses terms and phrases specific to school mathematics but that are often only loosely defined (Hill, 2005); teachers also aim to bridge the gap between children's home, or informal, mathematical language and the school mathematics curriculum (Pimm, 1987). The mathematics community, according to some, values more precision and accuracy in the use of terms—it has a more technical language with more shared meaning (Pimm, 1987; Smith, 2002). Accordingly, when policy asks teachers to talk like mathematicians, complications ensue. Such was the case in Eastern's mathematics policy.

To elaborate, state policy makers wanted teachers and students to use more authentic mathematical discourse. Eastern standards state that teachers "encourage students to use mathematical language, vocabulary, and notation to represent ideas, describe relationships, and model situations. . . ." This is a central, though often underrecognized, component of teaching mathematics to students. Children do not walk into classrooms using mathematical language, and teachers' tasks include helping them to transition from "lay" or "everyday" language to terms with more mathematical meaning and precision (Pimm, 1987). For instance, in this example a fourth-grade teacher corrected students' use of lay terms in discussing the multiplication table:

> TEACHER: What happens when you multiply zero by a number?
> STUDENT: Anything times zero is zero.
> TEACHER: Instead of saying "anything" let's use "number." We're in math now, and we should be using mathematical terms.

Throughout observations in Eastern, teachers worked to connect mathematical terms (e.g., "equal") to lay terms (e.g., "the same as"). Teachers also often corrected inexact terminology, such as "plussing," and replaced it with more mathematically appropriate terms, such as "adding."

In other cases, field notes from classroom observations suggest teachers simply missed opportunities to induct students into this more technical language. For example, one third-grade teacher implicitly endorsed students' use of the term "take-away" instead of "subtract":

> TEACHER: Your answer doesn't make sense. What should you do?
> STUDENT: Change it to take-away.
> [Teacher repeated this advice, and added that students should keep subtracting until the answer made sense.]

A fourth-grade teacher missed an opportunity to use the mathematical term "rotation" in geometry as she asked students to compare pictures of two 2-by-8 arrays as re-created in Figure 4.1.

> TEACHER: Is that different [pointing to the second array]?
> STUDENT: They're the same, just turned.
> TEACHER: . . . Remember, if it's going in a different direction, it's not different.

In this example, rather than noting that the array was "going in a different direction," this teacher might have elected to introduce (or reinforce) the nomenclature "rotation" to describe the relationship of one array to the other.

Viewed without reference to policy, one might argue that these teachers made sound decisions based on their students' prior understanding, developmental trajectories, or classroom discourse. However, viewed as a matter of implementation of the state standards, these teachers missed opportunities to move their students toward mathematically precise terminology.

Field notes also suggest some teachers increased confusion about the use and meaning of terms. For instance, in talking about characteristics of the number twenty, a third-grade teacher asked:

> TEACHER: Is twenty a square root?
> STUDENT: No.
> TEACHER: No it is not a square root.

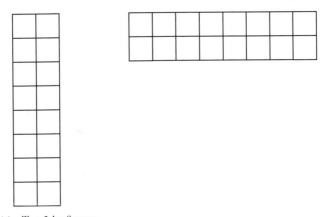

FIGURE 4.1   Two 2-by-8 arrays.

Of course 20 *is* a square root—of 400—yet this teachers' exchange with the student suggests both are confused about differences between the term "square" and "square root."

Similar confusions arose when a fifth-grade teacher taught a first lesson on permutations, a subject both of state policy (which called for more work on discrete mathematics, the curriculum strand that includes permutations) and a recent professional development session attended by this teacher. Permutations are an arrangement of objects in a definite order with no repetitions; for example, RAT, RTA, ART, ATR, TRA, and TAR are the complete set of arrangements for the letters R, A, and T (Billstein, Libeskind, & Lott, 2004, p. 422). The teacher used pattern blocks—colored hexagons, triangles, diamonds—as the concrete objects to be permuted and began class by asking students how many different arrangements they could make of one hexagon (1); of a hexagon and triangle (2); of a hexagon, triangle, and diamond (6); and so forth. Throughout the lesson, the teacher made many small and large errors with mathematical terminology. For example, the teacher referred to the pattern blocks themselves as permutations rather than as elements capable of representing permutations. He also, at the end of the lesson, attempted to link lay and mathematical terminology by asking and answering his own question "What's another word for permutations, one that begins with the letter *o*? Order." This teacher was attempting to connect this mathematical term and idea to lay terminology—a key task of teaching. Yet while permutations do involve the ordering of objects in unique ways, permutation and order are not mathematically equivalent terms.

Problems with square root, rotation, permutations, and other mathematical terminology run throughout the data. These problems stem in part from the linguistic straddling act policy demands of teachers. Teachers must negotiate between school mathematics language, students' home mathematical language, and mathematicians' language. They may reject more technically precise terms in their effort to make mathematical material more accessible to students or even to gain solidarity with students. As Bakhtin suggests (1981), individuals may have multiple "voices" that correspond to the three discourse communities outlined above and may choose to use particular languages to fit the needs of a particular situation.

But the examples suggest another equally important explanation for this phenomenon: teachers may lack a well-developed mathematical voice. Rotation and permutation, for instance, may simply not be topics with which most elementary teachers are familiar, making the accurate use of such terms difficult. Despite what policy asks, teachers often do not speak with the precision of mathematicians because they are not mathematicians—or more generally, they have not had access to the discourse of a mathematician's community. Further, Eastern's policy did not provide the resources to develop teachers' more accurate and wider use of mathematical terms—to induct teachers into mathematical language. Nowhere in professional development, curriculum materials or policy materials themselves was there explicit and well-developed attention to using mathematical terms more accurately in classrooms. This suggests that asking professionals to speak in a "voice" outside the one typically used in their work might be a common element of policy and cause common problems of implementation.

DISCUSSION AND CONCLUSION

Using basic insights from linguistics, this chapter has identified ways language and its use complicate implementation. When implementers and policy makers belonged to different discourse communities, as was often the case in Eastern, different meanings for the same terms resulted in implementation that deviated from policy design. And when policy makers asked implementers to use the "grammars" from communities to which they did not belong, additional complications ensued.

These observations support the utility of examining policy implementation using an interpretive method. Recent interpretive research focuses on individual cognition and highlights the ways prior experience, beliefs, and knowledge affect the interpretation of new social policy (Ball, 1990; Cohen, 1990; Cohen & Ball, 1990; Sherin, 1996, Spillane, 2000; Wilson, 1990). Other research in this vein examines the ways individuals' interpretations are shaped by the cultures, organizations, professions, and networks in which they take part (e.g., Coburn, 2001a; Hill, 2000; Lin, 2000; Spillane, 1998a; Yanow, 1996). The perspective outlined here is similarly interpretive in that it focuses on understanding. However, rather than searching for variation in how policy makers and implementers interpret policies writ large, this approach focuses on differences in how individuals understand and use the constituent elements of policies—that is, the words and phrases on which written policies rely. This approach helps reveal that language itself complicates the communication and implementation of policy and poses particular problems when implementers are asked to use language in new ways. (See also Yanow, 1996.)

This chapter also helps expand on the frequently observed fact that policies often contain ambiguities in their design. Brodkin (1990), for instance, notes that disputes over policy design are often not resolved not in official policy texts; such texts typically include compromise language that leaves terms of compliance ill-defined. Cohen and Ball (1999) likewise argue that some interventions (a term that can include policies) are ill-specified and poorly developed—consisting mainly of goal statements and principles with few plans for action and supporting materials. This chapter adds to these perspectives by noting that policies are not only ambiguous by design but because they rely on language as a medium for communication and because of features of the discourse communities to and in which policy is communicated. It reinforces Yanow's (1996) observation that simply making policy texts more clear and detailed, as many suggest (e.g., Mazmanian & Sabatier, 1989), will not solve the implementation problems sometimes created by policy ambiguity.

This chapter also has implications for the measurement of policy implementation. Specifically, if the meaning of terms varies, then more people can rightly claim to "do" elements of policy by some definition. But some definitions of "doing" may be more variable than policy makers might like. This potential variability complicates efforts to determine the extent of policy implementation via traditional survey techniques that require construct validity and consistent interpretation of terms. For example, in the illustrations above many teachers reported in surveys that they frequently use real-life problems and student explanations; however, observations across those classrooms turned up these practices at a much reduced rate. Thus traditional surveys may underestimate the extent of variation in implementation. This finding is consistent with Spillane & Zeuli, Stigler, Burstein, and others who have investigated the relationship between observational data and teacher reports of practice.

However, some findings from such teacher surveys seem more reliable in a traditional sense than others. Mayer (1999), for instance, found teachers do over report NCTM practices, but they overreport them consistently relative to one another. This means such reports cannot be taken as evidence that teachers *do* particular things in classrooms, but they can be used in multivariate analyses to search for predictors of teacher practices within teachers' self-reports or to explore the relationship of particular practices to student achievement. This is because when all measures constructed from such reports have the same amount of inflation, the interpretation of regression or other coefficients is unaffected.

A more complicated case arises when some practices are measured more accurately than others. Intuitively, it seems important that the hypothesized independent influences have roughly the same size error component proportionate to the size of the "true" signal. If the actual effects of two variables were roughly equal, but one were composed of mostly "true" signal and another mostly "error," the more accurately measured independent variable would appear more effective than the latter, despite the similarity in their actual size. This problem applies not only to the survey research reviewed here, but also to interviews, written materials, and other methods of communication that rely heavily on terms that might be defined in multiple ways. Better efforts to assess implementation do exist—for instance videotapes of mathematics teaching—but such efforts are expensive and often beyond the capacity of small research projects.

Policies are more or less affected by these characteristics of language depending on how those policies are designed, how professional communities are constituted, and how implementation proceeds. For instance, policies that rely more heavily on written words to communicate meaning will encounter more difficulties. Consider how Eastern's policy might have been different, for instance, if policy makers had made available a standard elementary curriculum filled with their version of "real-world" exercises or arranged professional development around a videotaped lesson filled with substantial mathematical explanations. Accompanying written words and phrases with these more concrete instantiations might improve the alignment of policy as implemented with policy as intended.

How language affects policy also depends on the distance between the communities at either end of the policy process—for example, differences between the discourse of mathematics education policy and classroom teachers. The greater the distance between the professional languages used by stakeholders in policy, the greater the opportunity for reinterpretations of policy. Conversely, policy may be made and implemented by two tightly connected communities, or policy may even be enacted by members of the community itself, thus ameliorating some problems with commonality of terms. Finally, the degree to which implementers share a technical language will also affect the number of complications induced by characteristics of language. Policies introduced into highly technical fields may also experience implementation difficulties but will likely encounter fewer problems of the type described here.

Given these concerns, policy makers who desire to get "more" of their policy implemented can take several actions. For one, educational policy makers might convey new standards not only through standards documents but also through curriculum materials, assessments, professional development, videotaped classroom instruction, descriptive case studies, and other forms. They might work explicitly on meaning by working with implementers to draw sharp lines around the practices "in" and "out" of this innovation (see Hill, 2000). Second, education policy makers might seek to draw more teachers into the policy community's discourse by educating implementers on what it means to use mathematical terms as mathematicians or to implement "real-world" problems. Third, although unlikely in this era of state standards, policy makers could devolve policy making to schools to further lessen the gap between policy making and implementation. In the longer term, policy makers might take steps to imbue education with a more technical language, either by working to standardize the use of terms through professional education, professional materials, or other means. And in the longer term policy makers would be well served if they paid closer attention to both teachers' language and the ways language affects implementation.

Notes

The author would like to thank David K. Cohen, Jay L. Lemke, Meredith Honig, and two anonymous reviewers for assistance with the thinking herein. All poor ideas, however, remain the property of the author. Research reported in this paper was supported by the Aspen Institute.

[1]For an elaboration on cognition and implementation, see the Spillane et al. chapter in this volume.

[2]Recent notable uses of such a perspective in education include an exposition of the politics within supposedly technical policy arguments (Lemke, 1995), and disjunctures across home/school language communities (e.g., Ogbu, 1999).

[3]I do not include a complete citation here to protect the anonymity of my research site.

[4]The wording of the survey did not exactly match the wording of the policy documents themselves. However, "real-world" and "real-life" are used interchangeably in the mathematics education community.

Chapter 5

Revisiting Policy Implementation as a Political Phenomenon

The Case of Reconstitution Policies

Betty Malen

For decades, public policy scholars have argued that political perspectives constitute valid and fruitful ways of looking at policy implementation (e.g., Bardach, 1977; Hargrove, 1975; Knapp, 1997). In these writings, policy implementation is characterized as "a reckoning stage" (Stone, 1980, p. 2) wherein social conflicts not fully recognized or effectively resolved during the initial adoption phase of the policy-making process resurface. These "enduring differences" (Bolman & Deal, 1991) are regulated through political exchanges in implementation in part because they are value-laden issues that cannot be resolved solely through the acquisition of empirical evidence or the application of technical expertise (Cuban, 1990; Pfeffer, 1981). The political bargaining and maneuvering that occurs as powerful interests interact to adopt policy continues during implementation as governing bodies, supervisors, and service providers anticipate and react to the diverse preferences of other influential players and to the contextual exigencies that condition what these various clusters of actors may be willing and able to do (Allison & Zelikow, 1999; Bardach, 1977). Whether the various actors "implicitly take each other into account" (Ingram, 1977, p. 502) or explicitly negotiate the purposes and parameters of policy, they forge political compacts that affect the extent to which policy may be broadly and faithfully implemented, or, routinely and strategically ignored, deflected, altered, or overturned.

Scholars who focus on policy implementation in public school contexts have followed suit (Cuban & Usdan, 2003; Malen & Ogawa, 1988; Muncey & McQuillan, 1998). They write that education policies often embody highly salient, value-laden issues that cannot be readily, fully or permanently resolved through rational deliberations or unanimous agreements. As a result, these policies tend to be adopted and implemented through political processes that reflect the relative power of contending groups more than the relative merits of policy options (Cuban, 1990; Levin, 2001; Murphy, 1971; Stone, et al., 2001; Weiler, 1993). Scholars also document that education policies often call for a reallocation of material resources and/or symbolic resources. As a result, these policies can awaken dormant conflicts, aggravate existing cleavages, and spark new battles about what constitutes an appropriate course of action or an appropriate distribution and utilization of time, attention, talent, money, and other individual or organizational resources (Henig, et. al. 1999; Levin, 2001; Muncey & McQuillan, 1998). For these and other reasons, education policies are likely to give rise to political challenges throughout implementation.

Scholars interpret these political challenges in various ways. "Politics" has been cast as a stock explanation for the unanticipated collapse of policies, as an endemic barrier to the consonant implementation of reforms (Muncey & McQuillan, 1998; Rich, 1996; Cuban & Usdan, 2003) and as an indispensable ingredient in ongoing efforts to improve the quality and equity of educational opportunities (Bryck, et al., 1998; Stone, et al., 2001). However cast, "politics" is an ever-present, at times pervasive force that can shape both the adoption and the implementation of education policies in vastly different but decisive ways.

This chapter revisits what it means to look at policy implementation from a political perspective and highlights why it is important to continue to do so. It outlines a conceptual framework that could be used to analyze the political dimensions of policy implementation in public school systems and draws on a recent study of a prominent high stakes reform option, school reconstitution, to illustrate its core components. The chapter then moves to a broader assessment of the utility of a political prism for understanding policy implementation in public education contexts and highlights the implications of that analysis for future research.[1]

A POLITICAL PERSPECTIVE ON POLICY IMPLEMENTATION

Scholars employ an array of models, metaphors, and constructs to examine the "politics" of policy adoption and implementation (or lack of same) in various education settings. Despite their distinctive orientation, scholars tend to view "politics" as a causal variable that helps explain why policies may be adopted and whether and how they may be implemented (McDonnell & Weatherford, 2000). And, they tend to incorporate some core concepts to depict the "politics" of policy developments across issues, levels of the system, and phases of the policy process. The conceptual framework offered here is comprised of a set of core concepts that undergird much of the research on the politics of policy adoption and implementation. A framework that brings together underlying and unifying concepts can help analysts examine the politics of policy implementation explicitly and empirically. The results of these investigations can be used to test current understandings and generate new insights.

The framework diagrammed in Figure 5.1 and discussed below reflects the cardinal assumption that policy implementation is a dynamic political process that affects and reflects the relative power of diverse actors and the institutional and environmental forces that condition the play of power. Since policy both regulates and precipitates conflict, the overarching analytic challenge is to get at the reciprocal relationship between politics and policy, to unpack how politics creates policy, and to uncover how policy creates politics (Lowi, 1972). Descriptive in its orientation, the framework does not provide criteria for judging the merits of either political exchanges or policy developments. Rather, it invites analysts to suspend normative judgments and to concentrate on capturing the realities and complexities of "politics" in whatever form those dynamics may take.

The framework draws heavily on Bardach's (1977) groundbreaking work on the politics of implementation and on the contributions of other scholars. Bardach employed the idea of "games" as a "master metaphor" to map the players, their stakes, resources, strategies, and tactics, and to discern the rules governing how clusters of actors influence policy implementation in their organizational contexts.[2] He also charted how various games affect "the process of assembling the elements required to produce a particular programmatic outcome" (Bardach, 1977, pp. 56–57). In so doing, he demonstrated that these familiar, foundational components of political analyses were serviceable tools

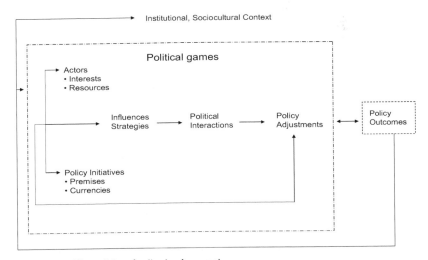

FIGURE 5.1   The politics of policy implementation.

for getting at the politics of implementation, that "special kind of politics . . . in which the very existence of an already defined policy mandate legally and legitimately authorized in some political process, affects the strategy and tactics" of the political struggles that are part and parcel of governmental and organizational life (Bardach, 1977, p. 37). The following framework includes a similar set of concepts that analysts can use to examine the political dynamics of policy adoption and implementation in public school systems.

CORE CONCEPTS AND THEIR ANALYTIC FUNCTIONS

The Roles of Actors in Bureaucratic and Public Arenas

Political perspectives reveal that actors at all levels of the system can influence policy implementation. They can do so by their choices regarding which policy options and designs to adopt and by their efforts to abandon or alter the purposes and provisions of policies throughout implementation (Firestone, 1989a; Malen & Hart, 1987; Hall & McGinty, 1997; Murphy, 1971). Thus, the first analytic task in implementation studies is to identify the relevant actors. This task involves arraying (1) the organizational authorities who have the formal power to make binding decisions in the various macro- and micro-arenas that comprise the education policy system; (2) the service providers, supervisors and intermediaries who are responsible for overseeing and supporting policy implementation; and (3) other "potential partisans" (Gamson, 1968) who may have an interest in the policy area and may shift from spectators to participants at any time (Schattschneider, 1960). A host of "visible and hidden" participants (Kingdon, 1995) such as government officials, educational administrators, teachers, students, parents, community groups, mayors, foundations, professional associations, corporations, education reform organizations, policy networks, and lay publics may play key roles in policy implementation (Henig, et al., 1999; Honig, 2004a, b; Muncey & McQuillan, 1998; Orr, 1999; Portz, et al., 1999; Shipps, 1997).

Developing the cast of characters involves more than situating actors in arenas, or what some term the sites, spaces, or "venues" (Baumgartner & Jones, 1993) in which actors vie for policy influence. It involves recognizing how the various venues shape the political dynamics. Simply put, the formal and informal arenas in which actors interact to influence policy developments are not neutral. Different arenas may be more or less open, accessible, and receptive to different players and their points of view. Moreover, different arenas have their own, often tacit, "rules" of participation and accommodation (Firestone, 1989a; Mazzoni, 1991). For example, more bounded organizational arenas such as school improvement teams, advisory councils, and task forces invite a very different style of play than the more open, public arenas may invoke, particularly if redistributive policies that implicate core stakes are at issue. In essence, arenas allocate access and advantage. As Mazzoni (1991) explains, "Arenas do more than locate decisive sites for decision-making action. They legitimate a set of participants, establish the institutional and social context—including 'the rules of the game'—mediate the potency of resources and strategies and encourage some means (and discourage other means) of reaching agreements. . . . Moving an issue to a new arena can change the key actors, relevant resources, incentives for action, influence relationships and governing rules—and hence winners and losers—in policy struggles" (Mazzoni, 1991, p. 116).

The Intersection of Actors' Interests and Policy Premises

Actors have different interests, here meaning the complex webs of values, views, orientations, dispositions, preferences, and convictions that shape their perceptions of public problems and the policy solutions that may be attached to them (Morgan, 1986). Generally speaking, actors seek to promote and protect their vested material and ideological interests; they seek to secure private benefits and to advance their diverse conceptions of the public good. Policies embody values, theories of intervention, and orientations to social and educational issues that may or may not conform to the ideas, interests, and ideals of the actors who were involved in their adoption or the expanded slate of actors who are involved in their implementation. These alignments and discontinuities matter. For example, policies that are not consistent with the beliefs of teachers (Muncey & McQuillan, 1998) or the ideology of powerful parents or other groups can encounter multiple forms of resistance (Wells & Serna, 1996; Zimmerman, 2002). The analytic task, then, is to examine how policy premises correspond with actors' interests, broadly construed. More specifically, the task is to gauge how actors are likely to interpret and respond to the policy; how clusters of actors with quite varied takes on the policy may align to support or resist its implementation; how sources of allegiance and resistance might be exploited; and how conflicts that arise reveal the stakes that actors attach to the initial policy and subsequent adaptations of it.

The Intersection of Actor Resources and Policy Currencies

Politics pivots on power—here meaning the relative capacity of actors to exert influence on policy developments. The actors' power can be gauged by analyzing the resources that actors can draw upon to exercise influence in organizational contexts (Dahl, 1984; Kanter, et al., 1992). Some refer to actors' resources as the capital that they command by virtue of their organizational position, individual attributes, social connections, professional networks and reputed stature (Orr, 1999; Stone, 1998; Wells & Serna, 1996). Taking stock of the actors' resources involves identifying both their assets and their liabilities, namely the forms of financial, informational, social, and cultural capital that may be necessary to wield influence in particular arenas but is unavailable or not under the control of the actors. The inventory of the actors' assets and liabilities serves as an initial indicator of the actors' power (Dahl, 1984; Dahl & Stinebrickner, 2003). Policies may augment or undermine the power of actors. Policies may carry ideational, regulatory, and financial resources that actors can draw on to cultivate and legitimate support for their agendas and to avert or reduce resistance to their initiatives. Since policies can "legitimate and empower new configurations of players at one level [of the system] or another" (Knapp, 1997, p. 234), the material and symbolic currencies accompanying policies (or missing from them) serve as an additional indicator of the actors' relative capacity to influence policy developments.

But actors' resources and policy currencies mean little unless actors have the "skill and will" to convert these assets into policy influence (Allison & Zelikow, 1999; Dahl, 1984). Indeed, "idea champions" (Daft & Becker, 1978) who persistently press others to accept new policies and practices and "policy entrepreneurs" (Kingdon, 1995) who astutely connect policy proposals to pressing problems at opportune moments can be important, arguably decisive players in both macro- and micro-arenas (Mintrom, 2000; Roberts & King, 1996; Mazzoni, 1991; Malen, 1994; Kanter, 1983). Thus the actors' ability and desire to capitalize on policy currencies as well as other power bases may be critical ingredients of policy influence.

The Efforts to Exert Influence: Strategies

Actors may use a variety of overt and covert strategies to convert their sources of power into policy influence. Classic treatments of political strategies direct attention to how actors may gain access to influential players and keep it from others (Truman, 1951); how they may exercise their voice and silence the voices of others (Cobb & Ross, 1997; Gaventa, 1980). Scholars have described familiar strategies, such as how actors may lobby, litigate, filibuster, demonstrate, or negotiate to promote and protect their interests and ideals. They also have described more subtle strategies including how actors may define problems, frame issues, fix decision premises, regulate participation, and control information in order to secure or sustain a power advantage (Morgan, 1986; Stone, 1997). Actors may invoke symbols to arouse or assuage various constituencies (Edelman, 1964). Some actors may work to contain the "scope of conflict" so that established interests can prevail while others may try to expand the "scope of conflict" so that less powerful groups might upset the dominant regime (Schattschneider, 1960). Actors may try to forge coalitions to acquire greater leverage, "shop" for "policy venues" and shift issues to more favorable decision arenas (Baumgartner & Jones, 1993; Holyoke & Henig, 2001; Mazzoni, 1991). In these and other ways, actors can directly or indirectly influence policy provisions and implementation developments.

The Impact of Institutional and Sociocultural Contexts on the Interplay of Influence

Policies unfold in nested contexts. These contexts provide the stage for political dramas and significantly shape those dramas (March & Olsen, 1989). Generally speaking, institutions and their broader environments "generate rules, regulations, norms and definitions of the situation" that affect how actors think and behave (Rowan & Miskel, 1999, p. 359). These institutional scripts are manifest in the education policy system's formal structures of authority, in its embedded habits, routines, and repertoires, and in the explicit and tacit "rules of the game." They also are manifest in the broader sociocultural values and in the reigning ideologies that shape conceptions of legitimate social problems, appropriate policy interventions, and acceptable political tactics (Dahl, 1984).

Like the arenas in which actors vie for influence, these broader institutional and sociocultural contexts are never neutral (March & Olsen, 1989; Mazzoni, 1991). Rather they infuse the policy system with presumptions, preferences, and prejudices that advantage some and disadvantage others. The institutional texts and the broader sociocultural forces transmit the core values, prevailing expectations, innovative impulses, and status-enhancing images that vulnerable organizations emulate to replenish their legitimacy, sustain the trust and confidence of key constituencies, and maintain the credibility and stability of the current regime (Weiler, 1993). In these and other ways, the institutional and sociocultural contexts mediate the power, preferences and incentives of the players and shape the adoption and implementation of education policies (Rowan & Miskel, 1999; Portz, et al., 1999; Ogawa, et al., 2003).

INTEGRATIVE METAPHORS AND THEIR ANALYTIC FUNCTIONS

To complete a political analysis of policy implementation, the core constructs used to map political dynamics must be combined to render interpretations of those dynamics and to link those dynamics to policy outcomes. The "games" metaphor (Bardach, 1977) and the broader "ecology of games" metaphor (Firestone, 1989a) can serve as integrative devices to characterize the political dynamics within and across arenas and to relate those dynamics to policy outcomes.

The Sets of Political Games

Identifying "games" involves characterizing how clusters of actors in particular arenas and contexts exercise their power to influence policy developments. Having used the preceding categories to examine the ingredients of the games, analysts are in a better position to name the games, to display the games, and to track their multiple effects on policy outcomes. But developing these lines of analysis is not a straightforward process. It requires that analysts discern the relative power of the contending actors, recognize the influence of the broad contextual forces that structure political dynamics and circumscribe human agency, and depict how these human and contextual forces interact to shape policy developments. Scholars suggest different ways analysts might address these complex matters (Clegg, 1989). For example, analysts can render well-reasoned judgments about the relative power of players by looking at (a) the content of specific decisions to see whose interests are served; (b) the clusters of actors who are reputed to be influential on particular issues, in particular arenas, at particular points in time; (c) their influence efforts to see whether the attributions of power constitute plausible explanations of the policy decisions and related developments; and (d) the opportunity structures in which actors vie for influence. Taken together, these indicators can help analysts render contextualized judgments[3] about players' influence on specific issues, in particular arenas and across phases of the process (Dahl, 1984; Geary, 1992), and characterize the interactions that produced policy influence (Bardach, 1977; Mazzoni, 1991).

Linking political "games" to policy outcomes is arguably the most difficult analytic challenge (Bryk, et al., 1999). Given the complex sets of factors that shape the production and distribution of valued educational outcomes, scholars have not, and, in all likelihood, will not be able to make credible claims about the direct effects of "politics" on such salient matters as students' academic accomplishments, occupational aspirations or civic commitments (Bryk, et al., 1999). But scholars have been able to chart how political interactions affect whether and how critical policy components get installed and sustained. Bardach's depiction of how political dynamics may divert resources, deflect goals, dissipate energies, create delays, and otherwise obstruct the construction of program elements required to produce the desired policy outcomes is an instructive case in point (Bardach, 1977). Firestone's (1989a) application of the ecology of games metaphor further illustrates how distinctive games that go on, concurrently, at all levels of the system, can alter the adoption and implementation of education policies. Since the sets of games that occur during policy adoption may shape policy implementation, those who seek to understand policy implementation should analyze policy adoption as well as implementation.

An Illustration of the Framework: The Case of School Reconstitution

The case study summarized below illustrates the key components of the framework and shows how the analytic categories traditionally used to examine policy adoption can be used to examine policy implementation. The case focuses on a timely topic yet tells a familiar tale about a flashy education reform that gets adopted then abandoned. It reveals how and why, in the late 1990s, the superintendent of a large, metropolitan district managed to enact a reconstitution initiative[4] that resulted in sweeping staff changes in six of the district's low-performing schools, and how and why he lost control of the initiative during implementation. Reported in detail elsewhere (Jones & Malen, 2002; Malen, et al., 2002), this case is based on documentary, interview, and observational data acquired by a research team that tracked the reconstitution reform from its initial enactment through the first two years of implementation (Finkelstein, et al., 2000). This abbreviated and oversimplified cut reflects data acquired from over 330 formal and informal interviews with district and school administrators, board members, union representatives, classroom teachers and others directly involved in the adoption and implementation of this initiative. It begins with the politics of adoption because these dynamics shaped how the politics of implementation unfolded.

The Politics of Adoption

Actors, interests, and resources
The superintendent decided to enact a bold, redistributive reform even though school systems generally adopt more incremental, less contentious policy alternatives. The superintendent advocated and authorized a school reconstitution initiative despite his public and repeated criticisms of the state decision to make school reconstitution a "remedy" for schools that consistently failed to meet state-defined performance standards. By virtually all accounts, the

superintendent embraced the idea as part of a desperate effort to curb state interventions in the district and to enhance the legitimacy of the district and its leaders. Key district administrators and board members reportedly feared the state might intervene and order its own changes. In their view, the autonomy of the system and the reputations and careers of its leaders were at stake. As a district official summarized: "The state had been pressing hard. . . . We had to find a way to fend them off. . . . [The superintendent] had to find a way to be victorious." Since reconstitution had political currency with state officials, it offered the superintendent an opportunity to demonstrate that he was willing and able to seize the initiative and to take what interview sources often termed "decisive action."

Amid and arguably because of intense pressures from state officials and smoldering concerns among select local constituencies, the superintendent made plans to reconstitute six of the district's low-performing schools. He had the formal power to reassign principals and redeploy staff. However, he had to make accommodations, particularly with union leaders who had the organizational resources to challenge administrative directives that run counter to the interests of union members (e.g., the ability to fuel negative publicity, flood the system with grievances, invoke "work to rule" in the schools, or otherwise disrupt the delivery of educational services).

Influence strategies

The superintendent's primary strategy was to control the "scope of conflict" (Schattschneider, 1960) through private interactions and proposal adjustments. In early discussions with key staff, the superintendent substituted the familiar language of "redesign" for the inflammatory rhetoric of "reconstitution," emphasized the opportunity to create "model schools" rather than punish failing schools, and drew on data on "the need for improvement" rather than on the efficacy of the reconstitution intervention. The superintendent then put these staff to work on identifying the schools to be reconstituted. The superintendent carried out "last-minute," low-visibility conversations with representatives of all the unions to reassure employees would be "reassigned without penalty." By most accounts, the union was "co-opted." The union extracted modest concessions, avoided the risk of being cast as resisting reform and acceded to the relatively small-scale "redesign" experiment. In conversations with school board members, the superintendent treated the initiative as an "information item," a move that made these exchanges a matter of professional courtesy, "not a request for board permission." In a climate characterized by the desire to "do something" to preempt further "state intrusion," the superintendent garnered a semblance of board support. Then, the superintendent met individually with the incumbent principals of the six targeted schools to inform them of their statuses (five were reassigned) and to ask them to "host" a meeting of faculty and staff at which the superintendent or his representatives would announce the initiative to the faculty and staff at the targeted schools.

Contextual forces, political games, and policy outcomes

The intense external pressure on the system and the superintendent's strategic choices converged to create an "insiders game" (Mazzoni, 1987; Polsby, 1984), wherein strategically located policy entrepreneurs shepherd a potentially divisive issue through the formal action channels with little public notice. They rely on their positional advantages and political skills to advance, or in this case, to authorize policy and to secure the neutrality if not the endorsement of actors who could delay enactment. Given the potential for conflict escalation, the price of protracted political battles, and/or the possibility of political gridlock, trying to institute a major, controversial change by circumventing, rather than by "meeting opposition head on and overcoming it" (Polsby, 1984, p. 159) can become, as it did in this instance, a promising way to secure an initial victory.

The Politics of Implementation

Actors, interests, resources

When the reconstitution initiative was made public, the slate of actors involved with the reform expanded to include the teachers affected, the parents of children in the targeted schools, and the media. Generally speaking, the teachers were "devastated" and "outraged" by a policy that came across as an unexpected, and in their view, unwarranted assault on their professional competence and commitment and an indefensible response to the concerns for teacher quality. The words of one capture the sentiments of many: "If teachers are weak, you can remove them or retrain them or even transfer them. . . . You don't have to annihilate a whole faculty to deal with a few bad apples who may mean well but do not teach well." Although a few viewed the initiative as "a real opportunity," most were appalled and angered by what they saw as a brutal, blanket indictment of their work and their worth. Some parents were concerned about the "unfair treatment" of teachers and the disruptive effects that massive teacher turnover could have on their children's education. The media also became a player, but not a promoter of the reform. Each set of actors had relevant resources that they used to influence policy developments. For example, teachers possessed expertise that the system relied on to deliver services and parents constituted a constituency the system relied on for legitimation and support. Thus their expressions of discontent signaled a problem the superintendent had to counter.

Influence strategies

The superintendent worked to rally support through a variety of appeals including public promises to give reconstituted schools substantial backing in the form of veteran teachers, instructional aides, small class sizes, computers, materials, ongoing professional development, and technical assistance. The superintendent and/or his designates met with faculty and staff and with parents to listen, to reassure employees that they had a job in the system and to reassure parents that "a change" was necessary, and that the superintendent's initiative was workable. But making promises, providing reassurance, creating forums to manage dissent, and offering justifications for the initiative in small group meetings and broader press releases were weak counters to the widespread disaffection that the initiative engendered and the media publicized in its coverage of the reform. Teachers voiced their opposition to the initiative and voted with their feet. When the initiative was announced, many reputedly capable and dedicated teachers refused to reapply for their positions. Many of their replacements also elected to leave the reconstituted schools at the end of the first and second year of implementation. Thus, the reconstituted schools had more vacancies than the superintendent anticipated. In a context characterized by chronic teacher shortages, the superintendent was not able to generate a strong pool of applicants and make good on his promise to staff the reconstituted schools with large cadres of master teachers. Nor could he make good on his promises regarding smaller class sizes, improved working conditions and the "unprecedented opportunity" to create "model schools." Simply put, the superintendent could not solidify support. The audience to be converted kept changing; disillusionment with the "broken promises" kept intensifying and prospects for creating coalitions of allies kept eroding.

Contextual forces, political games, and policy outcomes

In a context marked by numerous pressing problems and severe resource constraints, the superintendent could not deliver on the promises of substantial district support or offset the recurrent drain on human capital that occurred as many reputedly effective teachers left the reconstituted schools. By virtually all accounts, at the close of the second year of implementation, the initiative had "disappeared," save for the lingering sense of distrust and disillusionment it had engendered (Finkelstein, et al., 2000).

The implementation dynamics resembled an organizational "damage containment" game wherein actors scramble to overcome the problems that arise when initiatives are suspect, when efforts to mobilize stakeholder support have been delayed and contaminated by the politics of adoption, and when conflicts policy advocates sought to avoid in adoption erupt during implementation. Here, efforts to mobilize broad-based support started after the initiative was announced, rather than during its formulation when information and ideas from employees and other relevant constituencies can strengthen the policy design and the political campaign to secure the necessary backing (Kanter, 1983). They were encumbered by the suspicion that is generated when official mandates that have profound personal and professional ramifications arrive without notice or recourse. And, they were overpowered by the intense, negative reaction that occurred when the ramifications of restaffing reverberated in the schools and when the superintendent's promises were not kept. Given the decision to rely on the insider game to launch the reform, the superintendent lost the opportunity to test the waters, locate kindred spirits, implant compelling appeals, and garner the allegiance of the people he needed to assume positions in the reconstituted schools. When the conflict he sought to avoid in the adoption phase erupted in implementation, the superintendent lacked strong alliances and loyal recruits. Potential allies were dispersed; vocal resisters were outraged. The angry voice of opponents did not make the superintendent rescind his initiative but the resisters were incensed by the process as well as the proposal. Unchecked by the countervailing force of even a small, unified band of sympathetic if not stalwart supporters, they seized the exit option in numbers that severely damaged and eventually defeated the initiative.

THE UTILITY OF THE POLITICAL PRISM

As the preceding sections make clear, political perspectives on policy implementation have been around for quite some time and have guided numerous studies of policy adoption and policy implementation. These studies reveal that the types of games uncovered in the case study of school reconstitution are not the only types of games that occur as education initiatives wind their way through the education policy system. Some of the political games emphasized in the research literature operate to enervate policy initiatives while others operate to augment them.

A comprehensive analysis of the multiple games that may unfold lies beyond the scope of this chapter. However, I summarize several prevalent games here to highlight the contribution political perspectives can make to our understanding of policy implementation. To date, the primary contribution of politically anchored studies of policy implementation has been to help explain why translating policy into practice is not a straightforward, predictable, or controllable process (Bryk, et al., 1998; Kanter et al., 1992; McLaughlin, 1987; Pressman & Wildavsky, 1973). These studies document that in public school contexts, consonant policy implementation is a rare development (Berman & McLaughlin, 1975–1978; Smith, 2004). As some argue, the ambiguity required for political negotiation of policy purposes and provisions runs counter to the specificity required to give those responsible for implementation clear directions and workable action plans. As others point out, even more fully defined policies are subject to multiple interpretations (Yanow, 1996) and divergent responses. And, as many maintain, education systems are comprised of people with different preferences and priorities and relevant albeit unequal power bases that can be deployed to influence policy developments. For these and other reasons, a "politics of fidelity" may be an unrealistic expectation if not an oxymoron. Indeed, decades of research on the politics of policy implementation confirms that those who are interested in policy implementation may have to grapple with an array of political games that may affect policy initiatives in markedly different but decisive ways.

Political Games in Bureaucratic Arenas

The politics of policy dilution

One of the most prevalent and durable themes in the policy implementation literature is that "politics" is frequently and largely responsible for the dilution, if not the demise, of policy initiatives; that the "usual pattern is for social reform to be eroded by the particular interests of the implementers involved" (Stone, 1980, p. 22). Organizational actors who are not enamored with a policy may minimize its impact through bureaucratic games that obstruct implementation (Bardach, 1977). As multiple studies indicate, actors, through various combinations of simple neglect, subtle adaptation, overt resistance and creative defiance, can undermine the installation of new initiatives (Cuban & Usdan, 2003; Muncey & McQuillan, 1998; Rich, 1996).

Scholars offer different explanations for this pattern. Some point to the reluctance of policy makers to adopt robust policies. They argue, albeit for quite different reasons, that policy elites at the federal and state level may have "little appetite for the kind of prolonged struggle needed to get to the root cause of social problems. The course of least resistance for them is a succession of visible but superficial responses to problems" that have little chance of altering established political networks and the organizational priorities and routines those powerful interests support (Stone, 1980, p. 23; see also, Anyon, 1997; Stone, et al., 2001). They suggest that for policy makers who must stand for reelection, political credits tend to be gained or lost in the adoption of "flashy" policies that can be touted on the campaign trail, not in the development and implementation of comprehensive, coherent approaches to social and educational problems (Fuhrman, 1993, p. 11). In these and other ways, institutional structures and pluralistic bargaining among established interests create and perpetuate a political "incentives structure" (Chubb & Moe, 1988) that blunts policy initiatives (Plank, 1987). Even at the local level, deeply rooted traditions of incremental decision making and broadly held views about occupational survival may prompt district officials to select and enact policies that "attract . . . notice" and enhance legitimacy, but do not alter, fundamentally, the orientations and operations of the school system (Hess, 1999). While scholars may disagree on the reasons policy makers appear unwilling to adopt robust education reforms, they generally agree that if policies are weak in direction and design when they are injected into the education system, they are not likely to withstand the political challenges awaiting them in implementation (Fuhrman, 2001; McDonnell & Elmore, 1991).

Other scholars point to "the power of the bottom over the top" (Elmore, 1983) to explain why policies, be they deemed weak or strong, get diluted and derailed in implementation. The idea that "street-level bureaucrats" (Lipsky, 1980) have the power to unmake or remake policy faster than policy can influence organizational priorities and practices seems to capture many of the findings about policy implementation in education settings (Cuban, 1998; Elmore & Sykes, 1992; Rossman & Wilson, 1996; Weatherly & Lipsky, 1977). Some focus on the capacity of "local cartels" (Rich, 1996) to co-opt policy initiatives and community activists; others point to the demands of the workplace; the vague and, at times, contradictory policy provisions; the discretion afforded public school systems at the point of service delivery; and the strength of organizational norms, and routines. But overall, for a host of reasons, the targets of policy action seem to have the inclination, ability, and opportunity to convert new initiatives into conventional practices (Malen & Muncey, 2000). Whether this power advantage can be sustained in the wake of more stringent accountability policies remains to be seen. However, much research in this tradition suggests that even though service providers have little influence on policy adoption, they have considerable agency during implementation. This analysis has been used to assign considerable responsibility for policy outcomes to the service providers (Levin, 2001; Fuhrman & Elmore, 1990; Levin, 2001).

Other explanations look to the broad institutional forces that pressure school systems to adopt numerous "innovative" initiatives quickly to maintain legitimacy with key constituencies, including government officials, professional associations, and broad publics (Bryk, et al. 1993, 1998; Hess, 1999; Ogawa, et al., 2003). Since the pressure to enact multiple, fashionable reforms simultaneously can outstrip the capacity of school systems to implement them, policy initiatives may have little if any opportunity to improve organizational practices (Hatch, 2002; Hess, 1999; Malen & Rice, 2004). Doomed from the start, these initiatives fall victim to superficial attention and nonimplementation. In these and other ways, political pressures can dilute and derail implementation.

The politics of policy appropriation

A less prevalent contrasting theme suggests that while service providers and their immediate supervisors inadvertently or intentionally adjust policy in ways that dilute its distinctive features, these actors also "appropriate policies" (Fuhrman, Clune, & Elmore, 1988, p. 255). That is, they selectively and strategically embrace policies imposed from afar and then couple them in ways that advance their local interests (Firestone, 1989b; Fuhrman & Elmore, 1990; Wong, 1986). While the dynamics of appropriation or "accustomization" (Jung & Kirst, 1986) vary, this pattern is generally characterized by efforts to seize the opportunities that new initiatives may create and to use the new initiatives to advance the agendas of powerful players.

For example, drawing on the broad notion of "mutual influence" (Fuhrman & Elmore, 1990, p. 83), scholars suggest that state policies have influenced practices in schools and classrooms in part because they "coincided with, were preceded by, or were closely followed by corresponding district policies" that reinforced state policies (Fuhrman & Elmore, 1990, p. 92). While data on the "active appropriation" of federal or state education policies are limited (Chrispeels, 1997; Firestone, 1989b; Malen & Hart, 1987; Wong, 1986), they suggest that the prospects for cultivating a politics of appropriation may be contingent on (1) the degree of perceived congruence between policy premises and provisions and dominant local priorities and preferences, (2) the presence of local capacity and will, (3) the creation of forums for meaningful service-provider participation on implementation issues of import to them, (4) the size and stability of state and federal revenues attached to the policy, and (5) the ability of local leaders to clearly and continuously articulate how the policies emanating from higher levels of government relate to local initiatives and priorities. Comparative studies of local efforts to implement initiatives that call for professional and community collaboration suggest that the "co-construction" of new roles for parties involved in collaborative work (Marsh, 2002) and/or a reconceptualization of roles, particularly for district administrators also may enable local actors to appropriate policies and build on them (Honig, 2003).

Political Games beyond Bureaucratic Boundaries

The politics of policy nullification[5]
One of the most striking themes in the politics of policy implementation literature centers on efforts to nullify or revoke policy. Actors may seek to revoke policy through established channels of legislation and litigation. Propositions regarding school vouchers, bilingual education, or educational services for immigrant children and formal petitions regarding the appropriateness of special education services illustrate these options. Alternatively, actors may work to overturn policy through third-party intervention, secured by formal appeals to relevant authorities or informal links with organized groups that augment

the power of local actors (e.g., parents) who seek to halt the implementation of instructional programs or social programs that run counter to their views and values (Zimmerman, 2002). Actors may dilute policy to the point of nullification or they may ignore it altogether. But actors also may incorporate venue-changing strategies that shift decision-making from the circumscribed and orderly arenas of educational bureaucracies to the unbounded and volatile amphitheaters of public protests and "street brawls" (Schattschneider, 1960). Generally speaking, these dramatic shifts in arenas occur as policy conflicts escalate and erupt. Redistributive policies that challenge prevailing ideologies and entitlements, redefine rights and responsibilities, or otherwise alter the allocation of power and privilege are especially susceptible to this explosive form of politics wherein school communities can become, literally and figuratively, the battleground on which broad sociocultural wars are fought.

Studies of early efforts to desegregate public schools illustrate these dynamics (e.g., Armor, 1995; Crain, 1968; Orfield & Seaton, 1996; Peterson, 1976; Stout & Sroufe, 1970). In simplified terms, local officials charged with the responsibility for desegregating their public schools generally viewed desegregation as a dangerously disruptive venture. Even those who embraced the principles embodied in desegregation decrees reportedly feared the political controversies these decrees could encounter. These initiatives "laid bare the schism between words and deeds," between "the creed of equality" and the reality of inequities in the education system and the broader society (Rist, 1979, p. 22). They appealed to broad principles of justice and fairness and exposed deep divisions based on class, race, and culture. If dramatized by "condensational symbols" (Edelman, 1964), these core stakes could enable advocates and opponents to expand the "scope of conflict," turn spectators into participants, instigate confrontational tactics, and alter not only the rules of the game, but also the game itself (Schattschneider, 1960; Cobb & Elder, 1983).

Some communities avoided the public protests, violent eruptions, and combative tactics in part through the mature leadership of school boards and municipal leaders who advocated orderly, peaceful compliance (e.g., Crain, 1968) and in part through the incorporation of multiple mechanisms to diffuse conflict. For example, some plans relied on voluntary rather than mandatory bussing; created magnet school options; made minor adjustments in the reassignment of students; shifted the responsibility for developing plans to various advisory committees, task forces, and consulting groups; and retained structures like tracking that maintained segregated classes within desegregated schools (e.g., Crain, 1968; Peterson, 1976; Rist, 1979; Stout & Sroufe, 1970). In other communities, however, expressions of dissent moved beyond the bounds of voice and exit and into the realm of militant action. Riots, bus burnings, school boycotts, mass demonstrations, and other scope-expansion and conflict-escalation strategies polarized communities and paralyzed efforts to desegregate schools (Armor, 1995). Irreconcilable differences, intense emotions, and salient stakes meant that key parties were unwilling to negotiate differences, develop compromises, or accede to the legal authority embodied in desegregation decrees and related action plans. Additional factors, such as the action and inaction of state and federal authorities, the constellations of players who entered the fray, and the legacies of racial conflict and class division shaped the local political dynamics surrounding school desegregation. But the anticipation of violence and the incidence of it also altered power relationships within schools and communities (e.g., Rist, 1979). By some accounts, layers of volatile political dynamics, legacies of racial injustice, vestiges of fear, and shifts in the demographic, economic, ideological and governmental landscape converged to create exceedingly complex patterns of politics that have contributed, over time, to the "quiet reversal of Brown v. Board of Education" (Orfield & Seaton, 1996; Rosenberg, 2004).

The politics of policy amplification
Research in this vein examines how education systems and their surrounding communities might develop the governance structures and the cross-sector coalitions that are deemed necessary to install and sustain major education reforms, particularly in urban centers (e.g., Stone, et al., 2001). The analytic emphasis shifts from studies of how professional educators and school officials typically operate to buffer schools from external interference to how they might bridge schools and communities in ways that create a steadfast commitment to and a dependable foundation for education reform (Honig & Hatch, 2004). Externally focused, this brand of politics aims to create stable, durable relationships among powerful actors within and beyond the public school system. Ideally, issues are framed in terms of broad, collective benefits. Participation in the design and implementation of education reforms is strategically cultivated by education leaders who seek to establish strong linkages with policy elites, such as leaders of civic, corporate, and municipal organizations, and other stakeholders. Theoretically, group interactions enable participants to develop shared understandings of issues and interests, to forge new relationships based on mutual trust and respect, and to dedicate personal reserves and public resources to educational reform.

Several lines of work illustrate this form of politics. For example, some scholars have used the concept of "democratic localism" to identify various patterns of politics at the school level, to examine how these forms of communal interaction may be engendered, and to gauge how they may affect the capacity for and commitment to school improvement (Bryk, et al., 1998). Others have invoked the notion of "civic capacity" (Stone, et al., 2001) to examine how broad-based, stable coalitions committed to meaningful education reform might be created in a "high-reverberation" policy subsystem wherein the "frequent reshuffling of mobilized stakeholders, multiple and deeply held competing value and belief systems" and other factors complicate coalition formation (Stone, et al. 2001, p. 152; Shipps, 2003). Another has demonstrated how notions of "deliberative democracy" can be deployed to examine how efforts of educators and community residents to engage in "joint work" play out in political contexts marked by "power imbalances, competing belief systems, and variable organizational cultures and climates of trust" (Marsh, 2002, p. iv). While these and other related studies of coalition formation and community action employ different orienting constructs, they reach similar conclusions regarding the complexities of civic engagement, conflict mediation, collective commitment and collaborative work (e.g., Baum, 2003). In so doing, they expose the intricate political challenges embedded in both the formal adoption and the ongoing implementation of comprehensive, reform-oriented policies in public school contexts.

SUMMARY AND IMPLICATIONS

As this chapter demonstrates, studies that view policy implementation as a political phenomenon bring the complexities and uncertainties inherent in education policy pursuits to the fore. Taken together, the studies highlighted here suggest that policy implementation is a messy process marked by combinations of contests, contingencies, and disruptions that can not be fully anticipated let alone readily controlled. Bringing that reality into view is arguably an important service. The tendency to oversimplify social problems, political processes, and policy "solutions" and to "underestimate difficulties, over promise results and avoid any evidence of incompatibility and conflict . . . has the potential of a fatal flaw" (Moynihan, 1969, p. xii–xviii; House, 1974). That tendency fosters the creation of well-intentioned but ill-conceived policies that end up being marked more by fanfare than follow-through. It also increases the likelihood that exhaustion, frustration, disillusionment, and alienation may turn out to be the most discernible and dependable outcomes of education reforms (Jones & Malen, 2002).

Clearly, those who expect policy research to yield parsimonious theories, precise predictions, and prescriptive advice will be disappointed by the modesty of the analytic framework presented here, by the absence of propositions to test in future research, and by the omission of recommendations for enhancing policy implementation. Others also may be disappointed because this chapter provides a limited look at the political dimensions of policy implementation. These and other conspicuous shortcomings forecast the work that lies ahead.

Perhaps the most obvious task is a comprehensive, integrated review of the literature. This chapter samples rather than mines this resource. It pulls together threads of evidence about how politics may vary across issues and arenas as well as how patterns of politics may reflect different conceptions of power. A more extensive and systematic review could provide a more complete profile of the various patterns of politics evident in policy implementation and the conditions that give rise to them. It could array and compare the distinctive features, process dynamics, and policy consequences of various political games that occur within and beyond the bureaucratic boundaries of public school systems. Such an analysis might generate more explicit models of politics and uncover new ways of thinking about how various actors might influence those dynamics.

Another fairly obvious task is to address the stark empirical gaps in the literature. For example, studies of the "politics of policy dilution" tend to focus on how actor roles, relationships and interactions at the school level operate to convert "new" policies into conventional practice (e.g., Malen & Ogawa, 1988). In-depth treatments of how political exchanges carried out in district offices (e.g., Rogers, 1968), state education agencies (e.g., Madsen, 1994), or federal units may affect policy implementation are relatively scarce. Multilevel and longitudinal analyses that track the political interactions which operate to dilute a policy across units of the system and over time are also in short supply (e.g., Hall & McGinty, 1997; Malen & Hart, 1987; Muncey & McQuillan, 1998; Murphy, 1971). Such gaps may skew our explanations of policy dilution by placing primary responsibility for those patterns on service providers and their immediate supervisors. A more fulsome exploration might expose how actors throughout the system affect policy implementation not only by the initiatives they authorize and the political games they play to enact policy, but also by the roles they assume or avoid during implementation. Such an analysis also might unveil opportunities to enhance policy development and to derive more empirically balanced understandings of actor roles and responsibilities. Studies of countercases wherein actors appropriate rather than dilute policies could be used to enhance our understanding of both patterns through carefully crafted comparisons of the conditions under which these dynamics evolve, the resources and strategies that sustain them, and the ways different political dynamics bring about discernible policy adjustments.

Further, opportunities to examine politics beyond the bureaucratic boundaries of public school systems are available. The ongoing shifts in desegregation policy provide natural laboratories for tracing how the "politics of policy nullification" may evolve over time, as well as across communities. Other initiatives such as efforts to protect the rights of gay and lesbian students, to distribute condoms in secondary schools, or to make clinical services and day care centers part of the school program, particularly when cast as litmus tests of personal morality, have been met with evangelical responses, public protests, school boycotts and other confrontational tactics that can alter, in fundamental ways, the politics of policy implementation (e.g., Apple, 1996; Zimmerman, 2002). These developments create natural laboratories for examining different renditions of the politics of nullification.

While another form of public politics, namely "the politics of policy amplification," may be more an ideological ideal than an empirical reality, studies that examine approximations of this pattern would be welcome additions to a literature that has emphasized how politics tends to impede rather than enable policy implementation (Stone, et al., 2001). Efforts to unpack what it means and what it takes to engender a "pulling together" dynamic that enhances civic capacity and civic commitment to meaningful education reform are underway (Shipps, 2003). Some of this work looks at the role of mayors in this process (Henig & Rich, 2004); some focuses on identifying "which local political arrangements and coalitions are compatible with various versions of reform" (Shipps, 2003, p. 841); some concentrates on how university, school, and community partnerships might operate to create and sustain an infrastructure that might enable education reform to take hold (Baum, 2003). While a political dynamic that supports the development of robust education policies may be hard to create, it is too important to dismiss. Work in this area may help us discover ways to reach across economic, sociocultural and partisan divisions, to move beyond the protection of narrow base interests, and to develop the collective capacity and commitment required to address the full range of social, economic and educational conditions that severely and unfairly limit the learning opportunities and life chances of many students in public schools.

A particularly important task is to capitalize on the extant and emergent research to develop conceptual addenda to the conceptual framework outlined here. This fairly generic framework is a rugged heuristic—a familiar metaphor, not a refined theory. It is a serviceable point of departure for ongoing effort to map the political landscape, to identify the political games in the broader "ecology of game" (Firestone, 1989a), and to generate insights about facets of the policy process. It can elicit the descriptive detail required to refine concepts, articulate relationships, render midrange explanations of recurrent patterns of politics and develop more refined models of how politics and policy interact during and after the formal adoption of policy (e.g., Kingdon, 1995; Mazzoni, 1991; Sabatier, 1999). Thus, it is a sensible and serviceable conceptual tool.

However those interested in policy implementation elect to proceed, there is work to consult and work to attend to. The political dimensions of implementation both warrant and require thoughtful examination, not because the politics surrounding educational issues and initiatives can be tamed, but because politics is a reality that shapes what we have the inclination, capacity, and opportunity to do as policy actors, professional educators, and civic agents. Insofar as political perspectives sensitize us to that reality, they may enable us to appreciate why policy implementation is such a complex, iterative, and uncertain process and to uncover the avenues through which actors at all levels of the system might devise strategies to influence that process.

NOTES

[1]I am indebted to Ed Andrews, Bob Croninger, Sue Geary, Meredith Honig, Tim Mazzoni, and Donna Muncey for the ideas and citations they shared in conversations about this chapter.

[2]Here, "games" is simply a sensitizing device that can help analysts describe in detail the dynamic interplay of influence among diverse actors. The term is not to be confused with game theory, a tradition of work in economics and political science that develops mathematical models to predict how political games may play out (Ostrom, 1999).

[3]While it may be tempting to try to develop more global appraisals of an actor's power, the more global assessments are frequently misleading (Kingdon, 1995).

[4]School reconstitution initiatives seek to replace a school's administrators and teachers (or large percentages of them) with others who are presumably more capable and committed.

[5]I am grateful to Tim Mazzoni for encouraging me to include a discussion of what he termed the politics of nullification.

Chapter 6

Connections in the Policy Chain

The "Co-construction" of Implementation in Comprehensive School Reform

Amanda Datnow

What I have learned in my many years is what happens from legislation to the school level is a very torturous path. . . . One might as well have traveled to another planet where they speak another language and have another worldview.

—State Department of Education staffperson

In this statement, a state department of education staffperson is commenting on the policy implementation process with respect to the federal Comprehensive School Reform (CSR) Program. Expressed here is a common implementation lament that multiple levels of government impede implementation at the bottom of hierarchical educational systems. CSR provides an interesting case for revealing how more specifically connections among levels of government shape implementation processes and outcomes. Unlike policies of the past, its design specifically names states, districts, and schools as well as "design teams" as key implementers in ways that highlight the importance of cross-governmental relationships to implementation. This chapter demonstrates that understanding intended and unintended connections between these levels provides new insights into why policies developed at "higher" levels of the system may or may not be implemented as intended in schools. More specifically, the case of CSR illuminates what colleagues and I have called the "co-construction" theory of policy implementation. (See Datnow, Hubbard, & Mehan, 2002 for a full explanation of the theory.) In this chapter, I draw on that theory to illustrate how activities at various policy levels—federal, state, district, design team, and school—influence the implementation of comprehensive school reform in one state, Florida, and the impact of reform implementation on two schools in that state.

Conceptual Framework

Explanations for policy failed in implementation tend to be influenced by two dominant approaches: the technical-rational perspective and the mutual adaptation perspective (Snyder, Bolin, & Zumwalt, 1992). Here we develop a "co-construction" perspective as a departure from technical-rational models and an elaboration on mutual adaptation (atnow et al., 2002).

To elaborate, the technical-rational perspective traditionally has been the most extensively used approach for understanding policy implementation. It builds on classical management theory which places a premium on planning, organization, command, coordination, and control. Many educational reforms originated by the U.S. government circa 1965 until 1980 (e.g., Follow Through, Education for All Handicapped Students, Vocational Education) exemplify this perspective. A key presumption underlying these policy designs was that ". . . authority and responsibility should flow in a clear unbroken line from the highest executive to the lowest operative. . . ." (Masie, 1965, quoted in Smith & Keith, 1971, p. 241). In this view, the causal arrow of change travels in one direction from active, thoughtful designers to passive, pragmatic implementers.

Studies of reform implementation that exemplify the technical-rational perspective include Hall and Loucks (1981) and Gross, Giaquinta, and Bernstein (1971). In these studies, implementation is measured according to an objectified standard: fidelity to the policy design. The technical-rational perspective is more likely to frame local variation in implementation as a dilemma rather than as inevitable or potentially desirable (Snyder, Bolin, & Zumwalt, 1992).

By contrast some researchers have argued that technically driven reforms have not been as successful as planners envisioned because policy makers have not been sensitive to the culture of schools or the daily lives of educators (Berman & McLaughlin, 1978; Sarason, 1982). In this view, "context" appears as part and parcel of the school change process. The phrase "mutual adaptation" was first coined by Berman and McLaughlin (1978) in the Rand Change Agent Study to characterize this dynamic conception of context. Berman and McLaughlin argued that implementation should be seen as "a mutually adaptive process between the user and the institutional setting—that specific project goals and methods be made concrete over time by the participants themselves" (McLaughlin, 1976, cited in Snyder, Bolin, & Zumwalt, 1992). As Berman and McLaughlin imply, not only was mutual adaptation inevitable; it was desirable. Negotiation, flexibility, and adjustment on the part of educators and reform designers were keys to successful reform (Snyder, Bolin, & Zumwalt, 1992). Numerous other studies have adopted this perspective on reform (e.g., Mehan et al., 1986; Popkewitz, Tabachnick, & Wehlage, 1981; Smith & Keith, 1971). These studies all suggest generally that reform implementation involves an active and dynamic interaction between local educators, the reform policy, and the social, organizational, and political life of the school.

In the theory of co-construction, we build on the concept of mutual adaptation by elaborating more specifically how interrelations between actors in schools and the wider social and political sphere shape implementation (Datnow, Hubbard, & Mehan, 2002). In the process, our theory draws on work in the sociocultural tradition especially Rogoff (1995) and Tharp (1997) who identify personal, interpersonal, and community "levels" or "planes" of interaction and McLaughlin and Talbert (1993) who depict organizations as comprised of successively contextualized layers.

To elaborate, our theory of co-construction rests on the premise of multidirectionality: that multiple levels of educational systems may constrain or enable implementation and that implementation may affect those broader levels. In this view, political and cultural influences do not simply constrain reform in a top-down fashion. Rather, the causal arrow of change travels in multiple directions among active participants in all domains of the system and over time. This grammar makes the reform process "flexible" and enables people who have "different intentions/interests and interpretations [to] enter into the process at different points along the [reform] course. Thus many actors negotiate with and adjust to one another within and across contexts" (Hall & McGinty, 1997, p. 4).

The co-construction framework has a number of specific dimensions (Datnow et al., 2002). Most important is the idea of a *relational sense of context*. By this we mean that people's actions cannot be understood apart from the setting in which the actions are situated, and reciprocally, the setting can not be understood without understanding the actions of the people within it. Moreover, because contexts are inevitably interconnected (Sarason, 1997), contexts throughout the social system must be considered (Datnow et al., 2002, p. 12). A relational sense of context does not privilege any one context; rather it reveals the reciprocal relations among the social contexts in the policy chain (Hall & McGinty, 1997). Of course, at a given point in time, a researcher will foreground interactions among social actors in one context and locate others in the background. But in order to allow for a complete analysis, the interconnections among contexts throughout the social system are described (Sarason, 1997; McLaughlin & Talbert, 1993; Hall & McGinty, 1997).

This relational sense of context builds on but also moves beyond the embedded sense of context notion that has dominated many analyses up to now. While definitions vary, embedded context typically refers to classrooms as nested in broader systems layers (Fullan, 1991) or interactional "planes" (Rogoff, 1995). This conception is important because it calls attention to the fact that face-to-face interaction occurs within wider dimensions of social life. However, it often puts only one site in the center. Furthermore, the embedded sense of context can be susceptible to the conceptual traps of structural determinism and unidirectionality, implying that policy only travels in one direction, usually from the top down (Knapp et al., 1991). By contrast, the relational sense of context does not automatically assign a sense of importance to any one context but rather highlights relationships among contexts as a key focus for analysis.

POLICY BACKGROUND ON COMPREHENSIVE SCHOOL REFORM (CSR)

This chapter will bring to life and extend the co-construction perspective of policy implementation, and specifically the connections between policy levels, through an examination of comprehensive school reform. CSR, also known as the Obey-Porter initiative, allocates federal funds to schools for the adoption of "research-based" school reform models. The "purpose [of CSR] is to stimulate schools to revamp their overall educational operation by implementing a comprehensive reform program" (U.S. Department of Education, 2002). In 1998, $145 million were initially allocated for CSR and by 2003 the federal allocation increased to $310 million. Most of the funds have been designated for "Title I" schools or schools that meet federal definitions of serving high numbers of low-income students.

In drafting the CSR legislation, policymakers initially delineated nine[1] components of comprehensive school reform which include: (1) effective, research-based methods and strategies; (2) comprehensive design with integrated components including instruction, assessment, classroom management, professional development, parental involvement, and school management; (3) professional development; (4) measurable goals and benchmarks; (5) majority of faculty/staff members support model implementation; (6) parental and community involvement; (7) external technical support and assistance; (8) evaluation strategies; and (9) coordination of resources (U.S. Department of Education, 2000). The federal government's interest in whole school reform and in research-based programs is evident not only in CSR, but also in the No Child Left Behind legislation.

Most schools apply for CSR funds to pay for the costs associated with implementing externally developed, comprehensive school reform models, such as Success for All, Accelerated Schools, and the Comer School Development Program, among others. Though the reform models differ in their approaches to change, common to many of them is an interest in whole-school change, strong commitments to improving student achievement, new conceptions about what students should be expected to learn, and an emphasis on prevention rather than remediation (Oakes, 1993). Numerous CSR models have been associated with gains in student achievement (see Borman et al., 2002; Herman et al., 1999; Slavin & Fashola, 1998; Stringfield et al., 1997).

While CSR is a federal program, execution of the program takes place mainly at the state level. State educational agencies typically make decisions about which schools should receive funds. While the CSR legislation lists seventeen reform models as examples, schools can apply for funding for any whole school reform they wish (including a model of their own creation), providing it has research support. States make decisions regarding whether the schools' applications meet the federal criteria. It is estimated that over 6,000 schools have received CSR funding since the program's inception.

CSR has increased federal and state involvement in the implementation of comprehensive school reform and thus provides an interesting case for examining how multiple layers of educational systems interact over the course of implementation. Federal Title I funds have been available since 1994 to pay for the costs associated with whole school reform models as a regular part of Title I implementation. However, CSR signals a significantly expanded federal role in supporting comprehensive school reform. Moreover, it involves states in ways heretofore unseen in the comprehensive school reform movement. Policies like CSR require that implementation researchers move beyond old implementation models in which levels of government are seen solely as impediments to change. Rather, in the current policy context, the state level is a key implementer of reform and the federal government a key supporter. This design of CSR provides an important opportunity to consider how these broader layers of government may hinder or help implementation.

PRIOR RESEARCH ON COMPREHENSIVE SCHOOL REFORM

Much of the prior research on comprehensive school reform has focused on school-level issues such as school-level processes of selecting a CSR model (Bodilly, 1998; Consortium for Policy Research in Education, 1998; Desimone, 2000; Education Commission of the States, 1999; U.S. Department of Education, 1999b), the level of teacher support for CSR (Berends, 1999; Datnow & Castellano, 2000; Smith et al., 1998), and leadership in CSR schools (Hall & Placier, 2003; Murphy & Datnow, 2003). In general, this research tends to downplay or regard as "background" key dimensions of context. In doing so, prior research tends to miss some important elements of how the CSR implementation process unfolds.

For example, state accountability systems have been found to affect the implementation of reform efforts. However, because these studies tend to foreground schools and to examine state systemic reform as part of the background context in which the CSR schools, they miss different ways in which schools and states interact to produce sometimes different outcomes. For example, in one study, low scores on state tests seem to be what propelled schools to take on CSR models in the first place (Desimone, 2002). However, other studies have shown that when state testing and accountability demands were high, reform strategies were then later abandoned in favor of test preparation activities (Bodilly and Berends, 1999; Datnow, Borman, & Stringfield, 2000). Because these studies focus mainly on school responses to state policy, they fail to capture how schools and states interact in sometimes different ways to produce differential outcomes.

Other studies that examine state and district contexts in CSR implementation mainly highlight context as implementation barrier. For example, in a study of whole school reform in New Jersey schools, an effort that resulted from a state court mandate in the 1998 case of *Abbott v. Burke V,* Erlichson, Goertz, and Turnbull (1999) found that early CSR implementation efforts were thwarted when schools did not receive the resources from the state that they were expecting in order to pay for materials and training.[2] This outcome was further driven by a lack of capacity for school-based budgeting and insufficient direction from states and districts.

By contrast, several CSR studies have foregrounded the role of school-state and school-district relationships in the implementation process and have revealed important implementation lessons. For example, Hamman and Lane (2004) specifically focus on the role of states as intermediaries in CSR and find that states can forge positive relationships that support CSR implementation. Also for example, Berends et al. (2003) state that, "Many of the [New American Schools] NAS districts failed to provide organizational, public, and instructional leadership to the schools implementing the designs. Even where initial support existed, often it came from one individual, the superintendent, rather than the central office staff" (p. 127). They further add: "In many districts, the failure to protect the NAS reform effort from conflicting regulations and mandates put in place by district leaders anxious to show improvement again caused the reform to be virtually abandoned" (p. 127). Datnow (2005) similarly found that when district leadership and policy changes occurred, schools engaged in reform often looked on this as an opportunity to drop reform efforts. Only those schools that had reforms well institutionalized were able to sustain them in the absence of district support for the models.

In short, the literature on CSR is poised to move beyond lessons about states and districts as implementation barriers to more clearly reveal how schools, districts, and states may interact in particular ways to enable implementation.

METHODS

This chapter draws on data gathered in a longitudinal case study of comprehensive school reform in two schools in the state of Florida. These schools are part of a larger, twelve-school study that I conducted with a team of colleagues at Johns Hopkins University and the University of Toronto. I decided to focus on a subset of two case study schools and districts for this chapter, rather than reporting on the full study, in an effort to provide rich detail about their reform efforts and illuminate the connections between policy levels in each case.

Our case study data gathering at each school took place over a period of four years (1999–2003). For this chapter, I draw primarily on data gathered in interviews with educators and administrators at the school, district, and state levels. At each school, we conducted extensive interviews with teachers and administrators. In most cases, we interviewed teachers once; however, in some cases, teachers were interviewed more than once on consecutive visits, particularly in small schools, or when we wished to follow up with particular teachers. We interviewed principals and other key informants at the school level (e.g., reform coordinators) at least four times. We also interviewed numerous district administrators in each of the districts and personnel in the state departments of education in each of the three states. All interviews were conducted in person and then taped and transcribed verbatim, with the exception of the interviews with state department personnel that were conducted over the phone and not taped.

I consulted notes from classroom and school observations, documents (e.g., school improvement plans, publicly available statistics on the schools) and information about CSR that was available on state department of education Web sites. I also draw from detailed case reports that our research team has written on each school. These case reports have been updated after each site visit. For the purposes of confidentiality, pseudonyms are used in this chapter for all individuals and schools.

Site Selection

We selected the schools in this study according to several criteria. We chose states that supported the federal CSR program at varying levels and those that had state testing accountability systems, allowing us to assess the effects of these demands on school reform. We chose Florida in particular because it supported CSR at a high level. Five percent of Florida schools received CSR funds in 1998—on the high end across the country where the percentages of schools receiving CSR funds ranged from 1 to 5 percent of a state's total schools.

We chose to study whole-school reform designs as identified in the Northwest Regional Laboratory *Catalog of School Reform Models* (1998) instead of partial-school programs. We also chose only reforms that are the most popular, as evidenced by their presence on the list of top thirty models receiving CSR funds in 1998 and schools and districts in a diverse range of locations. We chose only Title I schools, or in the case of middle and high schools, those that served a majority low-income population. We created an initial list of potential schools using the Southwest Educational Development Laboratory's online database of schools nationwide that have received CSR funds and then solicited school principals and district personnel to participate.

The particular schools discussed in this chapter were implementing the ATLAS and Success for All reform designs. The major components of these reform designs are described in the Appendix. Table 6.1 lists the demographics of the two schools.

EXAMINING CSR IMPLEMENTATION AT THE STATE LEVEL

Through our interviews with state personnel and a review of publicly available documents, we have put together a portrait of Florida's state context with respect to standards and accountability and CSR. This portrait allows

TABLE 6.1
Description of School Sample

	Grades	Size	Race/Ethnicity					Free-Lunch Status	LEP Status	CSR funds	Location
			% Afr Am	% Asian or Pac Isl.	% Latino	% White	% Native	% Eligible	% LEP		
Success for All Elementary School	K–5	206	17	0	4	83		73	0	Yes	Rural
ATLAS High School	7–12	855	51	0.1	3	45	0.1	46	0	Yes	Rural

Note: All data reported are for 2000–2001.

for an examination of how state level policies serve as structural enablers or constraints to CSR at the local level. It also lays the groundwork for understanding the interconnections between the state and the federal, district, and local levels. Accordingly, we begin with the portrait and then move to a broader discussion.

Testing and Accountability in Florida

Florida's state testing and accountability began in 1999 under the leadership of Governor Jeb Bush. The state test, called the FCAT (Florida Comprehensive Assessment Test), is closely aligned with the state Sunshine Standards which have been in place since 1996. Students in grades 3–10 are tested, which is an increase from prior years when students were only tested in four grades. Schools receive letter grades (A–F) according to their performance on state tests. Schools that exceed targets receive financial bonuses, often of more than $100,000, and the state provides support for improvement to schools that receive the lowest grades.

The state's policy is controversial in that it allows students in schools that receive F grades for two years (within four years) to receive tuition vouchers to attend the private schools of their choice. This aspect of the state's system has been constrained by legal battles, however, and the fact that in at least two of the past three years there have been no schools with F ratings. Some state lawmakers use the latter as an indicator that the state's testing and accountability system is working to improve schools. A state department of education staff person whom we interviewed explained, "In Florida, there has been a real strong focus on student achievement. Everyone from the teacher to the parent to the custodian knows the school's rating, so there is an incentive to do something about it."

The CSR program in Florida is linked to the state's accountability system but not entirely. To be eligible for CSR, a school needs to be either eligible for Title I funds *or* have a C, D, or F rating on the state report card. When eligible schools apply for CSR funds, however, they are not judged on their performance on the state accountability measures (that is, solely by need) but rather on the proposals themselves.

CSR has been quite popular and competitive in Florida. In the first year, 126 schools received $50,000 each for one year of implementation. After the first year, participating schools were asked to submit a plan to meet the unmet benchmarks and a budget to support it and each school got the funding it asked for. In essence, Florida used the second installment of CSR funds to give additional money to these first cohort schools instead of funding a whole new cohort. The end result has been an increase in the per-school budget for CSR.

For example, in the 2002-2003 academic year 277 schools applied for CSR funding and 81 schools received $145,000 for one year.

During the period of our study, Florida was active in encouraging schools to apply for CSR funds. The state also held regional meetings to alert educators to CSR and a reform model fair before the application deadline. At the fair, the state helped educators to complete applications and consider how models would fit with their school improvement plans. Educators in Florida were provided with the rubric that would be used in evaluating their CSR applications. Each district had to submit plans on how it would work with schools.

The Florida Department of Education did not favor any particular CSR models in choosing which schools to fund. This choice was in part guided by a belief in local control. As one staff member explained, "We provide information and let them make the decisions. How would I know what is best for a school in Ft. Lauderdale or Escambia?" In the end the state did not receive many applications for locally developed models but that could be explained by close alignment between the state standards and available national models. As one state staff person explained, "I don't know of any models that are contrary to the Sunshine State Standards. But again, it is not just the model that helps them meet the standards. It is the way that school does business."

In Florida, CSR schools must adopt a formative testing program such as EduTest. This is an assessment tool, separate from the FCAT, which is used to give teachers feedback on their students' progress. In assessing the progress of CSR schools, the state looks at test scores, student attendance, and teacher absentee rates as indicators, and they administer surveys to principals and parents. They also reportedly make annual visits to each of the new CSR schools; however, the schools we studied had been visited only once during their three years in the CSR program. The state department planned to contract with expert educators and regional office staff to provide technical assistance to schools as needed during the implementation phase; however, again, this was not something that the first cohorts of CSR schools experienced.

The state department enhanced its support to CSR schools during the period of our study. A state department of education staff member stated, "We think that technical assistance and establishing good things at the beginning are key to the success of this program . . . If you treat CSR as just another funding source, you're not going to get anything." In addition to the support described above, the state is preparing to provide leadership training to all new CSR grantees. These were recent changes, however, and the earlier cohorts of CSR schools in Florida (including the sites in our study) did not have the same opportunities for support.

The state department staff person we interviewed was very pleased with the progress of CSR in Florida and expressed wishing only that there were more resources available so that they could fund more schools. As the person we interviewed stated, "Overall, CSR is showing that it is working in Florida. Our data are showing that it is working." This positive report however is not entirely consistent with outcomes in the school in our study, as I explain later in this chapter.

Moreover, as Hamman and Lane (2004) have also noted, it is important to note the role of individuals in shaping the level of connections that states have with schools with respect to CSR. The director of CSR in Florida whom we interviewed was proactive in working with schools. Hence, the level of support for CSR and the relative importance of CSR in a state's overall school improvement agenda may be due in part to the circumstances, priorities, and knowledge of the individuals placed in charge of CSR at the state level. At the same time, that there are differences in everything from funding guidelines to criteria for selection from state to state (see Datnow, 2004) with regard to CSR also points to the relatively loose connections between states and the federal government regarding CSR and among the states themselves.

EXAMINING CSR IMPLEMENTATION AT THE DISTRICT AND SCHOOL LEVELS

In this section, I examine schools' involvement with CSR, making connections to the district, design team, state, and federal levels. By foregrounding the school level in this instance, we are better able to see how reforms are co-constructed, given the state and federal policies regarding CSR as enablers and constraints to reform. As mentioned before, I profile two schools—a high school that implemented ATLAS and an elementary school that implemented Success for All—and their districts.

The ATLAS High School

The high school (grades 7–12) that we studied in Florida—the result of a merger between a middle and a high school that were the original focus of our study—is located in a rural area and serves one of the poorest counties in the state. Problems common to some rural districts were evident here, including a paucity of resources, nepotism, and petty politics; difficulties with teacher and administrator recruitment; high student dropout rates, and resistance to change. The community was described by a district staff member as "very small, very rural, and very political . . . They protect their own turf . . . They're not willing to give up tradition."

The district first became involved in comprehensive school reform, and CSR in particular, when the district's Title I director heard about the CSR funding opportunity at a state meeting. In interviews, she reported viewing CSR opportunistically—as a chance to bring substantial funding into the impoverished district. She believed its chances of being funded were good, given that the district had three schools with low grades on the state report card.

Before the merger, the ATLAS middle and high schools, both of which had D ratings before CSR (and still do), struggled considerably with implementation. At the high school, there was a lack of staff support, an absence of leadership for the reform, and a change of principals. At the middle school, virtually all of the same problems existed. School-level challenges notwithstanding, the lack of training in ATLAS appears to have been the most powerful constraint to implementation. Both schools received what they perceived to be inadequate support from the ATLAS design team. According to school personnel, the design team did not visit the schools regularly, apparently finding its remote, rural location difficult to get to.

Not surprisingly, implementation of ATLAS in both schools was very limited. Teachers in both schools spent the first year and half engaged in study groups; however, these seemed to produce few changes at the school. Only the small number of teachers who had the opportunity to attend training at Harvard in the ATLAS model was supportive of the reform. Others had a limited understanding of what the model was and were frustrated by the lack of direction they received. Teachers defined ATLAS in rather different ways, which was revealing of a lack of shared knowledge about the reform. One teacher described ATLAS as, "Generally looking at your own situation, doing some kind of surveying or otherwise collecting information, which, [when] upon looking at the information, you could deduce where the problems were." Whereas, another teacher described ATLAS as follows: "I know it has something to do with improving the students with their basics with reading and their math and those basic skills that they need. . . . So that's really all I can tell you about it because we really haven't done much with it." Yet a third teacher described ATLAS as "almost like integrating the different disciplines together."

We found that by and large, teaching to state standards influenced more of what teachers did in the classroom than CSR. As one teacher stated, "We base everything on our standards. I practically have them all memorized. I mean we're looking at them every other day if not every day. . . . That's really shaped our curriculum a lot." Another teacher remarked, "ATLAS hasn't changed my way of teaching at all. FCAT has, though." A number of teachers noted that ATLAS did not seem to cohere with the FCAT; some described

ATLAS-style learning is more "creative, outside-the-walls, and not standards-based."

In the third year of our study, the middle school closed and the students formerly attending that school, as well as from the other two K–8 schools, were moved to the high school. Part of the rationale for adding seventh and eighth grades to the high school was to create an overcrowding situation at that site which would help the school to obtain a building grant from the state for a new high school building. It was mentioned by administrators at both schools, however, that by combining the schools, the CSR monies could be stretched further as they would now have to pay for CSR support services for only one school. In the end, given a variety of inhibiting factors and slow pace of implementation, we were not surprised to find that the school abandoned the ATLAS model when the CSR funds ran out.

In sum, while the district Title I director supported CSR, it was not a major priority for high level administrators. The state test again governed much of what happened in classroom, much more so than the ATLAS model. Even early on, the conditions at the school also suggested that reform efforts were unlikely to continue after the CSR funding has ended. The enthusiasm for ATLAS was simply not present among most staff, many of whom never saw the value in reform to begin with.

The Success for All Elementary School

By contrast, our study also included a small, rural elementary school in Florida in a different part of the state that had a different implementation experience. The school served less than 200 students, most of whom were white and eligible for free or reduced-price lunch. The surrounding community was described as socioeconomically "very deprived" and the annual median family income was approximately $20,000. However, unlike the ATLAS high school's district, the district in which this school is located is quite large and more coordinated in its efforts.

For several years, the school had tried various methods to help improve student's reading skills. However, various reports indicated that nothing seemed to make a difference. A school psychologist told the principal about Success for All (SFA). She suggested that he visit an inner-city school nearby in order to observe the program. After the visit, the principal and a few teachers convinced the staff to vote to implement the program at their school. The principal explained, "It was the first program that we looked at that I really felt could work here." The decision to adopt SFA was made before investigating CSR as a funding source. In the spring of 1999, the school applied for and received a federal CSR grant to support the program. The school received $50,000 a year for three years.

At the time of initiation, district support for the school's decision to implement SFA was described by the principal as "very strong." An interview with a high-level district staff member confirmed this support, but in a qualified way. He pointed out that while he is "100% supportive of the school doing SFA," if a school implements a reform, and that program does not have a positive effect on student achievement, the district will ask that school to look into alternatives. The district did not commit resources to help fund SFA.

Implementation got off to a fast and relatively successful start. By the end of the first year, most teachers at the school were satisfied with SFA program. While some expressed difficulties with the rigid structure and lack of creativity, most teachers thought the program was making a difference and they wished to continue with it. For example, one teacher said. "I was one of those who were really, really nervous with it. It just seemed like it was just so much, and oh my gosh, how am I going to get all of this done? But, now it's smooth, it's working." Teachers explained that SFA helped to improve their teaching practices and had a positive affect on students' motivation to read. The school also had a positive relationship with the design team. The principal described the design team staff as "wonderful." Describing their experiences, teachers stated, "we have always enjoyed their visits and their help" and "we've really had great people."

In spite of these promising signs, the reform was discontinued at the end of the 2001–2002 school year due to a myriad of factors, including a lack of funding, a drop in state test scores, and a change in leadership. First, when the CSR funds ended, the school did not have other funds to continue. District cutbacks and ongoing funding issues at the state level made it difficult to support the reform, which was rather costly. The school did receive Title I funds, but not enough to support SFA. Second, while SFA had improved students' reading scores on SFA-developed assessment, this was not reflected on the Florida state assessment test. After year two of SFA implementation, the school dropped eleven points in reading, a major disappointment since the school adopted the program to address this specific problem. As a result, the district office no longer supported the SFA program. Third, since the implementation of SFA began, the school had changed principals twice. The principal who initiated the program left the second year after implementation. The new principal was neither overly enthusiastic nor negative toward the reform. This undoubtedly affected the attitudes of some of the teachers. The subsequent principal had very little knowledge about the program.

In sum, with respect to the Success for All school in Florida, we saw a high level of reform implementation, particularly within the first two years. This was facilitated in part by a strong connection between the school and the design team. Initially, there was also support from the district level; however, the district was by no means pushing SFA. And, when test scores failed to improve, the district no longer supported the reform. Ultimately, because what is measured matters, the outcomes on the state test figured strongly in the decision to drop the reform. While the state of Florida's accountability system strongly influenced the reform, the CSR program at the state level did not. The school had little interaction with the state regarding CSR, even though Florida is a state that purports to provide support to its CSR schools now. Nevertheless, it was the federal CSR funding that allowed the school to adopt SFA in the first place. Yet when funds ran out, it was impossible for them to continue. Overall, the story of reform at this school points to the fact that the sustainability, or lack thereof, of CSR was a joint accomplishment or co-construction of actors and events occurring at multiple policy levels, each important in its own right as a shaping force in the reform process.

DISCUSSION AND CONCLUSION

By looking at events and actions across various contextual levels in the policy chain, we find that indeed conditions at the federal, state, district, school, and design-team levels all co-constructed CSR implementation efforts. Whereas the technical-rational policy implementation literature would suggest that implementation is an activity restricted to a group of people in schools at the bottom of the policy chain, we see here that policy implementation is a systemwide activity, even when the desired change is mainly at the school level, as is the case in CSR.[3] However, the various policy levels have varying degrees of influence, and varying levels of connection with each other in the two schools and districts. These findings point to the need for viewing events in broader contextual levels not just as "background" or "context," but as important, dynamic shaping forces in the reform process.

The findings of this study also suggest that high-level policies are not as enabling of true reform as one might think. In theory, the "highest" policy levels (the federal government and state) would serve as important supports for CSR at the local level. To be sure, the findings of this study suggest that CSR provides financial support, which is much needed by schools. At the same time, the connections between what is happening in schools and what happens in these broader contextual spheres are quite loose. Perhaps this is not surprising as the CSR policies at the federal and state levels were latecomers to the entire CSR movement and were laid on top of (or had to exist alongside) state accountability systems, which had much more importance than CSR for the schools in this study.

Events at the school level and schools' connections with districts and design teams seem to be most critical to reform implementation, at least with respect to CSR. The primacy of school-level implementation activities has been documented in other studies of policy implementation more generally (Odden, 1991a, b). Many of the prior findings about the need for teacher support, strong leadership, ample resources, capacity for change, and a clear vision for how the reform fits into the school's broader improvement plan are supported by this study. Moreover, this study suggests that reforms need to help schools achieve state test outcomes in order to be sustainable. Taken more broadly, one can then draw the implication that some policies simply have more force than others in shaping reform at the local level.

The findings of this study also point to districts as important midlevel policy actors in the implementation chain. That is, we do see some patterns with regard to CSR support (or lack thereof) when we look at particular districts. In the case of the ATLAS school, we saw an absence of clear, ongoing district support for CSR from high-level administrators. There was more support in the case of the Success for All school, but certainly not advocacy for the reform. With respect to the design-team level, we find (just as many others before us) that ongoing design-team support is critical for successful implementation. Strong connections between design teams and schools were not apparent in the ATLAS school. In part, this school suffered from a lack of support from the design team in part because of their remote location. The Success for All school, on the other hand, benefited from close ties with their design team, which were in part facilitated by the fact that the design team staff were located in Florida.

Our study also reveals several other findings with regard to the role of the state and federal levels in policy implementation more generally and with regard to CSR in particular. We see that time, perspective, and level of experience with the policy make a difference in how much support and infrastructure is provided from the state and federal levels to schools and districts. As noted, the schools in this study were part of the first cohort of CSR schools. With the state in the developmental stage of their CSR programs, the state appeared to have roughly the same amount of interaction—minimal—with individual schools. As CSR matured and the state's experiences with the program deepened, support from the state level seemed to be increasing, but this did not change the experience for the early CSR schools that were part of our study. As Knapp et al. (1991) noted, there is a tendency for programs to settle in over time: "Just as the perception of a very new program will probably exaggerate its defects, the perception of a long standing program or set of programs will exaggerate its benefits (p. 122)."

Second, the findings suggest that a federal policy like CSR could motivate school reform and improvement, but this was not a given. In part, this is because of loose connections between systemic levels and the fact that the policy was co-constructed by individuals throughout the policy chain. Indeed, CSR operated as an incentive for schools to adopt a reform (though adoption does not equate to implementation or improvement), as the legislation and funding intended (U.S. Department of Education, 2002). For example, the ATLAS school was motivated by the CSR funding, and without it, would likely not have pursued any reform efforts. Yet, in this school, reform efforts barely got off the ground and were not sustained beyond the CSR grant period, but we cannot entirely fault CSR for this. In this school and district, there was an overall lack of capacity for reform. On the other hand, in the SFA school, CSR was not the primary motivator for reform initiation; it was a funding source used to support a reform effort already chosen. In theory, the outcomes could be better in such cases. As one state department official explained, "You can't impose whole school reform on folks. By pre-selecting eligible schools, that limits the motivation for schools to consider change." Just because educators in schools feel as if they must change due to low performance levels, this does not necessarily mean that they truly support the reform effort or that the reform will spur them on toward whole-school change. An educator in the ATLAS school reinforced this belief:

> I think [the reform] is simply a tool that we can use . . . Well, they will provide tools and training for us to use to help improve student achievement. And I think maybe that's something that none of us really understood going into Comprehensive School Reform, is that nobody's going to be able to bring in a packaged thing. Change has to come from within.

In sum, what we found is that the goals of whole school improvement and components that guided the creation of the CSR project did not fully make the transition from the federal legislation to the state to the district and to the school in this study. In part, this is due to loose connections among the policy levels and the fact that CSR appears to be overshadowed by state accountability systems. These findings about policy implementation are clearly not unique to this particular case, but the multiple policy levels implicated in CSR help to show the need for tighter connections among the levels and more explicit implementation activities at multiple levels.

APPENDIX

TABLE 6.2
Description of Comprehensive School Reform Designs

Design	Major characteristics
ATLAS Communities (Authentic Teaching Learning, and Assessment for All Students)	*Developer:* Coalition of Essential Schools, Education Development Center, Project Zero, School Development Program *Primary goal:* Develop pre-k–12 pathways organized around a common framework to improve learning outcomes for all students. *Main features:* 1. Pre-k–12 pathways 2. Development of coherent educational programs for every student so that they develop the habits of mind, heart, and work they will need as informed citizens and productive workers 3. Authentic curriculum, instruction, and assessment 4. Whole-faculty study groups 5. School/pathway planning and management teams For grades K–12, training provided
Success for All	*Developer:* Robert Slavin, Nancy Madden, and a team of developers from Johns Hopkins University. Now based at the non-profit Success for All Foundation in Baltimore. *Primary goal:* To guarantee that every child will learn to read. *Main features:* 1. Research-based, prescribed curriculum in the area of reading 2. 90-minute reading period; one-to-one tutoring; family support team; cooperative learning; on-site facilitator; and building advisory team For grades pre-K–6, materials and training provided

Source: The Catalog of School Reform Models: First Edition. Oak Brook, IL: Northwest Regional Educational Laboratory. Downloaded from http://www.nwrel.org/scpd/catalog/index.shtml.

NOTES

An earlier version of this paper was presented at the annual meeting of the American Educational Research Association, April 2003, Chicago, IL. The work reported herein was supported by a grant from the Institute for Education Sciences, U.S. Department of Education (No. R-117-D40005). The content or opinions expressed herein do not necessarily reflect the views of the Department of Education or any other agency of the U.S. Government. I wish to thank the participants of this research study for permitting us into their schools and offices and allowing us to interview and observe them engaged in reform efforts. I also wish to thank past and present colleagues on the research team, including Shelly Brown, Leanne Foster, Elizabeth Kemper, Gina Hewes, Sue Lasky,

Veronica Lotkowski, Judi Paver, Laura Rachuba, Camille Rutherford, Michele Schmidt, Sam Stringfield, Stephanie Sutherland, and Janet Thomas.

[1]Two additional components have since been added.

[2]For further discussion of *Abbott v. Burke*, see the Dumas and Anyon chapter in this volume.

[3]I am indebted to Meredith Honig for phrasing this important implication in this way.

Chapter 7

Building Policy from Practice

Implementation as Organizational Learning

Meredith I. Honig

Recent shifts in education policy increase the urgency to understand how school district central office administrators can support the implementation of school-community partnerships. In previous decades, such partnerships occasionally grew in neighborhoods across the country thanks largely to the initiative of local leaders and to funding from private foundations (e.g., Center for the Study of Social Policy, 1995; Clapp, 1939; Covello, 1958; Tyack, 1992). Now such partnerships appear as a frequent component education policy at federal, state, and local levels. For example, federal and state policies to strengthen instruction in reading, science, and bilingual education encourage, recommend, or require participation of families, health and human services agencies, youth organizations, and businesses, among others to help schools achieve ambitious academic standards (Honig & Jehl, 2000). Comprehensive school reform designs and after-school programs include community collaboration as a basic feature (California Department of Education, 1999; U.S. Department of Education, 1997, 1998a, 1999a).

These policies create new opportunities for school improvement but also new demands on central office administrators who aim to support their implementation. Arguably, when community partnerships appeared as a voluntary or occasional improvement strategy, central office administrators could more easily avoid participation. The incorporation of partnerships into a significant number of education policies ups the ante on central office administrators' more productive participation.

The research reported in this chapter informs the implementation of policy that fosters school-community partnerships—what I call collaborative education policy—by defining roles and capacity for central office administrators who aim to help with implementation. I use organizational learning theory to elaborate that collaborative education policy requires central office administrators to forge supportive rather than traditional regulatory or control relationships with school principals and other neighborhood leaders. Their new roles involve allocating resources and otherwise building central office policy from the practice of school-community partnerships rather than mandating local practice with policy. Findings come from an in-depth case study of Oakland Unified School District (CA). In the concluding section, I discuss implications of this analysis for education policy implementation research.

BACKGROUND

Studies of collaborative education policy largely have examined school-level implementation, including school principals' roles, not district central offices or central office administrators (e.g., Barfield et al., 1994; Cahill, 1993; Center for the Study of Social Policy, 1995; Cibulka, 1994; Crowson & Boyd, 1993; David and Lucile Packard Foundation, 1992; Jehl & Kirst, 1992; Levy & Shepardson, 1992; Mawhinney & Smrekar, 1996; Philliber Research Associates, 1994; Rossman & Morley, 1995; Smrekar, 1994; Smylie et al., 1994; SRI International, 1996; Wehlage, Smith, & Lipman, 1992). This school focus in the research makes sense given that historically, district central offices (and state and federal governments for that matter) have not participated in the implementation of school-community partnerships. Prior to the early 1990s, private philanthropic foundations, not public agencies, supported most major efforts to promote school-community partnerships for school-age children and families (e.g., Center for the Study of Social Policy, 1995) and typically focused directly on schools and neighborhoods and, sometimes, on state/county health and human services agencies. District central offices occasionally appeared in these and other school studies as impediments to implementation because they imposed categorical mandates and policy frameworks that diverted resources from school-community partnerships (Cunningham & Mitchell, 1990; David and Lucile Packard Foundation, 1992; Mawhinney & Smrekar, 1996). Past research thus highlights the importance of central office administrators' participation to collaborative education policy implementation but offers few guides for what such participation entails.

An analysis of collaborative education policy designs reveals that these policies typically call for at least three types of change: (1) Schools are to forge partnerships with community agencies such as health and human services organizations and Boys and Girls Clubs; (2) those school-community partnerships are to choose their own, shared goals and collaborative strategies for improving a range of student outcomes; and (3) central office administrators are to enable and support the implementation of partnerships' local, collaborative decisions (Honig, 2001). For example, policy guidance on schoolwide programs, comprehensive school reform, and school-linked services initiatives in California, Kentucky, Missouri, and other states asks schools and community agencies to form school-community governance teams. These local decision-makers are directed to study the status of youth and families through a community assessment process and to choose goals and strategies for their partnerships that they believe best address their local circumstances. These local choices are often presented in strategic planning documents submitted as part of applications for funding (e.g., California Department of Education, 1998; Family Investment Trust, 1995; Kentucky State Board for Elementary and Secondary Education, 1994). Policy designs either specify or imply that district central offices should not dictate partnerships' goals and strategies but help partnerships select and implement their own goals and strategies (Foundation Consortium for School-linked Services, 2002; Honig, 2001).

Collaborative education policies stem from a theory of action or set of underlying assumptions, shared with some site-based management programs and other bottom-up reform initiatives (Honig, 2004a). Namely, school principals, youth agency directors, and others who work with students day-to-day have valuable and immediate information about students' needs and strengths that is important to good and relevant decisions about school improvement. Central office administrators typically lack this local knowledge and have limited if any jurisdictional authority to mandate goals and strategies for the community partners who dominate the membership rosters of many school-community partnerships. These central office realities call for a policy design that features school-community partnerships determining their own goals and strategies and central office administrators marshalling support for those decisions.

These policies typically do not prescribe specific central office supports but leave those determinations to central office administrators. Given available central office policy tools, such supports may range from changes in individual central office administrators' day-to-day work to broader reforms of central office procedures and resource allocation. In other words, central office administrators' demands in collaborative education policy implementation relate to new processes for central office policy development: Central office administrators build central office policy from the practice of school-community partnerships—that is, they learn about partnerships' decisions and experiences and use that information to guide central office policy with the explicit goal of enabling partnerships' decisions.

Traditional models of implementation, bureaucracy, and policy making do not provide appropriate guides for what building policy from practice involves and actually focus on the opposite—how to mandate practice with policy. For example, implementation research and experience generally concern relationships in which central office administrators and other policy makers (also called principals or superiors) seek to direct the actions of schools (agents or subordinates) within their single-sector, hierarchical chain of command (e.g., Honig, 2001; Kreps, 1990; McDonnell & Elmore, 1987; Wildavsky, 1996). Local discretion appears as a problem to be harnessed through regulations, feedback, and other instruments of top-down control (Elmore, 1979–1980; Weatherley & Lipsky, 1977). Some say American state builders designed school district central offices and other public policy-making bureaucracies to reinforce centralized expertise at the expense of local knowledge and to limit local and other external influences on resource allocation and other public policy decisions (Skowronek, 1982). Studies of knowledge utilization by governmental agencies suggest that agency staff members tend to use information to control, not to support, implementers' decisions (Weiss & Gruber, 1984). District central office administrators have a particularly weak track record as participants in public policy implementation in general and specifically in forging relationships with schools that foster schools' collaborative decisions (Malen, Ogawa, & Kranz, 1990; Spillane, 1996). Case studies of central office administrators operating as so-called school support providers typically feature central office administrators helping schools implement district central office decisions, not schools' own decisions (e.g., Elmore & Burney, 1997).

CONCEPTUAL FRAMEWORK

Branches of organizational learning theory based in sociology, political science, and economics highlight specific activities involved when organizational actors such as district central office administrators collect information from outside their organization (i.e., information about partnerships' goals, strategies, and experiences) and use that information as the basis for organizational change (i.e., central office policy development). In particular, organizational learning involves two broad processes: the search for information outside the organization and the use or the incorporation of that information (or the deliberate decision not to incorporate that information) into rules regarding the behavior of individual organization members and the organization as a collective.

Search, also called exploration (Levitt & March, 1988) and knowledge acquisition (Huber, 1991), refers to a variety of processes by which information enters an organization. Information may be identified and brought into an organization by individual organizational members. For example, an organization may hire new staff members who carry new information with them or designate individuals, organizational subunits, and other so-called boundary spanners to venture outside an organization to gather information (Gladstein & Caldwell, 1985; Huber, 1991; Kanter, 1988). Information may also be sent into an organization as when state educational agencies provide funding guidelines to school district central offices.

Various factors stimulate search. Among them, an organization's failure to reach its goals may prompt exploration for new ideas. Successful organizations, faced with an excess of resources that accumulate when they exceed their targets, search for information for a number of purposes including to maintain their advantage (March, 1994a). Organizations may search for new information to reinforce or expand their control over subordinate organizations (Weiss & Gruber, 1984), to increase their repertoire of responses to future challenges or because search is part of their professional identities and purposes (Feldman, 1989).

Use refers to the incorporation of new information or deliberate decisions not to incorporate new information into an organization's collective wisdom, collective mind, or organizational rules. I consider these concepts, rarely applied to public policy settings, analogous to the development of organizational policy. Although terms vary, theorists generally agree that using information involves the following subprocesses:

- Interpretation. Once information has been identified and brought into an organization, organizational members make sense of the information and decide whether and how to incorporate it into organizational policy (Weick, 1995). Sense making is essential because, typically, various policy responses or nonresponses may fit a given situation (Yanow, 1996).
- Storage. Interpreted information is encoded as rules or "any semi-stable specification of the way in which an organization deals with its environment, functions, and prospers" (Levinthal & March, 1981, p. 307; see also, Argyris, 1976; Argyris & Schon, 1996; Cohen, 1991; Huber, 1991; Levitt & March, 1988). In policy contexts information may be viewed as stored when it becomes part of agency policy. Central office policies, for example, take various forms including administrative bulletins, school board decisions, resource allocations, and individual administrators' decisions about their own work (Weatherley & Lipsky, 1977).
- Retrieval. Organizational members draw on or retrieve the information, reformulated as organizational policy, to guide their subsequent choices and actions (Levitt & March, 1988).

Organizational learning involves both search and use. Too much search could result in central office administrators' continual failure to use information they have already collected to inform policy, their inability to make decisions, or their inundation over time with more information than they can manage (Argyris, 1976; March, 1994a). An exclusive focus on using information already collected could result in central office administrators' developing policy based on outdated information and on their improved performance with a finite set of competencies not necessarily appropriate to implementation demands (Argyris & Schon, 1996).

Organizational learning may result in either first-order or second-order change (sometimes called single-loop or double-loop learning). First-order change refers to alterations in day-to-day organizational structures and procedures. Second-order changes alter the underlying premises, beliefs, values, and logics that guide day-to-day decisions (Argyris & Schon, 1996). Scholars debate the value of these changes in different circumstances, but they generally agree that organizational learning may result in one or both types of change. An organization also "can learn something in order not to change"—meaning that decisions not to alter policy also comprise learning (Cook & Yanow, 1996, p. 439).

Scholars disagree about the relationship between organizational learning and improvement in ways that have important implications for this inquiry. According to one view, organizational learning leads to demonstrable improvements in organizational performance (e.g., Fiol & Lyles, 1985). Theories of organizational learning as organizational improvement are those most often applied to school systems to distinguish productive, high-achieving schools from ineffective schools (Bryk, Camburn, & Louis, 1997; Kruse, Louis, & Bryk, 1995; Leithwood, Jantzi, & Steinbach, 1995; Leithwood, Leonard, & Sharratt, 1998; Leithwood, & Louis, 1998; Marks & Printy, 2002; Marks, Louis, & Printy, 2000; Scribner, 1999; Scribner, Cockrell, Cockrell, & Valentine, 1999). A second view, seldom applied to schools or school district central offices, posits that success in certain arenas is inherently ambiguous both because feedback on performance tends to lag behind practice and because any available feedback may be interpreted in multiple ways. Given such ambiguity, organizational actors aim to behave appropriately—in ways that legitimate authorities consider valuable—regardless of the objective results of their actions (Feldman, 1989; March, 1994a). In this view, organizational learning occurs when central office administrators search for and use information as described above regardless of whether such actions can be linked to objective improvements in student outcomes or other outcome measures (Argyris, 1976; Argyris & Schon, 1996).

This process view of learning seems particularly appropriate to central office administrators in this case. Implementation of school-community partnerships can take three to five years to produce gains in students' school performance (Knapp, 1995; Rossman & Morley, 1995; SRI International, 1996).

Partnerships' goals and strategies may change as school principals and other partnership leaders receive feedback about their work and as their problems and populations evolve over time. Even if student outcomes appear to improve, the complexity of school-community partnerships makes it difficult to attribute such outcomes to the partnership or district central office policy (Knapp, 1995). Accordingly, measures related to the process of central office policy development guided this inquiry.

Models of organizational learning under ambiguous conditions also highlight that organizational learning for central office administrators involves managing risk. In classic economic terms, risk may be measured by the variance in the distribution of possible gains and losses associated with a particular choice. During search, central office administrators cast broad nets into their environments to fish for new information. Search thereby increases the amount of information central office administrators have to consider and widens the distribution of possible decisions and outcomes. Broader distributions mean greater risks of achieving extreme successes but also extreme failures. Conversely, when central office administrators use information they already have collected, they limit the range of alternatives under consideration and, accordingly, lessen their risk of extreme failures and successes (March, 1994b; March & Shapira, 1987).

Certain conditions tend to support organizational learning under conditions of ambiguity. These conditions include a warrant for change (Leithwood et al., 1995; March, 1994b) including threats to organizational survival. Past experiences may increase an organization's internal receptivity to new information (Cohen & Levinthal, 1990; Kimberly, 1981). For example, individuals who have searched before without negative consequences may perceive search as less risky and search more readily than others (March, 1994a). Learning occurs not by accident but intentionally—because organizational members set out to engage in such activities (Kanter, 1988; Lave, 1993; Wenger, 1998). Organizational learning requires occasions for organizational-environmental interactions (including interactions with other organizations in their environments) (Lave, 1993; Wenger, 1998) through which organizational members access new information and negotiate its meaning socially rather than individually. The designation of individual members or organizational units to specialize in search, sometimes called boundary spanners, can be important to organizational learning (Gladstein & Caldwell, 1985; Kanter, 1988). Individuals in subunits on the periphery of private-sector organizations may have more opportunities to search than those deeper within organizations. The latter may be well placed to incorporate information into new organizational policies (March & Olsen, 1975; Scott, 1995).

In sum, organizational learning theory clarifies that building policy from practice may demand that central office administrators search for and use information about the practice of school-community partnerships continuously and under inherently ambiguous conditions. Because of the ambiguity inherent in the enterprise, these activities themselves comprise appropriate measures of organizational learning. This theory also highlights conditions potentially conducive to organizational learning that provide criteria for selecting a strategic research site—a place where organizational learning may be possible—as elaborated below.

METHODS

I used a qualitative case study design to examine the implementation of four collaborative education policies in a single school district. Oakland, a mid-sized, urban California school district, provided a strategic research site (Hartley, 1994; Merton, 1987; Phillips & Burbules, 2000) in part because in the 1990s Oakland met many of the conditions theoretically conducive to organizational learning (see above). Oakland also was implementing multiple collaborative education policies that challenged central office administrators to build policy from practice.

Since 1992, the *Healthy Start* initiative of the California Department of Education (CDE) has awarded time-limited grants to school-community partnership sites annually through a competitive grant process. In their applications, school-community leaders outline their chosen goals and strategies and a plan for their implementation. CDE holds school district central offices accountable for enabling implementation of these local plans and for sustaining partnerships over the long term.

Supported by an annual set-aside of the city general fund since 1996, the *Oakland Fund for Children and Youth* funds community agencies and school-community partnerships based on their local plans for improving youth development and learning along specific indicators. With funding from the DeWitt Wallace–Readers Digest Fund, a consortium in Oakland (including the school district central office, city government, and community-based organizations) awarded grants to school and community leaders to develop and implement school-community partnerships—called *Village Centers*—governed by locally chosen school-level collaborative boards. The *Oakland Child Health and Safety Initiative,* funded by the Robert Wood Johnson Foundation, supported the reform of city-level governmental agencies to improve student outcomes. Oakland's plan focused on ongoing support for Village Center implementation.

I collected data between 1998 and 2000 but I examined events between 1990 and 2000 to capture Oakland's early experiences potentially relevant to implementation of the four focal policies (Cznariawska, 1997). Sustained observations of meetings between central office administrators and site directors were primary data sources (Barley, 1990). Meetings included regular school board and city council sessions, meetings of the mayor's education commission, and regular, formal gatherings of central office administrators and partnership representatives convened to help with implementation of the four focal policies (called "intermediary meetings" in Honig, 2004b). In all, I directly observed approximately 160 meeting hours.

I triangulated data from observations with semistructured interviews and record data (Miles & Huberman, 1994; Yin, 1989). I interviewed central office administrators who participated most often in the meetings identified above. These individuals tended to occupy positions on the periphery or frontlines of the central office dedicated to regular, direct contact with school-community partnerships (i.e., search) and had professional titles such as Director of Village Centers and Healthy Start Director. I call them "frontline central office administrators" to highlight their distinct central office positions. I used a snowball sampling technique (Miles & Huberman, 1994) to select other central office administrators including superintendents who did not participate directly in the meetings with school-community partnerships but whom the frontline central office administrators identified as essential to central office policy development (i.e., use). I call them "senior central office administrators" to reflect their broader authority within the central office. I interviewed school-community partnership leaders—called site directors here—who frequently attended the regular meetings with central office administrators, including school principals, heads of community-based organizations, and other individuals in site leadership roles. I interviewed directors of nonprofit organizations who convened the central office-site meetings and school board and city council members and county government representatives whom central office administrators identified as knowledgeable about the four focal policies. In all, I conducted forty-two, 60–150 minute interviews with thirty-three individuals about central office-site interactions and instances of search, use and the subactivities identified above.

I reviewed record data (e.g., official meeting minutes; implementation reports) that provided particularly important evidence of central office policy development over the course of the 1990s. I used NUD*IST software to code the interview and observation transcripts and electronic record data using codes related to organizational learning theory such as search and use and factors that enable and constrain search and use.

Findings

Various respondents indicated in interviews and observations that implementation involved learning in ways consistent with organizational learning theory:

CENTRAL OFFICE ADMINISTRATOR: We become servants to the neighborhoods.

SCHOOL BOARD MEMBER: I guess what I am trying to resist is the notion that there needs to be one model and that the [school] board needs to impose it. I mean that is why I really like the idea of school-by-school assessment and then working together between the district and the city and county to meet the needs at each school site.

DIRECTOR OF A CITYWIDE NONPROFIT ORGANIZATION: [Implementation for the central office means] being very clear about what the best practices are and being willing to be a learning organization like being willing to reevaluate how you do what you do on a regular basis. . . .

LEADER OF A COMMUNITY-BASED NONPROFIT ORGANIZATION: It's about [the central office] providing technical assistance immediately and capturing that information on what people [sites] are needing and sorting it to translate to broader policy.

Over the course of the 1990s, central office administrators frequently demonstrated specific organizational learning concepts in practice. I found critical incidents of learning in combinations of policy documents, observation notes, and interview transcripts over time and across all four policies, making discrete, brief displays of data challenging. The following example of site implementation in one Oakland neighborhood, presented in narrative form, captures how central office administrators used information about sites' practice to build policy as contrasted with traditional modes of information sharing in public policy settings such as advocacy campaigns and public hearings. This example is also typical in terms of its content. Although Oakland had almost ten years of experience with collaborative education policy implementation at the time of study, most sites were still in their infancy. Early implementation concerns, in Oakland as elsewhere, tended to involve concrete, practical challenges of launching sites including securing facilities, turning the water on, hiring staff members, designing programs, establishing relationships, and as in this example, ensuring the safety of youth and adults on school campuses when campuses opened their doors to community residents and other non–school staff members on a regular basis (SRI International, 1996).

Early in implementation, school principals, directors of community-based organizations, and parents at a school-community site in one Oakland neighborhood had grown increasingly concerned that unsafe conditions at and near the two participating schools jeopardized students' well-being, school performance, and the viability of the school-community partnership itself. Multiple conflicts had erupted among students after school. Service providers were reluctant to visit the school campuses. The school principals appeared apprehensive about opening their school doors to various community members. Safety problems were not new to this neighborhood. For several years, neighborhood leaders had tried to direct the attention of Oakland Unified School District and the City Manager's Office to neighborhood safety concerns through traditional avenues. For example, Community Organization,[1] a long-standing advocacy group, had organized campaigns and rallies to make information about neighborhood concerns available to central office administrators, police, and other government officials. Community Organization's leaders and community residents also gave reports during periods for public testimony at school board and city council meetings. These traditional avenues—advocacy campaigns and public hearings—had not led to changes in school district or city policy or to improved neighborhood safety by other means.

Community Organization's assistant director indicated that through these traditional avenues, he just could not "get the district's [central office administrators' and the school board's] attention." He recalled, "We [were] at a stage where the community [was] poised to make a change, but resources [were] not being put to where they [were] needed to help the community take the next step." The assistant director and others pointed to their participation in the Village Center Initiative as a turning point in their efforts to establish relationships with what they called "government," "the system," "the district," and "policy makers," regarding safety as well as their broader student achievement and community development goals. As part of the Village Center Initiative, a citywide nonprofit organization convened regular meetings of central office administrators, site directors, and others specifically, in the words of the nonprofit's director, "to connect government resources with community concerns." In early 1999, Community Organization's directors presented their safety challenges at one of these meetings.

Accustomed to traditional advocacy relationships, the Community Organization directors at first demanded a complete overhaul of the school campus and city policing systems. Over a six-week period, central office administrators, site directors, and others reviewed the neighborhood community safety report from which Community Organization directors had derived their initial policy recommendations. Subsequently, central office administrators, city staff members, and site directors agreed not to pursue large-scale police reform. Instead, they identified fights in a two-block radius around a specific street intersection as a place to start. Because most fights seemed to occur at this particular intersection, a reduction in the number of fights there potentially would lead to demonstrable improvements in neighborhood safety.

Community Organization's assistant director committed to increase the presence of parents in and around the schools during and after school. District central office administrators and representatives of the City Manager's Office pursued changes in city and central office policy. Several respondents involved in these events indicated that they knew they had special opportunities at that particular time to pursue such policy changes because, concurrently, the city manager and interim superintendent were in the process of reorganizing the school district's safety system. With the help of a citywide nonprofit director, central office administrators and city officials examined using the Village Center neighborhoods as "test cases" for the broader reorganization. To facilitate planning, the nonprofit director convened a series of meetings between the chief of police, central office administrators, and site directors.

Several aspects of this extended example illustrate organizational learning in action. First, central office administrators' participation in meetings and informal conversations illustrates search—the regular collection of information about sites' practice. Central office administrators also worked with site directors and others to translate that information into various policy responses and strategic nonresponses. In traditional advocacy relationships, parties outside government typically present not their practice but specific policy recommendations; by contrast, the Village Center meetings provided extended forums for examining and interpreting experience. Information about the safety concerns and the proposed and pursuant policy changes were stored in a variety of forms. For example, the community safety report became a part of Oakland Unified School District's policy manual-in-progress for the Village Center Initiative. City officials and senior central office administrators indicated that the reorganization of school police, in conjunction with the neighborhood-based parent involvement effort, were viable strategies to address the safety concerns. Accordingly, the reorganization may be viewed as part of an effort to encode sites' experiences into policy. As evidence of ongoing search and use, site representatives used their weekly meetings with central office administrators and others to revisit their implementation concerns. The interim superintendent agreed to use safety in Community Organization's neighborhood as one measure of the effectiveness of the broader policy changes.

Capacity for Building Policy from Practice

Particular threshold conditions and forms of capital proved consequential to whether central office administrators adopted these new roles. Threshold conditions were factors that appeared necessary but not sufficient for building policy from practice. Capital included those resources on which central office administrators relied in aiming to build policy from practice.

Threshold contextual conditions
Warrant for change. Throughout the 1990s, Oakland faced a performance "crisis" including substandard school achievement and resources

(e.g., Coburn & Riley, 2000; Commission for Positive Change in the Oakland Public Schools, 1990; Gammon, 2000). During that decade, the school district grappled with at least three formal threats of state takeover due to alleged fiscal mismanagement students' poor performance (Honig, 2001). Most respondents indicated that the central office operated with a high degree of urgency for reform.

Past experiences. Central office administrators typically referred to Oakland's relatively long history of activist politicians and experiments with community control of schools and government as a source of guidance and inspiration for collaborative education policy implementation (McCorry, 1978). By the late 1990s, central office administrators and others reported that they had accumulated significant experience with school-community partnerships (Oakland School Linked Services Work Group, 1999; Urban Strategies Council, 1992, 1993).

Sustained interactions between central office administrators and sites over time. Central office administrators highlighted at least three formal opportunities for regular site interactions. The site-level partnerships that governed site operations typically included school principals, parents, students, directors/ staff members of youth organizations, and, occasionally, central office administrators. Four intermediary organizations—new organizations generally composed of frontline and senior central office administrators and site leaders— were established specifically to help with implementation of each policy initiative and provided regular (weekly or monthly) opportunities for interactions (Honig, 2004b). Central office administrators and site directors both pointed to city council and school board meetings as opportunities to connect with the superintendent and elected officials for policy decisions requiring high levels of authority.

Threshold central office organizational conditions

Intentionality. An analysis of policy documents and interview and observation notes revealed that Oakland leaders believed that implementation involved new learning relationships between the central office and sites. In addition to the quotations noted above, by the mid- to late 1990s, senior administrators (primarily interim and assistant superintendents) reported school-community partnerships among their top three priorities for Oakland public schools. The interim superintendent promoted reinventing government reforms that had at their core the retraining of central office administrators specifically to support schools' collaborative decision making (Barzelay, 1992; City of Oakland, 2000). As partial evidence of central office administrators' intentionality, by the end of the 1990s, at least half of

Oakland's ninety-one public schools received funding to participate in one of these four collaborative policy initiatives.

Designation of boundary spanners. The central office designated certain frontline central office administrators to serve as liaisons with sites and to bring site information back to the district central office (i.e., to search). These individuals seemed particularly well suited to their "boundary spanning" roles. All reported that they enjoyed the daily unpredictability of their roles and that they believed that the highest rewards came from taking the greatest risks. Many of them claimed that they had worked for years as community organizers and that they had direct experience leading school-community sites. They described themselves as the "movers and the shakers" who worked "out of the box." Their offices were located on the periphery of the central office—literally outside but close to the main central office building.

Preemptive policy action. Central office administrators jump-started implementation when they identified and addressed in advance certain predictable site implementation challenges that only they had the authority to remedy. Interviews and observations confirmed that when central office administrators did not take such preemptive policy actions, these issues often overwhelmed their interactions with sites and otherwise diverted time and resources from the mostly unpredictable challenges that ultimately arose. For example, all four collaborative policy strategies potentially involved community organizations using school buildings after regular school hours, which required costly building permits and other agreements regarding facilities. Early in implementation, a citywide nonprofit organization convened central office administrators (specifically, business managers) and one pioneering site to discuss potential facilities concerns. Many central office administrators and site directors attributed early implementation successes at that site to preemptive actions taken as a result of these meetings. One central office administrator highlighted that such preemptive actions helped avoid "reinventing the wheel"—negotiating individually for resources that all sites needed.

Threshold site conditions

Site readiness proved fundamental to learning. Specifically, sites' designation of boundary spanners meant that individual site directors were available to interact with central office administrators. In addition, sites' development and initial implementation of goals and strategies meant that sites had a practice from which the central office might build policy. Several central office administrators observed that their conversations with sites stalled when site leaders did not clearly represent a broad site-based constituency and when they could not articulate partnership goals and strategies (Oakland School Linked Services Work Group, 1999).

Central office administrators' collaborative capital

Many of these threshold conditions were met in the early 1990s, but respondents reported remembering no examples of building policy from practice during that period. By contrast, an analysis of events at the end of the 1990s revealed instances of search and use. Multiple data sources confirmed that three forms of capital, built mainly in the second half of the decade, were fundamental to this shift: site and systems knowledge, political/social ties to sites and policy systems, and particular administrative tools.

Knowledge about sites and policy systems. Consistent with organizational learning theory, the Oakland case revealed that building policy from practice requires information—in this case, knowledge about sites and policy systems. One central office administrator captured the overall importance of site knowledge when he commented, "[Without site knowledge] then it's bureaucrats . . . sustaining their employment. It's [administrators saying] what they think for whatever reason—some maybe good reasons some maybe not—that people [sites] need." In other words, central office administrators frequently made a variety of policy decisions related to collaborative education policy implementation. Whether or not those decisions stemmed from sites' practice appeared associated with central office administrators' knowledge of that practice.

Site knowledge provided evidence that frontline central office administrators described as essential to their advocacy for central office policy changes. After all, frontline administrators' peripheral position provided some flexibility for search beyond the central office, but these positions also conferred limited authority to effect policy changes within the central office. These central office administrators reported and demonstrated in their day-to-day activities that securing policy changes often required that they lobby senior central office administrators and elected officials for assistance; detailed site knowledge helped them to lobby more effectively. Many frontline central office administrators learned this lesson from critical instances when they lacked site knowledge. As one long-time central office administrator recalled,

> All we had to do was a little basic arithmetic. . . . Is the county willing [to provide additional site resources]? Not unless we could really prove . . . that it was to their benefit. . . . I don't think that kind of basic work [documentation of site experiences, needs, and accomplishments] was ever really accomplished to prove the case.

Site knowledge also helped central office administrators and others understand in concrete terms what specific central office policy changes might advance site implementation. This concrete understanding proved particularly important because collaborative education policy documents tended to articulate abstract goals about learning and community responsiveness that some central office administrators found difficult to translate into actual central office policies. As one nonprofit leader observed,

> Like, if we know we want the district [central office] to be more community friendly we can work through that together with the district and we can move the district on being more open to community involvement and other broad themes of the initiative. . . . Being able to work through those negotiation issues on a small level around four [sites] is doable. . . . Forcing the district to have to be more community friendly in general—I mean, how would you do that?

Central office administrators also spoke about the importance of systems knowledge—knowledge about the rules and procedures of the district central office and other governmental agencies—to their ability to use or to help other central office administrators to use site knowledge to develop central office policies. As one central office administrator observed,

> The individual [administrator] whoever oversees this really needs to be hooked into someone . . . that has a firm understanding of how our district [central office] operates. Sometimes the mere act that because an assistant superintendent's calling helps [to leverage policy changes]. But most times it's because they've been around and they know what is happening, what is not happening, or why something might not be working [that makes them helpful].

When central office administrators claimed or demonstrated a lack of systems knowledge, they tended to ignore or fail to act on site knowledge. For example, Oakland's sites almost invariably involved non–school personnel (e.g., health and human service providers, parents) working on school campuses. Site directors typically knew that the district central office required background screenings for any adults working with youth at schools but questioned whether their status as a "Village Center" or "Healthy Start School" might qualify them for exemptions from these costly requirements and potentially embarrassing inquiries into the personal lives of community members with whom they were trying to establish partnerships. Site directors raised these issues with frontline central office administrators who, unbeknownst to sites, were unaware that requirements stemmed from unambiguous state and federal laws, not district policy. Even if the district pursued waivers, sites would still face the regular requirements in the meantime. Frontline central office administrators responded to sites' questions by suggesting that the rules were unclear, and they appealed to the district's legal office for guidance. In the process, these central office administrators raised sites' hopes that the requirements could be adapted. While waiting for a legal ruling, frontline central office administrators and site directors consumed over a month (approximately 6 hours and 35 minutes of formal meeting time) debating what should constitute district policy—time that proved wasted when participants realized they did not have the flexibility to craft their own rules. Nor did participants consider whether the federal and state rules actually inhibited site implementation. The omission of such consideration suggests a disconnection between the proposed policy and sites' practice or, in organizational learning terms, limited interpretation of site information.

Knowledge of public systems other than the district central office also proved fundamental to building policy from practice. Sites comprised multiple agencies from various jurisdictions and therefore the city and county had potentially important roles to play in policy development. Central office administrators and other policy makers with limited cross-systems knowledge tended to make decisions about site support not based on sites' practice but according to what they believed their own agency could provide. As one city administrator explained,

> Sites' demands are complex, complicated. I am not sure who [which agency] needs to do which piece. . . . I tend to think about it more in terms of what we [my agency] can offer. I don't know if they need it but I'm assuming that we should be able to provide . . . support.

A county agency director observed that when central office administrators built policy from their own expertise instead of sites' practice, they increased sites' fervor to advocate for specific policies rather than to share information about their practice: "Until we have people out in the field doing the analysis, we just have conjecture. Then you get 100 providers in line who want to provide certain services. They [sites] will want to find problems that feed these solutions."

Social/political ties with sites and systems. Observations and interviews revealed the importance of central office administrators' social/political ties with sites and within policy systems. With regard to site ties, central office administrators typically indicated that sites' funding applications and contracts provided information about sites' intentions and that similar documents were primary sources of information about schools for their central office colleagues in curriculum, evaluation, and business services. They highlighted that for them the "real deal"—meaning information about sites' actual day-to-day practice—came through direct relationships with sites that they established over time. When asked whether and how they shared information about their goals and strategies with the district central office, sites often referred to individual central office administrators with whom they had developed long-term direct relationships. Almost all respondents indicated that such ties between individual central office administrators and site directors were critical especially in Oakland where years of city-level governments' nonresponsiveness to neighborhood concerns fueled sites' unwillingness to share information. As further evidence of this government-neighborhood rift, site directors typically pointed out that in general they did not trust the school district with detailed information about their implementation experiences, but that they did share such information with the individual central office administrators with whom they had worked over at least several years.

For example, one long-standing frontline central office administrator indicated that individual site directors contacted him at least weekly and site directors confirmed this tally. However, during multiple meetings, site directors expressed significant dissatisfaction with that central office administrator. In interviews, these site directors explained that even though other central office administrators were typically more responsive, they would rather share information with a central office administrator who was a "known quality" and "trustworthy" rather than risk the information "falling into the wrong hands." A newer frontline central office administrator, characterized by sites as "with-it," "professional," and "responsive" had to make frequent site visits, as the central office administrator explained, "to establish the kinds of partnerships with principals and lead [community] agencies so the information comes more easily."

Strong systems ties—relationships within the district central office—also proved important, particularly for frontline central office administrators. As indicated above, using site knowledge often required district central office action beyond what frontline administrators could accomplish within their own span of authority. The frontline central office administrators who most frequently attempted to usher policy changes through the central office pointed to their regular communication with senior central office administrators and the school board as the key to their success. These "connected" frontline central office administrators stated and demonstrated that their communications with senior central office administrators increased the likelihood that these senior administrators trusted them and would take action on their requests. Frequent contact also helped frontline central office administrators understand how to translate complex site experiences into terms palatable to senior central office administrators and elected officials. As one central office administrator explained with regard to his lack of such ties,

When we [a colleague and myself] go to them [senior administrators and school board members] for . . . funding [for sites], they are always asking, why are you doing this . . . ? We don't have products, something that is tangible and concrete [specific recommendations for policy changes]. We invite them so infrequently to events and as a marketing thing they don't see that this matters to [academic] achievement. They don't link it, because of the infrequency of it. As a personal thing they don't have a reason to return our calls.

Administrative tools. Central office administrators pointed to specific administrative tools—the structure of their workday, their overall workload, and particular resource allocation mechanisms—as essential both to connecting with sites (search) and to developing policy (use). First, observations and interviews revealed that the structure of frontline central office administrators' workday and their overall workload significantly affected their ability to search. These administrators typically pointed out that capturing information about sites' practice required that they spend considerable time engaging with site directors. Even frontline central office administrators who previously had directed sites indicated the need for time on site to keep them up to date on sites' plans and challenges. The central office increased the sheer number of person hours spent with sites by dedicating central office administrators to site work, by hiring consultants, and by adding site work on to the responsibilities of other central office staff.

In addition, new resource allocation mechanisms seemed essential. These included budgeting systems that could handle nontraditional payment categories and complex, individual site budgets rather than the routine, uniform allocation of funds across sites or by preset formula. Such mechanisms also included procedures for adjusting budget categories quickly and on a site-by-site basis. In addition, site directors frequently pointed out with some urgency at meetings with central office administrators that sites typically did not have budgets sufficient to weather the many unforeseen costs that arose during implementation and bill the district central office after the fact, as was typical central office practice for disbursing funds to non–school agencies.

Central office administrators across all four policy initiatives most often relied on Memoranda of Understanding (MOUs)—contracts with each site—for such site-by-site policy development, including resource allocation and accountability for advance site payments. Unlike some other forms of contracts that specified sites' responsibilities, MOUs typically delineated both site and central office commitments. For some, MOUs made the difference between policy talk and action. According to one prominent education advisor in Oakland, "Everything we do should lead to some legislative or similar recommendations that can be enacted, become MOUs. Concrete policy changes versus talk about policy changes." MOUs also increased demands on central office administrators' time and the urgency for the workload adjustments described above. Central office administrators reported that developing MOUs involved negotiating with various parties, crafting agreements, and securing approval from senior central office administrators, central office lawyers, and school board members.

Systematic Variations in Capital and Challenges over Time

Frontline central office administrators tended to have stronger site knowledge and ties and to search more often than senior central office administrators. As partial evidence of this differential capital, during interviews, frontline central office administrators described in detail the strengths and weaknesses of specific sites whereas senior central office administrators deferred to frontline "staff members" to answer site-specific questions. Observations and records of central office-site meetings revealed that frontline central office administrators participated in the vast majority of these meetings. Site directors named frontline central office administrators as their main central office contacts; some site directors highlighted that they called particular frontline administrators several times a week to discuss various implementation challenges.

Senior central office administrators typically had the systems knowledge and ties that frontline central office administrators lacked. These resources stemmed in part from senior central office administrators' longer central office tenures and from their professional authority to set central office policy. However, senior central office administrators tended not to have site knowledge and ties to guide central office policy changes. For example, when asked what they knew about site implementation, senior central office administrators almost invariably reported familiarity with one long-standing, well-publicized site (Oakland School Linked Services Work Group, 1999) or deferred to the frontline central office administrators to address those questions.

In the short term, central office administrators' positions within the central office seemed to increase their site knowledge and ties at the expense of their systems knowledge and ties. Over time, these administrators faced pressures to develop their systems knowledge and ties, and in the process, they seemed to weaken their site knowledge and ties. Paradoxically, their frontline positions seemed to facilitate search *and* to increase pressures that limited search. As indicated above, individuals hired into frontline central office positions typically had site rather than systems experience. When asked about their job responsibilities during their first three to six months on the job, frontline central office administrators often reported spending most of their time working on site implementation challenges and otherwise increasing their site knowledge and ties. During subsequent months, senior central office administrators added new responsibilities to frontline central office administrators' caseloads that often involved work with other central office administrators "across the street." Frontline central office administrators invariably reported that these new responsibilities increased their knowledge of and ties to the central office but diverted time from their work and from their development of site knowledge and ties.

Frontline central administrators reported that they did not receive instructions to prioritize their additional, more traditional central office responsibilities but that in the face of competing demands they typically focused on their traditional responsibilities. Organizational learning theory offers an additional explanation. According to theory, decision makers in ambiguous situations receive little definitive feedback on their performance and tend to look for models of appropriate and legitimate behavior to serve as professional guides irrespective of objective outcomes (March & Olsen, 1975, 1976). Oakland's frontline central office administrators would have been particularly eager to find such models. They received little feedback on the effectiveness of their own work, and as new central office employees, they had weak job security and strong incentives to demonstrate their value if for no other reason than to keep their jobs. Frontline central office positions were relatively new and the central office offered few models of appropriate and legitimate frontline practice but multiple models of traditional practice (i.e., mandating practice with policy). Given such conditions, frontline central office administrators would have been inclined to seek professional role models, to find and follow models inconsistent with their nontraditional roles, to weaken their site knowledge and ties, and ultimately, to curtail their search activities. In sum, the very qualities that made frontline central office administrators inclined to search—nontraditional experiences and roles—also, over time, limited their resources for search and their actual choices to search.

In support of this interpretation, during interviews many frontline central office administrators expressed concerns about whether they were "doing it right" (fulfilling their frontline central office responsibilities). When asked about professional role models, frontline central office administrators typically pointed to central office administrators across the street as their formal or informal mentors. Chances are that the frontline central office administrators' primary professional guides were not skilled at search. A comprehensive state audit of the district central office reported that most central office administrators were not trained to support sites' decision making (Fiscal Crisis and Management Assistance Team, 2000). Two frontline central office administrators reported relatively high confidence in their frontline performance and seemed to maintain their site knowledge and ties over longer periods of time than others. These respondents attributed their relative confidence to visits to other districts where they met with their central office counterparts who were grappling with similar challenges. They indicated that on these trips they learned that Oakland was not underperforming relative to other districts and that they were not alone in their professional struggles. One central office administrator indicated that she could take risks because she did not fear losing her job: "I don't care what he [the interim superintendent] says. I don't need this job. I can go always go back [to my school]."

IMPLICATIONS FOR IMPLEMENTATION RESEARCH

This study highlights organizational learning theory as an important framework for examining the implementation of complex change efforts such as collaborative education policy. This study rests on the shoulders of several education scholars who put organizational learning on the school improvement map. I extend organizational learning research in education and other sectors in several ways that have implications for future implementation research. First, I draw on theories of organizational learning under conditions of ambiguity. This theoretical strand highlights that organizational learning occurs not within single organizations such as a school or a school district central office but between organizations; a view of Oakland's implementation process solely from within the district central office would have omitted the multiple conditions external to the district central office that affected implementation and obscured the search process almost entirely. Educational researchers may find this strand of organizational learning theory appropriate to studies of school improvement and various other policy demands. Second, much of the original empirical groundwork for organizational learning theory comes from studies of private firms. The Oakland case shows that public bureaucracies too can learn and that public sector learning may require various forms of capacity not captured by private sector studies. These findings raise the following question: Does the capacity for organizational learning in the public sector identified here apply to private firms?

Third, this study confirms that models of nontraditional professional practice may be essential to the implementation of new professional practice. However, the following question remains for direct investigations of settings in which appropriate models are more readily available: Given the availability of such models—a condition not adequately met in Oakland—under what conditions will central office administrators actually choose those models over others? Oakland's frontline central office administrators operated in a system with at least two logics of appropriate action: one promoting nontraditional frontline roles and one reinforcing traditional forms of central office administration. Under what conditions will frontline central office administrators choose nontraditional roles over the long term? Would other supports steer central office administrators' choices such as limiting frontline central office administrators' additional responsibilities or increasing their sense of job security?

Importantly, findings from this study come from a single albeit strategic case. Findings from such cases are not directly generalizable to populations but may define concepts to inform theory and to guide future research. This study's findings present a set of concepts that can focus research in other settings. Research that shines a light specifically on the constructs elaborated here may deepen understanding of how these constructs play out in practice in other districts and broaden knowledge of their applicability to public and private sector bureaucracies.

ACKNOWLEDGMENT

A previous version of this chapter was published as: Honig, M. I. (2001). Building policy from practice: District central office administrators' roles and capacity for implementing collaborative education policy. *Educational Administration Quarterly, 39*(3), 292–338. For this chapter, all sections have been shortened and implications for practice have been omitted.

NOTE

[1]Community Organization is a pseudonym.

Chapter 8

Toward a Critical Approach to Education Policy Implementation

Implications for the (Battle)Field

Michael J. Dumas and Jean Anyon

I'm gonna stay on the battlefield
I'm gonna stay on the battlefield
I'm gonna stay on the battlefield
'Til I die.

—Traditional Black American spiritual

In June 1990, the New Jersey State Supreme Court ruled in *Abbott v. Burke* that the state had failed to meet its constitutional requirement to provide educational opportunity in New Jersey's poor and predominantly Black urban communities. In its ruling, the court ordered a range of educational reforms to address the vast disparities in public education funding between urban districts comprised mainly of low-income students of color and suburban districts serving more affluent students. Most significantly, the justices determined that, as a result of decades of destabilization and disregard, poor districts were entitled to *more* funding than wealthy districts and ordered the state to raise funds for poor urban schools by increasing property taxes and reducing aid to suburban districts.

Abbott v. Burke is a significant case for exploring dynamics of education policy implementation, because it is so strikingly a story of *non*implementation. It is also instructive as an example of the inextricable link between education policy implementation and larger political, economic, and cultural processes. As we will make clear, education policy cannot be understood fully if considered distinct from broader social policy and ideological discourses within specific communities. To this end, we must analyze the

149

ideological, political, and cultural contexts within which education policy is created and implemented.

Abbott v. Burke is also a testament to the possibility of implementing education reform through the judiciary and evidence of entrenched opposition to education finance equity in many states. An understanding of the nature and substance of opposition in education policy implementation is essential to fully elucidating the challenges in reforming or, more substantially, *transforming* urban education. We argue that education policy implementation must be understood as a site of struggle and employ critical social science to explain the nature of this struggle and to assist in developing effective strategies for intervention.

We do not argue that class and race fully explain or account for challenges in implementing urban education policy. For example, in the New Jersey case, we might also call attention to the role of judicial intervention in shaping education policy; conflicts and negotiations between all three branches of government; the specific character of metropolitan regions in New Jersey; the relative influence of suburban and urban sectors of the electorate; and the complex process of administering state-mandated initiatives in local municipalities and school districts. Rather, we contend that critical analyses must inform these other investigations that are seemingly only about judicial, electoral, and/or administrative processes.

This chapter utilizes a critical framework best described as *cultural political economy*. Our approach to cultural political economy is informed here by Marxian political economy, Foucault's concept of power/knowledge, and critical race theory. Following our discussion of this theory, we offer a cultural political economy of *Abbott v. Burke*, which emphasizes the relationship between the cultural, political, and economic contexts within which the resulting policies were created and contested. We then examine the opposition to the implementation of the Abbott rulings through the lens of our focal theories. Our analysis reveals how various participants employed class and race to reify existing power relations and to undermine efforts to implement changes that could have helped improve urban schools. The chapter concludes with implications of our analysis for education policy implementation research and practice.

Borrowing from Michel Foucault (1980) and Black folk music tradition, we use the spatial metaphor of the battlefield to conceptualize the struggle involved in implementing social justice. Interestingly, the Abbott case involves a battle over the distribution of material resources within quite literal geographic fields—New Jersey's wealthy suburban districts and the economically depressed urban districts, where most of the state's poor residents are concentrated. More symbolically, the battlefield is meant to connote the site of ideological conflict over the educational rights of poor children and the responsibility of the state to provide equal opportunity for all its citizens. On this battlefield, the interests of the powerful hold sway; here, the ways in which education policies are implemented, or not implemented, continue to have deleterious consequences for children and families in urban communities.

CRITICAL THEORY AND EDUCATION POLICY IMPLEMENTATION: UNDERSTANDING SOCIAL POLICY AS A SITE OF STRUGGLE

To understand education policy implementation, it is crucial to examine the contexts within which it is "done." That is, education policy implementation must be conceptualized as a social practice that takes place upon a social terrain. Social theory seeks to explain how and why we do what we do on this social terrain. As elaborated in this section, *critical* social theory has come to denote a range of theoretical approaches that share a critique of the determinism of orthodox Marxism and seek to understand how humans exercise agency against new forms of domination in a rapidly changing world. Critical theories, as an approach to social analysis and cultural criticism, seek to illuminate how power shapes those constructs and processes that in turn inform how we understand what is, what should be, and what is possible. Our discussion of the intricacies, contradictions and trajectories within and across critical theories is necessarily incomplete in this brief chapter; our primary interest here is in synthesizing concepts and ideas that contribute to our understanding of the cultural political economy of education policy implementation, particularly in "raced" and "classed" urban contexts.

Cultural political economy is a critical approach that we believe offers great insight into educational policy implementation as a social practice on social terrain. Cultural political economy has its roots in two fields: political economy and cultural studies. Political economy is the social analysis of economic forces within a society and how these forces structure human experience and action. Traditional political economy analyses, with their focus on systems and economics, tend to ignore issues of culture and the lived experience of those subject to institutional constraints. In turn, cultural studies analyses are limited in their explanatory power because they fail to account for the ways in which "race," "culture," and "identities" are shaped within, and responsive to the political economy.

Cultural political economy "emphasizes the lifeworld aspects of economic processes—identities, discourses . . . and the social and cultural embedding of economic activity" (Sayer, 2001, p. 688). Cultural political economy allows us, in one moment, to step in for a close examination of the meaning of a specific act or utterance, and in another moment (or often simultaneously), to step back in order to bring into view the various social, historical, economic and cultural contexts within which actions and utterances are situated. In so doing, we can make connections between the global and local, between ideology and social practice, and between institutional structures and individual human agency that drive policy implementation.

We begin our discussion of cultural political economy with some explanation of the Marxian tradition in political economy and how it has influenced those in the cultural studies tradition. We then turn to the issue of discourse, a central concern in the field of cultural studies. Michel Foucault's concept of power/knowledge helps us understand how language shapes, defines and reifies material conditions (which are the primary focus of political economy). Finally, we bring critical race theory into the conversation, in order to gain some clarity about the roles of race and racialized discourse (which are always also about class and material realities) in shaping education policy implementation. In bringing these theories together, we do not imply that they are wholly compatible. However, we do argue that for those interested in education policy implementation, these theories—brought together here to inform a cultural political economy— offer invaluable lessons for research and practice.

Marxian Political Economy

Dominant notions of capitalist political economy present a system in which individuals compete for economic profit in a beneficent, open marketplace. Marxian political economy, on the other hand, offers a more critical perspective on material relations. Marxians begins with the proposition that economic production is primarily a social activity in which humans act based on where they are situated within the class structure. In Marx's conceptualization of capitalist political economy, the ruling class (or capitalists) controls the means of production, and exploits the labor of the working class (or proletariat) to reproduce conditions that increase profits for the ruling class and secure their own dominance. Importantly, political institutions reflect the interests of the capitalist ruling class.

Under capitalism, everything becomes a commodity—something to be bought and sold for profit. In capitalist political economies, commodification occurs because worth is reduced to economic gain. The fetishism of commodities alienates us from our own individual and collective human potential. "Fetishism," Gottlieb (1992) explains, "occurs when social relationships which derive from human activity are perceived to be the product of inhuman, unchangeable forces" (p. 21). In other words, social conditions persist (and resist policy and other efforts to change them) when people are convinced that

present economic exploitation is a natural, unavoidable fact, rather than a product of history. To counter this kind of fetishism, Marxian political economy offers a necessary counternarrative by emphasizing the historicity of our current social condition. That is, in order to raise consciousness about how unnatural and unnecessary oppressive social relations really are, Marxian analysis emphasizes how the history we make (and which in turn makes us) reproduces class relations within society.

Scholars influenced by Marx have offered some of the most serious critiques of what has come to be called neoliberalism. The neoliberal economic model that has dominated the United States and Britain, beginning with Reaganism and Thatcherism, has impaired efforts to implement educational equity. Neoliberalism, as ideology, emphasizes free enterprise and market solutions to economic and social problems. Neoliberal social policy prescribes that the state limit itself to providing basic infrastructure and maintaining some civil and financial order, but leave economic activity to the markets (Wacquant, 2001). In terms of public policy, this means a retreat from public investment in the social good; in the cultural sphere, neoliberalism fosters the notion that certain groups simply have themselves to blame.

One main criticism of Marxian political economy is that it suffers from economic reductionism or what Gramsci referred to as "economism." That is, there is a tendency to reduce all social relations and human organization to economic explanation. Economism is more characteristic of Marxian scholarship than Marx's own work and suggests that classes are fixed, that members of social classes always act immediately and predictably in their own interests, and that economic structures determine all other social formations.

Recent Marxian analyses have offered more complex explanations of the political-economic terrain. For example, David Harvey, a leading Marxian urban geographer, argues that capitalism feeds, and feeds off of racism (Merrifield, 2002). The market functions on scarcity, which is the basis for competition. Without competition, profits would not increase and the system would falter. In urban centers, scarcity is achieved by allowing poor neighborhoods, primarily inhabited by Black and Latino/a residents, to decay until the need for urban expansion raises the profits gained by urban development. Of course, in nearly all cases, this means that poor people of color are displaced by those who (1) can afford to pay the rising costs of living, and (2) are convinced that the neighborhood is no longer "undesirable"—that is, inhabited by undesirables. Conditions in the neighborhood then improve, but not for poor people of color. By this time, they have been pushed out to other economically depressed areas, not yet deemed ripe for economic exploitation.

Here, race has what Stuart Hall (1996) has called "determining" power. As a social formation, race shapes class relations and identities. Critiquing classical Marxian analysis on this point, he states, "Approaches which privilege the class, as opposed to the racial, structuring of working classes or peasantries are often predicated on the assumption that, because the mode of exploitation *vis-à-vis* capital is the same, the 'class subject' of any such exploitative mode must be not only economically but politically and ideologically unified" (p. 437). Hall makes clear here that poor people do not always identify with other poor people simply on the basis of shared economic status, and may instead choose to identify with those of the same racial identity, regardless of class standing. Hall offers us a more culture-conscious political economy, which holds on to Marx's analysis of the impact of economic forces on human lives, but also attends to *how social formations impact the economic structure of society*.

Foucault's Power/Knowledge

The notion that power shapes implementation is not new in implementation studies. (For example, see Malen, this volume.) But critical theorists put forth a particular conception of power that emphasizes how power, acting through discourse, shapes the very construction of knowledge. As Michel Foucault (1980) cautions us, although individuals or specific groups may put forth seemingly independent ideas, we must attend to the working of power in the articulation, dissemination and consumption of these various forms of knowledge.

But what is power? Foucault would argue that there is no such thing as power in and of itself. Rather, there is "an ensemble of actions which induce others and follow from one another." Power does not "exist universally in a concentrated or diffused form"; rather, "it exists only when it is put into action" (quoted in Yarbrough, 1999, p. 35). Power is a kind of force, but not a thing-in-itself. It is not embodied in any one person or group, but instead serves as a construct to understand relations between persons and groups, between events and other events, as a cause of this phenomenon and an effect of that set of phenomena.

Power in the Foucauldian sense "establish[es] the norms for rational discourse, systematically excluding any other discourses on the grounds that they are irrational, perverse, or insane" (Surber, 1998, pp. 214, 215). It "operates in and through discourse as the other face of knowledge" (Gubrium & Holstein, 2000, p. 494). That is, "discourse puts words to work, it gives them their meaning, constructs perceptions, and formulates understanding and ongoing courses of interaction" (p. 495). Discourse takes words from their state as simple utterances and embodies them with effect. The task of critical researchers and practitioners, Foucault would say, is to provide "a topological and geological survey of the battlefield" (p. 62) on which the formation of power takes effect through discourse and other means:

There is an administration of knowledge, a politics of knowledge, relations of power which pass via knowledge and which, if one tries to transcribe them, lead one to consider forms of domination designated by such notions as field, region and territory. . . . Endeavoring . . . to decipher discourse through the use of spatial, strategic metaphors enables one to grasp precisely the points at which discourses are transformed in, through and on the basis of relations of power. (pp. 69, 70)

Critical Race Theory

Toni Morrison has noted that "the habit of ignoring race is understood to be a graceful, even generous, liberal gesture." She continues, "To notice it is to recognize an already discredited difference. To enforce its invisibility through silence is to allow the black body a shadowless participation in the dominant cultural body" (1992, pp. 9–10). Critical race theory (CRT) "rudely" interrupts the hushed silence of liberalism, and seeks to make visible the manifestations of race in everyday life, specifically the ways in which people of color remain subjugated. Critical race theorists would argue that ultimately, our aim as critical researchers and practitioners is to advance policy that supports liberation from racial dominance.

CRT, although not a single unified theory, seeks to understand: (1) how white supremacy and oppression of people of color is constructed and maintained in the United States, particularly the relationship between institutionalization of white dominance and constitutional precepts such as "the rule of law" and "equal protection," and; (2) how to transform the "vexed bond between law and racial power" in which law reinforces white dominance, even and perhaps especially through its assertion of color-blindedness (Crenshaw et al., 1995, p. xiii).

One of the premises of CRT is that racism is a normal fixture in the social and cultural life of the United States. Racism is not, as many might assume, a few historical aberrant acts, but is permanently embedded within the institutions, values, and norms of society. CRT is particularly helpful in analyzing "the ongoing dynamics of racialized power, and its embeddedness in practices and values which have been shorn of any explicit, formal manifestations of racism" (p. xxix). For critical race theorists, legal decisions and resulting institutional policies needn't have an explicit reference to race in order to have racial intent and effect. For example, policies on curriculum, school funding, and teacher training and promotion may be crafted and implemented without any mention of race, and yet have racially "curious" effects, such as a reduction in the number of people of color in leadership positions, or as we shall detail in this chapter, fewer fiscal resources in schools serving communities of color.

Such policies needn't have an explicit reference to race in order to have racial intent, racial effect, or both.

CRT has also advanced the notion of *interest convergence* (Bell, 1995). Interest convergence proposes that laws and policies that benefit people of color are only implemented when there is also a benefit to whites. When that benefit to the dominant group is either unclear or simply is not present, opposition grows, and the policy is likely to be defeated or significantly weakened in its effectiveness.

Critical race theorists illuminate the role of discourse in maintaining white supremacy. They argue that power is maintained in social policy and everyday life through rhetoric which constructs whites as innocent victims, most often of African Americans. Thomas Ross points out that when whites are invoked as innocent victims of affirmative action, for example, there is an assumed "defiled black taker." He states, "This implicit personification is made explicit by the second part of the rhetoric, the questioning of the 'actual victim' status of the black person who benefits from the affirmative action plan. The contrast is between the innocent white victim and the undeserving black taker" (2000, p. 640). When innocence is defined in individualistic terms, Ross argues, whites can present themselves as racial victims. However, if we examine the many advantages whites have received by reason of their racial group membership, we might wish to ask, as Ross does, "What white person is 'innocent,' if innocence is defined as the absence of advantage at the expense of others?" (p. 636). As we shall see, whites often, and quite powerfully, claim individual innocence in matters of race, even as they lend active support, passive support, or both to policies that solidify (collective) white racial dominance.

The dismissal of oppression as a collective experience is the foundation of CRT's critique of liberalism and liberal approaches to policy implementation. Gloria Ladson-Billings explains, "CRT argues that racism requires sweeping changes, but liberalism has no mechanisms for such change. Rather, liberal legal practices support the painstakingly slow process of arguing legal precedence to gain citizen rights for people of color" (1998, p. 12). The problem with the liberal approach to education policy implementation is that there is no space for consideration of the broader social and historical context of race and racial power. The assumption is that there is a social will to extend equitable access to education to people of color, and that this can and should be done without any conscious consideration of racism. To the contrary, critical race analyses of the history of African Americans in the courts and civil society reveal a continuing pattern of legal decisions and social policies that replace one form of inequity with another, usually more covert form. Liberal policy proposals have no way to account for, or combat this entrenched, systemic racism. Thus, it ensures that each new iteration of "reform" will lift up a chosen or random few, but fail to alleviate the oppression of the masses of people of color.

A CULTURAL POLITICAL ECONOMY OF THE (NON-)IMPLEMENTATION OF *ABBOTT V. BURKE*

Much of the conflict over educational fiscal equity is a result of how schools are funded in the United States. Public school financing relies primarily on local property taxes, supplemented by varying levels of state aid, and very limited federal assistance. In general, large urban school districts receive about 42 percent of their funds from local sources, about 47 percent from state governments, and approximately 11 percent from the federal government (Anyon, 1997). Property wealth and education spending have always been unequal when compared between and within states. However the drastic social and economic transformations of the mid-twentieth century concentrated poor people, and particularly poor African Americans, in central cities as never before (Massey & Denton, 1993). In the 1930s and 1940s, urban industrialization brought thousands of African Americans from the rural South to the center of Northern cities, where good-paying jobs could be found, even for those with limited formal education. As Black people began to integrate the cities, whites moved into the suburbs. The jobs soon followed, creating what the Brookings Institution has identified as a "spatial mismatch" between black people and jobs (Raphael & Stoll, 2002; Anyon, 2005).

Many scholars have argued that federal "redlining" policies and white supremacy (i.e. the economic, political, and cultural systems that advance or give credence to white dominance) prevented Black people from moving beyond defined geographical spaces. Kantor and Brenzel explain:

> In the 1940s and 1950s . . . white hostility toward minorities together with the use of restrictive covenants that prohibited white homeowners from selling to minorities, Federal Housing Authority policies that discouraged loans to racially mixed neighborhoods in favor of those to all-white residential developments in the suburbs, and suburban zoning practices designed to preserve residential class segregation all effectively closed the suburbs to minority families. (p. 371)

Even after the passage of antidiscrimination laws in the 1960s and 1970s, "the persistence of discrimination continued to keep the majority of African-American families in the city, while the process of ghettoization in the suburbs confined most black suburbanites to areas already housing blacks or abandoned by whites" (p. 371).

Many middle-class families, regardless of race or racial animus, increasingly alarmed by the relatively poor quality of public education in the cities, took their children and tax dollars to more affluent areas. Poor urban residents could not afford homes, and those working-class residents who owned homes saw their property values plummet. Reduction in home ownership and new home construction, a decrease in existing property values and an increase in crumbling and abandoned residential properties translated into reduced tax revenues, which in turn had a deleterious effect on the financial stability of urban school systems.

Advocates for educational finance equity framed the equity problem as a civil rights issue and turned to the courts for redress. They argued that the life chances of urban poor children were limited by their lack of access to an education that would prepare them to compete with their more well-to-do suburban peers; the inequitable funding of education deprived poor people of a quality education and thereby relegated them to lives of poverty (Anyon, 1997)

In 1971, in the case of *San Antonio Independent School District v. Rodriquez,* the U.S. Supreme Court ruled that education is not a federal constitutional right. Following *Rodriquez,* then, attention turned to the states, whose constitutions invariably included clauses, inserted in the nineteenth century, guaranteeing some form of free education. The specific phrase added to the New Jersey Constitution in 1875 obligated the state to provide each child a "thorough and efficient" education (New Jersey Constitution, art. VIII, sec. 4, para. 1). The first New Jersey Supreme Court ruling on school funding, *Robinson v. Cahill,* was handed down in 1973. The court ruled that the state's system of school funding was unconstitutional since it deprived urban children of a "thorough and efficient" education. The justices argued that the obligation to fund education rested with the state, which could not simply pass on the responsibility to local municipalities, particularly those poor urban cities with a limited tax base. They demanded that the legislature institute a new "constitutionally sufficient" funding plan. Over the next few years, the court clarified its initial ruling, indicating that a "thorough and efficient" education required equity in funding, but also equity in curricular offerings, such that each student would be equipped for her "role as a citizen and as a competitor in the labor market" (*Robinson v. Cahill* 1976, 459–460, in *Abbott v. Burke* 1990, p. 309).

In 1975, the state legislature passed the Public School Elementary and Secondary Education Act (PSEA). However, they did not provide any funding for the measure. A year later, the legislature still had not funded PSEA. In response, the courts ordered the schools to be closed. Within a matter of weeks, legislators passed the state's first-ever income tax to cover the cost of implementing PSEA. However, the legislature did not rectify the unconstitutionality of the funding structure. Local municipalities were still largely responsible for raising tax revenues to improve schools, and middle-class and wealthy districts continued to receive the same amount of funds from the state as the more impoverished districts. Rather than inject funds into poor urban schools, legislators simply capped local school district expenditures, and instituted as a minimum standard a basic skills curriculum that relied heavily on rote memorization, skill-drill exercises, and standardized examinations. While cities only had funds for this basic curriculum, suburbs continued to offer more advanced innovative courses utilizing pedagogies that encouraged creativity and critical thinking (Anyon, 1997).

In the years of the PSEA, financial disparities between suburban and urban districts actually increased. Although in violation of the court mandate, local revenues, primarily collected through property taxes, provided the majority of funds for schools. Wealthy and middle-class suburbs raised funds to cover what state aid did not, while poor urban municipalities simply could not. In only two of the fiscal years between 1975 and 1985 did the legislature fully fund PSEA (Anyon, 1997).

After several more years of increasing inequities, the Newark-based Education Law Center filed a new lawsuit on behalf of urban schoolchildren. This lawsuit challenged the PSEA as inadequate to ensure a thorough and efficient education. *Abbott v. Burke*, initiated in February 1981 on behalf of 20 plaintiffs from Camden, East Orange, Irvington, and Jersey City, contended that the state's public education financing law relied too heavily on local property wealth and thereby denied students from poor districts an adequate education. Further, they denounced the existing statute as in violation of equal protection clauses in the state and federal constitutions. Marilyn Moreheuser, lead counsel for the plaintiffs and executive director of the Education Law Center, compared the Abbott case to the desegregation cases of the 1950s and 1960s. "This is separate but equal all over again. We're saying that we should at least make them equal" (Peterson, 1987). The state, for its part, argued that education financing provisions have no influence on student performance. Instead, they asserted, educational inequities result from sociopolitical factors, such as fiscal mismanagement, poor school leadership, and unstable home environments in which children receive inadequate parental guidance.

In 1985, the New Jersey Supreme Court assigned *Abbott v. Burke* to administrative law judge Steven Lefelt, who was charged with hearing the factual arguments in the case. After a nine-month-long trial in 1986–1987, Judge Lefelt issued a 600-page decision in August 1988 finding for the urban children. In his ruling, Lefelt characterized the current financing system as "broken" and recommended a complete overhaul. Lefelt further voiced concern about the state's responsibility to its citizens and praised resilient students who endure conditions in impoverished urban schools: "I believe the case comes down to whether the state desires to enhance the educational opportunity of students living in poor urban areas. This case has illuminated for me the prodigious efforts which must be undertaken by those urban youths who make it through the current system into productive lives." And finally a warning: "If we do not wish to spend monies easing these students' entry into contemporary society, then there are those who argue that we will have to spend the funds later in welfare, Medicaid, job training and prisons" (Sullivan, 1988, August 26, p. B-2). Lefelt noted in his administrative ruling that only the New Jersey Supreme Court could declare the funding law unconstitutional.

The case moved to the Supreme Court, which handed down the final ruling on June 5, 1990. The ruling declared the state's funding system unconstitutional and ordered equalization of funding between suburban and urban districts. Significantly, the court demanded that the state provide supplemental programs in urban districts to respond to existing disadvantages. As in *Robinson v. Cahill*, the court noted that tax-poor urban municipalities could not carry the burden of providing the bulk of funding for their schools. Disagreeing with the state's argument that financial and programmatic disparities were unrelated to educational outcomes, the justices argued that students in poor urban schools "simply cannot possibly enter the same market or the same society as their peers educated in wealthier districts" (*Abbott v. Burke*, 368, in Anyon, 1997).

On the issue of curriculum, the court rejected the state's claim that urban students were simply unsuited for sophisticated courses:

> Our constitutional mandate does not allow us to consign poorer children permanently to an inferior education on the theory that they cannot afford a better one or that they would not benefit from it. (*Abbott v. Burke*, 340, in Anyon, 1997)

In January 1990, after spending eight years in office opposing education finance reform, New Jersey Governor Thomas Kean in his final State of the State Address admitted that the existing system was unfair. In May 1990, the new governor, James Florio, anticipating the ruling in *Abbott v. Burke*, introduced the Quality Education Act (QEA), an extensive plan to increase income taxes by $1.1 billion to achieve equitable funding between suburban and urban districts (and also to reduce the budget deficit he inherited from Kean).

However, the new bill did not go over well with suburban taxpayers. The Democratic-controlled legislature, citing fears of retribution at the polls, diverted $360 million to property tax relief, in order to assuage the anger of middle-class suburban residents, who comprised the majority of the electorate (Kerr, 1991). According to New Jersey Senate President John Lynch, "We are skimming some money that would have otherwise been distributed to the state's urban centers in the form of school aid and using it instead to reduce municipal tax rates everywhere" (Kerr, 1991, January 8, p. B1).

This diversion of funds amounted to a shift in resources from poorer urban districts that lost the property tax funding to wealthier suburban areas that saved on their property taxes and effectively gutted the Quality Education Act. In response, the Education Law Center decided to reactivate the *Abbott* case. Once again, the court declared the state's funding plan unconstitutional and ordered that an equitable plan be instituted. This new plan was unveiled by Republican Governor Christine Todd Whitman, who had been elected largely by white suburban voters angry over Florio's increase in property taxes. Whitman and a number of Republican legislators swept into office in 1994 on a platform promising income tax cuts.

Whitman did cut taxes, but then had to find an alternative way to meet the court's funding equalization requirements. Her plan emphasized school improvement by emphasizing curriculum standards rather than finance equity. The Comprehensive Education Improvement and Financing Act (CEIFA) she signed into law in December 1996 reduced spending in all districts and left urban districts with what the court assessed in May 1997 to be inadequate funds to meet the constitutional standard of a "thorough and efficient" education.

In May 1998, the New Jersey Supreme Court ordered an unprecedented range of new programs in urban school districts, including full-day kindergarten for all three and four year olds, new facilities to alleviate overcrowding, increased security, health and social services, technology, alternative education, and after-school and summer-school programs. Since that time, the state has failed on several occasions to either fully fund or expeditiously implement various components of the ruling. Each time plaintiffs have returned to court, and in nearly every case the state has been at fault of violating urban students' constitutional rights.

For example, in January of 2004 a three-judge Appeals Court ruled that the New Jersey Department of Education could not remove $124 million in previously approved K–12 supplemental programs from the current (2003–2004) budgets of *Abbott* districts. The Court gave the Department of Education ten days to restore the funds that had been withheld largely based on the department's claims that they were short on funds. In March 2004, the Education Law Center reported that the state's budget for fiscal year 2005 failed to fully fund full-day kindergarten in urban districts, one of the provisions of the Supreme Court rulings. Furthermore, the proposed state budget fell over $200 million short of achieving parity between urban and suburban districts. The current governor and suburban lawmakers, who make up the majority of the State Legislature, may fear that further taxing middle- and upper-class residents could well lead to a suburban rebellion and cost them the next election. For now, then, it seems clear that Abbott is not being fully implemented in New Jersey, and that each attempt to implement parts of the law will continue to be met with fierce resistance.

The (Non-)Implementation of the Abbott Rulings: Lessons from Cultural Political Economy

Several lessons can be learned from analyzing the implementation of *Abbott* through the critical lens of cultural political economy. First, this approach highlights how the historical convergence of neoliberal economic policies and cultural discourses on race and class undermined the implementation of *Abbott*. Policies like *Abbott* that demand state investment without guarantee of financial profit are seen as threats to the free reign of the markets. The liberal argument is that investment in education yields economic benefits in terms of a more highly-skilled workforce. The neoliberal response is that there is no need to artificially produce social conditions. After all, what if there is *more* profit to be gained from creating and maintaining a large *poorly* skilled labor pool, whose competition for low-skill jobs can keep wages low (and thereby guarantee even more profits for the owning classes)?

In the 1980s, this neoliberal ideology converged with a white cultural struggle to reclaim a kind of political and moral certainty that was widely perceived to have been lost in the 1960s and 1970s (Gresson, 1995; Kincheloe et al., 2000). Ronald Reagan's focus on rugged individualism and individual responsibility resonated with a white population who felt threatened by changes in policy and the culture that they believed were biased toward Black people and other marginalized groups (Gresson, 1995; Kincheloe et al., 2000; Omi & Winant, 1994).

The public face of the beneficiaries of the *Abbott v. Burke* decision in New Jersey was that of poor urban African Americans even though all racial/ethnic groups were intended to benefit from the new initiatives. As we are reminded by critical race theorists, whites often close racial ranks across class lines, even though the economic condition of many white people is closer to that of poor people of color (Anyon, 2005). Thus, the neoliberal triumph of capital over the common good is compounded by the cultural triumph of race(-ism) over the common sense of addressing the shared economic interests of working-class people of all colors.

Second, the economic and political isolation of urban centers in New Jersey ensured that no dominant group interests would be served by "extending" educational opportunity to poor urban African Americans. Several social scientists have documented the concentration of poverty in urban centers

(Anyon, 1997; Fine & Weis, 1998; Massey & Denton, 1993; Wilson, 1996). In New Jersey, every resident is classified by the United States Census as an urban dweller but more than half of New Jerseyans live in what could be characterized as small towns with populations under 10,000. Less than 10 percent of state residents live in the largest cities, and most of these are Black or Latino/a and poor (Anyon, 1997). Data collected by Jean Anyon during the early years of the Abbott case revealed that, at the time, these city residents had little representation in the state legislature, which was dominated, as in most other states, by legislators from suburban districts (Anyon, 1997).

In terms of public schools in New Jersey in the mid-1990s, just over half of African American children attended schools that were 90 percent to 100 percent students of color and nearly 75 percent attended schools that were at least half Black. This racial segregation correlated with poverty concentration and low levels of school funding. Anyon, concluded, "The isolation of the minority poor and their children would impact significantly on decisions made by legislators who appeared to feel that urban Black and Latino students were 'other people's children' for whom suburbanites had no responsibility" (1997, p. 134).

In such an economic and cultural climate there is no political motivation to rush to fund urban schools. Poor urban people of color have little recourse in the legislature, and even less in the executive branch. Judicial processes can be contested, and as the record shows, effectively resisted such that mandated policies are never fully carried out on the ground. Further, as we have shown, not "extending" educational opportunity contributes to economic decline in urban centers, thus enhancing the cost-benefit for capitalist exploitation. As Stephen Haymes explains, "Black spaces in the city are represented as spaces of pathology, as spaces of disorder, without any consideration of how the colonizing of space by mainstream white institutions in the city removed and destroyed the communal living spaces, the home places of urban blacks" (1995, p. 118–119). Racist discursive representations of urban space only help make clearer the path to profit by offering a sense of legitimacy to this kind of "ethnic cleansing."

Third, education has become fetishized as a commodity, and is thus constructed as something that the poor simply have to do without. When New Jersey state education commissioner Fred Burke opined in 1976 that urban students (read: children of color) simply could not expect to perform as well academically as suburban students (that is, affluent whites), he was, as he stated, "just being honest." However, we shouldn't miss another assumption in his statement: education and educational opportunity are commodities purchased by middle-class property owners. As Foucault might contend, discourses normalizing property owners' right to a better education inform how power operates in shaping policy implementation. In taking as natural that those who live in communities with larger tax bases deserve a higher quality of education, Burke and other state leaders fetishize education as a commodity. Critical race theory challenges this fetishization on the grounds that "ownership" of property and of education has been, and in less overt ways, continues to be racially distributed. No one now has to commit a conscious act of discrimination, since the property and hence, the ownership is either passed on or made more readily available to those already privileged by class and race membership.

Staying on the Battlefield

Even when court cases such as *Abbott v. Burke* are won in favor of social justice, there are few guarantees that the rulings in themselves will actually lead to positive social change. In reference to the struggle for Black education, Derrick Bell states, "Even successful school litigation will bring little meaningful change unless there is continuing pressure for implementation from the Black community." Unjust laws, he notes, are "invariably a problem of distribution of political and economic power. The rules merely reflect a series of choices by the society made in response to these distributions" (1995, p. 18). The history of *Abbott v. Burke* suggests that Derrick Bell's assessment is also applicable to New Jersey: Liberal leadership, individual initiatives, and even class-action lawsuits have been insufficient to ensure full implementation of educational finance equity policy. If Bell is right in saying that what is needed is "continuing pressure for implementation," what can we do specifically as critical practitioners and researchers? We conclude this chapter by offering some implications from critical theory for practitioners and for researchers.

Implications for Critical Practitioners

First, practitioners must understand that race and class matter in education policy implementation. What does it mean to say that race and class matter? By race and class here, we mean to include raced and classed identities, race- and class-based collective action, cultural dimensions (i.e., discourses, everyday practices) of racism and classism, and structural constraints and material limitations that result from an historical legacy of persistent subjugation of poor people and people of color. The myriad ways in which these things matter is documented in recent work on race, class, and urban education reform (Anyon, 1997; Henig et al., 1999; Lipman, 2004; Orr, 1999). This body of work supports our argument in this chapter that decisions at each step of the implementation process are informed by race and class. In the cities studied—

from Newark to Baltimore to Chicago to Atlanta—similar dynamics emerge: historical patterns of legal housing discrimination, economic disinvestment in predominantly poor communities of color, white flight to the suburbs, and more recently, in some cases, new efforts to deterritorialize urban centers to make room for more upwardly mobile inhabitants. These dynamics inform implementation by creating an environment such as we described in New Jersey, in which polarized communities fight over fiscal resources, and the threat of economic scarcity converges with the threat of Black encroachment on white privilege. All of this stagnates and derails implementation so that it becomes more accurate to speak, as we do here, of policy *non*implementation.

Practitioners may need to confront the more fundamental problems of race and class inequity and the power of raced and classed cultural discourses as part of the process of education reform. Although exactly how to do this is beyond the scope of this chapter, some scholars argue that developing strategic political alliances across differences and territorial boundaries may be key (Henig et al., 1999; Dreier, Mollenkopf, & Swanstrom, 2001). Other scholars, most prominently Michael Apple (2001), provide some direction on how to counter oppressive discourses. Among other things, he proposes that we publicly challenge "common sense" about race, class, and education, rather than let those on the right control this discussion. We infer from Apple that the struggle for policy implementation is not won solely in the courts or by lobbying legislators, but also by engaging people through various media in ways that help them make connections between the promise of progressive education policy and their everyday lives.

Second, we must take into account that all stakeholders do not have the same access to power in the process of implementation. Ensuring that policies are implemented is a concern of legislators, jurists, administrators, businesspeople, educators, community activists, parents and young people. It is often said that it is important for everyone to have a voice at the table, and that all should take responsibility for the process. However, some parties have more influence than others in determining the course of implementation. For example, corporate leaders can impede implementation of policies that threaten their profits by threatening to move operations out of the state (or nation), and by pouring money into the coffers of politicians who support their interests. Suburban voters, in the New Jersey case, have disproportionately higher numbers of representatives in state government than those who live in the urban centers, making it possible to erect legislative roadblocks to implementing policies that benefit those who live in the cities. Even on the "community" level, there is differential access to power. Recent research on education reform reveals that some Black community leaders advance the interests of the Black middle class at the expense of the mass of poor Black people in their communities. This often takes the form of patronage politics, in which "white elites could secure black leaders' cooperation for a relatively low price in contracts, jobs . . . and a host of personal services" (Orr, 1999, p. 62). This kind of patronage means that those who most need access to power find themselves shut out of the process. This is perhaps why Derrick Bell is so convinced the people themselves—activists, parents, young people—must, "in the last analysis . . . provide an enforcement mechanism" (1995, p. 18). Critical practitioners understand that people in power have no interest in truly hearing and responding to all voices, and engage in struggle by making spaces for this kind of grassroots "enforcement."

Third, for those involved in education policy implementation as practitioners, the critical perspective suggests the need to attempt to operate outside the confines of liberalism. However appealing, piecemeal solutions that assist a select few should be supplemented or replaced by policies that address the needs of communities as a whole. The Abbott case reveals the interconnections between education funding policy and policies related to taxation, housing, urban development, health care and employment. We need to make sure that we constantly remind policy makers and the public of these connections. We also need to continue to mobilize members of the community to demand implementation policies with more transformative potential than those currently being offered.

Implications for Critical Researchers

First, researchers can develop richer theories about how intersectionalities of race, class, and gender mediate policy implementation. Our analysis makes clear that class and race are intrinsically connected social constructs. As O'Connor, Lewis, and Mueller (2003) state in their critique of Black education research: "It is African-Americans' racialized social location that increases the likelihood that they will be poor and without key economic resources. Thus, for example, if Blacks as a group are being held back in school more often because of reasons related to their collective lack of wealth, they are collectively without wealth in large part because they are Black (n.p.)." The authors argue that race needs to be understood as socially produced in relation to other social constructs as opposed to being posited as a biological or cultural essence. To not do so may "attribute to race significance it does not have, and ignore meaning it does have" (O'Connor, Lewis, & Mueller, 2003, n.p.).

For example, scholars and policy makers often cast problems of poverty as problems of culture, which offers a kind of discursive power to dismiss the problems as valid, since culture in turn signifies the chosen lifestyles of racialized others. Conversely, others have been tempted to suggest that racism is no longer a barrier to the social mobility of people of color, and that the primary culprit is class. However, as Stuart Hall (1996) reminds us, class never works alone. In public discourse, "urban poor" is meant to connote colored faces; public resistance to providing for the social welfare of urban poor people is therefore never simply about class domination, but is also wrapped up in racist notions in the minds of middle-class people, regardless of racial identity, and even internalized by poor people of color themselves.

Although we did not examine gender in the *Abbott* case, we maintain that further research may show its relevance in analyzing opposition to implementation of education reforms in New Jersey and throughout the nation. A most obvious example is Ronald Reagan's discursively powerful construction of "welfare queens," those sassy Black mamas who keep having children due to their disdain of work and hyperactive sex drives. Here, race, class and gender collude to create an image employed on national and local levels to stir passions and shape policy against poor Black families (Kelley, 1997).

Second, researchers should seek out multiple truths related to policy implementation. Critical theory in general, and cultural political economy more specifically, point to how truth is socially constructed, usually in ways that support certain classes, and certain cultural readings of the world. Part of interrogating power is seeking out subjugated truths or what some scholars have called counternarratives (Giroux et al., 1997).

In order to be transformative, educational research must engage members of the communities directly affected by the (non)implementation of educational equity policies. From them, we need to learn how implementation is experienced, how community leaders exercise agency in attempting to shape implementation, and perhaps most important, how and under what conditions residents of poor urban communities take an active role in putting on the "pressure" that Bell (1993) argues is so crucial.

Linda Tuhiwai Smith (1999), in her articulation of an indigenous research agenda, situates research within a larger project of self-determination. She states, "Self-determination in a research agenda becomes something more than a political goal. It becomes a goal of social justice which is expressed through and across a wide range of psychological, social, cultural and economic terrains. It necessarily involves the processes of transformation, of decolonization, of healing and of mobilization of peoples" (1999, p. 116). Smith's model offers a glimpse of what it might mean for educational policy implementation researchers to take seriously the priorities of poor urban people of color. Guided less by contributing to the literature and more by contributing to liberation, researchers might ask members of communities what it is they already know and what it is they need to know in order to move closer to self-determination. Of course, there is a danger in romanticizing the voices of oppressed communities (Fine, 1994). However, if we truly listen to the poly-vocality within communities, we can engage the people in ways that complicate and extend our analyses, rather than sentimentalize them, which often allows researchers to look heroic, but does little for those who have revealed their lives to us.

Third, critical policy implementation researchers must *advance scholarship about "deep-structural" solutions.* We can do this in several ways. First, we can choose research designs that emphasize the relationships between educational policies and historical, cultural, political, and economic contexts. This helps reveal patterns in how power works across time and space, regardless of the good will of a few social actors. Second, we can theorize from the counternarratives of oppressed peoples rather than attempt to force-fit peoples' lives into the narratives of existing theories. This allows us to step outside of canonical discourses. This is not an eschewal of existing theories; rather, it is using theory in the service of freedom, rather than in the service of itself, or our status in the academy. Third, our analyses and recommendations should always present a vision of new structural relations that don't depend on economic or cultural exploitation. We are often compelled to offer "realistic" solutions, which usually amount to new initiatives deemed possible in the present historical moment such as increased funding for teacher education or new funds for parent involvement programs. Although these may be wonderful ideas, we should connect them to more "deep-structural" prescriptions (Anyon, 1997, p. 164), so that they are less likely to be read as sufficient in themselves. For example, in discussing parental involvement, we should remind readers that instituting a truly living wage would go a long way toward providing families with the economic and psychological stability to be involved in their children's education in a meaningful way.

Michelle Fine has noted that scholarship on social change "sits at the messy nexus of theory, research, and organizing. The raison d'être for such research is to unsettle questions, texts, and collective struggles; to challenge what is, incite what could be, and help imagine a world that is not yet imagined" (1994, p. 30). Researchers, parents, young people and other community organizers must collaborate in the process of imagining new ways of engaging dominance as it reveals itself not only in stark material inequities but also in oppressive discourses. Together, we must develop tactics to transform existing relations of power and create spaces where victories are possible. The battlefield is all around us.

Chapter 9

An Economic Approach to Education Policy Implementation

Susanna Loeb and Patrick J. McEwan

This chapter describes an economic approach to understanding education policy implementation. Economists helped establish policy analysis as a field of study in the middle of the last century and economic methods have long been brought to bear on examinations of various policy processes essential to education outcomes, from congressional voting behavior to education productivity (Becker, 1993; Hanushek, 1986, 1997). However, explicit discussions of the relationship between economic methods and education policy *implementation* are rare. Economists seldom use the term "implementation" when addressing policy processes and outcomes, not defining it as a separate field of inquiry from policy analysis. Yet, recent trends in education policy bring to light the utility of economic methods for education policy implementation studies. For example, economic constructs fit well with assumptions about incentives imbedded in accountability policies and alternative wage policies to increase teacher workforce supply and quality.

This chapter highlights the utility of an economic framework for understanding the implementation of contemporary education policies. The defining feature of this approach is its focus on individual actors at multiple levels of educational systems—teachers, principals, school board members, community residents, governors, and others—and how implementation is shaped by their decisions in the face of resource and knowledge constraints. This perspective highlights how these actors' interact to determine how implementation unfolds.

The approach to understanding policy implementation that we discuss in this chapter is broadly consistent with other approaches in the implementation literature. For example, McLaughlin (1991a,b) notes that implementation is fundamentally determined by local implementers, such as teachers, principals, and students. Their will to implement a policy, as well as their capacity to do so, determines the success of implementation. Likewise, we emphasize that preferences ("will") and resource and knowledge constraints ("capacity") determine individual behaviors that are at the foundation of policy implementation.

We start by elaborating these and other dimensions of an economic approach to examining policy implementation. In the subsequent section we illustrate how actors' preferences and constraints may affect policy implementation using examples from teacher policy, school choice, and accountability reforms.

AN ECONOMIC APPROACH TO IMPLEMENTATION

Economic approaches to a variety of social phenomena rest on models of individual decision makers guided by their preferences and constrained by their resources and knowledge. Economists use these approaches to predict future implementation outcomes as well as to explain current policy effects. At their most general level, economic approaches involve (1) identifying important policy participants, (2) predicting or assessing the preferences of these individuals, (3) determining how a given policy is likely to alter the incentives or constraints facing these individuals, and (4) using data about how individuals have responded to constraint changes in the past to predict how the relevant individuals will respond to the policy change and how this response will affect implementation and the achievement of the policy goals. Economists also exert substantial effort empirically, estimating the actual responses of the individuals and the implications of these responses for understanding policy effects.

To elaborate, in order to predict and explain how individuals will respond to policy changes, one must understand the preferences that guide individuals' decisions. As an example, economists have examined school finance formulas that compensated school districts for the added cost of special education students (e.g., Cullen, 2003). Such analyses identify district administrators as important actors in the system. They predict that these administrators have preferences for increased revenues in their district. If a special education finance reform provides more money to districts when a greater number of students are classified as special education students, economists then will predict that the policy provides incentives for administrators to increase the fraction of students classified as special education. This effect may be large, impacting the lives of many students, or it may be quite small and not important for the overall success of the policy. By examining data on districts that have undergone such a policy change, researchers have been able to predict and explain the extent to which the incentive change affects student classifications and other outcomes. Cullen (2003), for example, finds that fiscal incentives such as these can explain over 35 percent of the recent growth in student disability rates in Texas.

Not all individuals have the same goals. Attention to these differences across all the relevant actors is essential for understanding implementation. For example, in a given neighborhood, community members outside of school may have goals focused on the long-term success of the community, whereas students and their families may be more interested in benefits of education that accrue to them individually such as income, prestige or happiness. These differences in goals may lead to differences in which policy approach they favor. Similarly, teachers, administrators, and elected officials may have different goals. All are likely to be concerned about student outcomes, but they also care about their own income, working conditions, and opportunities for advancement. These self-focused goals may lead to decisions that conflict with stated goals of reforms.

Microeconomic theory offers explanations for how these preference differentials play out various contexts. For example, one theory frames differences between the goals of firms and the goals of employees as a "principal-agent problem" (Holmstrom & Milgrom, 1991). The worker or agent in the firm pursues individual goals of advancement, income, ease of work, and so on. When these goals are in line with the goals of the firm's owner, known as the principal, workers' practice tends to reflect firm interests. At other times, agents pursue strategies that promise to improve their own outcomes at the cost of the principal's goals. One aim of policy may be to align worker and owner goals, or in the case of education, the goals of teachers and administrators with the goals of parents and the community. In the firm example, such alignment may come from linking worker pay to firm profits. In the case of schools, rewards and sanctions based on student performance may help to accomplish such alignment.

This discussion points to the importance of understanding individuals' knowledge, as well as preferences and the incentives imbedded in reforms, when attempting to predict or improve implementation. When the principal has perfect knowledge of the output that the agent is producing, then he or she potentially can design the agent's compensation to be a function of this output—in other words, he or she can design an incentive system that aligns the agent's interests with the firm's goals. For example, the owner of a firm can pay a worker based on the number of units of the good that are produced, which serves to align the individual goal of increasing pay and the firm goal of increasing production. However, in many industries—and education is clearly one of these—organizational output is difficult to measure and even more difficult to match to particular employees.

Output is multidimensional and difficult to measure in education, and much of what a school "produces" in terms of increased test scores or graduation rates is the result of collections of actors engaged in various activities. In such a case, even without the ability to perfectly align workers' incentives with those of owners, some employment contracts and public policies are more effective than others at aligning the preferences and goals of an organization's actors. For example, special education finance policies that provide money to districts based on factors that generally cannot be manipulated by district administrators, such as the number of students in the district and the poverty rate, do not increase incentives to classify students as special education, and thus may reduce unnecessary classification as compared to finance policy, which does link funds to the number of students classified.

Such complexity of the education system comes not just from the complexity of the outputs. The input mix—teachers, administrators, and textbooks, for example—is also complex. Economists model the interactions within organizations, or *firms*, of individuals working together to produce a given output. Firms have a specific production process (also know as the production function) through which they produce tangible outputs—from books to automobiles—by combining inputs such as labor and machinery. The available technology, including both the workings of the machinery and the knowledge of how best to utilize resources and work together, determines how effective firms can be at transforming inputs into outputs. In the typical market, the firm's owner wishes to maximize profits. To do so, he or she chooses a quantity of output to produce, based on the inputs needed, the costs of those inputs, and the market price that can be fetched for the output. When inputs cost less, the firm can produce outputs more cheaply; when the technology of production improves, it can produce more with a given mix of inputs.

This portrait of firm decision-making based on profit maximization is clearly germane only to a few education firms, such as education management organizations that explicitly aim to maximize profits (Levin, 2002). In addition, while some firms can choose almost all of their inputs, education organizations often have more limited control over inputs. For example, while public school districts or public schools can choose how they spend some of their revenues, they often cannot control the level of revenues they receive.

However, despite these differences, certain aspects of the firm model can be generalized usefully to education. For one, as noted above, the firm model calls attention to how individual preferences shape implementation outcomes. In addition, the model of the firm highlights how production processes use inputs and the technology of production to affect student outcomes and other shared goals. Third, economic models of the firm applied to education routinely look beyond the school walls and rest on assumptions that student outcomes are produced by the cumulative application of a range of student, family, and school inputs.

By modeling production functions for education, researchers describe how inputs combine with the available technology (or processes) of production to produce student outcomes. In education, as in all other industries, firms are interested in improving the technology of production; because by improving technology, firms can then produce more outputs for a given level of inputs. This model then calls attention to how the search for new technologies such as curricula, teacher recruitment strategies, and school structures impacts preferences, decisions and the implementation of policies.

Economic studies of complex social phenomena like education are sometimes criticized for resting on assumptions that there is a straightforward process by which inputs are transformed into outputs—that technology is well understood and consistently implemented. However, economists have long realized that even in profit-maximizing industries, there is much about the current technology of production that is uncertain or ambiguous. For example, economic researchers grapple with how organizational structures or management practices affect worker productivity especially in large industries where less control over the means of production increases variation in the production process and difficulty in understanding the process that produces the outputs. These questions about control and scale are particularly applicable to education, given that a typical school's output is produced in semi-autonomous classrooms. Thus, the technology of education is often opaque and highly variable (Murnane, 1984). Indeed, quantitative social scientists have spent more than thirty years attempting to discern the technology by using regression analysis to estimate education production functions. Studies of the effects of inputs such as parental characteristics, smaller class size, and different curricula are aimed at discerning production technology (Burtless, 1996; Hanushek, 1997; Krueger, 1999).

The simplest economic models assume that firms are able to choose their inputs so as to produce the greatest output at the least cost, constrained only by the costs of their inputs. In reality, most firms are constrained by regulations, contracts, and previous investments in durable goods. Firms in the education industry, including public schools and districts, face even greater constraints. Accordingly, economic models of education policy implementation seek to illuminate the various constraints on actors' goals, preferences, and ultimate decisions. For example, many schools and districts are constrained by the dollars allotted to them by federal, state and local governments; school boards and other elected bodies hold them accountable for ensuring that expenditures on resources cannot exceed their revenues. Schools and districts are further constrained because their input mix is partially determined by federal and state regulations on class size, teacher characteristics, and other aspects of production. Finally, and perhaps most important, education firms generally do not choose their student and family inputs. These inputs are simply beyond school or district control, at least in the case of nonmagnet public schools and other schools with neighborhood-based enrollment policies. The completely autonomous firm can choose its resource mix. In this case, if there is a "best practice" way of maximizing outputs, this firm can choose its inputs to fit with this system. However, when one input is fixed at different levels across schools, these schools may each face different best practices for maximizing inputs. Schools and districts clearly fit into this group of firms for which there is likely to be no single best technology. In keeping with this understanding, much empirical work in economics explores the differential effect of resources such as class size, vouchers, and teacher characteristics in varying contexts.

In summary, an economic approach to education policy implementation calls attention to how preferences and constraints lead individuals to make decisions that affect policy implementation. Within this framework, models of firms describe the interactions of individuals with different and often competing preferences. They highlight the importance of incomplete knowledge, resource constraints, and technology of production for shaping policy outcomes. This approach moves beyond the simple view of education production that posits a firm in which the technology of production is well understood and implementation occurs without a hitch because of shared preferences and knowledge. Rather, economics provides tools for thinking about how divergent and multidimensional preferences, incomplete knowledge, and input constraints affect implementation. In the following sections we use examples from teacher policy, school choice, and accountability reforms to elaborate how economic tools can be used to capture the dynamics of policy implementation in the context of these constraints.

APPLICATIONS

Divergent Preferences and Goals

The case of teacher policy
Teachers make decisions based on a wide variety of preferences, only some of which involve student outcomes. For example, while most teachers care about the outcomes of their students, teachers are also responsive to wages in their decisions to enter or quit teaching as are workers in other occupations. When wages increase, more college graduates express interest in teaching. When wages in other occupations increase, more teachers leave teaching for alternative jobs (Baugh & Stone, 1982).

Nonwage job characteristics also affect teacher choices including attributes of students, class size, school culture, facilities, leadership, and safety. Research has found that teachers prefer to teach in schools with higher-achieving students. For example, when teachers switch schools, they are more likely to move to schools with higher achieving and higher–socioeconomic-status students (Hanushek, Kain, & Rivkin, 2004; Lankford, Loeb & Wyckoff, 2001). Teachers also choose schools that have better facilities or that offer more preparation time. A recent survey of California teachers shows that turnover is a greater problem and vacancies are more difficult to fill in schools with larger class sizes, where teachers share classrooms (multitracking), or where teachers otherwise perceive the working conditions to be less favorable (Loeb, Darling-Hammond, & Luczak, 2005). Principals also strongly affect the working conditions in a school; some principals are able to create environments that teachers find favorable, regardless of the facilities or the characteristics of the student body. Finally, teachers appear to care about school location. Most teachers prefer to teach close to where they grew up and in districts that are similar to the district that they attended for high school (Boyd, Lankford, Loeb, & Wyckoff, 2005).

Such preferences pose particular challenges to urban districts because the number of teacher recruits whose hometown is in an urban area tends to fall short of the number of positions that need to be filled in urban districts. As a result, these districts must attract teachers from other regions. To induce sufficiently qualified candidates whose hometowns are in suburban regions, urban schools must have salaries, working conditions, or student populations that are more attractive than those of the surrounding suburban districts. When urban districts do not offer these inducements, teachers with suburban hometowns who take jobs in urban areas are likely to be less qualified than those who teach in the suburbs. Many urban districts face a second disadvantage as a result of this preference for proximity. Historically, the graduates of urban high schools have not received adequate education, forcing cities to choose from a less-qualified pool of potential teachers, even if they do not hire teachers from other areas. Accordingly, preferences for proximity lead to the perpetuation of regional inequities in the qualifications of teachers (Boyd, Lankford, Loeb, & Wyckoff, 2005).

So how do teachers' preferences for wages, working conditions, and location affect policy implementation? Consider a policy that sets a uniform salary schedule at the state level. Within the state, some districts are in locations or have working conditions generally not preferred by teachers and beyond district control. Districts with poorer conditions will not be able to attract the same teachers as other districts even with equal salaries. The same phenomenon holds true within districts where schools vary by working conditions or other dimensions that resonate with teachers. This leads to the substantial sorting that we see in the characteristics of teachers across schools within large urban school districts, where schools with fewer poor and low-performing students have more experienced teachers who score higher on measures of academic achievement and teacher preparation (Lankford, Loeb, & Wyckoff, 2001). Thus, salary equalization policies that aim to strengthen teacher quality across districts and schools may result in substantial inequality in teacher characteristics across schools.

Teacher preferences also mediate the effects of requirements for entry into teaching. For example, suppose we know that certain forms of preservice and in-service training improve teachers' ability to teach reading; and that such knowledge leads policy makers to impose training requirements for teachers that include classes on methods for teaching reading. Raising education and certification requirements for entering teachers may improve skills and prepare potential teachers for the difficulties of classroom teaching. However, the additional requirements necessitate that teachers spend more time and money on training before entering the classroom. The greater this cost, the greater the wage needed to entice potential teachers into the profession. Thus, policies aimed to improve the quality of teaching through increased certification requirements may decrease teacher quality if they pose an inhibitive cost. Effective training requirements seek to minimize the costs of entry for teachers while providing skills needed to be successful in the classroom (Boyd, Lankford, Loeb, & Wyckoff, 2003).

Accountability and choice

The lack of goal alignment among various educational actors including superintendents, teachers, school principals, and community members has been a source of concern for policy makers. Accordingly, policy makers have developed various policy approaches to better align such goals based on the assumption that greater goal alignment will improve implementation and ultimately school performance. While empirical studies have illuminated the extent to which these policies seem associated with such outcomes, economic theory helps highlight the underlying reasons why such alignment policies do and do not play out as intended.

Teachers and administrators pursue a range of goals, not all of which are consistent with community (society) goals. This lack of alignment is a source of concern for policy makers. Two recent classes of policies, school choice and accountability, are motivated by the similar objective of realigning these goals. The common lever behind policies in both classes is to target resources toward administrators and teachers that work toward community goals and away from those who do not. A change in resource constraints facing school employees could, in theory, increase incentives for these employees to act in alignment with community goals.

While both choice and accountability policies aim to realign the goals of teachers and administrators, they represent different approaches to this realignment. Accountability policies usually reward or sanction schools for the performance of their students on standardized tests (Carnoy & Loeb, 2003; Hanushek & Raymond, 2002). Tests are designed to measure how well students are doing at reaching goals set forth by the state. Choice-based policies, by contrast, allow families to choose which school their child attends (Levin, 1991). Schools that are pursuing goals that are consistent with the goals of families presumably will be more popular among families, while those not performing well will lose students and funding. The process provides incentives for the schools that are not meeting parents' goals to improve. If they do not improve they should, in theory, be forced out of the market.

In the choice case, if the goals of the community are similar to the goals of individual families, then, ignoring differences in knowledge or resources, both policies should produce similar outcomes. For example, one might presume that state-level goals represented in accountability plans are focused on raising achievement in reading and mathematics, and that families broadly share these goals both for their own children and for other children in the community. Accountability systems reward schools for improved test scores. Choice systems allow parents to choose schools that are most effective at improving their children's reading and math ability.

However, if the goals of parents and of the community are not similar, then the results of the two systems may be quite different. As one example, consider the implementation of school choice plans and the issue of racial integration and segregation of schools. Integration of schools may have benefits for the society or community, either because it promotes an equitable distribution of achievement across groups or because it promotes other social benefits, such as cooperation among diverse students. Yet, it often has been noted that many families prefer that their children attend school with children of the same race or culture (Clotfelter, 2001; Schneider & Buckley, 2002). In a school choice plan that allows families choice among a wide range of schools, many families will indulge their preferences, potentially leading to sorting along racial or ethnic lines.

In accountability plans that directly reward or sanction schools that fulfill, or fail to fulfill, social goals, there is less potential for family preferences to triumph over community preferences. This is because, unlike choice plans, accountability policies don't reduce the barriers that keep parents from choosing which schools their children attend (though private schools and residential sorting are both commonly used methods of sorting). However, there are difficulties with accountability policies, as well. While the goal of accountability is to re-align the preferences of education actors, it is not a simple task for policies to re-align preferences of any group. In many accountability plans, the broad aim is to encourage principals and teachers to focus greater efforts on improving various measures of school performance, such as test scores. Early experiences with the implementation of such accountability plans suggest that these individuals will continue to pursue their own goals and preferences, while searching for low-cost ways to appear as though their behaviors have altered.

The growing body of empirical evidence on accountability suggests that such "gaming" occurs with some frequency. That is, teachers and school administrators search for ways to improve measured performance without improving actual performance. This might be accomplished by excluding low-performing students from testing (e.g., Cullen & Reback, 2002; Figlio & Getzler, 2002), coaching students on test-taking to the exclusion of actually improving what students know and can do (e.g., Glewwe, Ilias, & Kremer, 2003), outright cheating (Jacob & Levitt, 2003), or even increasing students' caloric intake on the day of the test (Figlio & Winicki, 2005).

Both choice and accountability policies illustrate the difficulty of aligning the diverse preferences of actors. School choice confronts problems because parental preferences are not the same as community preferences. Accountability faces problems because it is often easier to game the system than to implement different instructional strategies. Economic theory highlights that if policy designers do not attend to differential preferences across the system, they may miss opportunities in policy design to create adequate incentives for implementation.

Binding Resource Constraints

While successful implementation of policies and the achievement of policy goals may require the alignment of incentives, this is often a necessary but not sufficient condition for effective implementation. Actors may wish to carry out a given policy but may be limited by resources—knowledge in particular—that cannot be addressed by incentives alone. This section discusses the importance of these constraints to implementation using examples from teacher, school choice, and accountability policies as illustrations. It first addresses knowledge constraints and then other resource constraints.

Incomplete information and local actor advantage in teacher policy
If education administrators and policy makers could obtain perfect knowledge of teacher effectiveness, then they could use such knowledge to optimize teacher compensation and hiring policies, thus improving student outcomes. On the other hand, incomplete knowledge can limit the ability of policy makers to design teacher policy in ways that might lead to such improvements. That is, in keeping with the principal-agent model discussed above, when the principal cannot measure what the agent is producing, it is more difficult to create incentives to increase productivity.

There are two common approaches for measuring teacher effectiveness. Both involve inaccuracies that lead to problems when it comes to designing policies to improve teaching. The first approach is based on measures of teachers' knowledge. For example, the vast majority of states require teachers to pass an exam before they are certified to teach (Angrist & Guryan, 2003). The exams provide information concerning potential teachers' abilities to solve math problems and comprehend reading passages, among other skills. The second approach measures teachers' performance by the test-score gains of their students. Students are tested at the beginning of the school year or at the end of the prior school year and then again at the end of the school year; the gains during this time are attributed to the teacher. Yet, despite their prevalence, both approaches provide limited knowledge of teacher effectiveness. For example, researchers have found that certification tests are incomplete measures of teacher knowledge, and teacher knowledge is an incomplete measure of teacher effectiveness (Ferguson & Ladd, 1996). Similarly, student tests are single and necessarily limited measures of student knowledge and student knowledge is an incomplete measure of the student outcomes that families and communities value (Carnoy & Loeb, 2003).

Consider these knowledge constraints in the context of teacher hiring. Districts and schools often do not appear to be making wise choices when hiring teachers (e.g., Levin & Quinn, 2003). There are a number of reasons why poor hiring decisions occur. The goals of the hiring authority may not be aligned with the state goals, perhaps leading administrators to hire friends or family. Hiring authorities may be constrained by budget uncertainties that do not allow hiring until late in the season. But in addition, knowledge limitations also may lead to poor hiring decisions. When schools or districts are recruiting teachers, they do not know how good a teacher each candidate will be. They obtain some relevant information from where applicants received degrees, from prior work experience, and, in some cases, from interviews. Tests of basic knowledge provide another layer of information that can improve hiring decisions. Hiring authorities can balance the results of tests with other candidate characteristics such as experience working with children or youth.

Test results for teachers, thus, can provide information for hiring authorities. However, many policies distort the potential benefits of these tests. For example, according to some policy designs, teachers must pass exams for certification, but their test score results are not reported to schools or districts; hiring authorities simply may not employ uncertified teachers. This policy aims to improve hiring decisions; however, there are two drawbacks of this approach that reveal the importance of knowledge constraints on implementation. First, certification status does not provide hiring authorities with complete information about test scores and there may be a substantial difference in knowledge between teachers who perform just above the test score cutoff and those that perform at the top of the distribution. While this is not the only information relevant for identifying high-quality teachers, it may be useful.

The second drawback of this approach is that it does not allow the hiring authority flexibility in which teachers it hires at the lower end of the test score distribution. Some schools, especially those in high poverty areas, hire from a small applicant pool. The new requirements may remove the worst candidates from this pool, making this a beneficial policy. However, if requirements are imprecise in their ability to identify good teachers—perhaps driven by the relatively poor performance of nonnative English speakers—and local administrators have additional knowledge and are effectively choosing from the pool of candidates available to them, increased requirements may eliminate some of the candidates that are actually better in practice from an already insufficient pool and disadvantage these schools to a greater extent. Here the implementation of a policy aimed at improving teacher quality may have the perverse effect of lowering it in the most difficult-to-staff schools.

Measurement of teacher quality by the test-score performance of students further reveals the importance of considering knowledge constraints on school actors' choices. A few policies have attempted to link teacher pay to the test-score levels or gains of their students (e.g., Glewwe et al., 2003; Lavy, 2002; McEwan & Santibañez, 2004). The argument for this policy approach is similar to that for accountability: teachers' goals are not aligned with community goals for students; the tests measure society goals; thus, linking teacher pay to test-score gains aligns teacher and community goals and otherwise improves schools. However, most tests do not address the broad range of skills that teachers cover in the classroom. Accordingly, the policies may provide incentives for teachers to focus instruction on material contained in the test and neglect other important areas of the curriculum (Hannaway, 1992; Holmstrom & Milgrom, 1991). Moreover, these policies may discourage teacher interaction and colleagueship essential to school performance. This lack of interaction may, for example, increase the time it takes for new teachers to become effective and otherwise contribute to turnover if new teachers are dissatisfied by their abilities in the classroom.

Given these limitations, a merit pay plan that allows school principals some discretion in dispersing bonuses may have more success than one based solely on test scores. Administrators may use the information provided by student test scores, but could balance this data with more qualitative information on the students in each teacher's classroom and contributions that teachers make to the school as a whole. In a system with high-quality administrators, this would have the benefit of rewarding classroom effectiveness while avoiding the testing problems highlighted above. However, if administrators' goals are not aligned with community goals or if administrators do not have the knowledge to make use of the data available to them, then such a system may not be preferable to the current system of fixed salary schedules and state regulations. Many factors that plague the teacher labor market, such as the inequitable distribution of highly skilled workers, affect the administrator workforce as well. Administrators may not have the skills or inclination to use discretionary funds wisely. These failures can affect how teacher policy, however well intentioned, is eventually implemented.

These examples regarding teacher labor markets provide illustrations of two important policy considerations pertaining to the role of knowledge constraints in policy implementation. First, incomplete knowledge may require an alternative set of policies than would complete knowledge. The incomplete knowledge of teaching ability provided by student tests suggests that tests should only be one aspect of teachers considered when designing compensation policies. Second, the relative knowledge at different levels of the education system affects policy implementation. Given the importance of context for the optimal use of resources, schools may differ substantially in their optimal resource mix. However, local administrators may be able to incorporate the complexities of their local environments with the knowledge provided by the test score performance of teachers and their students. But if local administrators do not have the knowledge necessary to use test score data effectively or their goals are not aligned with societal goals, then hiring and compensation decisions may be better left to other actors.

School choice and accountability: Incomplete information, family advantage and inequality

School choice and accountability policies provide a second example of how attention to the importance of knowledge helps reveal how preferences and resources shape implementation. If the states had perfect knowledge of the optimal technology of production for each school, then they could require each school to use this production process with a given set of inputs. However, production processes in education are complex and likely to differ across schools, based on student populations, teachers' abilities, and other local factors. States have not been able to assimilate and regulate all the information needed to run schools effectively. The failure of statewide policies is, at least partially, a result of this limited knowledge. States are left to construct policies that utilize local knowledge, while aligning local actors with state and community goals. School choice and assessment-based accountability are examples of such policies.

Most school choice policies attempt to align the preferences of the actors in the education system with the preferences of the "choosers" (i.e., parents and children). Families will choose schools that best fit their goals; schools that are not meeting families' goals will fail to attract students. In traditional systems of neighborhood public schools, most parents, especially lower-income parents, are constrained in their choice of schools. In part, these constraints stem from the fact that to exit their local public school they would need to change residences or pay private school tuition (Levin,

1991). School choice policies aim to diminish these important constraints. In doing so, choice plans promise to provide incentives for actors in the public school system to cater more directly to parental preferences, or risk losing students and funding. If parents can identify the schools that best fit their needs, their choices will support these schools and encourage other schools to change in line with these preferences.

The ability of school choice systems to utilize the knowledge that parents have about the education their children are receiving is particularly important because the education production process is so complex that it is difficult for state government to accurately identify effective schools. Choice programs draw on local knowledge to realign schools toward shared goals. Yet, this simple theory of choice driven by parental preferences has not always been reflected in the implementation of choice plans. Many parents do not exercise choice and when they do they do not always choose "good" schools. School-level actors do not always respond by improving (McEwan, 2000).

While the use of local knowledge is a potential benefit of school choice policies, knowledge constraints at the local level may be partially responsible for unexpected hitches in their implementation. To elaborate, according to a simple theory of choice, all parents are assumed to possess full knowledge of each school's current outputs and inputs (both their current school and other potential choices). Moreover, they are assumed to possess full knowledge of each school's production technology (e.g., curriculum and instructional methods) and how their own child could benefit (or fail to benefit) from it. This knowledge, in concert with their preferences and resource constraints, is used to make decisions about whether and, if so, how to exercise school choice. If the presumption of full knowledge fails to hold, then the choice policy may be implemented in unexpected ways. For example, instead of realigning goals toward parent preferences, schools may use advertising or other nonacademic symbols to delude parents about the benefits of their schools (Hsieh & Urquiola, 2003; Cullen and Loeb, 2004). To the extent that this advertising is effective and leads parents to make poor decisions, school choice programs may do no more than take dollars away from the instructional goals of the schools.

Differences in knowledge among groups of parents may also lead to unwanted consequences. Some parents have less knowledge of schools and their production possibilities than other parents. The common concern is that families of lower socioeconomic status possess less knowledge (Levin, 1991). If that is the case, then such families may be less likely to exercise choice or more likely to make incorrect choices that are not aligned with their own preferences for better schools. Such families may have similar preferences for enrolling their children in better schools, but they may be harder-pressed to act upon those preferences if they have less knowledge of how schools are reflecting those preferences. Knowledge constraints may result in cream-skimming, in which families of higher-socioeconomic status exercise choice more actively (Hsieh & Urquiola, 2003; McEwan, 2000). In sum, school choice plans may benefit the education system by drawing on local knowledge, but lack of sufficient local knowledge may lead to implementation problems.

By contrast, instead of relying on parents to informally gauge school quality and how it aligns with their preferences, accountability plans remove that responsibility. Instead, they attempt to directly measure school quality, distribute information about it in school "report cards," and then administer a variety of rewards, sanctions, or assistance on the basis of such information (Carnoy & Loeb, 2003). These policies are similar to traditional state regulation policies except that they monitor and regulate school outputs (i.e., student achievement) instead of inputs. While the implementation of input-based regulation is severely constrained by the lack of knowledge at the state level concerning effective resource allocation and local production processes, accountability plans are constrained by incomplete knowledge of outputs such as student achievement.

To elaborate, in most states, a limited range of outcome measures (e.g., reading and mathematics test scores) are used to construct a single rating of school quality that is reported in a public forum (e.g., a school report card). State actors are unable or unwilling to fully measure and describe the multidimensional aspects of school quality that reflect community preferences. The policy aim is for schools to broadly improve when subjected to the provisions of accountability. However, it is more likely that teachers and administrators will seek to improve the specific measures of outcomes that are used to allocate rewards and sanctions. This may lead schools to reallocate efforts toward the improvement of outcomes that are emphasized, while neglecting others (e.g., science or art) that do not form part of the overall measure of school quality (Carnoy & Loeb, 2003; Hanushek & Raymond, 2002; Jacob, 2002).

Lack of knowledge about school effectiveness at the state level impedes the implementation of accountability policies. Lack of knowledge among parents may similarly curb the implementation of choice plans. In addition, knowledge constraints on the part of local-level actors in the education system may frustrate the successful implementation of both policy approaches. Imagine that in an accountability policy state-level actors succeed in fully describing school quality and attaching rewards and sanctions to such descriptions, or that in a school choice policy all parents have complete knowledge about the production process in each school in their area. Schools should respond by improving their quality (and the outcome measures used to describe quality). Yet, this presumes that the main constraint to improving school quality is a misalignment in preferences of various actors in the education system. Local actors may simply not know how to improve. Superintendents, principals, teachers, and other school personnel may not possess adequate knowledge of production technology to improve selected outputs, especially among the most challenging populations of students.

Legislators' uncertainty concerning whether low-performing schools are a result of local knowledge constraints or goal misalignment is reflected in the disparate ways that "bad" schools are treated in states' accountability schemes (Education Week, 2004). In some cases, direct sanctions are applied (e.g., school closure). In other cases, or often concomitantly, low-performing schools receive instructional assistance from more central levels. The apparent difference in the underlying assumptions of the two sets of policies reflects a recognition by states that schools may have low performance either because of misaligned preferences or because of knowledge constraints—and sometimes a combination of both.

Bought knowledge and monetary resources in teacher policy
Prior examples have illustrated how policies can fail to meet their goals because of divergent preferences or because of knowledge constraints. However, simple monetary resource constraints also affect implementation. While lack of knowledge clearly constrains education actors, many knowledge limitations can be reduced with additional investments in acquiring knowledge. For example, better-designed report cards can provide added knowledge to parents in school choice programs. Trained consultants can help administrators and teachers interpret student test-score results. Yet, not all resources are related to knowledge. Age-appropriate and well-designed textbooks are necessary to carry out many instructional strategies. Adequate art supplies and musical instruments facilitate teachers' ability to teach music and art. Inadequate buildings that are too cold, too hot, or too crowded may also reduce teacher effectiveness. To illustrate the importance of resource constraints for understanding an economic approach to policy implementation, we briefly return to an example of teacher policy.

Many education reforms ultimately aim to improve classroom teaching. Economic theory calls attention to ways in which the implementation of these policies may be hindered by resource constraints. Consider a hypothetical policy designed to improve students' computer knowledge. The policy provides computers to each classroom and professional development to teachers regarding the use of software and hardware. (See Rouse & Krueger, 2004, for an assessment of a similar policy.) Imagine that an assessment of students' knowledge indicates that the policy does not successfully improve student performance. The economic approach would identify important actors and their preferences and constraints. In this case students and teachers are clearly important actors. Teachers' preferences may hinder successful implementation if they do not believe that student knowledge of computers is important.

Resource constraints may also affect implementation. While the program provides professional development, it does not provide the technical support that teachers might need to successfully utilize the computers. This can be viewed as either a knowledge constraint or a monetary constraint, since dollars can buy the extra support needed. Alternatively, teachers may simply not have the skills to effectively operate computers and integrate them into their classroom, even with the basic knowledge of the software and technical support. This skill may also be bought, although the cost may be prohibitive. For example, schools may need to spend more to hire skilled teachers or to send their current teachers back for substantial additional education. Many schools are constrained in their ability to hire and fire teachers, and these limitations combined with expenditure limits lead to resource constraints affecting the implementation of policies that require highly skilled teachers.

Inherent costs, bought knowledge and institutional constraints in school choice and accountability policies

Resource constraints among families or school actors may also constrain implementation of school choice and accountability policies. In school choice plans, families may remain in poor schools, not opting to exercise choice, due to resource constraints. For example, voucher plans may require additional tuition payments (so-called add-on payments) that are not feasible for low-income families. This is typical among privately funded choice programs, though less likely in publicly funded programs (McEwan, 2000). There may also be transportation costs associated with choice (Levin, 1991). In addition, some schools of choice demand additional time commitments by families, perhaps as classroom volunteers or in another capacity. The sacrifice of time represents an additional cost to families, albeit a nonmonetary one. There is also a cost to gathering information about schools, a necessary input to decisions about school choices. Many families have ready access to such information or find it relatively low-cost to obtain. For other families, obtaining and interpreting such information is onerous. Thus, resource constraints may be the proximal cause of the knowledge constraints discussed in the previous section. Some families lack knowledge, but can overcome this constraint by purchasing advice or data; this option is unavailable to other families.

The implementation of choice plans is also potentially hampered by resource constraints on the part of school actors. Let us presume that choice provides schools with strong incentives to respond to parental preferences for school quality, and that school-level actors possess sufficient knowledge to do so. They may still lack sufficient resources to adjust effectively. For example, schools may face binding constraints in their ability to move existing resources away from unproductive uses and toward productive uses. As discussed above, schools may be inclined to fire an incompetent teacher, and hire a better one, but face external constraints in doing so. These resource constraints may be particularly severe for schools that are losing students and, with them, dollars from the state. Students that leave traditional schools are often less costly than the average student in the school or district; yet the revenue loss is usually based on the average student. This drop in revenue may constrain response to choice incentives, especially if much of the remaining revenues are already committed.

In a similar vein, implementation problems in accountability plans may result from resource constraints. Sometimes schools lack knowledge about how to improve schools, but this knowledge can be acquired with additional resources, if available. As one example, many schools are inundated with reams of data on student outcomes. However, the data provide little usable knowledge for school improvement, unless additional resources—particularly the time of principals, teachers, and other staff—are expended on analysis. In other cases, knowledge constraints are more binding, and even additional resources are of little use.

CONCLUSION

This chapter began by describing an economic framework for understanding education production and the related issue of education policy implementation. The key to this framework is its focus on individuals. Individuals make decisions and take actions based on their preferences, as well as the knowledge and resource constraints that they face. In order to understand and predict policy effects, economists seek to identify important actors in the education system and the preferences that drive these actors' decisions. The economic approach then focuses on understanding how policies affect the constraints these individuals face. By understanding individuals' preferences and their changing constraints, economists identify potentially important processes resulting from policy changes. By estimating the extent and impact of these processes using available data or by drawing estimates from similar policy changes, this approach explains and predicts how policies are implemented. Economists have also expended considerable effort at developing empirical methods for estimating the responses of individuals and the effects of policy. The approach combined with the empirical methodology provides a broad but organized structure for analyzing education policy implementation.

Chapter 10

Social Capital and the Problem of Implementation

Mark A. Smylie and Andrea E. Evans

For some time now, we have recognized that implementation is a crucial link between the objectives and outcomes of policies, programs, and practices. We also have come to recognize that implementation, as a process of enactment or "carrying out," is inherently problematic (Hargrove, 1985). It is fraught with uncertainty and unpredictability. It is a process that is difficult to control and prone to failure.

Since the late 1960s much of the literature on implementation has focused on understanding factors that explain its success and failure. Initially, researchers looked to characteristics of policy development and delivery systems and to aims and characteristics of policies themselves to explain implementation. While useful, such explanations were soon seen as inadequate. It was not that policy characteristics and delivery systems were unimportant. Rather, it became clear that the will and capacity of local actors and local implementation contexts could compromise even the most well-developed policies and delivery systems. As Pressman and Wildavsky (1973) revealed, what local implementers do turns out to be what a policy becomes. (See also Lipsky, 1980.)

During the mid-1970s and 1980s, researchers began to explore in greater depth the ways in which local actors influenced implementation. A "second generation" of studies emphasized the importance of another set of factors that included local actors' motivation, attitudes, and commitment (e.g., Edwards, 1980; Nakamura & Smallwood, 1980); channels of communication and leadership (e.g., Mazmanian & Sabatier, 1983); and the knowledge and skills required to carry out a particular policy, program, or practice (e.g., Van Horn, 1979). Much of this work focused on the "will and capacity" of individual actors, but it paid little attention to the broader social and organizational contexts in which individual actors operated.

The Rand Change Agent Study—an investigation of planned educational change—was one of the first studies to look past individual actors to the significance of social organization in implementation (Berman & McLaughlin, 1977). Among other factors, this research identified interactions among teachers and between school personnel and external change agents as instrumental to implementation success. Subsequent studies of educational change also pointed to the importance of interaction—in particular collaborative interaction—between teachers and among teachers, principals, and local change agents to how implementation unfolded (e.g., Hargrove et al., 1983). The Rand Study and the research that followed had a substantial impact. It is difficult to find today a treatment of the subject of educational implementation or change that does not stress the importance of such relationships (e.g., Fullan, 2001a; Odden, 1991a,b).

While this literature marked a significant step in understanding how implementers matter to implementation, to some it did not go far enough. McLaughlin (1990b) observed that even as it stressed the importance of social relations in implementation, the Rand Change Agent Study underestimated their power. More recently, Knapp (1997) argued that we have come to see social relations in schools, particularly images of professional communities and communities of practice, as axiomatic to successful implementation and innovation. (See also Frank, Zhao, & Borman, 2004.) He concluded, however, that we have failed to delve deeply—empirically or theoretically—into how and why different social relations and social structures affect "capabilities for individual and collective action" and "define an organization's receptivity to reform ideas and ability to sustain them over time" (p. 254).

Following Knapp's (1997) lead, this chapter explores more deeply the role of social relations in implementation of educational reform using the theoretical concept of social capital. "Social capital" is used to describe the nature and function of social relations and their capacity to support individual and collective development and behavior. Gaining a great deal of attention in the late 1980s through the work of sociologist James Coleman, social capital has been applied most frequently to understanding the contributions of schools, families, and communities to the learning and development of children and youth (e.g., Dika & Singh, 2002; Goddard, 2003). It has also been applied to analyses of how the social organization of schools relates to teacher learning and development (e.g., Smylie & Hart, 1999). We believe, as does Knapp, that the concept of social capital also holds promise for understanding better how social relations in school organization function to promote or impede implementation and change.

We begin with a brief description of social capital and its components and an exploration of the implications of social capital for implementation. Then, we present examples of studies from the research literature as evidence of relationships between social capital and implementation. As we note later, there are few studies that look specifically at social capital formally defined. However, there is a good number of studies that focus on "like concepts" that provide enough evidence for us to draw some conclusions about the relationship between social capital and implementation. Our analysis of the literature highlights "positive" and "negative" cases of this relationship—a distinction we make to underscore that strong social capital is not necessarily conducive to successful implementation. After our discussion of the literature, we present findings from a recent five-year study of the Chicago Annenberg Challenge. The Chicago Challenge was a large-scale school improvement initiative that provided resources to schools to work with external partners in networks of other schools to promote school-level change. These findings, along with evidence drawn from the literature, suggest that social capital is a very useful concept to understand how social relations may support or impede implementation. We conclude with several observations about the development of social capital as a positive resource for implementation.

The Concept of Social Capital

"Capital" is generally defined as resources that can be accumulated and drawn on to promote productive activity (Bourdieu, 1986). The fields of economics, sociology, and political science distinguish among several forms of capital. Physical capital refers to material resources or physical implements. Fiscal or economic capital consists of monetary resources or resources that can be converted to monies. Cultural capital is composed of long-standing theories, dispositions, and goods from cultural and linguistic heritages. Political capital refers to power and influence. Human capital refers to individual and collective knowledge, skills, and other attributes that affect a person's capacity to do productive work.

By contrast, social capital consists of intangible and abstract resources derived from interactions among individuals and the social structures that frame them (Coleman, 1988). It is lodged neither in persons themselves nor in physical implements of their production. Social capital is not social interaction per se. Social capital is "produced" *through* social interaction. Like other forms of capital, social capital can promote certain behaviors within social structures and it can be accumulated and drawn on to achieve otherwise hard to attain objectives.

Components of Social Capital

Social capital is generally thought to consist of three major components: (1) social trust; (2) channels of communication; and (3) norms, expectations, and sanctions (Coleman, 1988, 1990; Smylie & Hart, 1999). First, social trust concerns confidence in the reliability and integrity of individuals and their social relations. In general, trust involves a calculation whereby a person decides whether or not to engage in an interaction with another individual that embodies some degree of risk (Bryk & Schneider, 2002). Trust is compromised when people perceive that others are acting in a manner inconsistent with common understandings and commitments. According to Bryk and Schneider (2002), there are several sources of trust. Trust can be predicated on explicit transactions, such as contracts, that define specific obligations among individuals. Trust can also be a function of informal mutual understandings that develop out of sustained interpersonal or working relationships among individuals, each of whom, through assessment of behavior, intentions, and felt obligations, is expected to behave in normatively appropriate ways. Finally, trust can grow out of a belief in the moral authority of an organization that shapes expectations for and consequences of relationships within it.

Trust can influence behavior in several general ways. According to Coleman (1988), trust lays the foundation for collective activity, mutual assistance, and joint accountability. Bryk and Schneider (2002) associate trust with the predisposition toward cooperation and confidence that individuals have in one another, in leadership, and in the social group. In high trust organizations, the logic goes, there will be less conflict and fewer issues will be contested. In conjunction with social norms around which it may form, trust can serve as a control that supports some behaviors over others. Finally, trust can create a context of predictability, stability, and assurance that can support open communication and critique, examination of taken-for-granted assumptions, and risk-taking when individuals and the group are confronted with the need to change.

A second component of social capital, channels of communication can facilitate the flow of information among individuals and promote access to new information, both of which can influence individual and collective behavior. According to Coleman (1988), this component of social capital is not necessarily related to trust, although it is conceivable that restriction of communication and manipulation of information may lead to distrust. Instead, channels of communication extend a person's access to information that others in a social structure possess. Inasmuch as individuals may be members of multiple social structures, they may provide access to information from outside the immediate group. Channels of communication can influence behavior by introducing new information for making specific decisions and taking particular actions. Such information can be educative, fostering the development of knowledge and skills that may make individuals and groups more productive.

The third component of social capital, norms, expectations, and sanctions, can influence individual and group behavior in several ways (Coleman, 1988).

Group norms and expectations can influence individual behavior by encouraging some actions and constraining others. Norms and expectations can be enforced by internal or external sanctions, both positive and negative, including the distribution of social support, ostracism, designation of honor and status, conferral of rewards, and expression of approval and disapproval. By providing direction and control, norms, expectations, and sanctions can reduce deviant behavior in a group. At the same time, they can constrain innovative thought and action.

Social Structures and Social Capital

Coleman (1988) argued that all social relations produce some form of social capital, be it weak or strong. At the same time, certain properties of social structures in which those relations occur are more conducive than others for developing strong social capital. One property is closure or the interconnectedness among a group's members. According to Coleman, in completely closed structures all group members are connected to one another and to few if any others outside that immediate group. In open structures some group members are not directly connected to one another and members may be more strongly connected to others outside the group. The importance of closure to social capital lies in the ability of members of a social structure to develop and sustain shared norms and effective sanctions and in members' ability to develop a base of shared understanding and trust through common expectations and mutual obligations. Closed structures have greater potential for promoting these properties, because members are less likely to engage in external relations that compete or conflict with them. Open structures reduce the possibility for shared norms, collective sanctions, mutual obligations, and interdependence, but as noted below, open structures are likely to provide members with new information from outside the group.

Another important property of social structures is the strength of relations among people within those structures. Granovetter (1973) defined the strength of a relationship, or in his words a "tie," as a combination of experience, emotional intensity, intimacy or mutual confiding, and reciprocity. Strong ties are more likely to exist in closed structures. Weak ties are characteristic of open structures. Strong ties promote cohesiveness whereas weak ties lead to fragmentation. Granovetter argued that, paradoxically, weak ties, particularly those linking members of multiple groups, serve a broader integrative function not served by strong ties within social structures. Information can be passed to a larger number of people and traverse greater social distances through weak ties. Further, persons to whom individuals are weakly tied are more likely to move in circles different from their own and carry information distinct from that which they might otherwise receive. According to Granovetter, weak ties increase information available to individuals and promote levels of cohesiveness that could otherwise be achieved within a tightly closed social structure with strong ties.

Implications for Implementation

How might the different components of social capital and properties of social structures relate to the implementation of new policies, programs, and practices in education? Bryk and Schneider (2002) see trust operating in school reform in the following way:

> Organizational change involves risks and trust moderates uncertainty and vulnerability in times of reform and structural change.... Reform is said to move faster in high trust contexts because people are more likely to coalesce around a plan of action. In high trust contexts, roles obligations are clearer, which increases the likelihood of broad-based, high quality implementation of new improvement efforts.... [I]n high trust organizations, participants enact interrelated sets of mutual obligations on each other, embedding normative understandings and providing moral resource for improvement. (p. 34)

Implementation may also be enhanced by effective, open channels of communication that provide to all relevant actors information about an innovation and information necessary to put it in place (e.g., Frank et al., 2004). Often new policies, programs, and practices require the development of new knowledge and skills. Channels of communication can provide opportunities and the "material content" for such development. Finally, norms, expectations, and sanctions can provide the impetus and imperative for change. They can promote implementation by motivating and directing individual and collective behavior in ways that are consistent with new programs and policies.

The relationship between social capital and implementation is, of course, more complicated than this when differences in social structures are recognized. In education, the degree to which social structures may be open or closed reminds us that implementation may involve complex, multilevel systems of relationships that exist not only among individuals within schools but also between schools, central offices, external change agents, policy-making bodies, and other entities. The strength and influence of inter- and intralevel relationships may both be understood in terms of trust, communication, and norms, expectations, and sanctions. For example, the implementation of new programs and practices may be influenced as much by trust and shared beliefs and assumptions between a school and an external change agent or the central office as trust and shared beliefs and assumptions among teachers and administrators within the school.

The openness or closure of social structures and relative strength of ties also make problematic the assumption that strong social capital is always conducive to implementation. Social capital must be strong enough to support change. There must be enough closure in the structure of social relationships to promote shared understanding, common beliefs and assumptions, and levels of mutual obligation and trust that form the foundation for new behavior. At the same time, strong social capital, particularly in the context of closed structures, can promote change in directions not intended by policy. It can also act as a conserving force. Strong relationships formed around shared knowledge and norms contrary to new programs and practices that are enforced by powerful social sanctions, will likely impede implementation. This point is consistent with Goddard's (2003) observation that any analysis of social capital must not simply consider whether relations exist or whether they are strong or weak (or open or closed). It must consider the substance or "content" that flows through and is enforced by those relations. It must also recognize that the content of social relations is never neutral; it is value-laden and serves to shape thinking and behavior in particular ways and toward particular ends.

We would expect, then, that the relationship between social capital and implementation will be shaped not only by the strength of social capital but also by the extent to which the content of social capital reinforces the specific program, policy, or practice that is to be implemented. Thinking about the relationship between social capital and implementation this way provides not only for the "positive case," siutations where strong social capital supports implementation and weak social capital fails to support implementation. It also provides for the "negative case," situations where strong social capital hinders implementaiton. This is consistent with McLaughlin's (1993) observation about the dark side of teacher professional community: "Strong professional communities, by themselves, are not always a good thing. Shared beliefs can support shared delusions about the merit or function of instructional orthodoxies or entrenched routines. This collective agreement can generate rigidity about practice and a 'one best way' mentality that resists change or serious reflection" (p. 95). As suggested by the discussion of research that follows, the relationship between social capital and implementation may not depend so much on policy type as on more situational matching of social capital in particular contexts to specific programs, policies, and practices at hand.

Evidence of the "Positive Case"

Most of the research that examines the relationship of components of social capital or similar concepts to implementation provides evidence of the positive case. This literature reveals that where these components or concepts are strong, implementation is more likely to be successful. Where they are weak, implementation is less likely to be successful. This basic finding is evident in research on the implementation of variety of educational reform initiatives.

For example, in their case studies of Kentucky schools, Wolf, Borko, and their colleagues (2000) found that implementation of state assessments, involving the alignment of school curriculum and instruction with those assessments, was positively related to components of social capital and to several "like concepts" including a shared vision of the reform, communication and collaboration among colleagues, levels of trust, and the attendant willingness to take risks. In a set of cases in Washington, they found that implementation of state standards and assessments was positively related to schoolwide commitment to the reform and its goals (Borko et al., 2003). Implementation was also related to teachers' collective commitment to, responsibility for, and confidence in their ability to achieve those goals. Both sets of cases emphasized how collaboration among teachers and principals promoted exchange of information, development of trust, formation of shared expectations, and mutual accountability.

Scribner, Hager, and Warne (2002) found shared beliefs, trust, collective identity, and sharing local knowledge were key factors in the implementation of district-mandated standards and assessments in the two high schools they studied. In one school, strong trust between teachers and their principal, strong channels of communication with smooth flow of information, and teacher inclusion in decision making were associated with relatively successful implementation. In the other school, implementation problems were associated with weak trust relationships between teachers and the principal and efforts on the part of the principal to unilaterally reshape teachers' shared identity.

Frank and his colleagues' (2004) study of six elementary and secondary schools found positive, statistically significant relationships between several elements of social capital and teacher implementation, in this case, use of computer-based innovations. More specifically, this study identified positive relationships between implementation and teachers' reports of access to expertise concerning these innovations through helping relationships and informal talk among teachers. It also identified a positive relationship between implementation and social pressure for implementation felt by teachers through their social interactions. Indeed, this study found that the relationships between implementation of these two aspects of social capital—access to expertise through channels of communication and social pressure—were each slightly stronger than the relationships between implementation and more traditional predictors of perceived adequacy of resources to support use and perceived potential of computers to aid instruction and help students.

Similar findings of the positive case have been reported in studies of the implementation of whole-school reform initiatives and comprehensive school reform (CSR) designs. Desimone's (2002) review of literature stressed the importance of shared beliefs to teacher support of CSR designs. She highlighted collaborative working relationships and communication as crucial factors affecting implementation. Walker's (2004) study of whole school reform in New Jersey found that the strength of organizational culture—defined as a system of shared beliefs and values—at the school level mediated the impact of state-level action and the quality of local implementation. Spillane and Thompson (1997) contend that social trust is crucial to the implementation of mathematics and science reforms at the school district level as well. Using cases of contrasting school districts, one more successful than the other in implementation, they argued that social trust promotes implementation success by facilitating conversations about instructional reform and collaboration among educators. Such interactions enable both administrators and teacher leaders to develop a shared understanding about the reforms and help them craft strategies to enact that shared understanding districtwide.

A number of studies provide evidence of the positive case in the implementation of school-based improvement activities. These activities may be part of larger initiatives, but by-and-large they are developed or shaped and managed by schools themselves. For example, in their evaluation of the Annenberg Bay Area School Reform Collaborative, a multidistrict, school-based reform initiative in California, McLaughlin and Talbert (1999) found that initial levels of trust, collegial relationships, and shared sense of purpose were related positively to the implementation of a cycle of inquiry and school-level improvement activity that sprang from that process. In another study, this one of "reforming" mathematics departments in three California high schools, Talbert (2002) found that shared values concerning mathematics instruction, shared commitment to "higher order learning for all students," and joint work driven by that commitment were positively associated with teachers' implementation of intellectually challenging instructional practices.

Bryk and Schneider's (2002) comparative case studies of elementary schools illustrate relationships among different approaches to school governance, relational trust, and collective action for local school improvement under Chicago's 1988 decentralization reform. In one school, distrust associated with consolidated principal power impeded collective efforts for improvement. In another, high trust associated with democratic governance provided support for more collective, systematic approaches to local improvement activity. A third case illustrated tensions, strains, and slow progress where high trust relationships had not fully formed.

Similar evidence of the positive case is evident in Elmore, Peterson, and McCarthey's (1996) study of the implementation of different school restructuring and instructional improvement initiatives in three elementary schools. The schools they studied, considered "exemplary" in terms of organizational restructuring, varied substantially in their ability to implement intellectually challenging instructional practices for students. Elmore and his colleagues associated this variation to differences in the "deep structure" of social relations in these schools. In each school there was frequent professional development activity and active collaboration among principals and teachers on issues of teaching and learning. However, one school stood out from the others in terms of more consistent implementation of challenging instructional practices. Social relations in that school were characterized by a common vision among teachers and shared goals and expectations for each other's work. Norms that every teacher should have a particular intellectual interest and that learning and development were part of teachers' professional work pervaded the school. Teachers at this school exhibited a strong sense of trust in one another and accepted responsibility for each other's work. These strong relationships inside the school were complemented by relations to sources of learning and support outside the school. Although these external relationships did not seem as strong as their internal ones, they nonetheless served as an important link to new information that enhanced faculty learning and development and implementation.

In addition to research on implementation of local school improvement activity, there are several studies that illustrate the positive case with regard to the implementation of teacher leadership and professional development initiatives. Among the first empirical studies to examine teachers' social relations and professional development was Little's (1982) ethnographic research on urban elementary and high schools working to implement a court-ordered desegregation plan. This study pointed to the importance of collaboration for continuous teacher learning and support for change in classroom practice consistent with the plan. It also identified specific qualities of productive collaboration. These included shared norms of reciprocity, interdependence, and egalitarianism; mutual trust; and a common focus on teaching. While this study focused primarily on relationships among teachers, it recognized the importance of relationships between teachers and their principals. Indeed, the association of teacher collaborative relations to teacher learning and change was strongest in schools where principals actively endorsed and participated in collegial work.

Further evidence of the positive case can be found in more recent studies of particular teacher professional development programs. From a longitudinal study of a professional development project to improve reading instruction (Richardson, 1994), Placier and Hamilton (1994) made two significant and relevant findings. First, they observed that cooperative, convivial relationships among teachers in schools can rest on shaky foundations. When threatened by demands for true joint work and collaboration, as was the case in this professional development project, dissatisfaction, fear, and distrust can arise and compromise teacher learning and implementation of new instructional practices. Second, they found that new social relations that developed within groups of teachers who were part of the professional development project made more of a difference in teachers' learning and implementation of new practices than the social contexts of their schools. The social relationships that developed among participating teachers were grounded in new common conceptions of instruction promoted by the professional development program, trust, interdependence, and shared accountability in work.

Clift and her colleagues (1995) made similar findings in their study of a collaborative leadership and professional development project involving university-based participants and educators from several surrounding elementary, middle, and high schools. This study found that the implementation of new classroom practices was related significantly to the social contexts of the project. Among the most important social factors at work were trust to deal productively with disagreements, mutual obligations for participation and contribution, and subsuming individual needs and interests to agreed-on goals of the group.

Finally, a number of studies have examined the nature of school relationships with external change agents in the implementation of reform. For instance, Miles (1993) argued that a key variable in change agents' success was their ability to develop rapport and trust relationships with schools. He pointed specifically to the agent's ability to establish strong, stable, supportive, "contractually clear," and predictable ties with groups and individuals involved in change initiatives. Fullan (2001a) has echoed these points. A number of recent studies have found that external agents' success is related strongly to their capacity for working effectively with schools. These studies indicate that external agents, working as partners or as intermediary organizations, are more likely to promote change if they possess strong relational skills and are able to cultivate social capital (Berends, Bodilly, & Kirby, 2002; Finnigan & O'Day, 2003; Kronley & Handley, 2003; Pravetti et al., 2001). Agents must be able to establish effective channels of communication among all relevant actors. They must be able to gain access to schools and build and sustain relational trust. They must also be able to provide schools adequate, predictable, and stable levels of resources needed for successful implementation and institutionalization of change. Honig's (2004b) recent study showed how intermediary organizations can promote social capital, what she calls political/social ties, in their own relationships with schools and among schools, community agencies, and the district central office through meetings and other convening strategies. The ability of these agents to promote social capital was related in part to their technical expertise in the area of change and their experience working with schools. (See also Kronley & Handley, 2003.)

EVIDENCE OF THE "NEGATIVE CASE"

A smaller number of studies provide evidence of the "negative case." That is, they show how strong social capital or "like concepts," misaligned or inconsistent with change sought, may impede implementation. In one study, Datnow and her colleagues (2003) found that strongly held teacher beliefs had a negative effect on implementation of Comprehensive School Reform models in culturally and linguistically diverse elementary schools. This research revealed that strong, shared beliefs that students lacked ability to learn reduced teachers' receptivity of CSR models and compromised subsequent implementation. In another example, Scribner's (1999) study of the implementation of teacher professional development activity found that strong, shared faculty norms shaped teachers' expectations for professional development which in turn affected its implementation. Those norms shaped teacher trust of outside consultants associated with that activity, which also affected implementation. In one of the schools he studied, teachers shared beliefs that professional development as an enterprise was largely ineffectual. Those beliefs were associated with distrust of external agents who promoted it, which compromised implementation efforts.

Coburn's (2001a) study of the implementation of an interactive, inquiry-oriented, school-based improvement initiative provides a more detailed look at social processes that underlie the "negative case." Consistent with Granovetter's (1973) observations, she found that formal networks and informal relationships among teachers in one California elementary school shaped their "sense-making" about the initiative and its implementation. The social structures teachers occupied established different channels of communication that determined what information teachers received. Close, informal, self-selected structures were associated with strong, shared "worldviews" and practices. These structures generated a great deal of social support and, we might think, trust. They restricted the flow of new information into the group, which impeded learning about new instructional practices associated with the initiative, which in turn compromised their implementation. Coburn found that formal, less self-selective structures involving more heterogeneous groups of teachers were less likely to generate such strong social support or promote and reinforce such strong shared understanding. However, they were more likely to expose teachers to a wider range of information and challenge prevailing knowledge and assumptions. These structures were more conducive to innovation and to the implementation of new practices.

Research on teacher leadership also provides evidence of the "negative" case. In his review of the literature, Smylie (1997) found that the social contexts of schools had substantial influence over the development and implementation of different teacher leadership roles (e.g., master and lead teacher roles, mentoring roles, and participative decision-making roles). Shared beliefs and dispositions about teacher leadership, norms and obligations defining teachers' professional working relationships, channels of communication and the flow of information, precedent for collaboration, and levels of trust have all been found to be instrumental in the implementation of these roles. With regard to the negative case, this literature shows that in schools where teachers share strong norms of privacy, autonomy, and egalitarianism, teacher leadership roles have substantial difficulty developing and functioning. Difficulty can also be found in schools where teachers share work orientations focused solely on the classroom, on their own students, and on their own practice rather than also on the school, on all students, and on the faculty as a collectivity. In contrast, in schools with strong, shared norms of collective responsibility for all students, joint accountability, and collaboration, among other things, teacher leadership is more likely to be successful. More recent reviews by Murphy (2005) and York-Barr and Duke (2004) point to similar relationships.

VIEWS FROM THE CHICAGO ANNENBERG RESEARCH PROJECT

A recent five-year study of the Chicago Annenberg Challenge—the Chicago Annenberg Research Project—provides a number of specific insights about the role of social capital in the implementation of large-scale local school reform.[1] A look at the Chicago Challenge is important because it is an example of a growing class of decentralized reform initiatives that have been promoted and supported with substantial resources since the mid-1990s by major national education philanthropic foundations (e.g., the Annenberg Foundation and the Gates Foundation). These initiatives rely primarily on local initiative, rather than externally developed programs and practices, and many depend on the assistance of external partners. The Chicago Challenge is a good example for this chapter because by design its implementation and outcomes are largely dependent on the development and function of productive working relationships among members of school organization and between schools and external partners. The Chicago Challenge represents a "window" through which to view the role of social capital in the implementation of local school improvement.

That said, the Chicago Annenberg Research Project did not set out to study social capital per se. However, looking back to the work, we can point to several findings that speak to different components of social capital. These findings give insight into the importance of shared beliefs and values, communication, and trust in implementing school improvement initiatives, particularly those involving external partners. They also provide evidence of the "positive" and "negative" case. We first set the stage with a brief description of the Chicago Annenberg Challenge and what it accomplished.

The Chicago Annenberg Challenge

The Chicago Annenberg Challenge was established in January 1995 with a $49.2 million grant from the Annenberg Foundation.[2] It was one of six such projects funded that year or the year before. Other Challenges were established in New York, Philadelphia, Los Angeles, and the San Francisco Bay area. A nationwide network of rural schools also received a grant. Since 1995, additional projects were established in other cities.

The Chicago Challenge grew out of the city's 1988 school decentralization reform. It set out a broad vision for change, calling for the "enhancement of learning for all students through dramatically improved classroom practice and strengthened community relationships" (Hallet, Chapman, & Ayers, 1995). The Chicago Challenge promoted local school development through networks of schools and external partners. It followed a logic that schools that work together with an external partner will find more support for improvement than if they act alone. The Challenge operated much like a foundation. It awarded planning and implementation grants to networks and external partners and provided some professional assistance to grant recipients. The Challenge articulated general goals for improvement but did not specify any particular activities or processes for schools to follow. Instead, the Challenge maintained that educators, parents, and community members should identify their own ways to solve local problems.

By design, the scope of the Challenge was broad. Between 1995 and 2001, the life span of the Challenge, it awarded grants to forty-five networks and external partners. Through these networks, it provided funds to between 200 and 220 Chicago public schools, or 35 percent to 40 percent of all schools in the system. Characteristics of Challenge schools resembled closely those of the school system—largely low-income, predominantly minority and racially isolated, and low-achieving. Networks were supported by a diverse group of external partners that included Chicago-area colleges and universities, arts and other cultural institutions, education reform and advocacy groups, neighborhood organizations, business groups, regional educational organizations, teacher organizations, and foundations. Schools and partners focused on several areas of improvement including curriculum and instruction, student learning climate and social services for students and families, parent and community support and development. Within these areas they engaged in a large number of specific initiatives including parent education programs, literacy programs, the integration of arts and technology into the curriculum, health-science education, the creation of small schools, middle school restructuring, principal and teacher leadership development, and strengthening school-communities ties.

Grants made to schools and networks were relatively small. In 1999, at the peak of funding, Annenberg schools received on average about $47,000 from the Challenge in money or resources provided by external partners through grants. This was about one percent of a typical Annenberg school's annual operating budget, not including other grants that the school might have obtained. On average, external partners received about $160,000 per year to work with their networks. After 1999, average levels of funding dropped dramatically for all but a handful of selected schools, to $29,000 in 2000 and $2,600 in 2001. In addition to grants, the Challenge provided modest professional support to schools and external partners.

In 1999, the Challenge identified eighteen schools, called Breakthrough Schools, to receive sustained funding during its last two years. The Challenge intended to further promote improvement in these "promising" schools and to encourage them to serve as models for other schools. Breakthrough Schools were selected by Challenge staff on the basis of their leadership, working relationships among their teachers, and their record of participation in Challenge-sponsored activities. As a group these schools were similar to other Annenberg schools. While other Annenberg schools' average funding dropped in 2000 and 2001, funding provided to Breakthrough Schools was sustained at about $50,000 per year.

Outcomes of the Challenge

The research project found that the Chicago Challenge made important contributions to a number of local school improvement initiatives, but had no significant effect on school development or student academic outcomes across the large number of schools it supported. Analyses of Iowa Test of Basic Skills (ITBS) scores showed that student achievement improved overall across Annenberg schools, but that improvement was no different than improvement across the school system as a whole. Analyses of longitudinal teacher survey data indicated that during the first half of the Challenge, Annenberg schools improved on several indicators of organizational support for student learning. There were slight improvements in instructional quality and aspects of student learning climate. School leadership, teacher professional community, and relational trust also showed improvement. By the end, Annenberg schools had regressed on these indicators to a point where they looked much like they did at the beginning of the Challenge. With few exceptions, changes in Annenberg schools mirrored those in demographically similar Chicago schools that did not participate in the Challenge. Those exceptions included changes in several indicators of leadership, professional community, and trust that began to favor Annenberg schools midway through the Challenge. However, by the end of the Challenge these initial advantages had disappeared. In contrast, in the latter years of the Challenge, Breakthrough Schools began to develop in ways that distinguished them from other Annenberg schools. They were able to sustain or strengthen aspects of teacher professional community, leadership, and trust while other Annenberg schools were not.

The Role of Social Capital in Implementation

The research project attributed the failure of the Chicago Challenge to achieve an overall effect to several factors including shortcomings in the design of the Challenge, inadequate resources, variability in the capacity of external partners, and conflicting policy influences from the central office. The project also pointed to problems concerning Annenberg schools' capacity to "engage" in the Challenge—that is, their capacity to develop and enact local collaborative improvement processes with external partners. It is with respect to these problems that we gain insight into the role of social capital in implementation.

Initial base of social resources
A case can be made that in order for schools to have successfully engaged in the Challenge's "style" of reform, they would have needed a base of human and social resources conducive to collaborative, locally defined school improvement work involving principals, teachers, parents, and external partners (Timar & Kirp, 1987). These resources might well include shared values and expectations, communication, cooperation and joint accountability, and trust. The research project indicated that the Challenge supported a substantial number of schools that entered the Challenge with substantial weaknesses in such resources. There are a number of possible explanations for this choice, including that the Challenge underestimated their importance.

According to teacher survey data collected before and throughout the research project, at the beginning of the Challenge, one-in-five Annenberg schools lacked shared norms and practices promoting teacher learning, risk-taking, and innovation. One-in-five schools had no clear standards for teachers or students and no clear vision for improvement. One-in-four schools lacked a sense of community among teachers and principals and displayed limited levels of cooperation and collaboration. One-in-three schools did not have a collective focus on and responsibility for student learning and school improvement and the ability to share information and address problems adequately. Finally, one-in-five Annenberg schools displayed only minimal levels of trust between teachers and principals. More than half displayed minimal trust among teachers and more than 40 percent displayed minimal trust between teachers and parents. The study attributed the relative success of the Breakthrough Schools to a somewhat stronger base of social resources. When these schools were chosen to receive sustained financial support, they were stronger than other Annenberg schools with regard to teacher collaboration, shared focus on and collective responsibility for student learning, shared orientation toward innovation, and trust.

Relationships with partners
Further insight into the importance of social capital comes from external partners' experiences working with schools. From beginning to end of the Challenge, the research project interviewed and observed nearly half of the forty-five partners working in Annenberg schools. These partners reported that they often encountered social dynamics in schools that confounded their efforts (per the examples below). Some confronted strong norms of privacy and autonomy that made it difficult to engage teachers in collaborative school improvement activity. In many instances, partners met overt resistance from teachers and principals. In some schools, beliefs and norms were shared and oppositional to partners' initiatives. In others, they were disparate and provided little solid ground for partners' efforts to gain traction.

The partners learned quickly that to be effective they had to become an accepted, trustworthy member of the school community. They consistently pointed to the importance of trust as a foundation for risk-taking and change on the part of teachers and principals. Some partners anticipated the need to develop trust from the beginning of their work with schools. Others acknowledged that they had underestimated its importance. They all emphasized repeatedly that building trust takes time and patience. Some observed that only in the later years of their work with schools had teachers trusted them enough to commit to the work that they were do to together.

Partners learned that it was often quite difficult to develop trust without effective means of communication. And one aspect of working with schools that frustrated partners most was the difficulty they experienced communicating with school personnel. Systems of communications that partners took for granted—phones, voice mail, and e-mail—were either unavailable or inoperable in many Annenberg schools. Partners who needed to reach individual teachers directly could rarely do so. Simple tasks, such as relaying messages from the school office, could not be relied on. Few Annenberg schools were wired for e-mail and Internet communication. Those that were wired typically had not prepared their staffs to use the technology effectively. Most partners found that the best way to develop channels of communication was the most direct—being in the schools. Having a physical presence made communication more effective. It also created a foundation for building trust relationships.

Examples of two schools

The importance of social capital was readily apparent in longitudinal field research in nearly two dozen Annenberg schools. We give examples of two of these schools here. When the first school joined the Challenge, teachers were quite cordial to one another, although very few spent time working together. Even though the principal held whole school faculty meetings several times a year, teachers did not regularly discuss their work. Early in the Challenge, a small group of teachers began to work with their external partner to improve literacy instruction at the school. This partner put a great deal of effort into developing stronger collaborative relationships among these teachers. After two years, there were marked differences in the relationships among teachers who participated in the group. They began to develop a shared identity. They frequently used their time together to exchange information from professional development activity, giving short presentations about what they had learned at conferences, and discussing specific pedagogical issues. This group established a strong network of communication that promoted the development of trust and shared values about literacy instruction. In the end, according to the external partner, these teachers found in their new relationships support, knowledge, incentives, and sense of accountability to critique, experiment, and begin to implement new teaching practices.

The second school is an example of how social trust can support the implementation of improvement efforts and also an example of its fragility. On entering the Challenge, teachers at this school were uncomfortable visiting each others' classrooms and discussing their teaching. Through the efforts of an in-house literacy coordinator, who was supported by the external partner, trust among teachers began to develop. As it grew, teachers became more willing to join the school's literacy initiative, collaborate, and engage in professional development activity. The literacy coordinator built her relationships with teachers carefully. At first, she provided assistance only when asked. By being responsive and responsible, she laid a foundation of trust for the work to come. The coordinator viewed herself as a resource. Her dependability, patience, and support drew greater numbers of teachers into the work. And through their interactions with the coordinator, teachers began to trust one another more, take risks, and speak more openly about their teaching.

Over time, several factors undermined this sense of trust. Because of reductions in Annenberg funding, the external partner had to cut the time the coordinator spent in the school. Without her daily involvement, some teachers began to withdraw into their classrooms. At the same time, tensions developed between teachers and the principal over issues of curriculum and instruction, which challenged the relationship the coordinator had developed with teachers. Some teachers questioned whether the coordinator was working for their interests or was an agent of the principal. While these tensions did not destroy the relationships that had developed between the coordinator and teachers, at the end of the fieldwork those relationships were clearly strained and in need of repair. In the process, the progress made to improve literacy instruction at the school had been compromised.

CONCLUDING OBSERVATIONS

Taken together, these several findings from the Chicago Annenberg Research project and the findings from the literature we reviewed earlier illustrate both the "positive" and "negative" case of the relationship between social capital and the implementation of local school improvement initiatives. They indicate that while strong social relations can be an asset to implementation, it can also be an impediment. They also indicate that the content around which capital develops and functions is crucial to successful implementation. This suggests that the influence of social capital on implementation may be situational, affected by its strength and content in particular settings and its alignment with the particular programs, policies, and practices at hand. There is a good bit more research that can be done to understand the relationship between social capital and implementation more fully. Most published findings come from a limited number of case studies. Large-scale analyzes and replication case studies have not been conducted. And, as we have noted throughout this chapter, most research that speaks to the relationship does not focus on social capital as formally defined but on amalgams of "like concepts." One reason for this may be the relatively recent application of the concept to the study of educational implementation and school change. Nevertheless, the consistency of findings from the existing research, emergent and indirect as they are, gives us some confidence that social capital is something to which implementation researchers ought to pay attention.

Our analysis is reminiscent of an argument Elmore (1978) made almost thirty years ago that the "problem" of implementation may be explained by more than political conflict, lack of individual motivation and commitment among implementers, or a failure of systems management and bureaucratic process. The problem may also be one of social organization. Elmore observed that implementation is a function of individual and collective decision-making and that the "quality" of decision making depends a great deal on social relationships. In his view, relationships most conducive to effective decision making and implementation embody "mutual agreement on goals, open communication among individuals, mutual trust and support among group members, [and] full utilization of member's skills . . ." (p. 209). According to Elmore, this perspective turns the problem of implementation "on its head." Referring to the implementation of government programs and policy, Elmore observed:

> [T]he capacity to implement originates at the bottom of the organization, not the top. . . . The factors that affect the behavior of implementers lie outside the domain of direct management control—individual motivation and commitment and the interaction and mutual support of people in groups. . . . The maximum that one level of government can do to affect the implementation process is to provide general support that enhances the internal capacity of organizations at another level to respond to the necessity for change, independent of the requirements of specific policies. (pp. 215, 216–217)

The concept of social capital sheds light on how and why social organization matters in the implementation of new education policies, programs, and practices. It also helps us understand better the challenge of creating a context conducive to implementation. Elmore (1978) and others (e.g., Frank et al., 2004; Smylie & Hart, 1999) have argued that policy can do little to directly generate social capital in schools. Theoretically, social capital is produced during the course of interaction or relationships "in action." However, policy can do much to create or constrain contexts that promote and support the types of relationships and interactions that generate productive social capital. Useem and her colleagues (1997) suggest that some of the most serious obstacles that policy might address include principal and teacher attrition that disrupts the formation and function of social groups (although the departure of disruptive personnel may have a positive effect on working relationships and the production of social capital within a school); union work rules and central office mandates that constrain productive organization of time and activity; and overload and task conflicts that result from policies that are not aligned with one another or support collective activity. While policies can provide external support, most observers agree that social capital must be cultivated and nurtured from within the school organization. This task is most likely to fall to school leaders, particularly principals. As the Chicago Annenberg research suggests, external agents may also play an important role.

Smylie and Hart (1999) have explored several possibilities for principals. (See also Kochanek, 2005.) We suggest that these possibilities may extend to external agents. Principals can create structures and occasions for interaction and for social bonds to form. They can mobilize groups and establish broad support systems. Principals can also promote productive social relations within the structures they create. First, they can foster trust by exhibiting consistency and competence in their work and by modeling commitment to the school community. They can also foster trust by providing strong, dependable, and facilitative support of teachers, making teaching public and its improvement a collective enterprise, managing conflict fairly and effectively, and sharing authority and leadership broadly. Principals can create joint tasks and other avenues for teachers within a school to exchange ideas and information. They can create channels for teachers to obtain new information by bringing professional development opportunities into the school and by establishing linkages to external resources. Finally, principals can communicate norms and expectations of community and teamwork that become focal points around which social relations can form and function. They can communicate norms and expectations for behavior consistent with valued organizational objectives, and we might say the aims of policies, programs, and practices to be implemented. Principals can also hold teachers individually accountable for their actions and promote mechanisms of collective accountability and collegial control. Within the bounds of system-level policies and procedures, principals can recruit, retain, and dismiss or "encourage out" personnel to promote productive social relations and thus productive social capital. Finally, while principals must work hard to develop social relations within their schools and create enough closure in these relations to sustain their strength and cohesiveness, principals must also recognize the importance of connecting to external resources to gain access to information that may challenge current knowledge and assumptions and provoke new ideas and understanding.

None of this is easy to do and leadership must remain attentive to the pitfalls of developing social capital that may work against desirable change. Still, if we are right about the relationship between social capital and implementation, it makes sense to pay more attention to the role of social relations as a source of support or constraint. And, it makes sense to take seriously the time, the leadership, and the patience needed to develop and sustain productive relationships. If we do not, we may squander an important resource to support school improvement. Or we simply make the work that much more difficult.

NOTES

[1]The first author of this chapter was Director of the Chicago Annenberg Research Project. The project was supported by a grant from the Chicago Annenberg Challenge and administered through the Consortium on Chicago School Research at the University of Chicago. Our discussion here draws freely from several project reports (Newmann & Sconzert, 2000; Smylie & Wenzel, 2003; Sconzert, Smylie, & Wenzel, 2004).

Readers are referred to these reports for detailed accounts of the project's conceptual framework, research methodology, and findings. Interpretations of and conclusions presented here are those of the chapter authors. They do not necessarily represent those of the project, the Chicago Challenge, or the Consortium.

[2]For a more detailed description of the establishment and early organizational history of the Challenge, see Shipps, Sconzert, and Swyers (1999).

Chapter 11

Implementation Research in Education

Lessons Learned, Lingering Questions and New Opportunities

Milbrey W. McLaughlin

In the more than thirty years since Jeffrey Pressman and Aaron Wildavsky published *Implementation*, a volume many regard as the "birth announcement" of implementation research, we have learned many lessons about implementation problems and processes and how research can add to understanding for both policy and theory (Pressman and Wildavsky, 1973).[1] Cumulative research provides some solid conceptions of how to consider and support implementation and points to areas in which understanding is still evolving. These developing perspectives together with education policy's changed social, political, and economic context also raise some new questions and opportunities for implementation research. This chapter first considers what we have learned about the nature of implementation—in particular, its problems, processes, actors, and outcomes—and where additional attention by researchers and policy analysts is needed to deepen these understandings. It then takes up questions about the new opportunities to learn that this generation of policy responses presents for the next generation of implementation researchers.

LESSONS AND LINGERING QUESTIONS

Overarching lessons from past implementation research feature ways in which early analysts and reformers underestimated or misunderstood implementation. Various problems—in particular, those associated with narrow problem conceptions, dichotomous notions about the "most effective" location of authority, decontextualized models of implementation paths, and cost/benefit assessments—surfaced once policy analysts began to tackle implementation as a topic of study. As Chapter 1 elaborates, overtime researchers have uncovered relationships among policy, people, and places that matter to implementation and policy consequences. These lessons both complicate and deepen our understandings about implementation in specific ways. In particular, they implicate fundamental elements of policy implementation research—conceptions of the policy problem, the implementation site, actors, the process, and outcomes. I discuss these implications in the following subsections.

The Problem

First, students of implementation have discovered that how a policy problem is framed—what a policy concern is assumed to be a "problem of"—arguably is the most important decision made as a policy is developed. Specification of the problem to be addressed sets the course for both policy and research and pushes alternative conceptualizations of an issue off the table. Assumptions about the nature of the policy problem determine the policy solutions pursued and the logic of action advanced by a policy. And notions about preferred solutions also determine how policies are formulated—the policy target, nature of policy implements, level of support and regulatory structures, for example. Early implementation studies seldom made the problem problematic, but rather took it as stated. Policy researchers soon saw, however, how competing formulations of policy problems were just that—alternative ideas about the root causes of a social issue—and had fundamental implications for policy design and implementation.

Nowhere is contention about the "problem of the problem" more prevalent than in education, in part because of the sector's "people-dependent" processes, "soft" core technology, and contested terrain of governance, voice and authority. Is disappointing student achievement a problem of inadequate standards? Shoddy curriculum? Poorly prepared teachers? An overly bureaucratic education system? Disagreements about how to answer these questions about "the problem" have permeated education policy communities. And waves of reformers have stitched various problem statements into policy banners to champion reform initiatives as diverse as charter schools, standards-based accountability, and school decentralization. The most recent one, "No Child Left Behind," features testing and "evidence-based" curriculum and touches every state and district in the country.

We also have learned that few education problems are merely technical ones; rather most problems embody normative conflict about means and ends. Many problem statements in education not only represent different interpretations of social facts—what accounts for poor student outcomes, for example—but beliefs and values as well. As normative statements, they implicate ideological perspectives that are not amenable to analysis. Implementation researchers cannot, for example, reach conclusions about the "correctness" of the value systems that underlie such controversial policies as school vouchers, the privatization of public education or parent school site governance. Each of these policies takes warrant from a particular problem conception: beliefs about the role of markets in public policy undergird voucher strategies; ideas about private sector efficiencies generate privatization schemes; reformers invested in ideals of deliberative democracy advance schemes to enhance stakeholder control of their public schools. Implementation researchers can identify the ideological base of a policy and elaborate the consequences of policies derived from it, document consequences, and assess trade-offs. But research cannot and should not evaluate underlying beliefs.[2]

This compounding of ideologies and consequences poses challenging problems for implementation researchers, however, since often it is difficult to separate them analytically or practically. For instance, are the disappointing outcomes of a charter school a consequence of its underlying normative assumptions about bureaucracies? Or, do they reflect decisions about how the school was designed and staffed? The first question taps ideology about organizational autonomy while the second raises functional concerns about the quality of education provided; in fact, they are tightly intertwined.

The field has learned that most education policy problems, like issues in other social sectors, defy once-and-for-all solutions and that problems themselves shift over time. Problems and solutions are often ephemeral because the contexts within and through which they function change constantly—and so alter both the effectiveness of the policy response as well as the policy problem itself. Additionally, policy problems in education are rarely "solved," because even successful policy responses create new issues. For example, an effective strategy for addressing teachers' professional learning may address an immediate need but also generate new ones if demand for related resources outstrips supply. Similarly, the rush to develop new small schools builds on research that supports the strategy but has created a crisis in staffing— the pool of qualified principals is insufficient to meet demand. Or, the high-stakes testing and accountability programs featured in many states perhaps can claim increased student achievement, but associated with these gains are increased student drop-out and "push-out" rates.

A basic lesson for policy researchers, then, is that problem statements cannot be taken for granted. Instead both problems and the solutions attached to them have the same status as theories. As such they present an important area for empirical investigation—research that examines alternative formulations and attends both to context and downstream implications.

Implementation Site

Early implementation studies focused on the ultimate implementing site—the organization or agency that in the end had responsibility for carrying out policy directives. The strategic role played by each implementation site highlights the endogenity of policy making and has important implications for implementation research. Many implementation studies take the policy as formulated as the policy "input," and examine consequences in light of this official expression. However, hundreds of implementation studies testify to the fact that any given policy varies across and within implementing systems and sites and that the "policy" that matters ultimately is the one enacted within the system, not the one originated outside of it.

As we learned from Moynihan, Pressman and Wildavsky, Bardach and legions of succeeding implementation researchers, policy implementation is a multilayered phenomenon and each layer or level acts on the policy as it interprets intention, resources, and regulatory frameworks. Pressman and Wildavsky (1973) depicted the challenges posed when "successful implementation" depended on the cooperation of many semiautonomous agencies—from Washington, DC, to Oakland, CA—and Bardach (1977) described complexities associated with the multilayered systems implicated by federal social policies. Moynihan (1970) characterized the consequences of these policy responses as *maximum feasible misunderstanding,* observing that the meaning various actors assign to policy diverged in fundamental ways from policy makers' intent.

Analysts now recognize at least five system levels that directly and indirectly shape the character and consequence of public policies: national, regional, or multistate; state; substate areas; and local (Scott & Meyer, 1991, p. 126). Each level through which a policy must pass makes policy in a fundamental way as it translates and filters intent and regulatory language and so serves as an implementation site in its own right. However, even levels of the system not directly named in policy design can affect policy outcomes. For example, shifts in federal preferences regarding instruction and curriculum filter down to states and influence state-level choices. State-level adoption of high-stakes accountability structures has pushed other, locally preferred assessment strategies off the table at the local level. These interlevel relationships have made their way into contemporary implementation research though few researchers have focused explicitly on how implementation decisions at one level influence those at another. Janet Chrispeels's (1997) look at how state policy decisions and shifting policy contexts affected local actions provides one exception and demonstrates the value of theory and practice related to a multilevel implementation analysis.

Taking policy as wholly exogenous fundamentally misrepresents implementation realities in education. Amanda Datnow (this volume), for example, details the co-constructed nature of Comprehensive School Reform policy and how school innovations supported by this federal initiative were negotiated by distinctive levels of the school system. Coburn and Stein (this volume) highlight the process whereby communities of practice learn internally from one another, creating unique understandings of similar experiences. Similarly, Spillane, Reiser, and Gomez (this volume) describe how district personnel modify policy intent and principles as they interpret them through their own frames of experience. This research teaches policy analysts to consider elements of formal policy—regulatory frames, resources, timelines—as building blocks for implementers' responses, not as road maps for action.

In contrast to earlier decontextualized implementation studies, many contemporary implementation researchers look to the broader policy context within which implementation "targets" operate. Anyon and Dumas (this volume), for example, describe how New Jersey's school finance case was effectively derailed by education funding policy's necessary connections to housing, urban development, taxation, health care, and employment. In this vein, lessons learned about the implementation site as multilayered and connected to other systems direct researchers to consider the relevant implementing system in interorganizational terms, attending to both vertical and horizontal connections affecting policy implementation.

Researchers have paid less attention, though, to another set of factors affecting an implementing site's response to policy goals and instruments: the agency's capacity, internal administrative structures, and norms of action. As Smylie and Evans (this volume) reveal, attention to capacity within schools surfaces important explanations for how implementation unfolds. In addition, agency administrative design and institutional setting interact with policy design to produce a site-specific response. Relatively uncomplicated policies typically can be carried out more or less uniformly within and across levels of the system; for example, laws specifying school-leaving age are relatively easy for agencies to implement. When policies are administratively or technically complex, however, variation in policy response becomes an inevitable result of broad variation in implementing sites' administrative and institutional arrangements including funding, professionalization, and political authority.

For example, Title I of the 1965 Elementary and Secondary Education Act (ESEA), an ambitious federal effort to improve educational opportunities for disadvantaged children, operated significantly differently in states across the country (McDonnell & McLaughlin, 1982). Title I functioned as a tightly controlled state program in places like New York that had a highly professionalized, well-staffed, and proactive state department of education. In so-called local control states such as Iowa, however, ESEA's Title I operated more or less as a pass-through program to local districts; Iowa and similar states possessed neither the administrative apparatus nor the state level authority to assume a dominant role in this federal program. This interaction between policy design and agency characteristics represents an importance source of variation in policy implementation and a fruitful, but currently understudied, area for implementation research.

The Actors

Organizations do not act; people do. "Street-level bureaucrats" entered the policy research vernacular shortly after *Implementation* was published (Weatherley and Lipsky, 1977). Weatherley and Lipsky's classic analysis of the pivotal role of implementers at the "bottom" of the system led to an appreciation that change is ultimately a problem of the smallest unit; street-level bureaucrats' roles as interpreters of and responders to policy is as critical as that of policy makers at the "top" of the system who formulate policy. This research taught that implementers' incentives and identities matter—that "street-level bureaucrats" have professional and personal motivation to comply or carry out policy directives—or not.

Subsequent researchers focusing on individual implementers featured different explanations for the variable responses to policy goals and strategies seen at the street level. David Cohen's well-known narrative about "Mrs. Oublier," a California mathematics teacher carrying out the state's new math framework, showed how an implementer's knowledge and experience matter (Cohen, 1990).[3] Though "Mrs. O" was dutiful in her efforts to implement the state's math curriculum, she failed in fundamental ways to do so because she did not comprehend the framework's basic precepts for instruction. Mrs. Oublier could only do what she understood and build on the expertise she possessed. California's math framework provided no opportunity for her to gain the knowledge she needed to make the assumed changes in her classroom practice.

Spillane, Reiser, and Reimer's distributed cognition framework extends Cohen's analysis (Spillane, Reiser, & Reimer, 2002). They show how district leaders viewed reform proposals through their own experience and so missed policy makers' core intent and deeper principles for action. District administrators did not refuse, resist or retard reform policies—they simply didn't understand policy intent or strategies. In the same way, Coburn and Stein (this volume) take us into the school and beyond notions of institutional isomorphism to show how teachers' training, knowledge, and beliefs shape how and what they consider reading policies. Hill (this volume) amplifies how the language of policy texts mediates such processes. Each of these researchers elaborates how the oft-heard response from educators to reform strategies—"I'm already doing it"—many times reflects lack of understanding rather than any correspondence between their practices and reform strategies.

Loeb and McEwan (this volume) also highlight the role of individual implementers. They elaborate how individuals' goals and constraints differ across relevant actors in ways that influence policy implementation and frame implementation as a principal-agent problem. Where Cohen, Spillane, and colleagues, and Coburn and Stein see "knowledge constraints" as including mainly existing knowledge and experiential frames, Loeb and McEwan point to shortfalls in expertise and professional capacity—issues of capability rather than predisposition. However, research teaches that both elements are essential to support individual action consistent with policy goals.

Research into the actions, values, and thoughts of implementers shows that implementation is not about mindless compliance to a mandate or policy directive, and that implementation shortfalls are not just cases of individual resistance, incompetence or capability. Rather, implementation involves a process of sense making that implicates an implementer's knowledge base, prior understanding, and beliefs about the best course of action. Early implementation research focused on the technical properties of policy and individuals' ability to carry it out—what was to be accomplished and by what means—to the general neglect of institutional elements that affected how and whether individuals responded—their norms, values, beliefs. Contemporary researchers such as those included in this volume acknowledge how these normative factors may trump technical components of a policy. However, while these lessons about institutional contexts are key for both research and policy, policy research models include these factors with great difficulty since they are challenging to access and assess by means of standardized instruments and require more costly site-based, qualitative research to uncover.

The Process

Hard as it is to believe today, early observations that policy implementation did not proceed in a straightforward, unidirectional fashion across and through levels of the policy system—*ipso jure*—generated alarmed surprise in federal policy circles. Early implementation theorists took a similarly simple stance, basing their analytical starting point in a policy's regulatory language and ignoring both deals made earlier in the policy-making process and adjustments made as the policy made its way through the implementing system.[4] These analyses, stemming from the old public administration model, separated administration from politics and took the policy as a given. This analytical stance leaves implementation context and actors in the shadows. Implementation in this view was an "efficiency" problem and about "carrying out" policy directives—an administrative and apolitical process, as opposed to "getting something done" and all the messiness that implies.

The complex, powerful and multifaceted nature of the implementation process now is taken-for-granted. "Change is hard," a complaint that today produces rolled-eyed response from policy analysts and policy makers alike, was not an anticipated conclusion in the 1970s when policy was expected to be more or less self-implementing, given necessary resources, regulation, and resolve. For that reason, and for the litany of failed expectations, dashed hopes, and misjudged implementation processes, the first two decades of implementation research has been dubbed "misery research."[5]

Researchers and reformers are much more sophisticated today about the implementation process. We understand that disconnections occur up and down the system. We understand that bargains struck can shift as aspects of the context change. Datnow (this volume), for example, depicts implementation as a process of negotiation that is reciprocal not unidirectional; her research takes implementation analysis beyond traditions of structural determinism. We know that these bargains are likely to change over time, as policy is *re*formulated in light of shifting expectations or normative assumptions or learning based in on-the-ground experience. Similarly, Malen (this volume) casts this process as one of "political games" played within and beyond bureaucratic boundaries.

Power is an essential dimension of the implementation process and political scientists introduced considerations of power into the policy process in the 1960s. Theodore Lowi's typology of policy decisions remains among the most significant. Lowi differentiates among distributive, regulative, and redistributive policies and shows how politics determine policy choices in the context of each (Lowi, 1969). Contemporary implementation analysts continue to feature considerations of power and politics in part by focusing on how power is assigned to different groups. For example, Anne Schneider and Helen Ingram elaborated the ways in which political power determines the "social construction of target populations" as weak or strong and as dependent or deviant (Schneider & Ingram, 1993). This perspective provides insight about why some populations are the targets of punitive, coercive policies whereas others receive supports. Dumas and Anyon's analysis (this volume) of the *non*implementation of the New Jersey school finance ruling in *Abbott v. Burke* features reformers' frustrating struggle on a social terrain contoured by issues of race and social class—an implementation setting where not all stakeholders had equal access to power or voice in the process. Political power enables those possessing it to force their will on others; where power is distributed, implementation requires a process of negotiation.

Betty Malen (this volume) focuses explicitly on how power and politics take center stage as education policies are designed and implemented and shows how political conflicts and struggles for influence at all levels of the system determine education policy and responses to it. Malen highlights the crucial role of micropolitics in education policy implementation, a domain neglected by analysts whose interests have focused on macrolevel political struggles; she also highlights intra-agency politics and their effect on implementation, a topic little studied at any level.

Additionally, power considerations have led to the entry of new actors—advocacy organizations and coalitions—into the policy process throughout the policy system. These organizations entered the educational policy arena primarily as a means to give voice to populations at the margins of the policy system—children, especially poor children of color, ethnic minorities and other groups outside the mainstream. These actors now feature prominently in both how policies are formulated and how they are carried out, but too are little studied.

Implementation research also is moving beyond linear or staged conceptions of the process. Both the implementation process and the policy making process itself typically have been formulated in terms of discrete phases that follow one another. Models of change efforts or innovative programs, for example, generally have been depicted as a three-stage process—adoption (getting started), implementation (carrying it out), and continuation (carrying on once special project funding or oversight has ended). This conception represents change as involving three separate and sequential tasks. Yet experience shows that the policy process is neither linear nor a set of discrete phases—certainly not at the "bottom" of the system as new actors enter the scene, demands shift, resources change, and competing pressures divert attention.

We have learned that—excepting education policy implementation tasks involving narrow surface structures such as schedule changes or calendar modification—implementation, broadly conceived, often implicates all of these stages simultaneously. For example, teachers new to a school or district are "new adopters" of a reform initiative even though the program may have been in place for some time, while veteran teachers are working to deepen its practices in their classrooms. Or, districts acting to extend an effective initiative to new sites confront the challenge of providing supports for sustaining change in original sites, while at the same time providing start-up supports and resources in others. On the ground, implementation involves interplay of change and continuity, getting started and going deeper, learning and relearning as midcourse corrections are made. Despite this understanding, though, too many implementation research designs continue to adopt a "pathway" model, rather than deal directly with the actual simultaneity of different implementation tasks.

In line with this understanding about how the process unfolds, ideas have changed about the role of ambiguity in implementation directives and conflict

in the process. Public management models tended to view ambiguity and conflict as policy flaws to be ironed out of the process, rather than as inherent features to be anticipated and even exploited as opportunities.[6] However, experience documents the potentially dysfunctional effects of "goal clarity" and
prescribed implementation procedures and shows the benefits of ambiguity
that allows positive local adaptation and negotiation about strategies, indicators, and priorities. For example, Meredith Honig (2001 and this volume)
shows how the ambiguity of policy design prompted policy makers in Oakland, CA, to learn from actors at the "bottom" of the system about how to
make the "top" more effective and responsive. However, Honig also describes
risks: some of Oakland policy makers over time reverted to a more ritualized,
codified implementation strategy in part because of inadequate supports for
their learning efforts.

Implementation Outcomes

Chapter 1 discusses important issues related to identifying implementable and
successful policies. But, what ultimately constitutes "successful implementation"? Within both research and policy communities, disagreement exists about
the answer to this question. One point of disagreement concerns whether success means fidelity to policy makers' intent and specific directives or instead (or
also) includes other unintended benefits that may result from implementers'
action. Contention also stems from whether success should be measured by the
extent to which implementers achieved sought-after status changes or whether
process measures also should be considered. For example, a school restructuring
effort that aims to improve students' academic performance may result in the
construction of small learning communities desired by policy makers and
enjoyed by students and teachers, but if those learning communities do not
demonstrably improve student performance, was the effort a success?

    Another outcomes consideration involves assumptions about relevant
timelines. When short-term successes or bumps in performance persist, does
that signal implementation success? Or, conversely, do findings of "no significant difference" underestimate the longer-term policy gains or significant
delayed effects? Teachers' professional development programs are an example
of policy efforts whose payoffs may appear down the road in terms of teachers' knowledge base, motivation, and sense of professionalism, rather than in
terms of students' more immediate achievement gains. Similarly, reforms seeking significant change in practice often take time to mature and appear in
established practice. To this point, Paul Sabatier argues that implementation
should be studied in cycles of ten years in order to consider maturation and
policy learning (Sabatier, 1991).

Assessment of implementation outcomes also implicates context. How do outcomes look when viewed from the perspective of the broader implementing system? A highly touted arts program in a Midwestern district, for example, resulted in outstanding student accomplishment; however, resource requirements for the effort drained supports from other arts programs in the district, and so deprived students unable to participate in this special project. Was it a success, all things considered? Another example: A new reading initiative boosted student scores in a high-poverty school district. While these increases were statistically significant, students still performed substantially lower overall than did students in more advantaged settings, and significantly below the state average. How should this effort be judged—did it succeed in its ultimate goal of preparing competent, skilled students? Or, what is the assessment of success when a high school is able to boost graduation rates, the ostensible policy goal, but the high school diploma awarded by the school— the ultimate education standard—in fact means little in terms of academic accomplishment?

Concerns about sustainability pose different questions about relevant outcomes. Implementation research examining the extent to which innovative practices were continued after special funding went away generally found low levels of continuation (Berman & McLaughlin, 1978). One explanation for this disappointing observation centers on implementers' learning (McLaughlin & Mitra, 2001). Often reform efforts focus on activity structures such as materials and project routines to the neglect of the knowledge principles that motivated the innovation. Lacking this knowledge, teachers risk "lethal mutations" of the project in their classrooms as they modify or extend the practice. Or, teachers are unable to continue a project once special supports are withdrawn because they never learned *why* they were carrying out particular activities or routines. Teachers require knowledge of a reform's "first principles" if they are to sustain project activities on their own. This knowledge of foundational theoretical constructs comprises an essential implementation outcome and extends beyond the activity structures assessed to determine degree of project implementation. Likewise, important questions feature the relationship between individual and system capacity. What system supports are necessary for individual learning to continue and deepen, and how does individual learning become established in system routines and knowledge?

Important implementation outcomes, then, involve not only the consequences associated with project activities, but also the individual and system capacity developed to sustain, extend, and deepen a successful initiative. Just as problem formulations cannot be taken for granted lessons learned about the complexity of implementation outcomes also direct researchers to make outcomes problematic and an issue for empirical analysis.

New Opportunities to Learn:
Beyond "Misery Research"

Implementation studies are poised to move beyond "misery research." In particular, such studies can explore the new agents, agencies, and institutional relationships that have been created in part in response to what reformers have learned from previous implementation research and can seek to understand the unique and essential contribution of both macro- and microelements of the policy system. These aspects of contemporary implementation are not well understood but offer promising opportunities for the next generation of implementation research to take up.

New Organizations and Organizations New to the Process

New agents, agencies, and relationships have appeared on the education policy scene and play a prominent role in interpreting policy and carrying it out. Two types of organizations stand out as especially important for implementation research to understand: intermediary and hybrid organizations.

Intermediary organizations
Intermediary organizations of various stripes have been created or reassigned in response to the disconnections across levels of the implementing policy system and as acknowledgment that local knowledge matters to implementation outcomes. That is, an important lesson of the 1970s and 1980s involved "mutual adaptation," or the likelihood that local implementers would, for better or worse, modify policy goals and strategies to suit local conditions. Central planners, we learned, had little effective influence over microlevel factors and action and local context usually trumped macrolevel intent. The development of intermediary organizations in part reflected a view of local adaptation of policy goals and strategies as a positive to be encouraged. In this view, policy makers or reformers distant from implementers did not and could not possess the knowledge necessary to tailor policies to local contexts or the will to ensure effective implementation. Intermediaries comprise a strategic "middle," operating between the top and bottom of the implementing system.

Intermediary organizations established as stewards for children and youth and as "third party neutral" actors differ in form, function, and funding.[7] Some are community-level collaboratives created in response to the Balkanized nature of opportunities and resources available to children and youth and the incoherent youth policy contexts in which schools operate. Disconnected services, multiple funding streams, and incompatible regulatory structures have made it difficult for schools to work with community agencies to provide the range of services and opportunities their students needed to be successful in school. Local collaboratives provide a promising and efficient way to provide a range of supportive services. They aim not only to make opportunities for children and youth more effective and efficient but they also can serve as "knowledge managers," conveners, and resource brokers (Honig, 2004a, b).

In Redwood City, California, for example, the Redwood City 2020 collaborative involves city and county partners from education, health, community-based organizations, and other youth-related agencies around the community's opportunities and resources for children and youth. Through the 2020 infrastructure, partners join in grant-funded activities and initiatives that leverage their collective resources to create new assets for youth such as a high school health center or Family Resource Centers—benefits that none could have accomplished on its own. Other local collaboratives focus exclusively on education. In Portland and Multnomah County, Oregon, Schools Uniting Neighborhoods [SUN] initiated a community schools initiative that brings together nonprofit organizations and public and private agencies to provide students and families with an array of services. Over the past two years, SUN has expanded to over 46 of the county's 150 schools—a remarkable achievement in fiscally strapped Oregon.

Collaborative organizations face formidable challenges to their effective operation and stability, though, and more needs to be understood about their implementation experiences. Individual agency self-interests, for instance, often compete with collaborative goals, especially as budgets are developed. Strong collaboratives require significant levels of trust and mutual understanding —resources disrupted when personnel turn over or membership changes. How do these organizations manage such challenges? Eugene Bardach, in response to these concerns, proposes that collaboratives adopt a new management form, "craftsmanship," to overcome some of these obstacles (Bardach, 1998). Under what conditions can collaboratives grow and sustain such management? Collaborations that bring actors together across institutional lines produce new capacity; Clarence Stone and colleagues see implementation in this instance as a process of social production (Stone, Henig, Jones, & Pierannunzi, 2001). Little research exists, though, on the roles and operation of local collaboratives in the social production process and there is much for the field to learn about how they grow new capacity as partners in policy implementation.

Local Education Funds (LEFs), prominent local intermediaries, pose similar opportunities for education implementation research to reveal how organizations with explicit brokering and mobilizing missions operate. Since their inception in 1983, Local Education Funds across the country have played a major role in fostering district reform efforts and building broad-based community support for public education (Public Education Network, 2004). LEFs typically feature development of a community-held vision as they pursue a local education reform agenda from their unique position between school districts and their communities. For example, in Hamilton County, TN, the Chattanooga Public Education Fund successfully served as convener around a politically charged debate about whether to merge city and county school systems. The Boston Plan for Excellence supports the city schools through technical assistance, research, and minigrants for teachers and works in close partnership with the district to provide professional development for all teachers and principals. New Visions, New York City's very large and active LEF, has been the launching pad for the city's small school efforts. Since 2000, New Visions has done the community engagement work necessary to build support for over 70 new small schools.

Intermediary organizations such as these are emerging in communities and regions across the country. They fill gaps in the policy system by virtue of their flexibility, expanded capacity, and ability to manage from the middle. They provide a structure for diverse interests and organizations to join together to promote consistent standards of quality across sectors, to provide missing resources, and to leverage existing ones. However, these organizational forms are relatively new to the education policy system and raise complex implementation issues for research. One involves challenges of cross-sector work: How do organizations work together when they have different or rival institutional logics, sources of authority, funding, legitimacy, pressures, and standards of accountability? Though existing evidence supports the important contribution of successful collaboratives and intermediaries to various outcomes (see, for example, Blank, Brand, Deich, Kazis, Politz, & Trippe, n.d.; Honig, 2004b), experience also suggests that more often than not, these ventures stumble on institutional or normative differences or never develop the capacity necessary to take on more than superficial tasks of coordination. Important implementation questions center on how intermediaries navigate the practical and political issues that define their local landscape. And, absent regulatory authority, how do these organizations establish and maintain legitimate presence in the community?

Hybrid organizations

"Hybrid" organizations represent another policy response to the shortfalls seen in education policy and practice. School reform has failed to meet its goals, some claim, because the institution itself is not up to the task posed by contemporary students. Today's students come to class with a myriad of challenges for teachers: limited English language proficiency, health problems, home dysfunction, and the array of troubles that accompany poverty. Even if schools and instruction were significantly improved, reformers' goals would be unmet because schools alone cannot provide supports necessary for students' success.

Institutional hybrids surround teaching and learning with other resources that enable success for all students regardless of their personal backgrounds. Community schools blend schools and social service resources to operate as "full service schools" (Coalition for Community Schools, 2000; Dryfoos, 1998; Dryfoos, Quinn & Barkin, 2005). Other hybrids bring together educational institutions. Schools called "middle college high schools" blend secondary and postsecondary resources to provide activities designed to assist underperforming students to meet high academic standards and progress toward a community college degree. Jobs for the Future (JFF) supports yet another mix—that of secondary schools and the workplace. JFF works with employers to develop credit-carrying workplace-based courses, such as a chemistry course based in a hospital's blood laboratory, as a way to engage high school students in their studies and enhance the perceived relevance of their course work. While early evidence suggests the promise of these organizational hybrids, little is known about how these institutional mergers have worked in fact. Like collaborative arrangements, hybrids raise central questions of how partners manage issues of accountability, normative compatibility, logics for action, and day-to-day operation—all implementation questions of the first order.

Non-system actors

Non-system actors—actors outside the formal education policy system—can and do play an important role in how policies are carried out and to what ends. They shape political debate and influence the normative climate and accountability structures that effect how individuals respond to policy directives and goals. For instance, as elaborated below, community coalitions represent strategic interorganizational associations now actively involved in education policy. Advocacy organizations have sprung up at all levels of the education sector in part in response to concerns about resource allocation, equity, and voice. Neither group has been included significantly in either education policy or policy research. However, both are vital players in contemporary policy arenas and offer occasions for an expanded empirical and theoretical consideration of education policy implementation.

Community coalitions

Local coalitions, informal but relatively stable groups with access to institutional resources, play a vital role in shaping school reform and the character of education policy at all levels. Clarence Stone and colleagues provide compelling evidence about the influence of local coalitions on urban school reform and assign the failure of urban school reform over past decades to educators' inability to enlist the support of the influential civic groups that determine community priorities (Stone, et al., 2001). An engaged public plays an indispensable role in school reform and support for public education. *It takes a city,* advises the title of the Paul Hill, Christine Campbell, and James Harvey book on urban school reform (Hill, Campbell & Harvey, 2000). For example, efforts to improve low-performing schools in poor, urban communities and the rural south appear to be succeeding thanks in part to the mobilization of certain coalitions (Henderson & Mapp, 2002). Efforts such as San Diego Dialogue sponsor public events through which civic and business leaders come together to learn about the district's ambitious reform agenda.[8] Key stakeholders in this view of education reform policy implementation include not only professional educators and parents, but politicians, nonprofits, employers, seniors, and others. Absent organized civic engagement in school reform, urban systems find themselves in constant battle for resources and vulnerable to shifting tastes.

However, effective, broad-based community coalitions are difficult to build and sustain; few good examples exist. Education policy implementation would benefit from research examining the formation, operation and vitality of community coalitions. How do they get started? What sustains them? How can local educators foster and support community coalitions focused on the public schools? And, how do they function in the domain of education policy?

Advocacy organizations
Implementation researchers identified political power and politics as central elements in how policies were framed and carried out. In response to this fact of policy-making life, advocacy organizations at all levels of government act to influence power dynamics in ways that benefit youth and youth-serving institutions. Few would argue with the proposition that advocacy organizations comprise vital assets for children and youth growing up in urban America. History teaches that without effective political activism dedicated to their interests, urban children are likely to lose in the competition for community resources. Public schools and the children who attend them face stiff competition from the priorities of more entrenched and powerful community interests. Organizations that champion the interests of urban children and youth confront an especially difficult task. Their beneficiaries lack political voice and their interests must compete for attention in a civic agenda filled with issues more compelling to many voters (most of whom are not parents) and politicians. They also face the extraordinarily difficult task of mobilizing support across fractured, segmented interests.

Yet in some communities, advocacy organizations are responsible for bringing about significant change in the educational resources available to children and youth and have become significant players in the education policy arena. In Oakland, CA, for example, Oakland Community Organizations mobilized a faith-based grassroots campaign that led to district support for new small, autonomous schools in the community's most impoverished neighborhoods. In San Francisco, CA, Coleman Advocates mobilized broad community support to pass a proposition that set aside 2.5 percent of the city's budget for children, a notable accomplishment in a city with proportionally the lowest youth population of any urban area in the country. Books not Bars, an youth-advocacy group protesting the construction of a new megajail in Alameda County, CA, did not succeed in stopping the project altogether but did convince county supervisors to scale it back considerably, thereby retaining funds for education support.

Despite their importance as change agents, however, advocacy organizations are little studied. Scant systematic documentation or analytical understanding is available about the nature or design of advocacy organizations generally, and even less comprehensive information exists about organizations advocating for children and youth. Most material is descriptive, provides guides for action or features elements "best practices." Existing case analyses are generally decontextualized though we know that advocacy organizations structures and strategies shape and are shaped by their local social and political setting. The character and function of advocacy organizations at all levels of government provides relatively unexplored territory for researchers interested in education policy implementation and the nature of social movements.

Units of Analysis and the Change Process

With lessons about the essential complexity of policy implementation and the multiplicity of relevant system and nonsystem actors come conceptual and practical challenges for researchers. If implementation is not a straight-line process bound by the formal policy system, how might researchers draw meaningful borders around the policies, people, and places that matter to how it unfolds? Complexity and expanding conceptions of influence are difficult to wrap empirical or theoretical arms around.

Societal sector
The evolving model of a societal sector provides a promising theoretical frame to guide the next generation of implementation research by providing a unit of analysis that assumes relational complexity. The societal sector paradigm, as developed by W. Richard Scott and John Meyer, incorporates lessons learned from past implementation research about narrow constructions of problems, actors, implementation settings, and logics of action and represents the convergence of implementation research and institutional theory as applied to organizational fields. It focuses attention on all the organizations, actors, and relationships within a sector associated with a particular activity or service such

as education (Scott & Meyer, 1991). A societal sector framework draws boundaries around actors and organizations by their actual functions in policy processes, not by geography or formal bureaucratic responsibility for a particular policy, and so prompts researchers to look within and outside the formal policy system to the range of people who matter to implementation. In this way, the societal sector framework permits researchers to build on lessons learned about relationships, contexts and outcomes while also revealing new actors and associations.

Yet, contemporary implementation researchers, with few exceptions, generally train their lens on the formal policy system under study to the exclusion of nonformal relationships that extend across categorical or functional boundaries—such as those within nongovernmental organizations, professional organizations, or the private sector. A societal sector frame helps avoid these limitations. Implementation research that considers broader societal influences on education policy and practice has much to contribute to our understanding of the depth and complexity of policy issues and the implementation process.

Systems learning

A societal sector frame provides the boundary for research; it features relationships and a functional view of policy implementation. It provides less assistance, though, in understanding *processes* of change within a sector. Particularly important are questions of how the enacting systems and interorganizational networks that define the sector learn from experience, acquire and use new knowledge, adapt and sustain positive outcomes.

The focus on system learning has been largely missing in implementation research, especially in education. (For a recent exception, see Honig in this volume.) Organizational theorists have examined questions of organizational learning (Argyris, 1993; Brown & Duguid, 1991; March, 1991) and policy researchers have paid episodic attention to how ideas travel, but questions about how systems within the public domain learn are relatively unexamined. In part this lack of attention to system learning within education reflects the fact that only recently has the system been considered as a unit of change. Prior education policy research typically followed categorical policy streams, for example, or focused on particular policy domains such as teacher professional development or standards based reform. It focused on "trees" to the neglect of the "forest."

A key focus for future implementation research involves extending this work to adopt a system perspective on responses to exogenous policy goals and structures. Implementation researchers are beginning to broaden conceptions of relevant unit of analysis at local and state levels and to incorporate considerations of agency design. For example, education policy implementation researchers are beginning to highlight the essential role of the school district —the local system—as critical to how policies are interpreted, carried out and sustained (Hightower, Knapp, Marsh, & McLaughlin, 2002; Spillane, 1996). Longer-term and more fundamental issues, though, implicate questions of system *learning*. Ambitious policies generally seek sustained change in practice and culture, not episodic attention to goals or targets. However, innovation in public policy rarely is the consequence of radical shifts but rather the result of incremental improvements that are incorporated into existing routines and norms. As Lee Cronbach so aptly put it, there are few "slam bam" policy effects (Cronbach, 1982). Incremental improvements, organizational learning theorists demonstrate, require opportunities to regularly examine practice, consider alternatives, and make adjustments informed by experience. Similarly, change that is sustained and deepened assumes coherent and consistent supports within the enacting system—what Weick and Roberts call a "collective mind," a condition practitioners might describe as "everyone being on the same page" (Weick & Roberts, 1993).

Yet neither policy makers nor researchers have paid much attention to how systems would learn these new behaviors or acquire the knowledge necessary to a collective mind. How can systems learn from experience? How can policy systems generate and use new knowledge in ways that further reformers' goals? How does individual learning connect to system learning? For example, when education policy targets change in teachers' capabilities and practices, what are assumed connections between individual and district system learning? Currently, both policy and research usually overlook this essential link and so neglect the relationship between individual learning and improvement.

Or, by and large the accountability and evaluation structures associated with education policy situate "learning" outside the implementing system as compliance measures and assessments of policy investment. This stance, while valid from the perspective of a social account, overlooks the importance of the system as its own source of learning and in many instances displaces opportunities for system learning. How might education policy at all levels be more intentional about facilitating system learning? For instance, learning theorists stress the importance of "situated learning" and context specific interpretation of experience (Brown, Collins & Duguid, 1989, for example). Scholars contributing to the burgeoning "knowledge management" literature likewise underscore the importance of learning by doing, integrating learning and practice on a continuing basis. (See for example, Harvard Business Review, 1998.)

Implementation research aims to investigate the structures and processes that move policy goals into practice, and the field can take advantage of theoretical developments that inform these objectives from another perspective. A productive viewpoint for the next generation of implementation researchers would integrate lessons from implementation research with current ideas about learning systems and knowledge management to understand how enacting systems can learn as part of policy implementation.

Acknowledgment

This chapter benefited significantly from Meredith Honig's and W. Richard Scott's careful reading and thoughtful suggestions.

Notes

[1]Pressman and Wildavsky's book named the complex and often unpredictable process that other observers of the policy described as Kennedy-Johnson era Great Society social programs rolled out of Washington, D.C., in the 1960s. Other early challenges to then conventional ideas about policy implementation include Daniel Moynihan's 1970 *Maximum Feasible Misunderstanding,* which details the huge variation in state and local responses to federal poverty initiatives and Martha Derthick's 1972 portrayal of the federal government's inability to order other governments' compliance with the conditions of a new federal housing program, *New towns in town: Why a federal program failed.*

[2]Alice Rivlin, considering the ideological dimension of many social policies, advised researchers to pursue "advocacy social science," rather than present a facade of "value-free" social science.

[3]Michael Knapp's analysis of teachers' implementation of National Science Foundation sponsored reforms in mathematics and science echoes Cohen's conclusions about the piecemeal nature of reform implementation; he too describes the general failure of teachers to fully understand the vision or first principles of the reforms and instead to rely on what they already know (Knapp, 1997).

[4]Van Meter and Van Horn (1975) and Mazmanian and Sabatier (1983) exemplify this early implementation research. See review in Hill and Hupe (2002) and Matland (1995).

[5]Based on his review of the implementation literature, Swedish scholar Bo Rothstein describes implementation research as "misery research, a pathology of social sciences." Cited in Hill & Hupe (2002, p. 79).

[6]Betty Achinstein (2002) and Meredith Honig (2004) provide instructive exceptions to this general observation. Their research describes conflict and ambiguity as implementation resources.

[7]Meredith Honig (2004) provides a useful analysis of the distinctive functions of intermediary organizations engaged in education policy implementation and the factors that enable and constrain their work. Honig asserts that the primary job of intermediaries is to work in between organizations or parties to mediate and manage change for both.

[8]See http://www.sandiegodialogue.org/k12.htm for details of the organization's objectives and strategies.

Bibliography

Abbott v. Burke 119 NJ 287 (1990).

Achinstein, B. (2002). *Community diversity and conflict among schoolteachers.* New York, NY: Teachers College Press.

Allison, G., & Zelikow, P. (1999). *Essence of decision* (2nd ed.). New York, NY: Longman.

Anderson, B., Odden, A., Farrar, E., Fuhrman, S., Davis, A., Huddle, E., Armstrong, J., & Flakus-Mosqueda, P. (1987). State strategies to support local school improvement. *Knowledge: Creation, Diffusion, Utilization, 9*(1), 42–87.

Angrist, J. D., & Guryan, J. (2003). *Does teacher testing raise teacher quality? Evidence from state certification requirements* (Working Paper 9545). Cambridge, MA: National Bureau of Economic Research.

Anyon, J. (1997). *Ghetto schooling: A political economy of urban educational reform.* New York, NY: Teachers College Press.

Anyon, J. (2005). *Radical possibilities: Public policy, urban education, and a new social movement.* New York, NY: Routledge.

Apple, M. W. (2001). *Educating the "right" way: Markets, standards, God and inequality.* New York, NY: Routledge.

Argyris, C. (1976). Single-loop and double-loop models in research on decision making. *Administrative Science Quarterly, 21*(3), 363–375.

Argyris, C. (1993). *Knowledge for action: Overcoming barriers to organizational change.* San Francisco, CA: Jossey-Bass.

Argyris, C., & Schon, D. A. (1996). *Organizational learning II: Theory, method, and practice.* Reading, MA: Addison-Wesley.

Armor, D. J. (1995). *Forced justice.* New York, NY: Oxford University Press.

Aronowitz, S. (1981). *The crisis in historical materialism.* South Hadley, MA: Bergin.

Askew, B. J., Fountas, I. C., Lyons, C. A., Pinnell, G. S., & Schmitt, M. C. (1998).

Reading Recovery review: Understandings, outcomes, and implications. Columbus, OH: Reading Recovery Council of North America.

Austin, J. L., & Howson, A. G. (1979). Language and mathematical education. *Educational Studies in Mathematics, 10*(3), 161–197.

Bakhtin, M. M. (1981). *The dialogic imagination: Four essays.* Austin, TX: University of Texas Press.

Ball, D. L. (1990). The mathematical understandings that prospective teachers bring to teacher education. *Elementary School Journal, 90*(4), 449–466.

Ball, S. (1994). *Education reform.* Philadelphia, PA: Open University Press.

Ball, S., & Lacy, C. (1984). Subject disciplines as the opportunity for group action: A measured critique of subject subcultures. In A. Hargreaves & P. Woods (Eds.), *Classrooms and staffrooms: The sociology of teachers and teaching* (X). Milton Keynes, UK: Open University Press.

Bardach, E. (1977). *The implementation game.* Cambridge, MA: MIT Press.

Bardach, E. (1998). *Getting agencies to work together: The practice and theory of managerial craftsmanship.* Washington, DC: Brookings Institution Press.

Barfield, D., Brindis, C., Guthrie, L., McDonald, W., Philliber, S., & Scott, B. (1994). *The evaluation of New Beginnings: A report for 1994.* Accord, NY: Philliber Research Associates.

Barley, S. R. (1990). Images of imaging: Notes on doing longitudinal field work. *Organization Science, 1*(3), 78–108.

Barley, S. R. (1996). Technicians in the workplace: Ethnographic evidence for bringing work into organization studies. *Administrative Science Quarterly, 41*(3), 404–441.

Bartelt, D. W. (1995). The macroecology of educational outcomes. In L. C. Rigsby, M. C. Reynolds, & M. C. Wang (Eds.), *School-Community Connections: Exploring Issues for Research and Practice* (pp. 159–191). San Francisco, CA: Jossey-Bass.

Barzelay, M. (1992). *Breaking through bureaucracy.* Berkeley, CA: University of California Press.

Baugh, W. H., & Stone, J. A. (1982). Mobility and wage equilibration in the educator labor market. *Economics of Education Review, 2*(3), 253–274.

Baum, H. S. (2003). *Community action for school reform.* Albany, NY: State University of New York Press.

Baumgartner, F., & Jones, B. (1993). *Agendas and instability in American politics.* Chicago, IL: University of Chicago Press.

Beck, J., Czerniak, C., & Lumpe, A. T. (2000). An exploratory study of teachers' beliefs regarding the implementation of constructivism in their classrooms. *Journal of Science Teacher Education, 11*(4), 323–343.

Becker, G. (1993). *Human capital: A theoretical and empirical analysis with special reference to education.* Chicago, IL: University of Chicago Press.

Bell, D. (1993). *Faces at the bottom of the well.* New York, NY: Basic.

Bell, D. (1995). Serving two masters. In K. Crenshaw, N. Gotanda, G. Peller, & K. Thomas (Eds.), *Critical race theory* (pp. 5–19). New York, NY: The New Press.

Berends, M. (2000). Teacher-reported effects of New American School Designs: Exploring relationships to teacher background and school context. *Educational Evaluation and Policy Analysis, 22*(1), 65–82.

Berends, M., Bodilly, S. J., & Kirby, S. N. (2002). *Facing the challenges of whole-school reform: New American Schools after a decade* (MR-1498-EDU). Santa Monica, CA: Rand Corporation.

Berends, M., Bodilly, S. J., & Kirby, S. N. (2002). Looking back over a decade of whole-school reform: The experience of New American Schools. *Phi Delta Kappan, 84*(2), 168–175.

Berends, M., Bodilly, S., & Kirby, S. (2003). District and school leadership for whole school reform: The experience of New American Schools. In J. Murphy & A. Datnow (Eds.), *Leadership for school reform: Lessons from comprehensive school reform designs* (pp. 109–131). Thousand Oaks, CA: Corwin Press.

Berends, M., Kirby, S., Naftel, S., & McKelvey, C. (2001). *Implementation and performance in New American Schools: Three years into scale-up.* Santa Monica, CA: Rand Corporation.

Berman, P., & McLaughlin, M. (1976). Implementation of educational innovation. *The Educational Forum, 40*(3), 345–370.

Berman, P., & McLaughlin, M. W. (1977). *Federal programs supporting educational change: Vol VII. Factors affecting implementation and continuation.* Santa Monica, CA: Rand Corporation.

Berman, P., & McLaughlin, M.W. (1978). *The Rand change agent study, Vols. 1–8.* Santa Monica, CA: The Rand Corporation.

Bidwell, C. E., & Yasumoto, J. Y. (1999). The collegial focus: Teaching fields, collegial relationships, and instructional practice in American high schools. *Sociology of Education, 72*(4), 234–256.

Billstein, R., Libeskind, S., & Lott, J. W. (2004). *A problem solving approach to mathematics for elementary school teachers.* San Francisco, CA: Pearson/Addison Wesley.

Blank, M., Brand, B., Deich, S., Kazis, R., Politz, B., & Trippe, S. (n.d.). Local intermediary organizations: Connecting the dots for children, youth and families. Available on-line from http://www.communityschools.org.

Blase, J. (1998). The micropolitics of educational change. In A. Hargreaves & A. Lieberman & M. Fullan & D. Hopkins (Eds.), *International handbook of educational change* (pp. 544–558). Dordrecht, The Netherlands: Kluwer Academic Publishers.

Blau, P. M. (1963). *The dynamics of bureaucracy.* New York, NY: John Wiley.

Bodilly, S. (1998). *Lessons from New American Schools' scale-up phase.* Santa Monica, CA: Rand Corporation.

Bodilly, S. (2001). *New American Schools' concept of break the mold designs: How designs evolved and why.* Santa Monica, CA: Rand Corporation.

Bodilly, S. J., & Berends, M. (1999). Necessary district support for comprehensive school reform. In G. Orfield & E. H. DeBray (Eds.), *Hard work for good schools: Facts not fads in Title I reform* (pp. 111–119). Boston, MA: The Civil Rights Project, Harvard University.

Bolman, L. G., & Deal, T. E. (1991). *Reframing organizations.* San Francisco, CA: Jossey-Bass.

Borko, H., Wolf, S. A., Simone, G., & Uchiyama, K. P. (2003). Schools in transition: Reform efforts and school capacity in Washington state. *Educational Evaluation and Policy Analysis, 25*(2), 171–201.

Borman, G. D., D'Agostino, J. V., Wong, K. K., & Hedges, L. V. (1998). The longitudinal achievement of Chapter 1 students: Preliminary evidence from the Prospects study. *Journal of Education for Students Placed at Risk, 3*(4), 363–399.

Borman, G., Hewes, G., Overman, L., & Brown. (2002). *Comprehensive school reform and student achievement: A meta-analysis* (Report No. 59). Baltimore, MD: Center for Research on the Education of Students Placed at Risk.

Bouillion, L., & Gomez, L. (2000). Designing for culturally and linguistically diverse communities: A case study of the role of local context in shaping curricular adaptation. In B. Fishman & S. O'Connor-Divelbiss (Eds.), *Proceedings of the Fourth International Conference of the Learning Sciences* (pp. 302–309). Mahwah, NJ: Erlbaum.

Bouillion, L. M. (2002). Teachers' locally-mediated sensemaking of a curricular design for "real world" learning: Developing design principles to support mutual adaptation in the use of education innovations. Unpublished doctoral dissertation, Northwestern University.

Bourdieu, P. (1986). The forms of capital. In J. G. Richardson (Ed.), *Handbook of theory and research for the sociology of education* (pp. 241–258). New York, NY: Greenwood.

Bourdieu, P. (1990). *The logic of practice.* Stanford, CA: Stanford University Press.

Bower, G. H., Black, J. B., & Turner, T. J. (1979). Scripts in memory for text. *Cognitive Psychology, 11*(2), 177–220.

Bower, G. H., & Morrow, D. G. (1990). Mental models in narrative comprehension. *Science, 247,* 44–48.

Boyd, D., Lankford, H., Loeb, S., & Wyckoff, J. (2005). The draw of home: How teachers' preferences for proximity disadvantage urban schools. *Journal of Policy Analysis and Management, 24*(1), 113–132.

Brewer, W. F., & Nakamura, G. V. (1984). The nature and functions of schemas. In R. S. Wyer Jr. & T. K. Srull (Eds.), *Handbook of social cognition,* Vol. 1 (pp. 119–160). Hillsdale, NJ: Erlbaum.

Brodkin, E. (1990). Implementation as policy politics. In D. J. Palumbo and D. J. Calista (Eds.), *Implementation and the policy process: Opening the black box* (pp. 107-118). Westport, CT: Greenwood Press.

Bronfenbrenner, U. (1979). *The ecology of human development: Experiments by nature and design.* Cambridge, MA: Harvard University Press.

Brown, J. (1998). *After being California's governor, why run for mayor of Oakland?* (Vol. 1). Oakland, CA: Oaklanders First.

Brown, J. S., Collins, A., & Duguid, P. (1989). Situated cognition and the culture of learning. *Educational Researcher, 18*(1), 32–42.

Brown, J. S., & Duguid, P. (1991). Organizational learning and communities-of-practice: Toward a unified view of working, learning, and innovation. *Organization Science, 2*(1), 40–57.

Brown, J. S., & Duguid, P. (1995). Organizational learning and communities-of-practice: Toward a unified view of working, learning, and innovation. In M. D. Cohen & L. S. Sproull (Eds.), *Organizational learning* (pp. 58–82). Thousand Oaks, CA: Sage.

Brown, J. S., & Duguid, P. (2000). *The social life of information.* Cambridge, MA: Harvard Business School Press.

Brunsson, N., & Olsen, J. P. (1993). *The reforming organization.* London, England: Routledge.

Bryk, A., Camburn, E., & Louis, K. S. (1997). Professional community in Chicago elementary schools: Facilitating factors and organizational consequences. *Educational Administration Quarterly, 35*(1), Suppl. 751–781.

Bryk, A. S., Kerbow, J. Q., Rollow, S. G., & Sebring, P. A. (1993). *A view from the schools: The state of reform in Chicago.* Chicago, IL: University of Chicago, Consortium on Chicago School Research.

Bryk, A. S., Lee, V. E., & Holland, P. B. (1993). *Catholic schools and the common good.* Cambridge, MA: Harvard University Press.

Bryk, A. S., & Schneider, B. (2002). *Trust in schools: A core resource for improvement.* New York, NY: Russell Sage Foundation.

Bryk, A., & Sebring, P. (1991). *Achieving School Reform in Chicago: What we need to know. A research agenda.* Chicago, IL: Consortium on Chicago School Research.

Bryk, A. S., Sebring, P. B., Kerbow, D., Rollow, S., & Easton, J. Q. (1998). *Charting Chicago school reform.* Boulder, CO: Westview Press.

Burch, P. (2000). *Moving from the margins to the mainstream: Teaching and learning reform in local policy context.* Unpublished doctoral dissertation, Stanford University.

Burch, P. (2002). Constraints and opportunities in changing policy environments: Intermediary organizations' response to complex district contexts. In A. Hightower, M. Knapp, J. Marsh, & M. McLaughlin (Eds.), *School districts and instructional renewal* (pp. 111–126). New York, NY: Teachers College Press.

Burch, P., & Spillane, J. (2003). Elementary School Leadership Strategies and Subject Matter: Reforming Mathematics and Literacy Instruction. The *Elementary School Journal, 103*(5), 519–535.

Burch, P., & Spillane J. (2004). How the subjects matter: Instructionally relevant policy in central office redesign. *Journal of Education Change, 5*(4), 51–76.

Burstein, L., McDonnell, L. M., Van Winkle, J., Ormseth, T. H., Mirocha, J., & Guiton, G. (1995). *Validating national curriculum indicators.* Santa Monica, CA: Rand Corporation.

Burtless, G. (Ed.). (1996). *Does money matter? The effect of school resources on student achievement and adult success.* Washington, DC: Brookings Institution.

Cahill, M. (1993). *A documentation report on the New York City Beacons Initiative.* New York, NY: Youth Development Institute, Fund for the City of New York.

California Department of Education. (1998). *Healthy Start request for applications.* Sacramento, CA: Author.

California Department of Education. (1999). *After-school learning and safe neighborhoods partnership program request for applications.* Sacramento, CA: Author.

Cantor, N., & Mischel, W. (1979). Prototypes in personal perception. In L. Berkowitz (Ed.), *Advances in experimental social psychology, 12* (pp. 3–53). New York, NY: Academic Press.

Cantor, N., Mischel, W., & Schwartz, J. C. (1982). A prototype analysis of psychological situations. *Cognitive Psychology, 14*, 45–77.

Carey, S. (1985). *Conceptual change in childhood.* Cambridge, MA: MIT Press.

Carnoy, M., & Loeb, S. (2003). Does external accountability affect student outcomes? A cross-state analysis. *Education Evaluation and Policy Analysis, 24*(4), 305–331.

Center for the Study of Social Policy. (1995). *Building new futures for at-risk youth: Findings from a five-year, multi-site evaluation.* Washington, DC: Author.

Chase, W. G., & Simon, H. A. (1974). Perception in chess. *Cognitive Psychology, 4*(1), 55–81.

Chi, M. T. H., Feltovich, P., & Glaser, R. (1981). Categorization and representation of physics problems by experts and novices. *Cognitive Science, 5*, 121–152.

Chinn, C. A., & Brewer, W. F. (1993). The role of anomalous data in knowledge acquisition: A theoretical framework and implications for science instruction. *Review of Educational Research, 63*(1), 1–49.

Chrispeels, J. H. (1997). Educational policy implementation in a shifting political climate: The California experience. *American Educational Research Journal, 34*(3), 453–481.

Chubb, J. E. & Moe, T. M. (1988). Politics, markets and the organization of schools. *American Political Science Review, 2*(4), 1065–1087.

Cibulka, J. G. (Ed.). (1994). [Special issue]. *Educational Administration Quarterly, 30*(3).

City of Oakland. (2000). *Blueprint for reinventing Oakland city government.* Retrieved January 9, 2001, from www.oaklandnet.org.

City of Oakland, Office of the Mayor. (1999). *Mayor's goals for 1999–2001. City of Oakland.* Retrieved August 20, 1999, from www.oaklandnet.com/government/mayor/goals.

Clapp, E. (1939). *Community schools in action.* New York, NY: Viking.

Clark, B. (1983). *The higher education system: Academic organization in cross-national perspective.* Berkeley, CA: University of California Press.

Clegg, S. R. (1989). *Frameworks of power.* Newbury Park, CA: Sage.

Clift, R., Veal, M. L., Holland, P., Johnson, M., & McCarthy, J. (1995). *Collaborative leadership and shared decision making: Teachers, principals, and university professors.* New York, NY: Teachers College Press.

Clotfelter, C. T. (2001). Are whites still fleeing? Racial patterns and enrollment shifts in urban public schools, 1987-1996. *Journal of Policy Analysis and Management, 20*(2), 199–221.

Clune III, W. H. (1983). A political model of implementation and implications of the model for public policy, research, and the changing roles of law and lawyers. *Iowa Law Review, 47,* 47–125.

Coalition for Community Schools (2000). *A policy approach to create and sustain community schools.* Washington, DC: Author.

Cobb, P., McClain, K., Lamberg, T. D., & Dean, C. (2003). Situating teachers' instructional practices in the institutional setting of the school and district. *Educational Researcher, 32*(6), 13–24.

Cobb, R. W., & Elder, C. D. (1983). *Participation in American politics.* Baltimore, MD: Johns Hopkins University Press.

Cobb, R. W., & Ross, M. H. (1997). *Cultural strategies of agenda denial: Avoidance, attack and redefinition.* Lawrence, KS: University Press of Kansas.

Coburn, C. E. (2001a). Collective sensemaking about reading: How teachers mediate reading policy in their professional communities. *Educational Evaluation and Policy Analysis, 23*(2), 145–170.

Coburn, C. E. (2001b). Making sense of reading: Logics of reading in the institutional environment and the classroom. Unpublished doctoral dissertation, Stanford University, Stanford.

Coburn, C. E. (2003). Rethinking scale: Moving beyond numbers to deep and lasting change. *Educational Researcher, 32*(6), 3–12.

Coburn, C. E. (2004). Beyond decoupling: Rethinking the relationship between the institutional environment and the classroom. *Sociology of Education, 77*(3), 211–244.

Coburn, C. E. (2005). The role of nonsystem actors in the relationship between policy and practice: The case of reading instruction in California. *Educational Evaluation and Policy Analysis, 27*(1), 23–52.

Coburn, K. G., & Riley, P. A. (2000). *Failing grade: Crisis and reform in the Oakland Unified School District.* San Francisco, CA: Pacific Research Institute.

Cohen, D. K. (1982). Policy and organization: The impact of state and federal educational policy on school governance. *Harvard Educational Review, 52*(4), 474–499.

Cohen, D. K. (1990). Revolution in one classroom: The case of Mrs. Oublier. *Educational Evaluation and Policy Analysis, 12*(3) 311–329.

Cohen, D. K., & Ball, D. L. (1990). Policy and practice: An overview. *Educational Evaluation and Policy Analysis, 12*(3), 347–353.

Cohen, D. K., & Ball, D. L. (1999). *Instruction, capacity and improvement.* Philadelphia, PA: Consortium for Policy Research in Education.

Cohen, D. K., & Barnes, C. (1993). Pedagogy and policy. In D. Cohen, M. W. McLaughlin, & J. E. Talbert (Eds.), *Teaching for understanding: Challenges for policy and practice* (pp. 207–239). San Francisco, CA: Jossey-Bass.

Cohen, D. K., & Hill, H. C. (2000). Instructional policy and classroom performance: The mathematics reform in California. *Teachers College Record, 102*(2), 294–343.

Cohen, D. K., & Hill, H. C. (2001). *Learning policy: When state education reform works.* New Haven, CT: Yale University Press.

Cohen D. K., & Spillane, J. P. (1993). Policy and practice: The relations between governance and instruction. In S. H. Fuhrman (Ed.), *Designing coherent education policy: Improving the system* (pp. 35-88). San Francisco, CA: Jossey-Bass.

Cohen, D. K., & Weiss, J. A. (1977). Science and social policy. *Educational Forum, 41*(4), 393–413.

Cohen, D. K., & Weiss, J. A. (1993). The interplay of social science and prior knowledge in public policy. In H. Redner (Ed.), *Studies in the thought of Charles E. Lindblom.* Boulder, CO: Westview.

Cohen, M. D. (1991). Individual learning and organizational routine: Emerging connections. *Organization Science, 2*(1), 135–139.

Cohen, W. M., & Levinthal, D. A. (1990). Absorptive capacity: A new perspective on learning and innovation. *Administrative Science Quarterly, 35*(1), 128–152.

Cole, M., & Engeström, Y. (1993). A cultural-historical approach to distributed cognition. In G. Salomon (Ed.), *Distributed cognitions: Psychological and educational considerations* (pp. 1–46). Cambridge, England: Cambridge University Press.

Coleman, J. S. (1988). Social capital in the creation of human capital. *American Journal of Sociology, 94* (Suppl.), 95–120.

Coleman, J. S. (1990). *Foundations of social theory.* Cambridge, MA: Harvard University Press.

Collopy, R. (2003). Curriculum materials as a professional development tool: How a mathematics textbook affected two teachers' learning. *Elementary School Journal, 103*(3), 287–311.

Commission for Positive Change in the Oakland Public Schools. (1990). Good education in Oakland: Community agenda for positive change. Oakland, CA: Author.

Consortium for Policy Research in Education. (1998). *States and districts and comprehensive school reform*. CPRE Policy Brief. Philadelphia: University of Pennsylvania Graduate School of Education.

Cook, S. N., & Yanow, D. (1996). Culture and organizational learning. In M. D. Cohen & L. S. Sproull (Eds.), *Organizational learning* (pp. 430–459). Thousand Oaks, CA: Sage.

Covello, L. (1958). *The heart is the teacher*. New York, NY: McGraw-Hill.

Crain, R. L. (1968). *The politics of school desegregation*. Chicago, IL: Aldine Publishing Co.

Crenshaw, K, Gotanada, N., Peller, G., & Thomas, K. (1995). *Critical race theory*. New York, NY: The New Press.

Cronbach, L. J. (1982). *Designing evaluations of educational and social programs*. San Francisco, CA: Jossey-Bass.

Crowson, R. L., & Boyd, W. L. (1993). Coordinated services for children: Designing arks for storms and seas unknown. *American Journal of Education, 101*(2), 140–179.

Cuban, L. (1990). Reforming again, again and again, *Educational Researcher, 19*(1), 3–13.

Cuban, L. (1993). *How teachers taught: Constancy and change in American classrooms, 1880–1990* (2nd ed.). New York, NY: Teachers College Press.

Cuban, L. (1998). How schools change reforms: Redefining reform success and failure. *Teachers College Record, 99*(3), 453–477.

Cuban, L., & Tyack, D. (1995). *Tinkering toward utopia*. Cambridge, MA: Harvard University Press.

Cuban, L., & Usdan, M. (2003). *Powerful reforms with shallow roots*. New York, NY: Teachers College Press.

Cullen, J. B. (2003). The impact of fiscal incentives on student disability rates. *Journal of Public Economics, 87*(7/8), 1557–1589.

Cullen, J. B., & Loeb, S. (2004). School finance reform in Michigan: Evaluating Proposal A. In J. Yinger & W. Duncombe (Eds.), *Helping children left behind: State aid and the pursuit of educational equity* (pp. 215–249). Cambridge, MA: MIT Press.

Cullen, J. B., & Reback, R. (2002). *Tinkering toward accolades: School gaming under a performance accountability system*. Unpublished manuscript, University of Michigan.

Cunningham, L. L., & Mitchell, B. (Eds.). (1990). Educational leadership and changing contexts in families, communities, and schools. *Eighty-ninth yearbook of the National Society for the Study of Education*. Chicago, IL: National Society for the Study of Education.

Czerniak, C. M., & Lumpe, A. T. (1996). Relationship between teacher beliefs and science education reform. *Journal of Science Teacher Education, 7*(4), 247–266.

Cznariawska, B. (1997). *Narrating the organization.* Chicago, IL: University of Chicago Press.

Daft, R., & Becker, S. (1978). *Innovations in organizations.* New York, NY: Elsevier North-Holland.

Dahl, R.A. (1984). *Modern political analysis* (4th ed.). Englewood Cliffs, NJ: Prentice-Hall.

Dahl, R.A., & Stinebrickner, B. (2003). *Modern political analysis* (6th ed.). Upper Saddle River, NJ: Prentice-Hall.

D'Amico, L., & Stein, M. K. (1999). *Observations, conversations, and negotiations: Instructional frameworks as anchors for administrator practice.* Paper presented at the Annual Meeting of the American Educational Research Association, Montreal, Canada.

D'Amico, L., Stein, M. K., & Harwell, M. (2001). *Examining the implementation and effectiveness of a district-wide instructional improvement effort.* Paper presented at the Annual Meeting of the American Educational Research Association, Seattle, WA.

Darling-Hammond, L. (1998). Policy and change: Getting beyond bureaucracy. In A. Hargreaves and A. Lieberman, M. Fullan, & D. Hopkins (Eds.), *International handbook of educational change* (pp. 642–667). Dordrecht, The Netherlands: Kluwer Academic Publishers.

Datnow, A. (2000). Power and politics in the adoption of school reform models. *Educational Evaluation and Policy Analysis, 22*(4), 357–374.

Datnow, A. (2004). Happy marriage or uneasy alliance? The relationship between Comprehensive School Reform (CSR) and state accountability systems. *Journal of Education for Students Placed At Risk, 10(1),* 113–128.

Datnow, A. (2005). The sustainability of comprehensive school reform in changing district and state contexts. *Educational Administration Quarterly, 41*(1), 121–153.

Datnow, A., Borman, G., & Stringfield, S. (2000). School reform through a highly specified curriculum: A study of the implementation and effects of the Core Knowledge Sequence. *The Elementary School Journal, 101*(2), 167–192.

Datnow, A., Borman, G. D., Stringfield, S., Overman, L. T., & Castellano, M. (2003). Comprehensive School reform in culturally and linguistically diverse contexts: Implementation and outcomes from a four-year study. *Educational Evaluation and Policy Analysis, 25*(2), 143–170.

Datnow, A., & Castellano, M. (2000). Teachers' responses to Success for All: How beliefs, experiences, and adaptations shape implementation. *American Educational Research Journal, 37*(3), 775–799.

Datnow, A., & Castellano, M. (2001). Managing and guiding school reform: Leadership in Success for All schools. *Educational Administration Quarterly, 37*(2), 219–249.

Datnow, A., Hubbard, L., & Conchas, G. Q. (2001). How context mediates policy: The implementation of single gender public schooling in California. *Teachers College Record, 103*(2), 184–206.

Datnow, A., Hubbard, L., & Mehan, H. (2002). *Extending educational reform: From one school to many.* London: Routledge Falmer Press.

David, J. L. (1989). Synthesis of research on school-based management. *Educational Leadership, 46*(8), 45–57.

David and Lucile Packard Foundation. (Ed.). (1992). [Special issue]. The Future of Children: School-Linked Services, 2.

Delgado, R., & Stefancic, J. (2000). *Critical race theory: The cutting edge.* Philadelphia, PA: Temple University.

Derthick, M. (1972). *New towns in-town: Why a federal program failed.* Washington, DC: Urban Institute.

Desimone, L. (2000). *Making comprehensive school reform work.* New York, NY: ERIC Clearinghouse on Urban Education.

Desimone, L. (2002). How can comprehensive school reform models be successfully implemented? *Review of Educational Research, 72*(3), 433–479.

Dika, S. L., & Singh, K. (2002). Applications of social capital in educational literature. A critical synthesis. *Review of Educational Research, 72*(1), 31–60.

DiMaggio, P. D., & Power, W. (1991). The iron cage revisited: Institutional isomorphism and collective rationality in organizational fields. In W. W. Powell & P. J. DiMaggio (Eds.), *The new institutionalism in organizational analysis* (63–82). Chicago, IL: University of Chicago Press.

Drake, C., Spillane, J.P., & Hufferd-Ackles, K. (2001). Storied identities: Teacher learning and subject-matter context. *Journal of Curriculum Studies, 33*(1), 1–23.

Dreier, P., Mollenkopf, J. & Swanstrom, T. (2001). *Place matters: Metropolitics for the twenty-first century.* Lawrence, KS: University Press of Kansas.

Driscoll, A. (1990). Exploring the relationship between organizational development and multicultural organizational development. Unpublished manuscript, University of Massachusetts, Amherst, MA.

Dryfoos, J. (1998). *Full-service schools: A revolution in health and social services for children, youth, and families.* San Francisco, CA: Jossey Bass.

Dryfoos, J., Quinn, J., & Barkin, C. (Eds.). (2005). *Community schools in action: Lessons from a decade of practice.* New York, NY: Oxford University Press.

Dweck, C.S. (1999). *Self-theories: Their role in motivation, personality, and development.* Philadelphia: Psychology Press.

Edelman, M. (1964). *The symbolic uses of politics.* Champagne-Urbana, IL: University of Illinois.

Editorial Projects in Education. (2001). A better balance: Standards, tests, and the tools to succeed. *Quality Counts, 20*(17).

Education Commission of the States. (1999). *Comprehensive school reform: Five lessons from the field.* Denver, CO: Author.

Education Week. (2004). Quality Counts, 2004. *Education Week*. Washington, DC: Author.

Edwards, G. (1980). *Implementing public policy*. Washington, DC: Congressional Quarterly Press.

Elementary and Secondary Education Act of 2002, 6301 Part F Comprehensive School Demonstration Program (2002).

Elmore, R. F. (1978). Organizational models of social program implementation. *Public Policy, 26*(2), 185–228.

Elmore, R. F. (1979–1980). Backward mapping: Implementation research and policy decisions. *Political Science Quarterly, 94*(4), 601–616.

Elmore, R. F. (1983). Complexity and control: What legislators and administrators can do about implementing public policy. In L. S. Shulman & G. Sykes (Eds.), *Handbook of Teaching and Policy* (pp. 342–369). New York, NY: Longman.

Elmore, R. F. (1983). Forward and backward mapping: Reversible logic in the analysis of public policy. Paper presented at the International Workshop on Interorganizational Implementation Systems, Rotterdam, The Netherlands.

Elmore, R. F. (1996). Getting to scale with good educational practice. *Harvard Education Review, 66*(1), 1–24.

Elmore, R. F., & Burney, D. (1997). *Investing in teacher learning: Staff development and instructional improvement in Community School District #2*. Philadelphia, PA: Consortium for Policy Research in Education.

Elmore, R. F., & Burney, D. (1999). Investing in teacher learning: Staff development and instructional improvement. In L. Darling-Hammond & G. Sykes (Eds.), *Teaching as the learning profession: Handbook of policy and practice* (pp. 263–291). San Francisco, CA: Jossey-Bass.

Elmore, R. F., & McLaughlin, M. W. (1988). *Steady work*. Santa Monica, CA: RAND.

Elmore, R. F., Peterson, P. L., & McCarthey, S. J. (1996). *Restructuring in the classroom: Teaching, learning, and school organization*. San Francisco, CA: Jossey-Bass.

Elmore, R. F., & Sykes, G. (1992). Curriculum policy. In P. Jackson (Ed.), *Handbook of research on curriculum* (pp. 185–215). New York, NY: Macmillan.

Engeström, Y., & Middleton, D. (1998). *Cognition and communication at work*. Cambridge, England: Cambridge University Press.

Erlichson, B., & Goertz, M. (2001). *Implementing whole school reform in New Jersey: Year two*. New Brunswick, NJ: Department of Public Policy and Center for Government Services, Rutgers, The University of New Jersey.

Erlichson, B., Goertz, M., & Turnbull, B. (1999). *Implementation whole school reform in New Jersey: Year one in the first cohort schools*. New Brunswick, NJ: Department of Public Policy and Center for Government Services, Rutgers, The University of New Jersey.

Family Investment Trust. (1995). The Caring Communities planning resource guide: Putting the pieces together. St. Louis, MO: Author.

Farrar, E., & Milsap, M. A. (1986). *State and local implementation of Chapter I*. Cambridge, MA: ABT Associates.

Feldman, M. S. (1989). *Order without design*. Stanford, CA: Stanford University Press.

Ferguson, R. F. & Ladd, H. F. (1996). How and why money matters: An analysis of Alabama schools. In H. F. Ladd (Ed.), *Holding schools accountable: Performance-based reform in education* (pp. 265–298). Washington, DC: The Brookings Institution.

Figlio, D. N., & Getzler, L. S. (2002). *Accountability, ability, and disability: Gaming the system* (Working Paper No. 9307). Cambridge, MA: National Bureau of Economic Research.

Figlio, D. N., & Winicki, J. (2005). Food for thought: The effects of school accountability plans on school nutrition. *Journal of Public Economics, 89*(2,3), 381–394.

Fine, M. (1994). Dis-stance and other stances: Negotiations of power inside feminist research. In A. Gitlin (Ed.), *Power and method: Political activism and educational research* (pp. 13–35). New York, NY: Routledge.

Fine, M., & Weis, L. (1998). *The unknown city: The lives of poor and working-class young adults*. Boston, MA: Beacon.

Fink, E., & Resnick, L. B. (2001). Developing principals as instructional leaders. *Phi Delta Kappan, 82*(8), 598–606.

Finkelstein, B., Malen, B., Muncey, D., Rice, J. K., Croninger, R. G., & Briggs, L. (2000). *Caught in contradictions: The first two years of a school reconstitution initiative*. College Park, MD: Department of Education Policy and Leadership, University of Maryland, College Park.

Finn, J.D., & Achiles, C.M. (1990). Answers and questions about class size: A statewide experiment. *American Educational Research Journal, 27*(3), 557–577.

Finnigan, K., & O'Day, J. (2003, July). *External support to schools on probation: Getting a leg up?* Philadelphia, PA: Consortium for Policy Research in Education.

Fiol, C. M., & Lyles, M. A. (1985). Organizational learning. *Academy of Management Review, 10*(4), 803–813.

Firestone, W. A. (1989a). Education policy as an ecology of games. *Educational Researcher, 18*(7), 18–24.

Firestone, W. A. (1989b). Using reform: Conceptualizing district initiative. *Educational Evaluation and Policy Analysis, 11*(2), 151–164.

Firestone, W. A., & Donner, W. W. (1981). *Knowledge use in educational development: Tales from a two-way street* (ERIC document 241583).

Firestone, W., Fitz, J., & Broadfoot, P. (1999). Power, learning, and legitimation: Assessment implementation across levels in the United States and the United Kingdom. *American Educational Research Journal, 36*(4), 759–793.

Firestone, W. A., Schorr, R. Y., & Monfils, L. F. (Eds.). (2004). *The ambiguity of teaching to the test*. Hillsdale, NJ: Lawrence Erlbaum Associates.

Fiscal Crisis and Management Assistance Team. (2000). Oakland Unified School District assessment and recovery plans. Sacramento, CA: Author.

Flavell, J. H. (1963). *The developmental psychology of Jean Piaget*. Princeton, NJ: Van Nostrand.

Foley, D. (1986). *Understanding capital*. Cambridge, MA: Harvard University Press.

Foucault, M. (1980). *Power/knowledge: Selected interviews and other writings 1972–1977*. New York, NY: Pantheon.

Foundation Consortium for School-linked Services. (2002). *Pilots to policy: Community systems supporting children to be safe, healthy, and ready for school each day* (Statewide conference proceedings). Sacramento, CA: Author.

Fountas, I. C., & Pinnell, G. S. (1996). *Guided reading: Good first teaching for all children*. Portsmouth, NH: Heinemann.

Franke, M. L., & Kazemi, E. (2001). Teaching as learning within a community of practice: Characterizing generative growth. In T. Wood, B. Nelson, & J. Warfield (Eds.), *Beyond classical pedagogy in teaching elementary mathematics: The nature of facilitative teaching* (pp. 47–74). Mahwah, NJ: Erlbaum Associates.

Freeman, D. (1993). Renaming experience/reconstructing practice: Developing new understandings of teaching. *Teacher & Teacher Education, 9*(5/6), 485–497.

Freeman, D. (1996). "To take them at their word": Language data in the study of teachers' knowledge. *Harvard Educational Review, 66*(4), 732–761.

Fuhrman, S. H. (1989). State politics and education reform (pp. 61–75). In J. Hannway & R. Crowson (Eds.) *The politics of reforming school administration: The 1988 yearbook of the Politics of Education Association Yearbook*. New York, NY: Falmer Press.

Fuhrman, S. H. (2001). *From the capital to the classroom: Standards-based reform in the states*. Chicago, IL: University of Chicago Press.

Fuhrman, S. H., Clune, W., & Elmore, R. F. (1988). Research on education reform: Lessons on the implementation of policy. *Teachers College Record, 90*(2), 237–258.

Fuhrman, S. H. (1993). The politics of coherence (pp. 1–34). In S. H. Fuhrman, (Ed.) *Designing coherent education policy: Improving the system*. San Francisco, CA: Jossey-Bass.

Fuhrman, S. H., & Elmore, R. F. (1990). Understanding local control in the wake of state education reform. *Educational Evaluation and Policy Analysis, 12*(1), 82–96.

Fullan, M. (2001a). *The new meaning of educational change* (3rd ed.). New York, NY: Teachers College Press.

Fullan, M. (2001b). *Whole school reform: Problems and promises*. Paper commissioned by the Chicago Community Trust. Toronto: Ontario Institute for Studies in Education, Canada.

Fullan, M. G. (1991). *The new meaning of educational change* (2nd ed.). New York, NY: Teachers College Press.

Gagliardi, P. (1990). Artifacts as pathways and remains of organizational life. In P. Gagliardi (Ed.), *Symbols and artifacts: Views of the corporate landscape* (pp. 3–38). Berlin, Germany: Walter de Gruyter.

Gallucci, C. (2003). Communities of practice and the mediation of teachers' responses to standards-based reform. *Education Policy Analysis Archives, 11*(35). Retrieved September 29, 2003 from http://epaa.asu.edu/epaa/v11n35.

Gammon, R. (2000, January 20). County says schools are over budget. *Oakland Tribune.* Retrieved January 20, 2000, from www.newschoice.com.

Gaventa, J. (1980). *Power and powerlessness.* Oxford, UK: Clarendon.

Geary, L. S. (1992). *Review of literature [on the meaning and measurement of power], in the policymaking process resulting in fiscal policy for special education in Utah.* Unpublished doctoral dissertation, University of Utah.

Gee, J. P. (1999). *An introduction to discourse analysis: Theory and method.* New York, NY: Routledge.

Geertz, C. (1973). *The interpretation of cultures: Selected essays.* New York, NY: Basic Books.

Gentner, D., Rattermann, M. J., & Forbus, K. D. (1994). The roles of similarity in transfer: Separating retrievability from inferential soundness. *Cognitive Psychology, 5*(25), 524–575.

Gentner, D. G., & Stevens, A. L. (Eds.) (1983). *Mental models.* Hillsdale, NY: Lawrence Erlbaum.

Gilman, D.A, & Kiger, S. (2003). Should we try to keep class sizes small? *Educational Leadership 60*(7), 80–85.

Giroux, H. A., Lankshear, C., McLaren, P., & Peters, M. (1997). *Counternarratives: Cultural studies and critical pedagogies in postmodern spaces.* New York, NY: Routledge.

Gladstein, D., & Caldwell, D. (1985). Boundary management in new product teams. Best Paper Proceedings of the National Academy of Management Meetings, San Diego, CA.

Glaser, B., & Strauss, A. (1967). *The discovery of grounded theory: Strategies for qualitative research.* Chicago, IL: Aldine.

Glewwe, P., Ilias, N., & Kremer, M. (2003). *Teacher incentives* (Working Paper No. 9671). Cambridge, MA: National Bureau of Economic Research.

Goddard, R. D. (2003). Relational networks, social trust, and norms: A social capital perspective on students' chances of academic success. *Educational Evaluation and Policy Analysis, 25*(1), 59–74.

Goggin, M. Bowman, A. O., Lester, J., & O'Toole, L. (1990). *Implementation theory and practice: Toward a third generation.* New York, NY: Harper Collins.

Gottlieb, R.S. (1992). *Marxism.* New York, NY: Routledge.

Granovetter, M. S. (1973). The strength of weak ties. *American Journal of Sociology, 78*(6), 1360-1380.

Grant, S. G. (1996). *Reforming reading, writing, and mathematics: Teachers' responses and the prospects for systemic reform.* New York, NY: Teachers College Press.

Greeno, J. G. (1989a). Situations, mental models, and generative knowledge. In D. Klahr & K. Kotovsky (Eds.), *Complex information processing: The impact of Herbert A. Simon* (pp. 285–318). Hillsdale, NJ: Lawrence Erlbaum.

Greeno, J. G. (1998b). The situativity of knowing, learning, and research. *American Psychologist, 53*(1), 5–26.

Greeno, J. G., Collins, A. M., & Resnick, L. B. (1996). Cognition and learning. In D. C. Berliner & R. C. Calfee (Eds.), *Handbook of Educational Psychology* (pp. 15–46). New York, NY: Macmillian Library Reference USA, Prentice Hall International.

Gresson, A.D. (1995). *The recovery of race in America.* Minneapolis, MN: University of Minnesota Press.

Gross, N., Gaicquinta, J., & Bernstein, M. (1971). *Implementing organizational innovations: A sociological analysis of planned educational change.* New York, NY: Basic Books.

Gubrium, J. B., & Holstein, J. A. (2000). Analyzing interpretive practice. In N. K. Denzin & Y. S. Lincoln (Eds.), *Handbook of qualitative research* (2nd ed., pp. 487–508). Thousand Oaks, CA: Sage.

Guthrie, J. W. (Ed.) (1990). *Educational Evaluation and Policy Analysis, 12*(3).

Hall, G., & Loucks, S. (1976). *A developmental model for determining whether or not the treatment really is implemented.* Austin, TX: Research and Development Center for Teacher Education, University of Texas.

Hall, P. M., & McGinty P. J. W. (1997). Policy as the transformation of intentions: Producing programs from statute. *Sociological Quarterly, 38*(3), 439–467.

Hall, P. M., & Placier, P. (2003). The Coalition of Essential Schools: Leadership for putting the Common Principles into practice. In J. Murphy & A. Datnow (Eds.), *Leadership lessons from comprehensive school reforms* (pp. 209–238). Thousand Oaks, CA: Corwin Press.

Hall, S. (1996). Gramsci's relevance for the study of race and ethnicity. In D. Morley & K. Chen (Eds.), *Stuart Hall* (pp. 411–440). New York, NY: Routledge.

Hallet, A., Chapman, W., & Ayers, W. (1995). *The Annenberg Challenge: Good schools for a great city.* Unpublished paper distributed at the press conference to announce the establishment of the Chicago Annenberg Challenge.

Hamann, E., & Lane, B. (2004). The Roles of State Departments of Education as Policy Intermediaries: Two Cases. *Educational Policy, 18*(3), 426–455.

Hammer, D., & Elby, A. (2002). On the form of a personal epistemology. In B. K. Hofer & P. R. Pintrich (Eds.), *Personal epistemology: The psychology of beliefs about knowledge and knowing* (pp. 169–190). Mahwah, NJ: Lawrence Erlbaum.

Hanks, W. F. (1991). Foreword. In J. Lave & E. Wenger (Eds.), *Situated learning: Legitimate peripheral participation* (pp. 13–24). Cambridge, England: Cambridge University Press.

Hannaway, J. (1989). *Managers managing: The workings of an administrative system.* New York, NY: Oxford University Press.

Hannaway, J. (1992). Higher-order thinking, job design, and incentives: An analysis and proposal. *American Educational Research Journal, 29*(Spring), 3–21.

Hanushek, E. A. (1986). The Economics of schooling: Production and efficiency in public schools. *Journal of Economic Literature, 49*(3), 1141–1177.

Hanushek, E. A. (1997). Assessing the effects of school resources on student performance: An update. *Educational Evaluation and Policy Analysis, 19*(2), 141–164.

Hanushek, E. A. (1999). Some findings from an independent investigation of the Tennessee STAR experiment and from other investigations of class size effects. *Educational Evaluation and Policy Analysis, 21*(2), 143–163.

Hanushek, E. A., Kain, J. F., & Rivkin, S. G. (2004). Why public schools lose teachers. *Journal of Human Resources, 39*(2), 326–354.

Hanushek, E. A., & Raymond, M. E. (2002). Improving educational quality: How best to evaluate our schools? (pp. 193–247). In Y. K. Kodrzycki (Ed.), *Education in the twenty-first century.* Boston, MA: Federal Reserve Bank of Boston.

Hargrove, E. C. (1985). *The missing link.* Washington, DC: Urban Institute.

Hargrove, E. C., Graham, S. G., Ward, L. E., Abernethy, V., Cunningham, J., & Vaughn, W. K. (1983). Regulation and schools: The implementation of equal education for handicapped children. *Peabody Journal of Education, 40*(4), 1–126.

Hartley, J. F. (1994). Case studies in organizational research. In C. Cassell & G. Simons (Eds.), *Qualitative methods in organizational research: A practical guide* (pp. 209–229). Thousand Oaks, CA: Sage.

Harvard Business Review. (1998). *Harvard Business Review on Knowledge Management.* Cambridge, MA: Author.

Harwell, M., D'Amico, L., Stein, M. K., & Gatti, G. (1999). *Professional development and the achievement gap in Community School District #2.* Unpublished manuscript, High Performance Learning Communities Project, University of Pittsburgh.

Hatch, T. (2002). When improvement programs collide. *Phi Delta Kappan, 83*(8), 626–639.

Hatch, T. (in press). The role of foundation support in building the capacity for school improvement. In R. Bacchetti & T. Ehrlich (Eds.) *Foundations and education.* San Francisco, CA: Jossey-Bass.

Haug, C. (1999). Local understanding, resources, and policies: Obstacles to standards-based mathematics education reform. Unpublished doctoral dissertation, University of Colorado, Boulder.

Haymes, S. N. (1995). *Race, culture, and the city: A pedagogy for black urban struggle.* Albany, NY: State University of New York Press.

Henderson, A. T., & Mapp, K. L. (2002). A new wave of evidence: The impact of family, school and community connections on student achievement. Austin, TX: Southwest Educational Development Laboratory.

Henig, J. R., Hula, R. C., Orr, M., & Pedescleaux, D. S. (1999). *The color of school reform: Race, politics and the challenge of urban education.* Princeton, NJ: Princeton University.

Henig, J. R., & Rich, W. C. (2004). *Mayors in the middle.* Princeton, NJ: Princeton University Press.

Herman, R., Aladjem, D., McMahon, P., Masem, E., Mulligan, I., O'Malley, A., Quinones, S., Reeve, A. and Woodruff, D. (1999). *An educators' guide to schoolwide reform.* Washington, DC: American Institutes for Research.

Herrington, C. D. (1994). Schools as intergovernmental partners: Administrator perceptions of expanded programming for children. *Educational Administration Quarterly, 30*(3), 301–323.

Hess, F. M. (1999). *Spinning wheels: The politics of urban school reform.* Washington, DC: Brookings Institute.

Hess, F. M. (2002). I say "refining" you say "retreating": The politics of high-stakes accountability, *Taking Account of Accountability: Assessing Politics and Policy.* Cambridge, MA: Harvard Program on Education Policy and Governance.

Higgins, E. T. (1996). Knowledge activation: Accessibility, applicability, and salience. In E. T. Higgins and A. W. Kruglanski (Eds.), *Social psychology: Handbook of basic principles* (pp. 133–168). New York, NY: Guildford Press.

High Performance Learning Communities Project. (2001). *Final Report.* Pittsburgh, PA: University of Pittsburgh.

Hightower, A. M., Knapp, M. S., Marsh, J. A., & McLaughlin, M. W. (Eds.). (2002). *School districts and instructional renewal.* New York, NY: Teachers College Press.

Hill, H. C. (2000). *Implementation networks: Non-state resources for getting policy done.* Unpublished doctoral dissertation, University of Michigan, Ann Arbor.

Hill, H. C. (2001). Policy is not enough: Language and the interpretation of state standards. *American Educational Research Journal, 38*(2), 289–318.

Hill, H. C. (2005). Content across communities: Validating measures of elementary mathematics instruction. *Educational Policy, 19*(3), 447–475.

Hill, M., & Hupe, P. (2002). *Implementing public policy: Governance in theory and practice.* London: Sage Publications.

Hill, P., Campbell, C., & Harvey, J. (2000). *It takes a city: Getting serious about urban school reform.* Washington, D.C.: Brookings Institution Press.

Hill, P. T., & Celio, M. B. (1998). *Fixing urban schools.* Washington, DC: Brookings Institution Press.

Holmstrom, B., & Milgrom, P. (1991). Multi-task principal-agent analysis: Incentive contracts, asset ownership, and job design. *Journal of Law, Economics and Organization* (7), 24–52.

Holyoke, T., & Henig, J. (2001, September). Shopping in the public arena: Venue selection and the advocacy behavior of charter schools. Paper presented at the Annual Meeting of the American Political Science Association, San Francisco, CA.

Honig, M. I. (2001). Managing ambiguity: The implementation of complex education policy. Unpublished doctoral dissertation, Stanford University.

Honig, M. I. (2003). Building policy from practice: District central office administrators' roles and capacity for implementing collaborative education policy. *Educational Administration Quarterly, 39*(3), 292–338.

Honig, M. I. (2004a). Where's the "up" in bottom-up reform? *Education Policy, 18*(4), 527–561.

Honig, M. I. (2004b). The new middle management: Intermediary organizations in education policy implementation. *Educational Evaluation and Policy Analysis, 26*(1), 65–87.

Honig, M. I., & Hatch, T. (2004). Crafting coherence: How schools strategically manage multiple external demands. *Educational Researcher, 33*(8), 16–30.

Honig, M. I., & Jehl, J. D. (2000). Enhancing federal support for connecting educational improvement strategies and collaborative services. In M. C. Wang & W. L. Boyd (Eds.), *Improving results for children and families: Linking collaborative services with school reform efforts* (pp. 175–198). Greenwich, CT: Information Age.

Honig, M. I., Kahne, J., & McLaughlin, M. W. (2001). School-community connections: Strengthening opportunity to learn and opportunity to teach. In V. Richardson (Ed.), *Handbook of Research on Teaching* (4th ed., pp. 998–1028). Washington, D.C.: American Educational Research Association.

House, E. R. (1974). *The politics of innovation.* Berkeley, CA: McCutchan.

Hsieh, C. T., & Urquiola, M. (2003). *When schools compete, how do they compete? An assessment of Chile's nationwide school voucher program* (Working Paper 10008). Cambridge, MA: National Bureau of Economic Research.

Huber, G. P. (1991). Organizational learning: The contributing processes and the literatures. *Organization Science, 2*(1), 88–115.

Hutchins, E. (1995a). *Cognition in the wild.* Cambridge, MA: The MIT Press.

Hutchins, E. (1995b). How a cockpit remembers its speeds. *Cognitive Science, 19*(3), 265–288.

Illig, D. C. (1997). *Reducing class size: A review of the literature and options for consideration.* Sacramento, CA: California State Library, Sacramento; California Research Bureau.

Ingram, H. (1977). Policy implementation through bargaining: The case of federal grants-in-aid. *Public Policy 25*(4), 499–526.

Jackson, P. W. (1968). *Life in classrooms.* New York, NY: Holt, Rinehart and Winston.

Jacob, B. A. (2002). *Accountability, incentives, and behavior: The impact of high-stakes testing in the Chicago Public Schools* (Working Paper 8968). Cambridge, MA: National Bureau of Economic Research.

Jacob, B. A., & Levitt, S. D. (2003). Rotten apples: An investigation of the prevalence and predictors of teacher cheating. *Quarterly Journal of Economics, 118*(3), 843–878.

Jehl, J., & Kirst, M. (1992). Getting ready to provide school-linked services: What schools must do. *Future of Children, 2*(1), 95–106.

Jennings, N. (1992). Teachers learning from policy: Cases from the Michigan reading reform. Unpublished doctoral dissertation, Michigan State University.

Jennings, N. E. (1996). *Interpreting policy in real classrooms: Case studies of state reform and teacher practice.* New York, NY: Teachers College Press.

Jones, D. R., & Malen, B. (2002). Sources of victory, seeds of defeat: Linking enactment politics and implementation developments. In W. Hoy & C. Miskel (Eds.) *Theory and research in educational administration* (pp. 41–76). Greenwich, CT: Information Age Publishing, Inc.

Jung, R. K., & Kirst, M. W. (1986). Beyond mutual adaptation into the bully pulpit: Recent research on the federal role in education. *Educational Administration Quarterly, 22*(3), 80–109.

Kanter, R. M. (1983). *The change masters.* New York, NY: Simon and Schuster.

Kanter, R. M. (1988). When a thousand flowers bloom: Structural, collective, and social conditions for innovation in organization. *Research in Organizational Behavior, 10*, 169–211.

Kanter, R. M., Stein, B. A., & Jick, T. D. (1992). *The challenge of organizational change.* New York, NY: The Free Press.

Kantor, H., & Brenzel, B. (1993). Urban education and the truly disadvantaged: The historical roots of the contemporary crisis, 1945–1990. In M. B. Katz (Ed.). *The underclass debate: Views from history* (pp. 366–402). Princeton, NJ: Princeton University Press.

Katz, M. B., Fine, M., & Simon, E. (1997). Poking around: Outsiders view Chicago school reform. *Teachers College Record, 99*(1), 117–157.

Kazemi, E., & Stipek, D. (2001). Promoting conceptual thinking in four upper-elementary mathematics classrooms. *The Elementary School Journal, 102*(1), 59–80.

Keil, F. (1989). *Concepts, kinds and cognitive development.* Cambridge, MA: MIT Press.

Keisler, S., & Sproull, L. (1982). Managerial response to changing. *Administrative Science Quarterly, 27*(4), 548–570.

Kelley, R. D. G. (1997). *Yo mama's disfunktional.* Boston, MA: Beacon.

Kellner, D. (1989). *Critical theory, Marxism, and modernity.* Baltimore, MD: Johns Hopkins University Press.

Kemp, E. K., Tzou, C. T., Reiser, B. J., & Spillane, J. P. (2002). Managing dilemmas in inquiry science teaching. In P. Bell, R. Stevens & T. Satwicz (Eds.), *Keeping learning complex: The proceedings of the Fifth International Conference of the Learning Sciences (ICLS)* (pp. 206–213). Mahwah, NJ: Erlbaum.

Kentucky State Board for Elementary and Secondary Education. (1994). *Planning for progress: The Kentucky Education Reform Act, 1994–95* (Strategic plan summary). Lexington, KY: Author.

Kerr, P. (1991, January 8). Democrats urge big shift in Florio plan. *New York Times,* p. B1.

Kimberly, J. R. (1981). Managerial innovation. In P. C. Nystrom & W.H. Starbuck (Eds.), *Handbook of organizational design: Adapting organizations to their environments* (Vol. 1, pp. 84–100). Oxford, UK: Oxford University Press.

Kincheloe, J. L., & McLaren, P. (2000). Rethinking critical theory and qualitative research. In N. K. Denzin & Y. S. Lincoln (Eds.), *Handbook of qualitative research* (2nd ed., pp. 279–313). Thousand Oaks, CA: Sage.

Kincheloe, J. L., Steinberg, S., Rodriguez, N. M., & Chennault, R. E., (Eds.). (2000). *White reign.* New York, NY: St. Martin's.

Kingdon, J. W. (1995). *Agendas, alternatives and public policies* (2nd ed.). New York, NY: Harper Collins.

Kirst, M., & Bulkley, K. (2000). "New, improved" mayors take over city schools. *Phi Delta Kappan, 81*(7), 538–546.

Kirst, M., & Jung, R. (1980). The utility of a longitudinal approach in assessing implementation. *Educational Evaluation and Policy Analysis, 2*(5), 17–34.

Klayman, J., & Ha, Y. W. (1987). Confirmation, disconfirmation, and information in hypothesis testing. *Psychological Review, 94*(2), 211–228.

Knapp, M. S. (1995). How shall we study comprehensive, collaborative services for children and families? *Educational Researcher, 24*(4), 5–16.

Knapp, M. S. (1997). Between systemic reforms and the mathematics and science classroom: The dynamics of innovation, implementation, and professional learning. *Review of Educational Research, 67*(2), 227–266.

Knapp, M. S., Bamburg, J. D., Ferguson, M. C., & Hill, P. T. (1998). Converging reforms and the working lives of frontline professionals in schools. *Educational Policy, 12*(4), 397–418.

Knapp, M. S., Stearns, M. S., Turnbull, B. J., David, J. L., & Peterson, S. J. (1991). Cumulative effects of federal education policies at the local level. In A. R. Odden (Ed.), *Educational Policy Implementation* (pp. 105–124). Albany, NY: SUNY Press.

Kolodner, J. L. (1983). Maintaining organization in a dynamic long-term memory. *Cognitive Science, 7*(4), 243–280.

Kreps, D. M. (1990). *A course in microeconomic theory.* Princeton, NJ: Princeton University Press.

Kronley, R. A., & Handley, C. (2003, April). *Reforming relationships: School districts, external organizations, and systemic change.* Providence, RI: Brown University, Annenberg Institute for School Reform.

Krueger, A. B. (1999). Experimental estimates of education production functions. *Quarterly Journal of Economics, 114*(2), 497–532.

Kruse, S. D., Louis, K. S., & Bryk, A. (1995). An emerging framework for analyzing school professional community. In K. S. Louis & S. D. Kruse (Eds.), *Professionalism and community: Perspectives on reforming schools* (pp. 23–44). Thousand Oaks, CA: Corwin Press.

Kunda, Z., & Thagard, P. (1996). Forming impressions from stereotypes, traits, and behaviors: A parallel-constraint-satisfaction theory. *Psychological Review, 103*(2), 284–308.

Ladson-Billings, G. (1998). Just what is critical race theory and what's it doing in a nice field like education? *Qualitative Studies in Education, 11*(1), 7–24.

Ladson-Billings, G. (1999). Preparing teachers for diversity: Historical perspectives, current trends, and future directions. In L. Darling-Hammond & G. Sykes (Eds.), *Teaching as the learning profession: Handbook of policy and practice* (1st ed., pp. 86–123). San Francisco, CA: Jossey Bass.

Lampert, M. (1999). Studying teaching as a thinking practice. In J. Greeno and S. G. Goldman (Eds.), *Thinking practices* (pp. 53–78). Hillsdale, NJ: Lawrence Erlbaum and Associates.

Lankford, H., Loeb, S., & Wyckoff, J. (2001). Teacher sorting and the plight of urban schools: A descriptive analysis. *Education Evaluation and Policy Analysis, 24*(1), 37–62.

Larkin, J. H., McDermott, J., Simon, D., & Simon, H. A. (1980). Expert and novice performance in solving physics problems. *Science, 208*(20), 1335–1342.

Latour, B. (1987). *Science in Action.* Cambridge, MA: Harvard University Press.

Lave, J. (1993). Situated learning in communities of practice. In L. Resnick, J. Levine, & T. Teasley (Eds.), *Perspectives in socially shared cognition* (pp. 63–82). Washington, DC: American Psychological Association.

Lave, J., & Wenger, E. (1991). *Situated learning: Legitimate peripheral participation.* Cambridge, England: Cambridge University Press.

Lavy, V. (2002). Evaluating the effect of teachers' group performance incentives on pupil achievement. *Journal of Political Economy, 110*(6), 1286–1317.

Lee, V. E., & Bryk, A. S. (1986). Effects of single-sex secondary schools on student achievement and attitudes. *Journal of Educational Psychology, 78*(5), 381–395.

Lee, V. E., & Smith, J. (1995). Effects of high school restructuring and size on gains in achievement and engagement for early secondary students. *Sociology of Education, 68*(4), 241–270.

Lee, V. E., & Smith, J. B. (1996). Collective responsibility for learning and its effects on gains in achievement for early secondary school students. *American Journal of Education, 104*(2), 103–147.

Leithwood, K., Aitken, R., & Jantzi, D. (2001). *Making schools smarter: A system for monitoring school and district progress* (2nd ed.). Thousand Oaks, CA: Corwin Press.

Leithwood, K., Jantzi, D., & Steinbach, R. (1995, April). *An organizational learning perspective on school responses to central policy initiatives.* Paper presented at the Annual Meeting of the American Educational Research Association, San Francisco, CA.

Leithwood, K., Leonard, L., & Sharratt, L. (1998). Conditions fostering organizational learning in schools. *Educational Administration Quarterly, 34*(2), 243–276.

Leithwood, K., & Louis, K. S. (Eds.). (1998). *Organizational learning in schools.* Lisse, The Netherlands: Swets & Zeitlinger.

Lemke, J. L. (1995). *Textual politics: Discourse and social dynamics.* Bristol, PA: Taylor & Francis.

Lennon, M. C., & Corbett, T. (Eds.). (2003). *Policy into action: Implementation research and welfare reform.* Washington, DC: The Urban Institute Press.

Leont'ev, A. N. (1981). The problem of activity in psychology. In Wertsch, J. V. (Ed.), *The concept of activity in soviet psychology* (pp. 37–71). Armonk, NY: M. E. Sharpe.

Levin, B. (2001). *Reforming education: From origins to outcomes.* New York, NY: Routledge Falmer.

Levin, H. M. (1991). The economics of educational choice. *Economics of Education Review, 10*(2), 137–158.

Levin, H. M. (2002). *The potential of for-profit schools for education reform* (Occasional Paper No. 47). New York, NY: National Center for the Study of Privatization in Education, Teachers College.

Levin, J., & Quinn, M. (2003). *Missed opportunities: How we keep high-quality teachers out of urban schools.* Boston, MA: The New Teacher Project.

Levinthal, D., & March, J. G. (1981). A model of adaptive organizational search. *Journal of Economic Behavior and Organization, 2*(4), 307–333.

Levitt, B., & March, J. G. (1988). Organizational learning. *American Review of Sociology, 14,* 319–340.

Levy, J. E., & Shepardson, W. (1992). A look at current school-linked service efforts. *Future of children: School-linked services, 2*(1), 44–55.

Lewis, D., & Maruna, S. (1998). Person-centered policy analysis. *Research in Public Policy Analysis and Management, 9,* 213–230.

Lieberman, A., & Grolnick, M. (1996). Networks and reform in American education. *Teachers College Record, 98*(1), 7–45.

Lieberman, A., & McLaughlin, M. W. (1992). Networks for educational change: Powerful and problematic. *Phi Delta Kappan, 73*(9), 673–677.

Lieberman, A., & Wood, D. (2001). When teachers write: Of networks and learning. In A. Lieberman & L. Miller (Eds.), *Teachers caught in the action: Professional development that matters* (pp. 174–187). New York, NY: Teachers College Press.

Lin, A. (1998). *To cope is also to act: Understanding variation across street-level bureaucracies.* Unpublished manuscript.

Lin, A. C. (2000). *Reform in the making: The implementation of social policy in prison.* Princeton, NJ: Princeton University Press.

Lipman, P. (2004). *High stakes education: Inequality, globalization and urban school reform.* New York, NY: Routledge Falmer.

Lipsky, M. (1980). *Street-level bureaucracy.* New York, NY: Russell Sage Foundation.

Little, J. (1993). Professional community in comprehensive high schools: The two worlds of academic and vocational teachers. In J. Little & M. W. McLaughlin (Eds.), *Teachers' work* (pp. 137–163). New York, NY: Teachers College Press.

Little, J. W. (1982). Norms of collegiality and experimentation: Workplace conditions of school success. *American Educational Research Journal, 19*(3), 325–340.

Little, J. W. (1984). Seductive images and organizational realities in professional development. *Phi Delta Kappan, 73*(9), 673–677.

Little, J. W. (1990). Conditions of professional development in secondary schools. In M. W. McLaughlin, J. E. Talbert, & N. Bascia (Eds.), *The contexts of teaching in secondary schools* (pp. 187–223). New York, NY: Teachers College Press.

Little, J. W. (2002). Locating learning in teachers' communities of practice: Opening up problems of analysis in records of everyday work. *Teachers and teaching: Theory and practice, 8*(3), 345–354.

Little, J. W. (2003). Inside teacher community: Representations of classroom practice. *Teachers College Record, 105*(6), 913–945.

Loeb, S., Darling-Hammond, L., & Luczak, J. (2005). How teaching conditions predict teacher turnover in California schools. *Peabody Journal of Education, 80*(3), 44–70.

Lortie, D. C. (1975). *Schoolteacher.* Chicago, IL: University of Chicago Press.

Louis, K. S. (1994a). Beyond "managed change": Rethinking how schools improve. *School Effectiveness and School Improvement, 5*(1), 2-24.

Louis, K. S. (1994b). Improving urban and disadvantaged schools: Dissemination and utilization perspectives. *Knowledge and Policy, 7*(4), 34–54.

Louis, K. S. (1998). Reconnecting knowledge utilization and school improvement: Two steps forward, one step back. In A. Hargreaves, A. Lieberman, M. Fullan, & D. Hopkins (Eds.), *International handbook of educational change, Part 2* (pp. 1074–1095). Dordrecht, The Netherlands: Kluwer Academic.

Louis, K. S., & Kruse, S. D. (1995). *Professionalism and community: Perspectives on reforming urban schools.* Thousand Oaks, CA: Corwin.

Louis, K. S., & Marks, H. M. (1998). Does professional community affect the classroom? Teachers' work and student experiences in restructuring schools. *American Journal of Education, 106*(4), 532–575.

Louis, K. S., Marks, H. M., & Kruse, S. (1996). Teachers' professional community in restructuring schools. *American Education Research Journal, 33*(4), 757–798.

Lusi, S. F. (1997). *The role of state departments of education in complex school reform.* New York, NY: Teachers College Press.

Lowi, T. (1969). *The end of liberalism.* New York, NY: Norton.

Lowi, T. (1972). Four systems of policy, politics and choice. *Public Administration Review, 11*(X), 298–310.

Madsen, J. (1994). *Educational reform at the state level: The politics and problems of implementation.* Washington, DC: Falmer Press.

Majone, G. (1989). *Evidence, argument, and persuasion in the policy process.* New Haven, CT: Yale University Press.

Malen, B. (1994). Site-based management: A political utilities analysis. *Education Evaluation and Policy Analysis, 16*(3), 249–267.

Malen, B., & Hart, A. W. (1987). Career ladder reform: A multi-level analysis of initial effects. *Educational Evaluation and Policy Analysis, 9*(1), 9–24.

Malen, B., & Muncey, D. (2000). Creating "a new set of givens"? The impact of state activism on site autonomy. In N. D. Theobald & B. Malen (Eds). *Balancing local control and state responsibility for K–12 education* (pp. 199–244). Larchmont, NY: Eye on Education.

Malen, B., & Ogawa, R. T. (1988). Professional-patron influence on site-based governance councils: A confounding case study. *Educational Evaluation and Policy Analysis, 10*(4), 251–270.

Malen, B., Ogawa, R., & Kranz, K. (1990). What do we know about school based management? A case study of the literature—A call for research. In W. Clune & J. Witte (Eds.), *Choice and control in American education, Volume 2: Decentralization and school restructuring* (pp. 289–342). Philadelphia, PA: Falmer Press.

Malen, B., & Rice, J. K. (2004). A framework for assessing the impact of education reforms on school capacity: Insights from studies of high stakes accountability initiatives. *Educational Policy, 18*(5), 631–660.

Mandler, J. (1984). *Stories, scripts, and scenes: Aspects of schema theory.* Hillsdale, NJ: Lawrence Erlbaum.

March, J. G. (1991). How decisions happen in organizations. *Human-computer interaction, 6*(1), 95–117.

March, J. G. (1994a). *A primer on decision making.* New York, NY: Free Press.

March, J. G. (1994b). *Three lectures on efficiency and adaptiveness in organizations.* Helsinki, Finland: Swedish School of Economics and Business Administration.

March, J. G., & Olsen, J. P. (1975). The uncertainty of the past: Organizational learning under ambiguity. *European Journal of Political Research, 3*, 147–171.

March, J. G., & Olsen, J. P. (1976). *Ambiguity and choice in organizations.* Bergen, Norway: Universitetsforlaget.

March, J. G., & Olsen, J. (1989). *Rediscovering institutions: The organizational basis of politics.* New York, NY: The Free Press.

March, J. G., & Shapira, Z. (1987). Managerial perspectives on risk and risk taking. *Management Science, 33*(11), 1404–1418.

Marks, H. M., Louis, K. S., & Printy, S. M. (2000). The capacity for organizational learning: Implications for pedagogical quality and student achievement. In K. Leithwood (Ed.), *Understanding schools as intelligent systems* (pp. 239–265). Stamford, CT: JAI.

Marks, H. M., & Printy, S. M. (2002). Organizational learning in high-stakes accountability environments: Lessons from an urban school district. In W. Hoy & C. Miskel (Eds.), *Theory and research in educational administration* (Vol. 1, pp. 1–40). Greenwich, CT: Information Age.

Markus, H. R. (1977). Self-schemata and processing information about the self. *Journal of Personality and Social Psychology, 35*(2), 63–78.

Markus, H., & Zajonc, R. B. (1985). The cognitive perspective on social psychology. In G. Lindzey & E. Aronson (Eds.), *Handbook of social psychology* (pp. 137–230). New York, NY: Random House.

Marsh, D. D., & Crocker, P. S. (1991). School restructuring: Implementing middle school reform. In A. R. Odden (Ed.), *Education Policy Implementation* (pp. 259–278). Albany, NY: State University of New York Press.

Marsh, J. A. (2002). Democratic dilemmas: Joint work, education politics and community. Unpublished doctoral dissertation, Stanford University.

Massell, D. (2001). The theory and practice of using data to build capacity: State and local strategies and their effects. In S. H. Fuhrman (Ed.), *From the capitol to the classroom: Standards-based reform in the states. One hundredth yearbook of the National Society for the Study of Education* (pp. 148–169). Chicago, IL: National Society for the Study of Education.

Massell, D., & Goertz, M. E. (2002). District strategies for building instructional capacity. In A. M. Hightower, M. S. Knapp, J. A. Marsh, & M. W. McLaughlin (Eds.), *School districts and instructional renewal* (pp. 43–60). New York, NY: Teachers College Press.

Massey, D. S., & Denton, N. A. (1993). *American apartheid: Segregation and the making of the underclass.* Cambridge, MA: Harvard University Press.

Mathematica & Decision Information Resources (2005). *When schools stay open late: The national evaluation of the 21st Century Community Learning Centers Program.* Washington, DC: Authors.

Matland, R. E. (1995). Synthesizing the implementation literature: The ambiguity-conflict model of policy implementation. *Journal of Public Administration Research and Theory, 5*(2), 145–174.

Mawhinney, H. B., & Smrekar, C. (1996). Institutional constraints to advocacy in collaborative services. *Educational Policy, 10*(4), 480–501.

Mayer, D. (1999). Measuring instructional practice: Can policymakers trust survey data? *Educational Evaluation and Policy Analysis, 21*(1), 29–46.

Mazmanian, D. A., & Sabatier, P. A. (1983). *Implementation and public policy.* Glenview, IL: Scott, Foresman and Company.

Mazmanian, D. A., & Sabatier, P. A. (1989). *Implementation and public policy.* New York, NY: University Press of America.

Mazzoni, T. L. (1987). The politics of educational choice in Minnesota. In W. L. Boyd & C. T. Kerchner (Eds.), *The politics of excellence and choice in education* (pp. 217–230). London: Falmer Press.

Mazzoni, T. L. (1991). Analyzing state school policymaking: An arena model. *Educational evaluation and policy analysis, 13*(2), 115–138.

McCorry, J. J. (1978). *Marcus Foster and the Oakland Public Schools: Leadership in an urban bureaucracy.* Berkeley, CA: University of California Press.

McDonnell, L. M., & Elmore, R. F. (1987). Getting the job done: Alternative policy instruments. *Educational Evaluation and Policy Analysis, 9*(2), 133–152.

McDonnell, L. M., & Elmore, R. F. (1991). Getting the job done: Alternative policy instruments. In A. R. Odden (Ed.), *Educational policy implementation* (pp. 157–184). Albany, NY: State University of New York Press.

McDonnell, L. M., & McLaughlin, M. W. (1982). *Education policy and the role of the states.* Santa Monica, CA: The Rand Corporation.

McDonnell, L. M., & Weatherford, M.S. (2000). Seeking a new politics of education. In L. M. McDonnell, P. M. Timpane, & R. Benjamin (Eds.), *Rediscovering the democratic purposes of education* (pp. 174–206). Lawrence, KS: University Press of Kansas.

McEwan, P. J. (2000). The potential impact of large-scale voucher programs. *Review of Educational Research, 70*(2), 103–149.

McEwan, P. J., & Santibañez, L. (2004). *Teachers' (lack of) incentives in Mexico.* Unpublished manuscript. Wellesley, MA: Wellesley College and Rand Corporation.

McLaughlin, M. W. (1987). Learning from experience: Lessons from policy implementation. *Educational Evaluation and Policy Analysis, 9*(2), 171–178.

McLaughlin, M. W. (1990a). *Educational policy and educational practice.* Stanford, CA: Center for Research on the Context of Secondary School Teaching, Stanford University.

McLaughlin, M. W. (1990b). The Rand Change Agent Study revisited: Macro perspectives and micro realities. *Educational Researcher, 19*(9), 11–16.

McLaughlin, M. W. (1991a). Learning from experience: Lessons from policy implementation. In A. R. Odden (Ed.), *Education policy implementation* (pp. 185–196). Albany, NY: State University of New York Press.

McLaughlin, M. W. (1991b). The Rand Change Agent Study: Ten years later. In A. R. Odden (Ed.), *Education Policy Implementation* (pp. 143–155). Albany, NY: State University of New York Press.

McLaughlin, M. W. (1993). What matters most in teachers' workplace context? In J. W. Little & M. W. McLaughlin (Eds.), *Teachers' work: Individuals, colleagues, and contexts* (pp. 79–103). New York: Teachers College Press.

McLaughlin, M. W., & Mitra, D. (2001). Theory-based change and change-based theory: Going deeper, going broader. *Journal of Educational Change, 1*(2), 2–24

McLaughlin, M.W., & Talbert, J. E. (1993a). *Contexts that matter for teaching and learning*. San Francisco: Jossey-Bass.

McLaughlin, M. W., & Talbert, J. E. (1993b). Understanding teaching in context. In Cohen, D.K., McLaughlin, M. W., & Talbert, J. E. (Eds.), *Teaching for understanding: Challenges for policy and practice* (pp. 167–206). San Francisco: Jossey-Bass.

McLaughlin, M. W., & Talbert, J. E. (1999). *Assessing the results: The Bay Area School Reform Collaborative, year three*. Stanford, CA: Stanford University, Center for Research on the Context of Teaching.

McLaughlin, M. W., & Talbert, J. E. (2001). *Professional communities and the work of high school teaching*. Chicago, IL: University of Chicago Press.

Mehan, H., Hertweck, A. L., & Meihls, J. L. (1986). *Handicapping the handicapped: Decision making in students' educational careers*. Stanford, CA: Stanford University Press.

Merrifield, P. (2002). *Metromarxism*. New York, NY: Routledge.

Merton, R. K. (1987). Three fragments from a sociologist's notebooks: Establishing the phenomenon, specified ignorance, and strategic research materials. *Annual Review of Sociology, 13*, 1–28.

Meyer, J. W., & Rowan, B. (1977). Institutionalized organizations: Formal structure as myth and ceremony. *American Journal of Sociology, 83*(2), 340–363.

Meyer, J., & Rowan, B. (1978). The structure of educational organizations. In M. Meyer (Ed.), *Environments and organizations* (pp. 78–109). San Francisco, CA: Jossey-Bass.

Miles, M. B. (1993). Forty years of change in schools: Some personal reflections. *Educational Administration Quarterly, 29*(2), 213–248.

Miles, M. B., & Huberman, A. M. (1994). *Qualitative data analysis: An expanded sourcebook* (2nd ed.). Thousand Oaks, CA: Sage.

Milward, B. (2000). *Marxian political economy: Theory, history and contemporary relevance*. London: Macmillan.

Mintrom, M. (2000). *Policy entrepreneurs and school choice*. Washington, DC: Georgetown University Press.

Mintrop, H. (2003). *Schools on probation: How accountability works (and doesn't work)*. New York, NY: Teachers College Press.

Mishel, L. (2004, September 23). Schoolhouse schlock: Conservatives flip-flop on standards for charter schools research, *American Prospect Online*.

Mitchell, D. E., & Encarnation, D. J. (1984). Alternative state policy mechanisms for influencing school performance. *Educational Researcher, 13*(5), 4–11.

Moe, T. M. (2000). The two democratic purposes of public education. In L.M. McDonnell, P. M. Timpane, & R. Benjamin (Eds.), *Rediscovering the democratic purposes of education* (pp. 127–147). Lawrence, KS: University Press of Kansas.

Morgan, G. (1986). *Images of organizations*. Beverley Hills, CA: Sage.

Morrison, T. (1992). *Playing in the dark*. Cambridge, MA: Harvard University.

Moynihan, D. P. (1969). *Maximum feasible misunderstanding*. New York, NY: The Free Press.

Moynihan, D. P. (1970). *Maximum feasible misunderstanding*. New York, NY: Free Press

Muncey, D., & McQuillan, P. (1998). *Reform and resistance in schools and classrooms* (pp. 148–164). New Haven, CT: Yale University Press.

Murnane, R. J. (1984). Production and innovation when techniques are tacit: The case of education. *Journal of Economic Behavior and Organization, 5*(3/4), 353–373.

Murphy, G. L., & Medin, D. L. (1985). The role of theories in conceptual coherence. *Psychological Review, 92*(3), 289–316.

Murphy, J. T. (1971). Title I of ESEA: The politics of implementing federal education reform. *Harvard Educational Review, 41*(1), 35–63.

Murphy, J. T. (2005). *Connecting teacher leadership and school improvement*. Thousand Oaks, CA: Corwin.

Murphy, J., & Datnow, A. (2003). *Leadership lessons for comprehensive school reforms*. Thousand Oaks, CA: Corwin Press.

Nakamura, R. T., & Smallwood, F. (1980). *The politics of policy implementation*. New York, NY: St. Martin's Press.

National Research Council (1989). *Everybody counts: A report to the nation on the future of mathematics education*. Washington, DC: National Academy Press.

Neal, J., Kelly, P., Klein, A., & Schubert, B. (1997). *Touching the future: Executive summary, California Reading Recovery, 1991–1997*. Fresno, CA: Central California Reading Recovery Project.

New Zealand Ministry of Education. (1996). *Reading for life: The learner as a reader*. Wellington, New Zealand: Learning Media Limited.

Newmann, F. M., Wehlege, G. G., Secada, W. G., Marks, H. M., Gamoran, A., King, M. B., et al. (1996). *Authentic achievement: Restructuring schools for intellectual quality*. San Francisco, CA: Jossey-Bass.

Newmann, F. M., King, M. B., & Youngs, P. (2000). Professional development that addresses school capacity: Lessons from urban elementary schools. *American Journal of Education, 108*(4), 259–299.

Newmann, F. M., & Sconzert, K. (2000). *School improvement with external partners*. Chicago, IL: Consortium on Chicago School Research.

Newmann, F. M., Smith, B., Allensworth, E., & Bryk, A. S. (2001). Instructional program coherence: What it is and why it should guide school improvement policy. *Educational Evaluation and Policy Analysis, 23*(4), 297–321.

Nisbett, R. E., & Ross, L. (1980). *Human inference: Strategies and shortcomings of social judgment*. Englewood Cliffs, NJ: Prentice-Hall.

Northwest Regional Educational Laboratory (1998). *Catalog of school reform models.* Portland, OR: Northwest Regional Educational Laboratory.

Novick, L. R. (1988). Analogical transfer, problem similarity, and expertise. *Journal of Experimental Psychology: Learning, Memory, and Cognition, 14*(3), 510–520.

Oakes, J. (1993). New standards and disadvantaged schools. Background paper prepared for research forum on Effects of New Standards and Assessments on High Risk Students and Disadvantaged Schools. Cambridge, MA: Harvard University.

Oakland School Linked Services Work Group. (1999). Partnership for change II. Oakland, CA: Author.

O'Connor, C., Lewis, A., & Mueller, J. (2003). Researching Black educational experiences and outcomes: Theoretical and practical considerations. Unpublished manuscript. Ann Arbor, MI: University of Michigan.

O'Day, J. A. (2002). Complexity, accountability, and school improvement. *Harvard Educational Review, 72*(3), 1–31.

Odden, A. (Ed.). (1991a). *Educational policy implementation.* Albany, NY: State University of New York Press.

Odden, A. (1991b). New patterns of education policy implementation and challenges for the 1990s. In A. Odden (Ed.), *Education policy implementation* (pp. 297–327). Albany, NY: State University of New York Press.

Odden, A., & Marsh, D. (1989). State education reform implementation: A framework for analysis (pp. 41–59). In J. Hannway & R. Crowson (Eds.), *The politics of reforming school administration: The 1988 yearbook of the Politics of Education Association Yearbook.* New York, NY: Falmer Press.

Ogawa, R. T., Sandholtz, J. H., Martinez-Flores, M., & Scribner, S. P. (2003). The substantive and symbolic consequences of a district's standards-based curriculum. *American Educational Research Journal, 40*(1), 147–176.

Ogbu, J. U. (1999). Beyond language: Ebonics, proper English, and identity in a Black-American speech community. *American Educational Research Journal, 36*(2), 147-184.

Olson, J. M., Roese, N. J., & Zanna, M. P. (1996). Expectancies. In E. T. Higgins & A. W. Kruglanski (Eds.), *Social psychology: Handbook of basic principles* (pp. 211–238). New York, NY: Guilford Press.

Omi, M., & Winant, H. (1994). *Racial formation in the United States.* New York, NY: Routledge.

Orr, M. (1998). The challenge of school reform in Baltimore: Race, jobs, and politics. In C. N. Stone (Ed.), *Changing urban education* (pp. 93–117). Lawrence, KS: University Press of Kansas.

Orr, M. (1999). *Black social capital: The politics of school reform in Baltimore, 1986-1998.* Lawrence, KS: University Press of Kansas.

Osborne, D., & Gaebler, T. (1992). *Reinventing government: How the entrepreneurial spirit is transforming the public sector.* Reading, MA: Addison-Wesley.

Ostrom, E. (1999). Institutional rational choice: An assessment of the institutional analysis and development framework. In P.A. Sabatier (Ed.), *Theories of the policy process* (pp. 35–71). Boulder, CO: Westview Press.

Pea, R. (1996). Seeing what we build together: Distributed multimedia learning environments for transformative communication. In T. Koschmann (Ed.), *CSCL: Theory and practice of an emerging paradigm* (pp. 171–186). Mahwah, NJ: Lawrence Erlbaum.

Perkins, D. N. (1993). Creating a culture of thinking. *Educational Leadership, 51*(3), 98–99.

Peterson, I. (1987, July 5). Civil-rights suit over Jersey school financing nears climax. *New York Times,* p. 24.

Peterson, P. (1976). *School politics Chicago style.* Chicago, IL: The University of Chicago Press.

Peterson, P. L. (1990). Doing more in the same amount of time: Cathy Swift. *Educational Evaluation and Policy Analysis, 12*(3), 261–280.

Peterson, P., Rabe, B., & Wong, K. (1986). *When federalism works.* Washington, DC: The Brookings Institution.

Peterson, P., Rabe, B., & Wong, K. (1991). The maturation of redistributive programs. In A. R. Odden (Ed.), *Education Policy Implementation* (pp. 65–80). Albany, NY: State University of New York Press.

Pfeffer, J. (1981). *Power in organizations.* Marshfield, MA: Pitman Publishing.

Philliber Research Associates. (1994). An evaluation of the Caring Communities program at Walbridge Elementary School. Accord, NY: Author.

Phillips, D. C., & Burbules, N. C. (2000). *Postpositivism and educational research.* Lanham, MA: Rowman & Littlefield.

Piaget, J. (1972). *The psychology of the child.* New York, NY: Basic Books.

Pillow, W. S. (2004). *Unfit subjects.* New York, NY: Routledge-Falmer.

Pimm, D. (1987). *Speaking mathematically: Communication in mathematics classrooms.* New York, NY: Routledge & K. Paul.

Placier, P., & Hamilton, M. L. (1994). Schools as contexts: A complex relationship. In V. Richardson (Ed.), *Teacher change and the staff development process: A case in reading instruction* (pp. 135–158). New York, NY: Teachers College Press.

Plank, D. (1987). Why school reform doesn't change schools: Political and organizational perspectives. In W. L. Boyd & C.T. Kerchner (Eds.), *The politics of excellence and choice in education* (pp. 143–152). New York, NY: Falmer Press.

Pollock, M. (2001). How the question we ask most about race in education is the very question we most suppress. *Educational Researcher, 30*(9), 2–12.

Polsby, N. W. (1984). *Political innovation in America: The politics of policy initiation.* New Haven, CT: Yale University Press.

Popkewitz, T. S., Tabachnick, B. R., & Wehlage, G. (1981). *The myth of educational reform: A study of school responses to a program of change.* Madison, WI: University of Wisconsin Press.

Portz, J., Stein. L., & Jones, B. B. (1999). *City schools and city politics: Institutions and leadership in Pittsburgh, Boston and St. Louis.* Lawrence, KS: The University of Kansas Press.

Pravetti, L, Derr, M. K., Anderson, J., Trippe, C., & Paschal, S. (2001). Changing the culture of the welfare office: The role of intermediaries in linking TANF recipients with jobs. *Economic Policy Review* (September), 63-76.

Pressman, J. L., & Wildavsky, A. (1973). *Implementation.* Berkeley, CA: University of California Press.

Pressman, J. L., & Wildavsky, A. (1984). *Implementation* (3rd ed.). Berkeley, CA: University of California Press.

Public Education Network. (2004). Taking responsibility: Using public engagement to reform our public schools. Washington, DC: Author.

Purkey, S. C., & Smith, M. S. (1983). Effective schools: A review. *Elementary School Journal, 83*(4), 427–452.

Radin, B. (2000). *Beyond Machiavelli: Policy analysis comes of age.* Washington, DC: Georgetown University Press.

Radin, B. A. (1977). *Implementation, change, and the federal bureaucracy: School desegregation policy in H.E.W., 1964–1968.* New York, NY: Teachers College Press.

Radin, B. A. (1997). Presidential address: The evolution of the policy analysis field: From conversation to conversations. *Journal of Policy Analysis and Management, 16*(2), 204–218.

Raphael, S., & Stoll, M. A. (2002). *Modest progress: The narrowing spatial mismatch between blacks and jobs in the 1990s.* Washington, DC: Brookings Institution.

Reiser, B. J., Spillane, J. P., Steinmuller, F., Sorsa, D., Carney, K., & Kyza, E. (2000). Investigating the mutual adaptation process in teachers' design of technology-infused curricula. In B. Fishman & S. O'Connor-Divelbiss (Eds.), *Proceedings of the Fourth International Conference of the Learning Sciences* (pp. 342–349). Mahwah, NJ: Lawrence Erlbaum.

Reiser, B. J., Tabak, I., Sandoval, W. A., Smith, B. K., Steinmuller, F., & Leone, A. J. (2001). BGUILE: Strategic and conceptual scaffolds for scientific inquiry in biology classrooms. In S. M. Carver & D. Klahr (Eds.), *Cognition and instruction: Twenty-five years of progress* (pp. 263–305). Mahwah, NJ: Lawrence Erlbaum.

Resnick, L. B. (1989). Introduction. In L. B. Resnick (Ed.), *Knowing, learning, and instruction: Essays in honor of Robert Glaser* (pp. 1–24). Hillsdale, NJ: Lawrence Erlbaum Associates.

Resnick, L. (1991). Shared cognition: Thinking as social practice. In J. Levine & S. Teasley (Eds.), *Perspectives on socially shared cognition* (pp. 1–20). Washington, DC: American Psychological Association.

Resnick, L. B., Elmore, R. F., & Alvarado, A. (1996). *Developing and implementing high-performance learning communities.* Proposal submitted to the Office of Educational Research and Improvement (solicitation # RC-96-1370).

Rich, W. C. (1996). *Black mayors and school politics: The failure of reform in Detroit, Gary and Newark.* New York, NY: Garland Publishing Company.

Richardson, V. (Ed.). (1994). *Teacher change and the staff development process: A case in reading instruction.* New York, NY: Teachers College Press.

Rist, R. C. (1979). *Desegregated schools.* New York, NY: Academic Press.

Roberts, N. C. & King, P. J. (1996). *Transforming public policy: Dynamics of policy entrepreneurship and innovation.* San Francisco, CA: Jossey-Bass.

Robinson v. Cahill 70 NJ 155 (1976).

Rochefort, D. A., Rosenberg, M., & White, D. (1998). Community as a policy instrument: A comparative analysis. *Policy Studies Journal, 26*(3), 548–568.

Rogers, D. (1968). *110 Livingston Street: Politics and bureaucracy in the New York City School System.* New York, NY: Random House.

Rogoff, B. (1990). *Apprenticeship in thinking: Cognitive development in social context.* New York, NY: Oxford University Press.

Rogoff, B. (1994). Developing understanding of the idea of communities of learners. *Mind, Culture, and Activity, 1*(4), 209–229.

Rogoff, B. (1995). Observing sociocultural activity on three planes: Participatory appropriation, guided participation, and apprenticeship. In J. V. Wertsch, P. Del Rio, & A. Alvarez (Eds.), *Sociocultural studies of mind* (pp. 139-164). Cambridge, NY: Cambridge University Press.

Rogoff, B., (1998). Cognition as a collaborative process. In W. Damon & D. Kuhn, & R. S. Siegler (Eds.), *Cognition, perceptions and language. Handbook of Child Psychology* (5th Ed., pp. 679–744). New York, NY: Wiley.

Romberg, T. (1983). *A common curriculum for mathematics.* Reading, PA: Addison-Wesley.

Rosenberg, G. (2004). Substituting symbol for substance: What did Brown really accomplish? *Political Science and Politics, 37*(2), 205–209.

Rosenholtz, S. J. (1985). Effective schools: Interpreting the evidence. *American Journal of Education, 93*(3), 352–358.

Rosenholtz, S. J. (1991). *Teachers' workplace: The social organization of schools.* New York: NY: Teachers College Press.

Ross, B. H. (1987). This is like that: The use of earlier problems and the separation of similarity effects. *Journal of Experimental Psychology: Learning, Memory, and Cognition, 13*(4), 629–639.

Ross, T. (2000). Innocence and affirmative action. In. R. Delgado & J. Stefancic (Eds.), *Critical race theory: The cutting edge* (pp. 635–647). Philadelphia, PA: Temple University Press.

Rossman, G. B., & Wilson, B. L. (1996). Context, courses, and the curriculum: Local responses to state policy reform. *Educational Policy, 10*(3), 399–421.

Rossman, S. B., & Morley, E. (1995). The national evaluation of Cities in Schools. Washington, DC: Urban Institute.

Rouse, C. E., & Krueger, A. B. (2004). *Putting computerized instruction to the test: A randomized evaluation of a "scientifically-based" reading program* (Working Paper 10315). Cambridge, MA: National Bureau of Economic Research.

Rowan, B., & Miskel, C. G. (1999). Institutional theory and the study of educational organizations. In J. Murphy & K. S. Louis (Eds.), *Handbook of research on educational administration* (2nd ed., pp. 359–383). San Francisco, CA: Jossey-Bass.

Rumelhart, D. E. (1980). Schemata: The building blocks of cognition. In R. J. Spiro, B. Bruce, & W. F. Brewer (Eds.), *Theoretical issues in reading and comprehension* (pp. 33–58). Hillsdale, NJ: Lawrence Erlbaum.

Sabatier, P. (1991). Toward better theories of the policy process. *Political Science and Politics, 24*(2), 129–168.

Sabatier, P., & Mazmanian, D. (1979). The conditions of effective implementation: A guide to accomplishing polilcy objectives. *Policy Analysis, 5*(5), 481–504.

Sabatier, P., & Mazmanian, D. (1980). The implementation of public policy: A framework of analysis. *The Policy Studies Journal, 8*(4), 538–560.

Sabatier, P. A. (1999). *Theories of the policy process.* Boulder, CO: Westview Press.

Sackrey, C., & Schneider, G. (2002). *Introduction to political economy.* Cambridge, MA: Dollars & Sense.

Sarason, S. (1982). *The culture of the school and the problem of change* (2nd ed.). Boston, MA: Allyn & Bacon.

Sarason, S. (1997). Revisiting the creation of settings. *Mind, culture, and activity, 4*(3), 175–182.

Sayer, A. (2001). For a critical cultural political economy. *Antipode, 33*(4), 687–707.

Schank, R. C. (1986). *Explanation patterns: Understanding mechanically and creatively.* Hillsdale, NJ: Lawrence Erlbaum.

Schank, R. C., & Abelson, R. P. (1977). *Scripts, plans, goals, and understanding.* Hillsdale, NJ: Lawrence Erlbaum.

Schattschneider, E. E. (1960). *The semi-sovereign people.* New York, NY: Holt, Rhinehart and Winston.

Schneider, M., & Buckley, J. (2002). What do parents want from schools? Evidence from the internet. *Educational Evaluation and Policy Analysis, 24*(2), 133–144.

Schneider, A., & Ingram, H. (1990). Behavioral assumptions of policy tools. *Journal of Politics, 52*(2), 510–529.

Schneider, A., & Ingram, H. (1993). Social construction of target populations: Implications for politics and policy. *American Political Science Review, 87*(2), 334–347.

Schram, S. F. (1995). *Words of welfare: The poverty of social science and the social science of poverty.* Minneapolis, MN: University of Minnesota Press.

Schwab, J. J. (1987). *Science, curriculum, and liberal education: Selected essays.* Chicago, IL: University of Chicago Press.

Sconzert, K., Smylie, M. A., & Wenzel, S. A. (2004). *Working for school improvement: Reflections of Chicago Annenberg external partners.* Chicago, IL: Consortium on Chicago School Research.

Scott, W. R. (1995). *Institutions and organizations.* Thousand Oaks, CA: Sage.

Scott, W., & Cohen, R. (1995). Work units in organizations: Ransacking the literature. In L. Siskin & J. Little (Eds.), *The subjects in question: Departmental organization and the high school* (pp. 48–67). New York, NY: Teachers College Press.

Scott, W., & Meyer, J. (1991). The organization of societal sectors: Propositions and early evidence. In W. W. Powell & P. J. DiMaggio (Eds.), *The new institutionalism in organizational analysis* (pp. 108–140). Chicago, IL: University of Chicago Press.

Scribner, J. P. (1999). Professional development: Untangling the influence of work context on teacher learning. *Educational Administration Quarterly, 35*(2), 238–266.

Scribner, J. P., Cockrell, K. S., Cockrell, D. H., & Valentine, J. W. (1999). Creating professional improvement process. *Educational Administration Quarterly, 35*(1), 130–160.

Scribner, J. P., Hager, D., & Warne, T. (2002). The paradox of professional community: Tales from two high schools. *Educational Administration Quarterly, 38*(1), 45–76.

Sherin, M. G. (1996). The nature and dynamics of teachers' content knowledge. Unpublished doctoral dissertation, University of California, Berkeley.

Shipps, D. (1997). The invisible hand: Big business and Chicago school reform. *Teachers College Record, 99*(1), 73–116.

Shipps, D. (2003). Pulling together: Civic capacity and urban school reform. *American Educational Research Journal, 40*(4), 841–878.

Shipps, D., Sconzert, K., & Swyers, H. (1999). *The Chicago Annenberg Challenge: The first three years.* Chicago: Consortium on Chicago School Research.

Siskin, L. S. (1991). Departments as different worlds: Subject subcultures in secondary schools. *Educational Administration Quarterly, 27*(2), 134–160.

Siskin, L. S. (1994). *Realms of knowledge: Academic departments in secondary schools.* Washington, DC: Falmer Press.

Sizer, T. R. (1985). A vote for "messiness". *Phi Delta Kappan, 67*(2), 125–126.

Sizer, T. R. (1986). Rebuilding: First steps by the Coalition of Essential Schools. *Phi Delta Kappan, 68*(1), 38–42.

Skowronek, S. (1982). *Building a new American state.* Cambridge, NY: Cambridge University Press.

Skowronek, S. (1982). *Building a new American state*. Cambridge, England: Cambridge University Press.

Slavin, R. E., & Fashola, O. (1998). *Show me the evidence!* Thousand Oaks, CA: Corwin.

Slavin, R. E., & Madden, N. A. (1998). *Disseminating Success for All: Lessons for policy and practice, Revised technical report*. Baltimore, MD: Center for Research on the Education of Students Placed At Risk, Johns Hopkins University.

Smith, C., Snir, J., & Grosslight, L. (1992). Using conceptual models to facilitate conceptual change: The case of weight-density differentiation. *Cognition and Instruction, 9*(3), 221–283.

Smith, F. (2002). *The glass wall: Why mathematics can seem difficult*. New York, NY: Teachers College Press.

Smith, J. P., diSessa, A. A., & Roschelle, J. (1993). Misconceptions reconceived: A constructivist analysis of knowledge in transition. *Journal of the Learning Sciences, 3*(2), 115–163.

Smith, M. L. (2004). *Political spectacle and the fate of American schools*. New York, NY: Routledge Falmer.

Smith, L., & Keith, P. (1971). *Anatomy of an educational innovation*. New York, NY: John Wiley & Sons.

Smith, L., Ross, S., McNelis, M., Squires, M., Wasson, R., Maxwell, S., Weddle, K,, Nath, L., Grehan, A., Buggey, T. (1998). The Memphis Restructuring Initiative: Analysis of activities and outcomes that affect implementation success. *Education and Urban Society, 30*(3), 276–232.

Smith, L. T. (1999). *Decolonizing methodologies: Research and indigenous peoples*. London: Zed.

Smith, M. S., Levin, J., & Cianci, J. E. (1997). Beyond a legislative agenda: Education policy approaches in the Clinton Administration. *Educational Policy, 11*(2), 209–226.

Smith, P. Molnar, A., & Zahorik, J. (2002). Class size reduction: A fresh look at the data. *Educational Leadership 61*(1), 72–74.

Smithmier, A. M. (1996, October 25-27). *Meeting children's needs through systems change: Will an alternative policy instrument work for integrated services?* Paper presented at the Annual Meeting of the University Council for Educational Administration, Louisville, KY.

Smrekar, C. (1994). The missing link in school-linked social service programs. *Educational Evaluation and Policy Analysis, 16*(4), 422–433.

Smylie, M. A. (1997). Research on teacher leadership: Assessing the state of the art. In B. J. Biddle, T. Good, & I. Goodson (Eds.), *International handbook of teachers and teaching* (pp. 521–592). Dordretch, The Netherlands: Kluwer.

Smylie, M. A., Crowson, R. L., Chou, V., & Levin, R. A. (1994). The principal and community school connections in Chicago's radical reform. *Educational Administration Quarterly, 30*(3), 342–364.

Smylie, M. A., & Hart, A. W. (1999). School leadership for teaching learning and change: A human and social capital development perspective. In J. Murphy & K. S. Louis (Eds.), *Handbook of research on educational administration* (2nd ed., pp. 421–441). San Francisco, CA: Jossey-Bass.

Smylie, M. A., & Wenzel, S. A. (2003). *The Chicago Annnenberg Challenge: Successes, failures, and lessons for the future.* Chicago, IL: Consortium on Chicago School Research.

Snyder, J., Bolin, F., and Zumwalt, K. (1992). Curriculum implementation. In P. Jackson (Ed.), *Handbook of Research on Curriculum* (pp. 402–435). New York, NY: Macmillan.

Songer, N. B., Lee, H. S., & Karn, R. (2002). Technology-rich inquiry science in urban classrooms: What are the barriers to inquiry pedagogy? *Journal of Research in Science Teaching, 39*(2), 128–150.

Spillane, J. P. (1996). School districts matter: Local educational authorities and state instructional policy. *Educational Policy, 10*(1), 63–87.

Spillane, J. P. (1998a). A cognitive perspective on the role of the local educational agency in implementing instructional policy: Accounting for local variability. *Educational Administration Quarterly, 34*(1), 31–57.

Spillane, J. P. (1998b). State policy and the non-monolithic nature of the local school district: Organizational and professional considerations. *American Educational Research Journal, 35*(1), 33–63.

Spillane, J. P. (1999). External reform initiatives and teachers' efforts to reconstruct their practice: The mediating role of teachers' zones of enactment. *Journal of Curriculum Studies, 31*(2), 143–175.

Spillane, J. P. (2000). Cognition and policy implementation: District policymakers and the reform of mathematics education. *Cognition and Instruction, 18*(2), 141–179.

Spillane, J. P. (2004). *Standards Deviation.* Cambridge, MA: Harvard University Press.

Spillane, J. P., & Callahan, K. A. (2000). Implementing state standards for science education: What district policy makers make of the hoopla. *Journal of Research in Science Teaching, 37*(5), 401–425.

Spillane, J. P., Diamond, J. B., Sherer, J. Z., Coldren, A. F. (2004). Distributing leadership. In M. Coles & G. Southworth (Eds.), *Developing leadership: Creating the schools of tomorrow* (pp. 37–49). New York, NY: Open Press.

Spillane, J. P., & Jennings, N. E. (1997). Aligned instructional policy and ambitious pedagogy: Exploring instructional reform from the classroom perspective. *Teachers College Record, 98*(3), 439–481.

Spillane, J. P., Reiser, B. J., & Reimer, T. (2002). Policy implementation and cognition: Reframing and refocusing implementation research. *Review of Educational Research, 72*(3), 387–431.

Spillane, J. P., & Thompson, C. L. (1997). Reconstructing conceptions of local capacity: The local education agency's capacity for ambitious instructional reform. *Educational Evaluation and Policy Analysis, 19*(2), 185–203.

Spillane, J. P., & Zeuli, J. S. (1999). Reform and teaching: Exploring patterns of practice in the context of national and state mathematics reform. *Educational Evaluation and Policy Analysis, 21*(1), 1–27.

SRI International. (1996). *California's Healthy Start School-Linked Services Initiative: Results for children and families.* Menlo Park, CA: Author.

Stangor, C., & McMillan, D. (1992). Memory for expectancy-congruent and expectancy-incongruent information: A review of the social and social developmental literature. *Psychological Bulletin, 111*(1), 42–61.

Stein, M. K., & Brown, C. A. (1997). Teacher learning in a social context: Integrating collaborative and institutional processes with the study of teacher change. In E. Fennema & B. S. Nelson (Eds.), *Mathematics teachers in transition* (pp. 155–191). Mahwah, NJ: Lawrence Erlbaum Associates.

Stein, M. K., & D'Amico, L. (2002). Inquiry at the crossroads of policy and learning: A study of a district-wide literacy initiative. *Teachers College Record, 104*(7), 1313–1344.

Stein, M. K., Harwell, M., & D'Amico, L. (1999). Toward closing the gap in literacy achievement. Unpublished manuscript, High Performance Learning Communities Project, University of Pittsburgh.

Stein, M. K., Silver, E., & Smith, M. S. (1998). Mathematics reform and teacher development: A community of practice perspective. In J. Greeno & S. V. Goldman (Eds.), *Thinking practices in mathematics and science learning* (pp. 17–51). Mahwah, NJ: Lawrence Erlbaum Associates.

Stein, S. J. (2004). *The culture of policy.* New York, NY: Teachers College Press.

Stigler, J. W., Gonzales, P., Kawanak, T., Knoll, S., & Serrano, A. (1999). *The TIMMS videotape classroom study: Methods and findings from an exploratory research project on eighth-grade mathematics instruction in Germany, Japan, and the U.S.* Washington, D.C.: National Center for Education Statistics.

Stone, C. N. (1980). The implementation of social programs: Two perspectives. *Journal of Social Issues, 36*(4), 13–34.

Stone, C. N. (1998). Introduction: Urban education in political context. In C. N. Stone (Ed.), *Changing urban education* (pp. 1–22). Lawrence, KS: University Press of Kansas.

Stone, C. N., Henig, J. R., Jones, B. O., & Pierannunzi, C. (2001). *Building civic capacity: The politics of reforming urban schools.* Lawrence, KS: University Press of Kansas.

Stone, D. (1997). *Policy paradox: The art of political decision making.* New York, NY: Norton.

Stout, R. T., & Sroufe, G. E. (1970). Politics without power: The dilemma of a local school system. In M. W. Kirst (Ed.), *The politics of education at the local, state and federal levels* (X). Berkeley, CA: McCutchan Publishing Corporation.

Strauss, A., & Corbin, J. (1990). *Basics of qualitative research: Grounded theory procedures and techniques.* Newbury Park, CA: Sage.

Strike, K. A., & Posner, G. J. (1985). A conceptual change view of learning and understanding. In L. H. T. West & A. L. Pines (Eds.), *Cognitive structure and conceptual change* (pp. 211–231). Orlando, FL: Academic Press.

Strike, K. A., & Posner, G. J. (1992). A revisionist theory of conceptual change. In R. A. Duschl & R. J. Hamilton (Eds.), *Philosophy of science, cognitive psychology, and educational theory and practice* (pp. 147–176). Albany, NY: State University of New York Press.

Stringfield, S., Millsap, M.A., Herman, R., Yoder, N., Brigham, N., Nesselrodt, P., Schaffer, E., Karweit, N., Levin, M., & Stevens, R. (with Gamse, B., Puma, M., Rosenblum, S., Beaumont, J., Randall, B., & Smith, L.). (1997). *Urban and suburban/rural special strategies for educating disadvantaged children. Final report.* Washington, DC: U.S. Department of Education.

Stringfield, S., & Ross, S. M. (1997). A reflection at mile three of a marathon: The Memphis Restructuring Initiative in mid-stride. *School Effectiveness and School Improvement, 8*(1), 151–161.

Sullivan, J. (1988, August 26). Jersey's funds for schools found flawed. *New York Times,* pp. B1–B2.

Surber, J. P. (1998). *Culture and critique: An introduction to the critical discourses of cultural studies.* Boulder, CO: Westview.

Sutton, M., & Levinson, B. (Eds.). (2001). *Policy as practice: Toward a comparative sociocultural analysis of educational policy.* Westport, CT: Ablex.

Talbert, J. E., & McLaughlin, M. W. (1994). Teacher professionalism in local school contexts. *American Journal of Education, 102*(2), 123–153.

Talbert, J. E. (2002). Professionalism and politics in high school teaching reform. *Journal of Educational Change, 3*(3/4), 339–363.

Tharp, R. G. (1997). From at risk to excellence: Research, theory, and principles for practice (Research report #1). Santa Cruz, CA: Center for Research on Education, Diversity and Excellence.

Timar, T. B., & Kirp, D. L. (1987). Educational reform and institutional competence. *Harvard Educational Review, 57*(2), 308–330.

Trope, Y. (1986). Identification and inferential processes in dispositional attribution. *Psychological Review, 93*(3), 239–257.

Truman, D. B. (1951). *The governmental process.* New York, NY: Alfred A. Knopf.

Tyack, D. (1992). Health and social services in public schools: Historical perspectives. *Future of Children, 2*(1), 19–31.

Tzou, C. T., Reiser, B. J., Spillane, J. P., & Kemp, E. K. (2002). *Characterizing the multiple dimensions of teachers' inquiry practices.* Paper presented at the annual meeting of the American Educational Research Association, New Orleans, LA.

Urban Strategies Council. (1992). *Partnership for change: Linking schools, services, and the community to serve Oakland youth.* Oakland, CA: Author.

Urban Strategies Council. (1993). *Data match: A tool for advocacy.* Oakland, CA: Author.

U.S. Department of Education. (1997). *Schoolwide programs.* Washington, DC: Author.

U.S. Department of Education. (1998a). *Guidance on the comprehensive school reform demonstration program.* Washington, DC: Author.

U.S. Department of Education. (1998b). *Waivers: Flexibility to achieve high standards. Report to Congress on waivers granted under the Elementary and Secondary Education Act.* Washington, DC: Author.

U.S. Department of Education. (1999a). *Twenty-first Century Community Learning Center Program application for grants.* Washington, DC: Author.

U.S. Department of Education (1999b). *CSR in the field: Fall 1999 update.* Washington, DC: Author.

U.S. Department of Education. (2002). Guidance on the Comprehensive School Reform Demonstration Program. Washington, DC: Author. Retrieved July 5, 2004, from http://www.ed.gov/programs/compreform/guidance/page_pg5.html?exp=0.

U.S. General Accounting Office. (1998). *Elementary and Secondary Education: EdFlex states vary in implementation of waiver process.* Washington, DC: Author.

Useem, E. L., Christman, J. B., Gold, E., & Simon, E. (1997). Reforming alone: Barriers to organizational learning in urban school change initiatives. *Journal of Education for Students Placed at Risk, 2*(1), 55–78.

Van Dijk, T. (1999). Discourse and the denial of racism. In A. Jaworski & N. Coupland (eds.), *The discourse reader* (pp. 541-558). London: Routledge.

Van Horn, C. E. (1979). *Policy implementation in the federal system.* Lexington, MA: Lexington Books.

Van Lehn, K. (1989). Problem solving and cognitive skill acquisition. In M. Posner (Ed.), *Foundations of Cognitive Science* (pp. 527–580). Cambridge, MA: MIT Press.

Van Maanen, J., & Barley, S. (1984). Occupational communities: Culture and control in organizations. *Research in Organizational Behavior, 6,* 287–365.

Van Meter, D., & Van Horn, C. E. (1975). The policy implementation process: A conceptual framework. *Administration and Society, 6*(4), 445–488.

Vaughan, D. (1996). *The Challenger launch decision: Risky technology, culture, and deviance at NASA.* Chicago, IL: University of Chicago Press.

Vesilind, E. M., & Jones, M. G. (1998). Gardens or graveyards: Science education reform and school culture. *Journal of Research in Science Teaching, 35*(7), 757–775.

Viadero, D. (2004a, September 1). AFT charter school study sparks heated national debate. *Education Week,* p. 9.

Viadero, D. (2004b, September 8). New data fuel current charter school debate. *Education Week,* p. 14.

Villegas, A., & Lucas, T. (2002). *Preparing culturally responsive teachers: A coherent approach.* Albany, NY: State University of New York Press.

Vosniadou, S., & Brewer, W. F. (1992). Mental models of the Earth: A study of conceptual change in childhood. *Cognitive Psychology, 24*(4), 535–585.

Wacquant, L. (2001). The penalisation of poverty and the rise of neo-liberalism. *European Journal on Criminal Policy and Research, 9*(4), 401–412.

Walker, E. (2004). The impact of state policies and actions on local implementation efforts: A study of whole school reform in New Jersey. *Educational Policy, 18*(2), 338–363.

Weatherley, R., & Lipsky, M. (1977). Street-level bureaucrats and institutional innovation: Implementing special-education reform. *Harvard Educational Review, 47*(2), 171–197.

Wechsler, M. E. (2001). A district community of practice: Understanding the relationship between a supportive district and its schools. Unpublished doctoral dissertation, Stanford University.

Wehlage, G., Smith, G., & Lipman, P. (1992). Restructuring urban schools: The New Futures experience. *American Educational Research Journal, 29*(1), 51–93.

Weick, K. E. (1976). Educational organizations as loosely coupled systems. *Administrative Science Quarterly, 21*(1), 1–19.

Weick, K. E. (1995). *Sensemaking in organizations.* Thousand Oaks, CA: Sage.

Weick, K. E., & Roberts, K. H. (1993). Collective mind in organizations: Heedful interrelating on flight decks. *Administrative Science Quarterly, 38*(3), 357–381.

Weiler, H. N. (1993). Control versus legitimation. In J. Hannaway & M. Carnoy (Eds.), *Decentralization and school improvement* (pp. 55–83). San Francisco, CA: Jossey-Bass.

Weiss, J., & Gruber, J. E. (1984). Using knowledge for control in fragmented policy areas. *Journal of Policy Analysis and Management, 3*, 225–247.

Weiss, J. A. (1989). The powers of problem definition: The case of government paperwork. *Policy Sciences, 22*(2), 97–121.

Weiss, J. A. (1990). Ideas and inducements in mental health. *Journal of Policy Analysis and Management, 19*(2), 1–23.

Wells, A. S. & Serna, L. (1996). The politics of culture: Understanding local political resistance to detracking in racially mixed schools. *Harvard Educational Review, 66*(1), 93–118.

Wenger, E. (1998). *Communities of practice: Learning, meaning, and identity.* Cambridge, England: Cambridge University Press.

Wildavsky, A. (1996). *Speaking truth to power: The art and craft of policy analysis.* New Brunswick, NJ: Transaction.

Williams, P. J. (1992). *The alchemy of race and rights.* Cambridge, MA: Harvard University.

Wilson, J. Q. (1989). *Bureaucracy: What government agencies do and why they do it.* New York, NY: Basic Books.

Wilson, S. M. (1990). A conflict of interest: The case of Mark Black. *Educational Evaluation & Policy Analysis, 12*(3), 293–310.

Wilson, W. J. (1996). *When work disappears: The world of the new urban poor.* New York: Knopf.

Wolf, S., Borko, H., Elliott, R., & McIver, M. (2000). "That dog won't hunt!": Exemplary school change efforts within the Kentucky reform. *American Educational Research Journal, 37*(2), 349–393.

Wong, K. K. (1986). Politics of local reform: Responses to federal redistributive school policy. *Issues in Education, 4*(3), 236–258.

Yancey, W. L., & Saporito, S. J. (1995). Ecological embeddedness of educational processes and outcomes. In L. C. Rigsby & M. C. Reynolds & M. C. Wang (Eds.), *School-community connections: Exploring issues for research and practice* (pp. 193–227). San Francisco, CA: Jossey-Bass.

Yanow, D. (1996). *How does a policy mean? Interpreting policy and organizational actions.* Washington, DC: Georgetown University Press.

Yarbrough, S. R. (1999). *After rhetoric: the study of discourse beyond language and culture.* Carbondale, IL: Southern Illinois University.

Yasumoto, J. Y., Uekawa, K., & Bidwell, C. E. (2001). The collegial focus and high school students' achievement. *Sociology of Education, 74*(3), 181–209.

Yin, R. K. (1989). *Case study research: Design and method.* Thousand Oaks, CA: Sage.

York-Barr, J., & Duke, K. (2004). What do we know about teacher leadership? Findings from two decades of scholarship. *Review of Educational Research, 74*(3), 255–316.

Zahorik, J., Halbach, A., Ehrle, K., & Molnar, A. (2004). *Teaching practices for smaller classes. Educational Leadership, 61*, 75–77.

Zimmerman, J. (2002). *Whose America? Culture wars in the public schools.* Cambridge, MA: Harvard University Press.

Contributors

Jean Anyon is the author of *Radical Possibilities: Public Policy, Urban Education, and a New Social Movement* (Routledge, 2005). Her 1997 book, *Ghetto Schooling: A Political Economy of Urban Educational Reform*, was reviewed in the *New York Times* and many other publications. It is widely used and cited. She has written extensively on the confluence of social class, race, and economic issues in schooling, and several of her articles have been reprinted in over forty edited collections. She teaches social and educational policy in the Doctoral Program in Urban Education at the Graduate Center of the City University of New York.

Cynthia E. Coburn is Assistant Professor in Policy, Organization, Management and Evaluation at the Graduate School of Education, University of California at Berkeley. Her research brings the tools of organizational sociology to understand the relationship between instructional policy and teachers' classroom practices in urban schools. She has studied these issues in the context of state and national reading policy, attempts to scale-up innovative school reform programs, and district-wide professional development initiatives. She was the recipient of a Spencer Foundation national dissertation fellowship in 1999 and won the 2002 Dissertation Award from Division L of the American Educational Research Association. Recent work has been published in *Educational Evaluation and Policy Analysis*, *Educational Researcher*, *Sociology of Education* and *Educational Policy*.

Amanda Datnow is currently an Associate Professor of Education at the USC Rossier School of Education, where she teaches in the Ed.D. and Ph.D. programs and is also the Associate Director of the Center on Educational Governance. She was formerly a faculty member at the Ontario Institute for Studies in Education at the University of Toronto and at Johns Hopkins University. Her research focuses on the politics and policies of school reform, particularly with regard to the professional lives of educators and issues of equity. Sociological perspectives inform her research on these topics, and her research methods are primarily qualitative. Recent books include *Extending Educational Reform: From One School to Many* (2002) and *Gender*

271

in Policy and Practice: Perspectives on Single Sex and Coeducational Schooling (2003, co-edited with Lea Hubbard).

Michael J. Dumas is a doctoral candidate in the Ph.D. Program in Urban Education at The Graduate Center of the City University of New York. His research interests include the history and politics of Black education, the political economy of urban education, and ethnographic methodology.

Andrea E. Evans is Assistant Professor of Educational Administration and Leadership at Northern Illinois University. Her research interests include the impact of organizational and social contexts of schools on African American students, school leadership, and leadership preparation. Evans received her Ph.D. in educational policy studies from University of Illinois at Chicago, her M.Ed. from DePaul University and her B.S. from University of Illinois at Chicago. She is a former high school science teacher and administrator.

Louis M. Gomez is Aon Professor of Learning Sciences, Professor of Computer Science, and Learning Science Program Coordinator at Northwestern University. Professor Gomez' primary interest is in working with school communities to create social arrangements and curriculum that supports school reform. Along with his colleagues, Professor Gomez has been dedicated to collaborative research and development with urban schools that will bring the current state-of-the-art in computing and networking technologies into pervasive use in urban schools so that they will transform instruction and support community formation. Prior to joining the faculty at Northwestern Professor Gomez was director of Human-Computer Systems Research at Bellcore in Morristown New Jersey. At Bellcore, he pursued an active research programs investigating techniques that improve human use of information retrieval systems and techniques which aid in the acquisition of complex computer-based skills. Professor Gomez received a B.A. in Psychology from the State University of New York at Stony Brook and a Ph.D. in Cognitive Psychology from the University of California at Berkeley.

Heather C. Hill is an associate research scientist at the University of Michigan. Her primary work focuses on developing measures of teachers' content knowledge for teaching mathematics, and using such measures to evaluate public policies and programs intended to improve teachers' understanding of this mathematics. Her other interests include the measurement of instruction more broadly, instructional improvement efforts in mathematics, and the role that language plays in the implementation of public policy. She received a Ph.D. in political science from the University of Michigan in 2000 for work analyzing the implementation of public policies in law enforcement and education. She is the coauthor, with David K. Cohen, of *Learning policy: When state education reform works* (Yale Press, 2001).

Meredith I. Honig is an assistant professor of education leadership and policy studies at the University of Washington in Seattle. Her research and teaching focus on policy design, policy implementation, and organizational change in cities. She is particularly interested in how urban, public-policy making bureaucracies such as school district central offices manage ambiguity, complexity, and innovation. Honig received her Ph.D. from Stanford University in 2001. Prior to joining the University of Washington faculty, Honig was an assistant professor and co-director of the Center for Education Policy and Leadership at the University of Maryland, College Park. She has served as a policy and research specialist at the California Department of Education and worked in other state and local youth-serving agencies. Her recent publications have appeared in *Educational Administration Quarterly, Educational Evaluation and Policy Analysis, Educational Policy, Educational Researcher,* and the American Educational Research Association's *Handbook of Research on Teaching* (4th ed.).

Susanna Loeb is an associate professor of education at Stanford University, specializing in the economics of education and the relationship between schools and federal, state, and local policies. She studies teacher labor markets, assessment-based accountability, poverty policy, and education resource allocation. Her recent work looks specifically at how teachers' preferences affect the distribution of teaching quality across schools and how policies can alleviate these differences. She is particularly interested in issues of equity. Susanna received her Ph.D. in economics in 1998 from the University of Michigan, where she also received a master's in public policy. Her dissertation won the American Education Finance Association Jean Flanigan Outstanding Dissertation Award and the Association for Public Policy Analysis and Management Dissertation Award. Susanna's recent papers include Estimating the effects of school finance reform: A framework for a federalist system, in the *Journal of Public Economics*; Examining the link between teacher wages and student outcomes: The importance of alternative labor market opportunities and non-pecuniary variation, with Marianne Page, in the *Review of Economics and Statistics;* and Teacher sorting and the plight of urban schools: A descriptive analysis, with Hamilton Lankford and James Wyckoff in *Education Evaluation and Policy Analysis.*

Betty Malen is a professor in the department of Education Policy and Leadership at the University of Maryland, College Park. Her research focuses on the politics of education reform. She has examined the enactment and implementation of a variety of education policies including initiatives that emphasize the decentralization of decision-making authority, the professionalization of teaching, and high-stakes accountability. She also has examined how these and other reform initiatives affect the balance of power between state government and local educational systems. Her research appears regularly in education policy and leadership journals such as *Education Evaluation and Policy Analysis, Educational Policy,* and *Educational Administration Quarterly,* in yearbooks sponsored by the Politics of Education Association and the American Education Finance Association; and in other outlets concerned with policy and leadership.

Patrick J. McEwan is an Assistant Professor in the Department of Economics at Wellesley College. He previously taught in the Departments of Educational Policy Studies and Economics at the University of Illinois at Urbana–Champaign. McEwan's research focuses on the economics of education, applied econometrics, and education policy in Latin America. He has evaluated education policies ranging from class-size reduction to private school vouchers throughout Latin America. Most of his work is conducted in

Chile, but he has also worked in Argentina, Bolivia, Colombia, Honduras, and Mexico. His research has been published in a wide range of economics and education journals as well as in three books. He has consulted widely on education policy and evaluation at the Inter-American Development Bank, the RAND Corporation, UNESCO, the World Bank, and the ministries of education of several countries. Currently, he is currently serving on the Executive Board of the American Education Finance Association. He received his Ph.D. from Stanford University in 2000 and his B.A. (summa cum laude) from the University of Illinois at Urbana–Champaign in 1994.

Milbrey W. McLaughlin is the David Jacks Professor of Education and Public Policy at Stanford University. McLaughlin codirects the Center for Research on the Context of Teaching and serves as Executive Director of the John W. Gardner Center for Youth and Their Communities, a partnership between Stanford University and Bay Area communities to build new practices, knowledge, and capacity for youth development and learning both in communities and at Stanford. She is the author or coauthor of books, articles, and chapters on education policy issues, contexts for teaching and learning, productive environments for youth, and community-based organizations. Her books include: *School Districts And Instructional Renewal* (with Amy Hightower, Michael Knapp, and Julie Marsh, Teachers College Press, 2002); *Communities of Practice and the Work of High School Teaching* (with Joan Talbert, University of Chicago Press, 2001); *Community Counts: How Youth Organizations Matter for Youth Development* (Public Education Fund Network, 2000); *Urban Sanctuaries: Neighborhood Organizations in the Lives and Futures of Inner-City Youth* (with Merita A. Irby and Juliet Langman, Jossey-Bass, 1994; 2001); and *Identity and Inner-City Youth: Beyond Ethnicity and Gender* (with Shirley Brice Heath, Teachers College Press, 1993).

Mark A. Smylie is Professor and Chair of the Policy Studies Area in the College of Education at the University of Illinois at Chicago. His research interests include urban school improvement, leadership, teacher learning and development, and the relationship of school organization to classroom teaching and student learning. Smylie received his Ph.D. in educational leadership from Peabody College at Vanderbilt University and his M.Ed. and B.A. from Duke University. He is a former high school social studies teacher.

James P. Spillane is the Spencer T. and Ann W. Olin Professor in Learning and Organizational Change at Northwestern University where he teaches in both the Learning Sciences and Human Development and Social Policy graduate programs in the School of Education and Social Policy and is a Faculty Fellow at the Institute for Policy Research. Spillane's work explores the policy implementation process at the state, school district, school, and classroom levels, focusing on intergovernmental relations and relations between policy and school leaders' and teachers' practice. He is the author of *Standards Deviation: How Local Schools Miss-Understand Policy* (Harvard University Press, 2004) and *Distributed Leadership* (Jossey-Bass, 2006) and numerous journal articles. He is director of Northwestern University's Multi-disciplinary Program in Education Sciences, a pre-doctoral training program involving students from Economics, Human Development and Social Policy, Learning Sciences, Psychology, and Sociology.

Mary Kay Stein holds a joint appointment at the University of Pittsburgh as Associate Professor of Administrative and Policy Studies and Research Scientist at the Learning Research and Development Center. Her work includes several studies that examine the influence of school and district contexts and group interaction on the learning and development of teachers of mathematics. Recent publications include (with Barbara Nelson) Leadership Content Knowledge that appeared in the 2003 special edition of *Educational Evaluation and Policy Analysis* and (with Hugh Mehan and Lea Hubbard) Reform ideas that travel far afield: The two cultures of reform in New York City's District #2 and San Diego, in *The Journal of Educational Change*. In addition to her current National Science Foundation-funded work on the Scaling Up Mathematics Project, Dr. Stein leads (along with Cynthia Coburn) a Spencer- and MacArthur -funded project on useful and usable knowledge for school improvement. Dr. Stein has served on several national panels and is also an elected member of the Riverview School District Board of Directors in Oakmont, Pennsylvania.

Author Index

Achinstein, B., 228–229
Allison, G., 83, 88, 229
Anderson, B., 8–9, 229, 260
Angrist, J.D., 179, 229
Anyon, J., 18–19, 21, 96, 123, 149–168, 213, 216, 229, 271
Apple, M.W., 103, 165, 229
Argyris, C., 129–130, 226, 229
Armor, D.J., 99–100, 229
Aronowitz, S., 229
Askew, B.J., 45, 229
Austin, J.L., 69, 230, 244–245

Bakhtin, M.M., 67, 78, 230
Ball, D. L., 11, 65–66, 75, 79, 230, 236
Ball, S., 47, 58, 230
Bardach, E., 6, 23, 83, 85–86, 90–91, 96, 212, 221, 230
Barfield, D., 126, 230
Barley, S.R., 58, 133, 230, 268
Bartelt, D. W., 19, 230
Barzelay, M., 137, 230
Baugh, W.H., 174, 230
Baum, H. S., 86, 89, 101, 103, 230
Baumgartner, F., 86, 89, 230
Beck, J., 54, 88, 169, 230, 238
Becker, G., 88, 169, 230, 238
Bell, D., 156, 164, 166–167, 231, 272
Berends, M., 12, 109–110, 197, 231–232
Berman, P., 7, 95, 106, 188, 219, 231

Bidwell, C. E., 27, 44, 231, 270
Billstein, R., 78, 231
Blank, M., 222, 231
Blase, J., 231
Blau, P.M., 231
Bodilly, S., 12, 109–110, 197, 231–232
Bolman, L.G., 83, 232
Borko, H., 63, 194, 232, 270
Borman, G.D., 109–110, 188, 232, 238
Bouillion, L., 57, 232
Bourdieu, P., 68, 189, 232
Bower, G.H., 50, 232
Boyd, D., 12, 126, 175–176, 232, 237, 247, 255, 259
Brewer, W. F., 49–50, 53, 232, 234, 262, 269
Brodkin, E., 66, 79, 233
Bronfenbrenner, U., 58, 233
Brown, J.S., 27–28, 226–227, 233
Brunsson, N., 233
Bryk, A.S., 2, 13, 18, 57, 90, 95, 97, 100, 130, 190, 192, 195, 233, 249–250, 257
Burch, P., 12, 16–17, 58, 63, 233–234
Burstein, L., 69, 80, 234
Burtless, G., 173, 234

Cahill, M., 126, 158, 160, 234, 261
California Department of Education, 125, 127, 234

277

Cantor, N., 49–50, 234
Carey, S., 50–51, 53, 234
Carnoy, M., 176, 179, 183, 234, 269
Center for the Study of Social Policy,
     126, 234
Chase, W. G., 51, 234
Chi, M. T. H., 234
Chinn, C. A., 53, 234
Chrispeels, J. H., 13, 98, 212, 234
Chubb, J. E., 96, 234
Cibulka, J. G., 126, 234
City of Oakland, 137, 235
Clapp, E., 125, 235
Clark, B., 58, 235
Clegg, S. R., 90, 235
Clift, R., 197, 235
Clotfelter, C. T., 177, 235
Clune III, W. H., 8, 235
Coalition for Community Schools, 223,
     235
Cobb, P., 17, 26–28, 38, 44, 235
Cobb, R. W., 88, 99, 235
Coburn, C. E., 11, 15, 17, 25–46, 49, 56,
     63, 65, 67, 79, 198, 213–215,
     235, 271, 275
Coburn, K. G., 137, 236
Cohen, D. K., 3, 8, 11, 17, 20, 25,
     47–49, 52, 54, 58, 65–67, 75,
     79, 82, 214–215, 228, 236,
     256, 272
Cohen, M. D., 129, 233, 236–237
Cohen, W. M., 131, 236
Cole, M., 236
Coleman, J. S., 188–191, 236
Commission for Positive Change in the
     Oakland Public Schools, 137,
     237
Cook, S. N., 130, 237
Covello, L., 125, 237
Crain, R. L., 99, 237
Crenshaw, K., 155, 231, 237
Cronbach, L. J., 227, 237
Crowson, R. L., 12, 126, 237, 242, 258,
     264
Cuban, L., 15–16, 25, 83–84, 96–97, 237
Cullen, J. B., 170, 178, 182, 237

Cunningham, L. L., 126, 237, 245
Czerniak, C. M., 54, 230, 237
Cznariawska, B., 132, 238

Daft, R., 88, 238
Dahl, R. A., 88–90, 238
D'Amico, L., 38–40, 238, 245, 266
Darling-Hammond, L., 21, 175, 238,
     240, 250, 252
Datnow, A., 2, 15, 18, 105–123, 198,
     212, 216, 231, 238–239, 244,
     257, 271
David and Lucile Packard Foundation,
     126, 239
David, J. L., 6, 8, 239
Delgado, R., 239, 261
Derthick, M., 5, 228, 239
Desimone, L., 109–110, 195, 239
Dika, S. L., 188, 239
DiMaggio, P. D., 56, 239, 263
Drake, C., 59, 63, 239
Dreier, P., 165, 239
Driscoll, A., 57, 239
Dryfoos, J., 223, 239
Dumas, M., 149–168
Dweck, C. S., 50, 239

Edelman, M., 89, 99, 239
Editorial Projects in Education, 239
Education Commission of the States,
     109, 239
Education Week, 184, 240, 268
Edwards, G., 187, 240
Elmore, R. F., 2–3, 5, 7–8, 11–12, 15,
     20–21, 27, 38, 46, 97–98, 128,
     196, 205–206, 240, 242, 255,
     261
Engestrom, Y., 236, 240
Erlichson, B., 110, 240
Evans, A., 187–208

Family Investment Trust, 127, 240
Farrar, E., 6, 229, 241
Feldman, M. S., 129–130, 241
Feltovich, P., 51, 234
Ferguson, R. F., 2, 179, 241, 249

Figlio, D. N., 178, 241
Fine, M., 16, 163, 167–168, 241, 248
Fink, E., 40–41, 241
Finkelstein, B., 91, 94, 241
Finn, J. D., 2, 241
Finnigan, K., 12, 19, 197, 241
Fiol, C. M., 130, 241
Firestone, W. A., 2, 47, 54, 86, 90–91, 98, 103, 241
Fiscal Crisis and Management Assistance Team, 145, 242
Flavell, J. H., 51, 242
Foley, D., 242
Foucault, M., 150, 152, 154, 163, 242
Foundation Consortium for School-linked Services, 127, 242
Fountas, I.C., 38, 45, 229, 242
Franke, M. L., 26, 242
Freeman, D., 68, 242
Fuhrman, S. H., 7–9, 63, 96–98, 229, 236, 242, 254
Fullan, M., 108, 188, 197, 231, 238, 242, 252

Gagliardi, P., 60, 243
Gallucci, C., 26–27, 31, 42, 243
Gammon, R., 137, 243
Gaventa, J., 88, 243
Geary, L. S., 90, 104, 243
Gee, J. P., 67–68, 243
Geertz, C., 70, 243
Gentner, D., 50–51, 243
Gilman, D. A., 2, 243
Giroux, H. A., 167, 243
Gladstein, D., 129, 131, 243
Glaser, B., 51, 70, 234, 243, 260
Glewwe, P., 178, 180, 243
Goddard, R. D., 188, 193, 243
Goggin, M., 3–5, 66–67, 243
Gomez, L. M., 47–64
Gottlieb, R. S., 152, 243
Granovetter, M. S., 191–192, 198, 243
Grant, S. G., 25, 63, 201, 244
Greeno, J. G., 49–50, 60, 244, 250, 266
Gresson, A. D., 162, 244
Gross, N., 53, 106, 244, 264

Gubrium, J. B., 154, 244
Guthrie, J. W., 230, 244

Hall, G., 106, 257
Hall, P. M., 86, 102, 107, 109, 257
Hall, S., 153–154, 167, 257
Hallet, A., 200, 244
Hamann, E., 18, 244
Hammer, D., 50, 244
Hanks, W. F., 28, 244
Hannaway, J., 17, 180, 245, 269
Hanushek, E. A., 2, 169, 173, 175–176, 183, 245
Hargrove, E. C., 83, 187–188, 245
Hartley, J. F., 132, 245
Harvard Business Review, 227, 245
Harwell, M., 38, 238, 245, 266
Hatch, T., 2, 13–14, 20, 97, 100, 245, 247
Haug, C., 53, 245
Haymes, S. N., 163, 245
Henderson, A. T., 224, 245
Henig, J. R., 84, 86, 89, 103, 164–165, 221, 246, 266
Herman, R., 109, 246, 267
Herrington, C. D., 246
Hess, F. M., 15, 97, 246
Higgins, E. T., 50, 246, 258
High Performance Learning Communities Project, 46, 246
Hightower, A. M., 16, 227, 233, 246, 254, 274
Hill, H. C., 15, 17, 19, 25, 27, 49, 52, 54, 58, 63, 65–82, 214, 236, 246
Hill, M., 228, 246
Hill, P., 224, 246
Holmstrom, B., 171, 180, 246
Holyoke, T., 89, 246
Honig, M. I., 1–23, 44, 82, 86, 98, 100, 104, 123, 125–148, 197, 218, 221–222, 226, 228, 247, 272–273
House, E. R., 101, 247, 254, 261
Hsieh, C. T., 182–183, 247
Huber, G. P., 128–129, 133, 247, 256
Hutchins, E., 60, 247

Illig, D. C., 2, 247
Ingram, H., 8, 13, 15, 83, 216, 247, 262

Jackson, P. W., 69, 240, 247, 265
Jacob, B. A., 178, 183, 247
Jehl, J. D., 11–12, 125–126, 247–248
Jennings, N., 25, 52, 248, 265
Jones, D. R., 54, 86, 89, 91, 101, 221,
    230, 248, 260, 266, 268
Jung, R. K., 6–7, 98, 248–249

Kanter, R. M., 88, 95, 129, 131, 248
Kantor, H., 157, 248
Katz, M. B., 16, 18, 248
Kazemi, E., 26, 65, 74, 242, 248
Keil, F., 49, 248
Keisler, S., 53, 248
Kelley, R. D. G., 167, 248
Kellner, D., 248
Kemp, E. K., 61, 122, 248, 267
Kentucky State Board for Elementary
    and Secondary Education, 127,
    248
Kerr, P., 160–161, 249
Kimberly, J. R., 131, 249
Kincheloe, J. L., 162, 249
Kingdon, J. W., 86, 88, 103–104, 249
Kirst, M., 6–7, 16, 18, 98, 126, 248–249,
    266
Klayman, J., 50, 249
Knapp, M. S., 2, 6, 8, 13, 16–17, 83, 88,
    108, 120, 130–131, 188,
    227–228, 233, 246, 249, 254,
    274
Kolodner, J. L., 50, 249
Kreps, D. M., 128, 249
Kronley, R. A., 197–198, 249
Krueger, A. B., 173, 184, 249, 262
Kruse, S. D., 27, 57, 130, 249, 252
Kunda, Z., 50, 250

Ladson-Billings, G., 1, 156, 250
Lampert, M., 68, 250
Lankford, H., 175–176, 232, 250, 273
Larkin, J. H., 51, 250
Latour, B., 60, 250

Lave, J., 26–27, 44, 131, 244, 250
Lavy, V., 180, 250
Lee, V. E., 2, 15, 27, 55, 57, 227, 233,
    250, 265
Leithwood, K., 130–131, 250–251
Lemke, J. L., 82, 251
Lennon, M. C., 5, 251
Leont'ev, A. N., 60, 251
Levin, B., 84, 97, 251
Levin, H. M., 172, 177, 181, 182, 185,
    251
Levin, J., 179, 251
Levinthal, D. A., 129, 131, 236, 251
Levitt, B., 128–129, 178, 247, 251
Levy, J. E., 126, 251
Lewis, D., 59, 63, 166, 251, 258
Lieberman, A., 9, 27, 231, 238, 251–252
Lin, A., 47, 49, 59, 67, 79, 251
Lipman, P., 21, 126, 164, 252, 269
Lipsky, M., 6, 97, 128–129, 187, 214,
    252, 269
Little, J. W., 9, 25–27, 29, 57–58, 196,
    221, 252, 255, 259, 263
Loeb, S., 20–21, 169–186, 215, 232, 234,
    237, 250, 252, 273
Lortie, D. C., 57, 252
Louis, K. S., 2, 16–17, 27, 57, 130,
    251–252
Lowi, T., 6, 85, 216, 252–253
Lusi, S. F., 18, 252

Madsen, J., 102, 253
Majone, G., 3, 21, 253
Malen, B., 8, 15, 17, 19, 83–104, 128,
    154, 216–217, 241, 248, 253,
    273
Mandler, J., 49, 253
March, J. G., 89, 128–131, 145, 161,
    226, 251, 253
Marks, H. M., 27, 130, 252, 254, 257
Markus, H. R., 49–50, 254
Marsh, D. D., 8–9, 254
Marsh, J. A., 16, 98, 101, 227, 233, 246,
    254
Massell, D., 1, 12, 19, 254
Massey, D. S., 157, 163, 254

Mathematica & Decision Information Resources, 2, 254
Matland, R. E., 228, 254
Mawhinney, H. B., 12, 126, 254
Mayer, D., 65, 69, 80, 254
Mazmanian, D. A., 6–7, 80, 187, 228, 254–255, 262
Mazzoni, T. L., 86–90, 93, 103–104, 255
McCorry, J. J., 137, 255
McDonnell, L., 8, 12, 63, 84, 97, 128, 213, 234, 255–256
McEwan, P. J., 20–21, 169–186, 215, 255, 273
McLaughlin, M. W., 2, 5, 7–10, 15–17, 20, 22, 25, 27, 31, 44, 58, 65, 95, 106–107, 169, 188, 193, 195, 209–228, 231, 233, 236, 240, 246–247, 251–252, 254–256, 267, 274
Mehan, H., 105, 107, 239, 256, 275
Merrifield, P., 153, 256
Merton, R. K., 132, 256
Meyer, J. W., 56, 212, 225–226, 256, 263
Miles, M. B., 133, 197, 256
Milward, B., 256
Mintrom, M., 88, 256
Mintrop, H., 13, 15–16, 256
Mishel, L., 2, 256
Miskel, C. G., 89, 248, 254, 262
Mitchell, D. E., 13, 126, 237, 256
Moe, T. M., 96, 234, 256
Morgan, G., 87–88, 257
Morrison, T., 155, 257
Moynihan, D. P., 101, 212, 228, 257
Muncey, D., 83–84, 86–87, 96–97, 102, 104, 241, 253, 257
Murnane, R. J., 173, 257
Murphy, G. L., 5, 49, 84, 86, 102, 109, 199, 231, 244, 257, 262, 265

Nakamura, R. T., 49–50, 187, 232, 257
National Research Council, 71, 257
Neal, J., 45, 257
New Zealand Ministry of Education, 38, 257
Newmann, F. M., 13, 27, 207, 257

Nisbett, R. E., 50, 257
Novick, L. R., 52, 258

Oakes, J., 109, 258
Oakland School Linked Services Work Group, 137, 139, 144, 258
O'Connor, C., 258
O'Day, J. A., 18, 21, 258
Odden, A., 3, 5, 8, 120, 188, 229, 249, 254–255, 258–259
Ogawa, R. T., 8, 83, 89, 97, 102, 128, 253, 258
Ogbu, J. U., 82, 258
Olson, J. M., 50, 258
Omi, M., 162, 258
Orr, M., 18–20, 86, 88, 164, 166, 246, 258
Osborne, D., 258
Ostrom, E., 104, 259

Pea, R., 60, 231, 245, 252, 259, 274
Perkins, D. N., 259
Peterson, I., 6, 27, 65, 99, 159, 196, 240, 249, 259
Peterson, P., 6, 27, 65, 99, 159, 196, 240, 249, 259
Pfeffer, J., 83, 259
Philliber Research Associates, 126, 259
Phillips, D. C., 132, 259
Piaget, J., 51, 242, 259
Pillow, W. S., 15, 259
Pimm, D., 69, 76, 259
Placier, P., 109, 196, 244, 259
Plank, D., 96, 259
Pollock, M., 17, 259
Polsby, N. W., 93, 259
Popkewitz, T. S., 107, 260
Portz, J., 86, 89, 260
Pravetti, L., 197, 260
Pressman, J. L., 5, 95, 187, 209, 212, 228, 260
Public Education Network, 221, 260
Purkey, S. C., 9, 260

Radin, B., 4–6, 260
Raphael, S., 157, 260

Reiser, B. J., 17, 25, 47–64, 67, 213–214,
    248, 260, 265, 267
Resnick, L. B., 40–41, 46, 49, 241, 244,
    250, 260–261
Rich, W. C., 84, 96–97, 103, 261
Richardson, V., 196, 261
Rist, R. C., 99–100, 261
Roberts, N. C., 88, 261
Rochefort, D. A., 13, 261
Rogers, D., 102, 261
Rogoff, B., 26, 60–61, 107–108, 261
Romberg, T., 261
Rosenberg, G., 13, 100, 261
Rosenholtz, S. J., 8, 27, 261
Ross, B. H., 51, 261
Ross, T., 156, 261
Rossman, G. B., 97, 126, 130, 262
Rouse, C. E., 184, 262
Rowan, B., 56, 89, 256, 262
Rumelhart, D. E., 49, 262

Sabatier, P., 6–7, 80, 103, 187, 218, 228,
    254–255, 259, 262
Sackrey, C., 262
Sarason, S., 106–107, 262
Sayer, A., 151, 262
Schank, R. C., 49–50, 53, 262
Schattschneider, E. E., 86, 89, 92, 99, 262
Schneider, A., 177, 262
Schneider, M., 8, 13, 15, 216, 262
Schram, S. F., 15, 20, 263
Schwab, J. J., 67, 263
Sconzert, K., 207–208, 257, 263
Scott, W. R., 56, 58, 131, 212, 225–226,
    263
Scribner, J. P., 130, 194, 198, 258, 263
Sherin, M. G., 79, 263
Shipps, D., 16, 86, 101, 103, 208, 263
Siskin, L. S., 15, 44, 58, 263
Sizer, T. R., 3, 9, 263
Skowronek, S., 128, 263–264
Slavin, R. E., 109, 122, 264
Smith, C., 53, 264
Smith, F., 69, 76, 264
Smith, J. P., 50, 264
Smith, L., 106–107, 109, 264

Smith, L. T., 167, 264
Smith, M. L., 95, 264
Smith, M. S., 13, 264
Smith, P., 2, 264
Smithmier, A. M., 13, 264
Smrekar, C., 12, 126, 254, 264
Smylie, M. A., 17, 19, 25, 27, 126,
    187–208, 213, 263–265, 274
Snyder, J., 106–107, 265
Songer, N. B., 55, 265
Spillane, J., 16–17, 19–21, 25, 27, 38,
    47–65, 67, 79–80, 82, 128,
    195, 213–215, 227, 234, 236,
    239, 248, 260, 265–267, 274
SRI International, 126, 130, 134, 266
Stangor, C., 53, 266
Stein, M. K., 25–46, 56, 213–215, 266,
    275
Stein, S. J., 15, 21, 266
Stigler, J. W., 69, 80, 266
Stone, C. N., 15, 18, 83–84, 88, 96,
    100–103, 221, 223, 266
Stone, D., 88, 266
Stout, R. T., 99, 266
Strauss, A., 70, 243, 267
Strike, K. A., 53, 267
Stringfield, S., 109–110, 123, 238, 267
Sullivan, J., 160, 267
Surber, J. P., 154, 267
Sutton, M., 21, 267
Talbert, J. E., 15, 17, 25, 27, 31, 44, 58,
    65, 107, 195, 236, 252, 256,
    267, 274

Tharp, R., 107, 267
Timar, T. B., 202, 267
Trope, Y., 49–50, 267
Truman, D. B., 88, 267
Tyack, D., 15, 125, 237, 267
Tzou, C. T., 61, 248, 267

U.S. Department of Education, 63, 108,
    121, 267–268
U.S. General Accounting Office, 268
Urban Strategies Council, 137, 268
Useem, E. L., 206, 268

Van Dijk, T., 268
Van Horn, C. E., 187, 228, 268
Van Lehn, K., 268
Van Maanen, J., 58, 268
Van Meter, D., 228, 268
Vaughan, D., 28–29, 268
Vesilind, E. M., 54, 268
Viadero, D., 2, 268
Villegas, A., 1, 21, 269
Vosniadou, S., 50, 269

Wacquant, L., 153, 269
Walker, E., 63, 195, 269
Weatherley, R., 6, 128–129, 214, 269
Wechsler, M. E., 38, 44, 269
Wehlage, G., 107, 126, 260, 269
Weick, K. E., 56, 129, 227, 269
Weiler, H. N., 84, 89, 269
Weiss, J., 3, 47–49, 128–129, 236, 269
Wells, A. S., 87–88, 269
Wenger, E., 26–34, 36, 38, 42–45, 131, 244, 250, 269

Wildavsky, A., 4–5, 95, 128, 187, 209, 212, 228, 260, 269
Williams, P. J., 269
Wilson, J. Q., 65, 79, 97, 163, 262, 270
Wilson, S. M., 65, 79, 97, 163, 262, 270
Wilson, W. J., 65, 79, 97, 163, 262, 270
Wolf, S., 194, 232, 270
Wong, K.K., 6, 98, 232, 259, 270

Yancey, W. L., 19, 270
Yanow, D., 49, 66–67, 79–80, 96, 129–130, 237, 270
Yarbrough, S. R., 154, 270
Yasumoto, J. Y., 27, 44, 231, 270
Yin, R. K., 133, 237, 270
York-Barr, J., 199, 270

Zahorik, J., 2, 264, 270
Zimmerman, J., 87, 99, 103, 270

Subject Index

Abbot v. Burke. See under court cases
accountability. *See under* Education
    Policy
  state accountability systems, 110, 121
  test scores, 28, 73, 114, 118–119, 171,
    177, 179–180, 183
  Sunshine State Standards (*see under*
    Florida)
Annenberg Challenge. *See* Chicago
    Annenberg Challenge
autonomy, 13, 92, 199, 203, 211

Brookings Institution, 157
Brown v. Board of Education. See under
    court cases

California, 8, 26, 32, 42, 45, 52, 54, 125,
    127, 132, 175, 195, 198, 214,
    221
  Bay Area School Reform Collabora-
    tive, 195
  California Department of Education,
    125, 127, 132
  California Mathematics Frameworks
    (*see* cognition and implemen-
    tation)
  Healthy Start School-linked Services
    Initiative, 132–133, 140
  Los Angeles, 200

Oakland (*see* collaborative education
    policy)
  San Francisco, 200, 225
capacity, 5, 8, 13, 15–16, 19–21, 65,
    80, 87–88, 97–98, 100, 103,
    110, 120–121, 125, 146–147,
    169–170, 185, 187–189, 197,
    202, 206, 213, 215, 219,
    221–222
central office. *See* district central office,
    school
Chicago Annenberg Challenge, 19, 189,
    199–200, 207
cognition and implementation, 47–64,
    65, 67, 79, 82
  experts, 46, 51, 55
  mental models, 50
  principled knowledge, 48
  schema, 50–52
  cognitive learning theory, 25
  distributed cognition, 48, 60, 214
  sense making, 21, 49, 215
  social cognition, 48, 60
cognitive learning theory. *See under* cog-
    nition and implementation;
    communities of practice
collaborative education policy, 125–127,
    134, 137, 139–140, 146–147
  boundary spanners, 131, 138

capacity for implementation of, 125, 136–147
central office administrators roles in, 125–147
community agencies' roles in, 126–127, 132, 142
school-community partnerships, 125–127, 130–133, 137
communities of practice theory, 25–46
boundary objects, 30–32, 38–39, 43
brokers, 30–32, 37–39, 43–44
cognitive learning theory, 25
joint enterprise, 26, 28, 30–31, 33, 35
mutual engagement, 26, 28–30, 33, 44
negotiation, 26, 29–31, 34, 39, 42–44
reification, 29–31, 33–39, 42–43, 46
shared repertoire of practice, 28
teacher professional community, 26–27, 44
complexity, 2–4, 13, 20, 22–23, 47, 131, 172, 219, 225–226
context, 2–4, 6–7, 13–14, 16, 19–21, 25, 33, 35, 37, 40–41, 46, 50, 56–60, 65–68, 71–73, 83–85, 87–90, 94–95, 101, 106–110, 112, 119, 129, 136, 150–152, 156, 168, 171, 174, 179, 181, 187, 190, 192–193, 197, 199, 206, 209, 211–213, 215–216, 219–220, 225–227
court cases
Abbot v. Burke, 110, 123, 149–150, 158–160, 162, 164, 216, 229
Brown v. Board of Education, 100
Robinson v. Cahill, 158, 160
San Antonio Independent School District v. Rodriguez, the U.S. Supreme Court, 158
critical race theory, 150, 152
culture, 9, 20–21, 26, 59, 60, 67–70, 72, 79, 85, 88–89, 99, 101, 103, 106–107, 149–155, 157, 162–168, 174, 177, 189, 195, 198, 200, 227

district central office, school, 12, 16–18, 128–130, 132
central office administrators, 16, 19, 125–147

economics of implementation, 149–186
capitalism, 152–153
economic theory, 21, 171, 176
economism, 153
finance reform, 160, 170
fiscal equity, 157
microeconomic theory, 171
equity, 15, 84, 150, 153, 156–158, 161, 164–165, 167, 223
education policy, 1–5, 8–10, 12–14, 16–18, 20–23, 31, 48, 70, 81, 86, 89, 95, 101, 125–127, 134, 137, 139–140, 146–147, 149–152, 156, 164–166, 169, 173–174, 186, 209–211, 217, 220, 222–228
accountability, 2–3, 12–13, 15, 19–20, 42–43, 58, 97, 110, 112–113, 119–121, 143, 169–170, 174, 176–178, 180–181, 183–186, 190, 194, 197, 199, 202, 204, 207, 210–212, 222–223, 227, 234, 237–238, 241, 246, 253–254, 256, 258, 273
developmental programs, 6
federal education policy, 8, 121, 215
Comprehensive School Reform (CSR) program, 12, 105, 108–122, 195, 198, 213
Elementary and Secondary Education Act (ESEA), 5–6, 10, 42, 109, 146, 158, 199, 210, 212–214, 216, 218, 220, 222, 224, 226, 228
No Child Left Behind Act, 10
Title I, 6, 10, 57, 108–109, 112–113, 116–118, 213
Great Society Period and, 5–7
Progressive Era and, 19
history of, 4–9
Wave 1, 5–6

Wave 2, 6–7
Wave 3, 7–9, 18
Wave 4, 9–22
large-scale school improvement, 189
mathematics, 15, 28, 52–55, 59, 62,
    65–66, 69–76, 78, 80–82, 177,
    183, 195, 214, 228
reading policy, 26, 32–33, 45, 57, 59
redistributive programs, 6
school reconstitution, 17, 84, 91, 95
school choice, 11–12, 20, 170, 174,
    176–178, 181–185
standards-based reform, 10, 13, 17, 48,
    53, 65–66, 70
teacher policy, 170, 174, 178, 181, 184
vouchers, 1, 98, 113, 174, 211
whole school reform, 8, 108–110, 121,
    195

federal education policy. *See under* Edu-
    cation policy
Florida, 106, 111–115, 117–119, 120
    FCAT (Florida Comprehensive
        Assessment Test), 113–114, 116
    State Department of Education, 105
    Sunshine State Standards, 114
Foucault, Michel, 150, 152, 154, 163

implementation as organizational learn-
    ing. *See* collaborative education
    policy; organizational learning.
institution, 85, 89, 157, 222–223
institutional capital, 20
institutional patterns, 18
institutional sector, 56
institutional setting, 19, 106, 213
intermediary organizations, 16, 137, 197,
    220, 228
Iowa Test of Basic Skills (ITBS), 201

Kentucky, 12, 127, 194

language and implementation, 65–82
    discourse community, 65, 68, 76
    grammar, 66, 68, 75–76, 79, 107
    interpretive perspective, 67, 70. 79

mathematics language, 78
policy language, 64, 66–68, 75
positivist perspective, 67, 70
slang, 66
technical language, 66, 69, 76, 81
leadership, 8, 19, 28, 38–39, 41–42, 63,
    99, 109–110, 113–114, 116,
    118, 120, 133, 155, 159, 164,
    174, 187, 190, 196–197, 199,
    201–202, 207

Marxian critical theory, 150–153
mathematics. *See under* education policy
Missouri, 127
mutual adaptation, 7, 106–107, 220

A Nation at Risk, 7
National Council of Teachers of Mathe-
    matics (NCTM), 59, 66, 71,
    74, 80
new institutionalism in sociology, 56, 89
    isomorphism, 214
    scripts, 35–36, 48, 89
New Jersey, 18, 110, 149–150, 158–165,
    167, 195, 213, 216
    Burke, Fred, 110, 123, 149–150,
        158–160, 162–164, 216, 229
    Comprehensive Education Improve-
        ment and Financing Act, 161
    Lefelt, Steven, 159–160
    Moreheuser, Marilyn, 159
    New Jersey State Supreme Court, 149
    Newark-based Education Law Center,
        159
    Whitman, Christine Todd, 161
New York City, 26, 32, 38, 45, 222
nonimplementation, 97, 149, 165, 216

Oakland, CA, 126, 132, 134–140,
    142–146, 212, 218, 224
    Healthy Start School-linked Services
        Initiative, 132–133, 140
    Oakland Child Health and Safety Ini-
        tiative, 132
    Oakland Community Organizations,
        224

Oakland Fund for Children and
Youth, 132
Oakland Unified School District, 126,
135–136
Village Centers, 132–133
organizational culture, 101, 195
organizational learning, 125–147,
226–227
change and, 126–128, 130–131,
135–136, 139–140, 142–144,
146, 226–227
organizational rules, 129
organizational-environmental interactions, 131
risk, 131, 138, 142, 146
search (for information), 129, 133,
136, 138–139, 143–146
use (of information), 127–129,
130–131, 133, 136, 139–140

Philadelphia, PA, 12, 200
policy, 1–23, 25–28, 30–34, 36–45,
47–60, 63–68, 70–91, 93–111,
113, 119–121, 125–147,
149–153, 155–156, 162–176,
178–184, 186–187, 192–193,
202, 206, 209–229
goals, 5, 10–12, 14–15, 20–21, 27, 31,
33, 46, 49–50, 55, 75, 90, 106,
108, 121, 126–129, 131–132, 135,
138–140, 142, 170–173, 176–182,
184, 194, 196–197, 200, 206,
213–215, 220–223, 226–227
core change, 11, 15, 20
discrete change, 10–11
large-cale change, 10–11, 135, 189,
199, 205
systemic, 38 (see large-scale change)
targets, 12–16, 97, 113, 129, 213, 216,
227
actors, school, 11–12, 107, 128,
169–170, 172–173, 176–178,
180–186
actors, non-school, 11–12, 18, 20,
58, 66, 70, 83, 85–91, 93–94, 96,
98–100, 102–104, 119–120, 130,

168, 181–186192, 194–195, 197,
202, 204, 206, 209–210,
212–213, 215, 217–218,
220–221, 223, 225–226, 228
formal, 14, 16–18
informal, 42, 49, 56, 61, 86, 145,
198, 223
tools, 7–8, 12–16, 26, 29, 38, 42–43,
59–60, 85, 121, 127, 139, 143,
174
capacity building, 8, 13
hortatory, 13
incentives, 6, 8, 12–13, 16
learning, 13, 16
levers of change, 12–13, 16
mandates, 8, 12–13, 15, 20, 95, 110,
126, 206
performance targets, 13
systems change, 8, 12–13, 16
policy implementation, 1–5, 8–10, 14,
16–18, 20–23, 25–28, 31–32,
41–45, 47–49, 51, 56, 59–60,
64–66, 68, 70, 79–80, 83–86,
89, 91, 95–98, 101–106, 108,
119–121, 126–128, 134, 137,
139, 149–152, 156, 163–170,
173–175, 181, 184, 186, 210,
212–215, 217, 221, 223–228
agency, 8–9, 14, 21, 56, 90, 97, 122,
127–129, 141, 151–152, 167,
212–214, 217, 221, 226
ambiguity of, 66, 80, 95, 130–132,
146, 217–218, 228
complexity and, 2–4, 13, 20, 22–23,
47, 131, 172, 219, 225–226, 273
context, 2–4, 6–7, 13–14, 16, 19–21,
25, 33, 35, 37, 40–41, 46, 50,
56–60, 65–68, 71–73, 83–85,
87–90, 94–95, 101, 106–110,
112, 119, 129, 136, 150–152,
156, 168, 171, 174, 179, 181,
187, 190, 192–193, 197, 199,
206, 209, 211–213, 215–216,
219–220, 225–227
dimensions of (see also policy, people
and places), 4, 14, 18–19, 21–22

economics of, 5, 21, 104, 128, 151,
    174, 189
language and, 17, 38, 52, 58, 60, 62,
    64–70, 72, 75–76, 78–82, 92,
    105, 152, 212, 214–215, 222
as organizational learning (*see* organizational learning)
"implementable" policy, 1–2, 22, 218
politics of, 9, 82, 84–86, 90–91, 94,
    96–100, 102–104, 115, 155, 165,
    215–217, 224
power in, 9, 13, 45, 56, 71, 83–90, 92,
    95–102, 104, 116, 150–156,
    163–168, 188–189, 193, 195,
    216–217, 224
sense making, 21, 49, 215
social organization, 188, 205–206
communities of practice theory and
    (*see* communities of practice)
cognition and (*see* cognition and
    implementation)
critical theory and, 164
uncertainty, 184, 187, 192
variance, 4, 6–7, 9, 19, 21–22, 27, 32,
    38, 51, 53, 57, 67, 74, 79–80, 106,
    131, 144, 173, 196, 202, 213–214
policy implementation research, 3–5,
    8–10, 17, 20–23, 60, 126, 150,
    167–168, 210, 226
place-based research, 19
political economy, 150–154, 162, 167
power. *See under* politics of policy implementation
principal-agent problem, 171, 178, 215

race, 5, 17–18, 21, 67, 92, 98–99,
    150–153, 155–156, 158, 162,
    164–167, 177, 216
racism, 153, 155–156, 164, 166, 191
RAND Change Agent Study, 6, 106,
    187–188
reading policy, 26, 32–33, 45, 57, 59
California, 26, 32, 45
New York City Community District
    2, 26, 32

Balanced Literacy Framework, 38–42
Reading Recovery, 37, 45
Running Records, 37–38, 45
Robinson v. Cahill. See under court cases

*San Antonio Independent School District v.
    Rodriguez*, the U.S. Supreme
    Court. *See under* court cases
school reform models, 108–109, 112,
    122, 198
Success for all, 109, 112, 115,
    117–120, 122–123
Accelerated Schools, 8, 109
Coalition for Essential Schools, 8
Comer Schools (Comer Developmental Program), 8, 109
social capital, 20, 188–194, 197–199,
    202–207
trust, 20, 189–204, 206–207
strong/weak ties, 191–192
social class, 153, 216
socio-cultural learning theory. *See* Communities of Practice
standards based reform, 10, 17, 48, 53,
    65–66, 70, 226
Sunshine State Standards (*see under*
    Florida)
state education policy, 38, 53, 57–59, 67,
    71–71, 76, 78, 110, 212
Public School Elementary and Secondary Education Act (PSEA),
    158–159
state accountability systems, 110, 121
state education agencies, 102
state-mandated initiatives, 150
sustainability, 119, 219
systems learning, 226–228. *See also* collaborative education policy;
    organizational learning

Title I. *See under* federal education policy

urban education policy, 150

What Works Clearinghouse, 1–4, 7–9, 22

44054900R00170

Made in the USA
San Bernardino, CA
05 January 2017